AND ITS SOCIAL AGENDAS

CLASS, GENDER, AND IDENTITY IN CLOTHING

DIANA CRANE

THE UNIVERSITY OF CHICAGO PRESS

CHICAGO AND LONDON

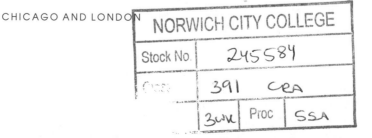

The University of Chicago Press, Chicago 60637
The University of Chicago Press, Ltd., London
© 2000 by The University of Chicago
All rights reserved. Published 2000
Printed in the United States of America
15 14 13 12 11 10 09   6 5 4 3

ISBN 0-226-11799-5 (paper)

Library of Congress Cataloging-in-Publication Data

Crane, Diana, 1933–
     Fashion and its social agendas : class, gender, and identity in clothing /
Diana Crane.
        p.   cm.
     Includes bibliographical references and index.
     ISBN 0-226-11798-7 (alk. paper)
     1. Costume—Social aspects.   2. Fashion—Social aspects.   3. Social class.
4. Gender identity.   5. Group identity.   6. Costume and sexuality.   I. Title.
GT525.C75   2000
391—dc21   99-088216

FASHION
AND ITS SOCIAL AGENDAS

FASH

*To Michel, who has always enjoyed fashion,
and to Adrienne, my companion on innumerable shopping trips*

CONTENTS

ACKNOWLEDGMENTS

During the eleven years that I have been researching various aspects of fashion and clothing choices, I have received assistance from many different sources. I am most grateful to the men and women who were interviewed for the study—designers, fashion forecasters, and public relations staff—and to the women (and a few men) who participated in the focus groups on fashion photographs and clothing advertisements.

The assistance of librarians was essential to this study. I thank particularly Françoise Blum and Michel Prat at the library of the Centre d'Etudes de Documentation, d'Information, et d'Actions Sociales in Paris, which owns a complete set of Frédéric Le Play's publications, for their assistance in obtaining copies of the case studies conducted by Le Play and his associates of French working-class families in the nineteenth century. I am especially grateful to Antoine Savoye, specialist in the works of Le Play, who made me aware of the existence of this unique archive.

I am also indebted to numerous reference librarians at the Bibliothèque Forney in Paris and at the Van Pelt Library of the University of Pennsylvania, and particularly Lauris Olson and Lee V. Pugh, assistant director of the Interlibrary Loan Department. I also thank Françoise Tétart-Vittu of the Musée de la Mode de la Ville de Paris (Musée Galliera).

In the early stages of my research, I received a Fulbright Senior Research Award. I thank the Department of Sociology at the University of Pennsylvania for providing a sabbatical year in 1995–96 and for allocating funds for research and clerical assistance in conducting and transcribing focus-group sessions.

Linda Mamoun and Kesha Moore provided invaluable assistance as focus-group leaders. Christine Holmes and Bonita Iritani performed the difficult job of transcribing the tapes. Tina Nemetz was always ready and able to solve administrative problems. I also thank Waddick Doyle at the American University of Paris for his assistance in locating focus-group participants.

I am grateful to Pierre-Michel Menger of the Centre de Sociologie des Arts in Paris for inviting me to spend a month at the Ecole des Hautes Etudes en Science Sociales and to present my research in his seminar at the Ecole during the year 1995–96.

Judith Adler, Susan Kaiser, and Toba Kerson devoted precious time to reading and commenting on an earlier version of the manuscript. Their advice and suggestions were invaluable. I especially appreciate Toba's interest in the study from its earliest stages, which manifested itself in the form of clippings and articles that would otherwise have been inaccessible to me.

I am grateful to Douglas Mitchell at the University of Chicago Press for his long-standing interest in my work and Robert Devens for his assistance with the onerous process of preparing a volume with fifty-eight illustrations for publication. I also thank the press for a small grant to partially cover photographic reproduction fees.

Finally, Michel Hervé and Adrienne Hervé provided moral support and were always available with advice and assistance. They exhibited their usual patience and stoicism when confronted with the ordeal of sharing their lives with a manuscript-in-progress.

Portions of the book, in somewhat different form, have appeared in the following publications.

"Fashion Design as an Occupation: A Cross-National Approach." Pp. 55–73 in *Current Research on Occupations and Profession*, vol. 8: *Creators of Culture*, ed. M. Cantor and C. Zollars. Greenwich, CT: JAI Press, 1994. Reprinted with permission.

"Postmodernism and the Avant-Garde: Stylistic Change in Fashion Design." *Modernism/Modernity* 4 (1997): 123–40. © 1997. The Johns Hopkins University Press.

"Globalization, Organizational Size and Innovation in the French Luxury Fashion Industry: Production of Culture Theory Revisited." *Poetics: Journal of Empirical Research on Literature, the Media, and the Arts* 24 (1997): 393–414. Copyright 1997. Reprinted with permission from Elsevier Science.

"Clothing Behavior as Non-Verbal Resistance: Marginal Women and Alternative Dress in the Nineteenth Century." *Fashion Theory* 3 (1999): 241–68. Reprinted with permission from Berg Publishers.

"Women Fashion Designers and Women's Experience." *Journal of American Culture* 22, no. 2 (summer 1999): 1–8. Reprinted with permission from Bowling Green State University Popular Press.

"Diffusion Models and Fashion: A Reassessment." *The Annals of the American Academy of Political and Social Science* 566 (November 1999): 13–24. © 1999 by The American Academy of Political and Social Science. Reprinted with permission.

"Gender and Hegemony in Fashion Magazines: Women's Interpretations of Fashion Photographs." *Sociological Quarterly* 40, no. 4 (Fall 1999): 541–63. © 1999 by The Midwest Sociological Society. Reprinted with permission.

1 FASHION, IDENTITY, AND SOCIAL CHANGE

Clothing, as one of the most visible forms of consumption, performs a major role in the social construction of identity. Clothing choices provide an excellent field for studying how people interpret a specific form of culture for their own purposes, one that includes strong norms about appropriate appearances at a particular point in time (otherwise known as fashion) as well as an extraordinarily rich variety of alternatives. One of the most visible markers of social status and gender and therefore useful in maintaining or subverting symbolic boundaries, clothing is an indication of how people in different eras have perceived their positions in social structures and negotiated status boundaries. In previous centuries, clothing was the principal means for identifying oneself in public space. Depending on the period, various aspects of identity were expressed in clothing in Europe and the United States, including occupation, regional identity, religion, and social class. Certain items of clothing worn by everyone, such as hats, were particularly important, sending instant signals of ascribed or aspired social status. Variations in clothing choices are subtle indicators of how different types of societies and different positions within societies are actually experienced.

Recently, sociologists have begun to understand the power of artifacts to exercise a kind of cultural "agency," influencing social behavior and attitudes in ways that we often fail to recognize. Technology embodied in machinery, architecture, and computers (to name a few) is a major influence in modern life (Latour 1988) and has tended to obscure the fact that nontechnological artifacts have been influencing human behavior for centuries. Clothes as artifacts "create" behavior through their capacity to impose social identities and empower people to assert latent social identities. On the one hand, styles of clothing can be a straitjacket, constraining (literally) a person's movements and manners, as was the case for women's clothing during the Victorian era. For centuries, uniforms (military, police, religious) have been used to impose social identities on more or less willing subjects (Joseph 1986). Alternatively, clothing can be viewed as a vast reservoir of meanings that can be manipulated or reconstructed so as to enhance a person's sense of agency. Interviews by social psychologists (Kaiser, Freeman, and Chandler 1993) suggest that people attribute to their "favorite" clothes the capacity to influence the ways they express themselves and interact with others.

Social scientists have not articulated a definitive interpretation of how a person constructs social identity in contemporary society. Recent theories conceptualize people as functioning today in a social structure more fluid and less constraining than those of the past. Contemporary societies are characterized as "postindustrial" and their cultures as "postmodern," implying a transformation in the relationships between different elements of the social structure and in the nature and role of culture.

In this book, I will examine fashion and clothing choices in nineteenth-century industrial and contemporary postindustrial societies, drawing examples from France, the United States, and England. In class societies, each class had a distinct culture which differentiated it from other classes, but at the same time it shared certain values, goals, and gender ideals with other classes. In contemporary, "fragmented" societies, class distinctions are important in the workplace, but, outside the workplace, distinctions are based on criteria that are meaningful to the numerous and diverse social groups in which they originate but not necessarily to members of other social groups. How do fashion and clothing choices differ in societies where social class and gender are the most salient aspects of social identity, as compared with societies where lifestyles, age cohorts, gender, sexual orientation, and ethnicity are as meaningful to people as social class in constructing their self-images and in their presentation of self? Changes in the dissemination of fashion and in clothing choices can be used to trace and interpret these transformations in class cultures.

CLOTHING AND SOCIAL CHANGE:
Status, Class, and Identity

Changes in clothing and in the discourses surrounding clothing indicate shifts in social relationships and tensions between different social groups that present themselves in different ways in public space. In previous centuries, increases in the availability of clothing to members of different social classes that were related to a gradual decline in the cost of clothing affected the origins and accessibility of fashionable styles. In the late Middle Ages, clothes in European societies began to resemble those we know today: shapeless gowns were replaced by tailored, fitted garments whose forms were generally influenced by fashions originating in the courts of kings or the upper classes. In some countries, sumptuary laws specified the types of material and ornaments that could be used by members of different social classes (Hurlock 1965). In relatively rigid social structures, attempts to use clothing to negotiate status boundaries were as controversial as analogous attempts to use clothing to negotiate gender boundaries in the twentieth century.

Until the Industrial Revolution and the appearance of machine-made clothing, clothes were generally included among a person's most valuable possessions. New clothes were inaccessible to the poor, who wore used clothing that had often passed through many hands before reaching them. A poor man was likely to own only a single suit of clothes. For example, among 278 people arrested in and around Paris in 1780, only twenty-eight possessed more than one outfit of clothing (Roche 1994:87). Those rich enough to own substantial wardrobes considered them valuable forms of property to be willed to deserving relatives and servants when they died. Cloth was so expensive and so precious that it constituted in itself a form of currency and frequently replaced gold as a form of payment for services (Stallybrass 1993:37). When funds were scarce, clothes were pawned, along with jewels and other valuables.

In preindustrial societies, clothing behavior indicated very precisely a person's position in the social structure (Ewen 1985). Clothing revealed not only social class and gender but frequently occupation, religious affiliation, and regional origin, as well. Each occupation had a particular costume. In some countries, each village and region in the countryside had its own variations on the costume of the period (Pellegrin 1989). As Western societies industrialized, the effect of social stratification on clothing behavior was transformed. The expression of class and gender took precedence over the communication of other types of social information. The essence of social stratification in industrial societies can be understood in terms of hierarchies of occupations (see, e.g., Goldthorpe 1987:39–42; and Le Play 1862), occupation being an indicator of control over property and other economic resources. Clothes for specific occupations disappeared and were replaced by clothing for types of occupations and by uniforms that signified a particular rank in an organization. Regional identification became less salient.

In nineteenth-century industrializing societies, social class affiliation was one of the most salient aspects of a person's identity. Differences in clothing behavior between social classes were indications of the character of interpersonal relationships between social classes in industrializing societies. The social "chasm" between the middle and upper classes and the lower class was enormous. At the end of the century, the lower class constituted the overwhelming majority of the population in this period (73 percent in France [Duroselle 1972:85], 85 percent in England [Runciman 1990:389]; and 82 percent in the United States [U.S. Bureau of the Census 1975, pt. 1:139]. Contacts between this class and other social classes occurred largely through services performed by members of the working class for the middle and upper classes. Such contacts were restricted, for the most part, to artisans and tradespeople, who were generally men, and to servants, who were usually female.

Even in the nineteenth century, clothes represented a substantial portion of a working-class family's possessions. In France, a working-class man's suit, purchased at the time of its owner's marriage, was often expected to last a lifetime and to serve a variety of purposes, including Sunday church services, weddings, and funerals. A young woman and her female relatives typically spent several years preparing her trousseau, which represented an important part of the resources she contributed to her future household and which contained clothes, undergarments, and bed linens that were intended to last for decades. In England, poor families formed clubs for the purpose of saving to buy clothes (de Marly 1986). Clothes were relatively unavailable to the working class but abundantly accessible to the upper class, for whom fashions were created. Members of other classes who wished to have a fashionable appearance were required to emulate that class.

By the late nineteenth century, clothes had gradually become cheaper and therefore more accessible to lower class levels. As the first widely available consumer item, clothes were sometimes an indulgence for rich and poor alike. Young, employed working-class women spent their wages on fashionable items. Middle- and upper-class women devoted substantial proportions of their families' incomes to clothes.

Costume historians have concluded that clothing was democratized during the nineteenth century, because all social classes adopted similar types of clothing (Steele 1989a). They argue that this transformation was most pronounced in the United States because of the character of its social structure. Class structures in industrializing societies during the nineteenth century were not identical. Since groups of people with similar positions in a class hierarchy tend to share distinctive, life-defining experiences (Kingston 1994: 4), variations in the nature of class hierarchies were visible in clothing behavior. The United States in the nineteenth century was widely believed to be a classless society, characterized by a high level of upward mobility. Tocqueville's assessment of the country in 1840 as one in which, "at any moment, a servant may become a master" apparently reflected popular attitudes at the time. The obsession with fashion among American women in the nineteenth century has been attributed to the high level of "status competition" engendered by "the fluidity of American society, the universal striving after success, the lack of a titled aristocracy, and the modest past of most Americans" (Banner 1984: 18, 54). Ironically, although *expectations* of upward mobility were higher in America than in other countries, actual levels of mobility were not (Kaelble 1986).[1]

The large numbers of immigrants in the second half of the nineteenth century made clothing in the United States particularly salient. Immigrants divested themselves of their traditional clothing as soon as they arrived, using clothes as a means of discarding their previous identities and establishing new ones (Heinze 1990: 90). The United States also experienced high levels of geographical mobility owing to internal migration from East to West, meaning that large numbers of people were establishing identities in new locations. In France, there was enormous variation in social environments. In Paris, which was at the forefront of social change and modernity and the focus of internal migration, the demand for fashionable clothing was very high. By contrast, in provincial cities, which were pale imitations of Paris, and farming communities in the countryside, which remained steeped in tradition, new clothing was less accessible.

Fashion, which appeared to offer possibilities for a person to enhance his or her social position, was only one aspect of clothing during this period. It has to be seen in relation to the various ways in which clothing was used as a form of social control, through the imposition of uniforms and dress codes. Although men's clothing was becoming simpler in comparison with the previous century, clothes in the workplace were becoming more differentiated as uniforms proliferated in bureaucratic organizations to indicate ranks in organizational hierarchies. In the workplace, social class differences were being made increasingly explicit by the use of uniforms and dress codes.

In the twentieth century, clothes have gradually lost their economic but not their symbolic importance, with the enormous expansion of ready-made clothing at all price levels.[2] The availability of inexpensive clothing means that those with limited resources can find or create personal styles that express their perceptions of their identities rather than imitate styles originally sold to the more affluent. While, in the past, the occasional working-class street style was documented, the proliferation of street styles representing diverse subcultures within the working class has only occurred in the past fifty years. Theoretically, fashion is available to people at all social levels, both for creating styles that express their identities and for adopting styles created by clothing firms.

The nature of fashion has changed, as well as the ways in which people respond to it. Nineteenth-century fashion consisted of a well-defined standard of appearance that was widely adopted. Contemporary fashion is more ambiguous and multifaceted, in keeping with the highly fragmented nature of contemporary postindustrial societies. Kaiser, Nagasawa, and Hutton (1991 : 166) refer to "the complex range and multitude of simultaneously 'fashionable' styles of clothing and personal appearance. . . . the range of choice in the marketplace contributes to a state of confusion bordering on chaos." Clothing choices reflect the complexity of the ways we perceive our connections to one another in contemporary societies.

THEORIZING FASHION IN THE NINETEENTH CENTURY: Class Cultures and Symbolic Boundaries

The best-known theory of fashion and clothing behavior is Simmel's theory of fashion change as a process of imitation of social elites by their social inferiors (1957). Writing at the beginning of the twentieth century, Simmel delineated the role of fashion as it had developed in nineteenth-century societies, in which social classes had relatively distinct class cultures. Simmel's model of fashion change was centered on the idea that fashions were first adopted by the upper class and, later, by the middle and lower classes. Lower-status groups sought to acquire status by adopting the clothing of higher-status groups and set in motion a process of social contagion whereby styles were adopted by groups at successively inferior status levels. By the time a particular fashion reached the working class, the upper class had adopted newer styles, since the previous style had lost its appeal in the process of popularization. The highest-status groups sought once again to differentiate themselves from their inferiors by adopting new fashions.

Although Simmel recognized that some trendsetters were working-class women who had become actresses or courtesans, he has been criticized for emphasizing the role of superordinate groups in initiating the contagion process. Others argue that upwardly mobile status groups were motivated to adopt new styles as status markers in order to differentiate themselves from groups subordinate to themselves, while the highest-status groups, whose eminence was secure and based on wealth and inheritance, tended to be relatively indifferent to the latest fashions (McCracken 1985: 40). Veblen's (1899) model of "conspicuous consumption" helps to explain the motivations of fashion adopters in some social strata.

Simmel's theory assumes that new styles were widely adopted, but the question of who did or did not adopt them is crucial for understanding the nature of fashion in nineteenth-century class societies. Were fashions circulating primarily in the upper strata of these societies? To what extent were fashionable styles adopted by the working class? Middle-class observers in the nineteenth century tended to generalize from experiences in their own social circles and exaggerate the extent to which new styles were widely adopted by the working class. Middle-class commentators in magazines and newspapers drew their conclusions about working-class clothing from the appearance of certain types of people who were particularly "visible," such as artisans and servants. Were those who were located in social positions that had little contact with the middle class less likely to adopt new styles? While costume historians have claimed that clothes were democratized during the nineteenth century, it would seem unlikely that members of the working class could emulate the extensive wardrobes of the middle class in anything more than a superficial manner.

Bourdieu's (1984) theory of class reproduction and cultural tastes is useful for understanding how different social classes respond to cultural goods and material culture in highly stratified societies. His theory suggests that the dissemination of fashion was more complicated than the process described by Simmel. Bourdieu describes social structures as complex systems of class cultures comprising sets of cultural tastes and associated lifestyles. Within social classes, individuals compete for social distinction and cultural capital on the basis of their capacity to judge the suitability of cultural products according to class-based standards of taste and manners. Cultural practices which include both knowledge of culture and critical abilities for assessing and appreciating it are acquired during childhood in the family and in the educational system and contribute to the reproduction of the existing social class structure. In class societies, the dominant and most prestigious culture is that of the upper class. Elites possess "the power to set the terms through which tastes are assigned moral and social value" (Holt 1997b:95). The social backgrounds and cultural practices of the middle and lower classes prevent them from fully assimilating the tastes of the upper class. The consumption of cultural goods associated with the upper and middle classes requires attitudes and knowledge that are not readily accessible to members of the working class.

According to Bourdieu's theory, the tastes of working-class men would be based on a "culture of necessity" characteristic of that class, in other words, clothing that was practical, functional, and durable rather than aesthetically pleasing and stylish. Those who moved into the middle classes would be expected to adopt the clothing behavior of that class but would not exhibit the same levels of taste and refinement owing to insufficient socialization and education.

Bourdieu's theory helps to explain how social classes and hence social structures are maintained over time but is less useful for understanding how people respond during periods of rapid social change. His emphasis on the acquisition of standards for making cultural assessments in childhood and in the educational system suggests that these standards and hence cultural tastes change relatively slowly. The outcome of incessant competition for social distinction is stability, rather than change, in the social structure. During the nineteenth century, rising standards of living, combined with rising expectations and greater access to information, led working-class men to participate more actively in public spheres and public spaces. Changing conceptions of themselves as citizens might have been signaled by their use of new types of clothing to indicate their changing perceptions of their social status. In general, as people's social networks expand and as their social contacts become more varied, they are exposed to and are likely to adopt new forms of culture (DiMaggio 1987; Erickson 1996:221–22).

Fashion histories tell us what was considered fashionable in specific periods, but it is more difficult to find out what ordinary people and particularly working-class people actually wore in the past. Here the work of another social scientist, Frédéric Le Play, who studied working-class families in France during the nineteenth century, is a major resource. Le Play was interested in understanding the character of nineteenth-century class societies, because he was concerned that changes brought about by the Industrial Revolution were leading to a decline in personal contacts between different social classes and an emphasis on materialistic values at the expense of moral sentiments. Le Play's goal in conducting case studies of families was to provide a complete picture of the economic and social life of each family and of the social environment in which the family resided. He and his associates collected a great deal of information about the financial situation of families and made detailed inventories of all their assets and possessions, including complete inventories of the wardrobes of all family members and the cost of each item of clothing. They published a series of case studies of eighty-one working-class families, conducted between 1850 and 1910, that provides a unique resource for studying facets of French working-class life in the nineteenth century not recorded elsewhere.[3] These studies come surprisingly close to fulfilling a need expressed by a British sociologist (Runciman 1990:392) for "intensive, longitudinal ethnography, in which different aspects of consciousness are located in the context of class practices."

Other sources of information about working-class life are studies of family budgets by American researchers, such as Carroll Wright, toward the end of the nineteenth century and during the twentieth century (Brown 1994). These studies provide information about clothing choices of American working-class families. Photographs culled by costume historians offer unique insights concerning the ways people perceived themselves and their clothing (Ginsburg 1988; Lee Hall 1992; Severa 1995).

FASHION IN THE TWENTIETH CENTURY: Theorizing the "Fragmented" Society

Social scientists agree that Western societies have changed in the past thirty years but disagree in their descriptions and interpretations of those changes and about their significance for the individual. Theories that have different conceptions of the nature of contemporary social structure, and particularly of the relationship between social structure and culture, have different implications for understanding how people consume cultural goods such as clothing.

Some scholars (e.g., Clark and Lipset 1991) imply that social class is becoming less salient in contemporary society, particularly in the context of politics, the economy, and the family, than before. American studies have found little support for the existence of separate class cultures. One reason is the high rate of interclass and intraclass mobility: classes in the United States are not intergenerationally reproduced social groups (Kingston 1994:36). This suggests that social class is becoming less important in the formation of a person's self-image. Kingston (1994) found that "class does not significantly affect a whole host of attitudes on social issues, values, and lifestyle tastes, and communal attachments and socializing."

Instead of class cultures, there is increasing fragmentation of cultural interests within social classes. In such a highly fragmented society, "the number of special interests and individual interests is almost too staggering to imagine" (Vidich 1995:381). "Multiple and overlapping institutionalized cultures" rely on very different standards and cannot be reduced to "a single calculus of distinction," such as that proposed by Bourdieu (John R. Hall 1992:260). Differences between lifestyles are being accentuated by segmentation of media channels and exploited by advertisers and marketing experts (Turow 1997:193). The result is "hypersegmentation," which isolates each lifestyle in its own niche. Turow believes lifestyles have begun to resemble "image tribes," nonoverlapping segments of the population whose members have distinct "problems, allegiances, and interests." Alternatively, Holt (1997a), who also emphasizes the diversity of lifestyles available to people in contemporary societies, implies that not only do these lifestyles evolve and change over time but also that individuals move from one to another as the salience of particular lifestyles changes.

Participation in a lifestyle as compared with membership in a social class presumes a greater level of agency on the part of the individual.[4] People make choices that require the continual assessment and evaluation of consumer goods and activities in light of their potential contributions to identities or images they are attempting to project. From time to time, a person is likely to alter her lifestyle, and, as large numbers of people engage in this process, the characteristics of lifestyles themselves evolve and change. Ultimately, social classes are less homogenous, because they are fragmented into different but continually evolving lifestyles based on leisure activities, including consumption.

The variety of choices in lifestyles available in contemporary society liberates the individual from tradition and enables her to make choices that create a meaningful self-identity (Giddens 1991). The construction and presentation of self have become major preoccupations as a person continually reassesses the importance of past and present events and commitments. A person constructs a sense of her identity by creating "self-narratives" that contain her understandings of her past, her present, and her future. These understandings change continually over time as she reassesses her "ideal" self in relation to her changing perceptions of her mental and physical selves on the basis of past and present experiences.

In his theory of postindustrial society, Bell (1976) argued that a person has unparalleled freedom to construct new identities outside the economic and political spheres; social identity is no longer based entirely on economic status. His theory suggests that people construct their identities differently in the workplace as compared with spaces they occupy in their leisure time. This is significant, because the amount of time available to a person for leisure pursuits has greatly increased during the twentieth century while the proportion of the person's lifetime during which he or she is employed has steadily decreased. The number of years spent in the educational system has risen, periods of unemployment have become more commonplace, and early retirement is acceptable. Time not devoted to gainful employment is considered "leisure," although "'leisure' is a global term in which there is a mixture of socially constrained time (family work), socially committed time (voluntary political activity), and time for oneself (leisure)" (Dumazedier 1989: 155). The increasing availability of time not devoted to paid employment has important social implications. The individual is free from constraints and "institutional norms imposed by work, family obligations, political and religious authority" (158). This implies that leisure is a "liminal" time when one can develop a sense of personal and social identity.

These theories suggest that the consumption of cultural goods, such as fashionable clothing, performs an increasingly important role in the construction of personal identity, while the satisfaction of material needs and the emulation of superior classes are secondary. Bocock (1993:81) states: "Style, enjoyment, excitement, escape from boredom at work or at play, being attractive to self and others, these become central life-concerns, and affect patterns of consumption in post-modernity, rather than copying the ways of living and consumption patterns of 'superior' social status groups." On the microlevel, the role of the consumer rather than that of the producer "has come to define the human experience. . . . Outside their homes . . . and their workplaces . . . consumers are spending most of their time in shopping environments" (Firat 1995:111–12). The postmodernist consumer is expected to be a sophisticated interpreter of codes so as to be able "to discriminate between alternatives, while at the same time identifying with chosen commodities, in order to articulate a particular persona" (Partington 1996:212). In postmodern cultures, consumption is conceptualized as a form of role-playing, as consumers seek to project conceptions of identity that are continually evolving.

What evidence exists about the prevalence of narcissistic, postmodernist consumers? Conceptualizing different types of consumers in contemporary societies is a complex task. One solution that is frequently used in market research is lifestyle typologies. Although most of these typologies classify the population only in terms of categories based on social class, certain types of values, and, to some extent, age, they indicate differences and similarities between major lifestyles within and across social classes.

Vals 2, a system widely used in market research, classifies the population into eight groups on the basis of (1) personal orientations: actions, status, and principles, and (2) resource constraints: income, education, and age (Waldrop 1994). These categories suggest that the American population is deeply divided in its orientation toward consumption.[5] According to this system, slightly more than half the population (57 percent) is influenced largely by traditional values, including four groups that belong to both middle- and working-class lifestyles.[6] The traditional segment of the population includes middle class "fulfilleds," who are well-educated and informed, older (50 percent are over fifty), and content with families, careers, and their social positions. The traditional segment also includes working-class "believers," poorly educated people with deeply rooted moral codes, one-third of whom are retired. A third working-class lifestyle, the "makers," although not oriented toward principles, have conventional attitudes and are not interested in consumption. A fourth group, the underclass "strugglers," are very poor; their greatest concerns are security and safety.

The four remaining groups, which constitute 43 percent of the population, appear to have the financial means and the appropriate attitudes for being postmodernist consumers. They include the upper-class "actualizers," who constitute the wealthiest segment of the population, and two younger middle-class groups, the "achievers" and the "experiencers." The latter are particularly oriented toward fashion and fads. A younger working-class group, the "strivers," is "image conscious" and interested in consumption of clothing. The "strivers" are blue-collar workers who may identify with the working class at work and with the middle class during leisure time, as Halle (1984) found in a study of factory workers.[7] These categories suggest that younger and more affluent groups are concerned with identity and have postmodernist attitudes toward the use of consumption to manipulate the presentation of identity, while older and generally less affluent groups have more traditional attitudes toward identity and lifestyle. Some marketing experts argue that age groups alone are sufficient to explain variations in lifestyles. They divide the population into three groups, those born between 1909 and 1945, those born between 1946 and 1964, and those born between 1965 and 1984 (Smith and Clurman 1997). They show that the three groups vary in attitudes and goals that affect the nature of their lifestyles.[8]

Although market segments identified for selling commodities are always less heterogeneous than the social segments and groups that actually exist in the population and that are constantly changing (Fiske 1997), it appears that postmodernist attitudes toward identity are confined to certain segments of the population and that there are major differences in orientations toward consumption both within and across social classes. Other market research studies show that consumers with the same demographic characteristics, such as education and income, do not select the same leisure activities or clothing (Crispell 1992), suggesting that lifestyles are more salient than class status. Studies also show that the majority of women say they are not interested in fashion and do not attempt to modify their appearance in order to conform to new styles (Gutman and Mills 1982; Gadel 1985; Krafft 1991; Valmont 1993). Only about one-third of the female population, mainly younger women, are interested in fashionable styles, and even fewer attempt to engage in something approaching postmodernist role-playing, continually adopting and discarding identities associated with clothing and its accessories (Rabine 1994).

The obsession with personal identity that is characteristic of some but not all lifestyles can be explained in part as a consequence of a society and culture that are increasingly complex and difficult to interpret. Younger people, whose careers are least stable and who are also the most active consumers of media culture, find it difficult to obtain a clear sense of what contemporary society is like and of its significance for them. Technological and organizational changes in the workplace have led to a situation in which employment histories are less predictable and less uniform in terms of generation and social background (Buchmann 1989). Age and social cohorts no longer share the same experiences; timing of experiences, such as education, first employment, marriage, and childbearing, has become more erratic. The concern with personal identity is one way of adapting to new forms of social and cultural disorganization.

Fashion contributes to the redefinition of social identities by continually attributing new meanings to artifacts. Davis (1992:17–18) argues that fashionable clothing is meaningful to the consumer because it expresses ambivalences surrounding social identities, such as "youth versus age, masculinity versus femininity, androgyny versus singularity . . . work versus play . . . conformity versus rebellion." The fascination of fashion lies in the ways in which it continually redefines these tensions and embodies them in new styles. The consumer uses various discourses to interpret the connections between her sense of her personal identity and the social identity that is conferred by membership in various social groups that wear similar clothing. According to Thompson and Haytko (1997:16), consumers use "fashion discourses to forge self-defining social distinctions and boundaries, to construct narratives of personal history, to interpret the interpersonal dynamics of their social spheres, to understand their relationship to consumer culture, . . . and to transform and . . . contest conventional social categories, particularly those having strong gender associations."

As Bell (1976) indicates, contemporary societies are characterized by a disjunction between the economy and culture, between work and leisure. This suggests that, on the basis of occupations and professions, the population is differentiated into discrete social classes whose members are expected to exhibit identities that are marked by distinctive types of attitudes and behavior in the workplace. Outside the economic sphere, the bases for stratification are cultural configurations based on lifestyles, values, and conceptions of personal and gender identity. Leisure activities, including consumption, shape people's perceptions of themselves and are more meaningful than work for many people.

Therefore it is necessary to examine how occupational clothing conveys different meanings compared with leisure clothing and how these types of clothing are used in different ways. Within the leisure sphere, social affiliations based on age, race and ethnicity, and gender and sexual orientation are particularly salient. People at all social class levels consume material culture in order to enhance their identification with specific groups but not with the society as a whole. They tend to identify with very narrow and very specific cultural interests (John R. Hall 1992; Holt 1997a).

Simmel's "top-down" model was the dominant form of fashion dissemination in Western societies until the 1960s, when demographic and economic factors increased the influence of youth at all social class levels. The enormous size of the baby boom generation and its affluence compared with that of previous generations of young people contributed to its influence on fashion. Since the 1960s, the "bottom-up" model, in which new styles emerge in lower-status groups and are later adopted by higher-status groups (Field 1970), has explained an important segment of fashion phenomena. In this model, age replaces social status as the variable that conveys prestige to the fashion innovator. Styles that emerge from lower socioeconomic groups are often generated by adolescents and young adults who belong to subcultures or "style tribes" with distinctive modes of dress that attract attention and eventually lead to imitation at other age and socioeconomic levels (Polhemus 1994). New styles also emerge from subcultures within middle-class strata, such as artistic and homosexual communities. In both models, the process of diffusion downward or upward has been accelerated by media exposure, which now leads to rapid awareness of new styles at all levels of the system. However, the trajectories of fashion diffusion are more complex than is suggested by either of these models (Davis 1992). An indication of the difficulties in using Simmel's top-down model today is seen in the fact that members of adolescent subcultures, often at low social class levels, are sometimes the most avid consumers of luxury fashion items, which they adopt soon after their appearance and discard before they have lost their fashionable cachet (de la Haye and Dingwall 1996).

The factors that lead to the circulation of styles from different sources and particularly from the working class to the upper class must also be posed as a question about the relationships between cultural organizations that produce and disseminate culture. It is sometimes assumed that fashion in a mysterious way epitomizes the essence of cultural trends at a particular time. What this conception of fashion ignores is the fact that fashion, like other forms of popular culture, emerges from sets of interacting organizations and networks that shape its content in various ways (Crane 1992; Peterson 1994). The meanings of cultural products are affected by the relationships between creators and publics and between managers and markets. When a particular set of cultural producers dominates a cultural market, as French fashion designers did until the 1960s, and as major Hollywood film studios do today, the nature of the styles or genres that are marketed is less diverse compared with those that appear when cultural producers located in different countries compete with one another. In the nineteenth century, fashion emanated largely from a single source, Paris, whose dictates were widely accepted in other industrial societies. In the twentieth century, the increasing importance of fashion worlds in other countries, of fashion leaders in media culture, and of subcultures centered on leisure activities, has made the relationship between clothing choices and fashion more complex. As their potential publics have expanded from local to national and from national to global, fashion organizations have been transformed. In the past, designers in small urban firms sought to acquire prestige and attract clients by associating themselves with the arts (Bourdieu 1993).

Today, because of enormous competition in global markets, fashion organizations find it very difficult to establish a business and survive. In this environment, clothing itself is less important than the frames that are used to sell it, which can be used in turn to sell licensed products. Consumers are no longer perceived as "cultural dopes" or "fashion victims" who imitate fashion leaders but as people selecting styles on the basis of their perceptions of their own identities and lifestyles. Fashion is presented as a choice rather than a mandate. The consumer is expected to "construct" an individualized appearance from a variety of options. An amalgam of materials drawn from many different sources, clothing styles have different meanings for different social groups. Like some genres of popular music and popular literature, clothing styles are significant to the social groups in which they originate or to whom they are targeted but are often incomprehensible to people outside these social contexts.

FASHION AND GENDER IN THE NINETEENTH AND TWENTIETH CENTURIES

Fashionable clothes are used to make statements about social class and social identity, but their principal messages are about the ways in which women and men perceive their gender roles or are expected to perceive them. In the nineteenth century, fashionable clothes generally expressed the gender roles of upper class women. The roles of working-class wives were ignored, while middle- and working-class employed women and middle-class women dress reformers developed alternative definitions of gender roles that were only tangentially reflected in fashionable dress.

The effect of nineteenth-century class structures on women was different than for men. Women at all social levels had few legal or political rights. Late nineteenth-century scientists argued that the differences between men and women justified different social roles. According to Russett (1989:11–12), "The overwhelming consensus . . . was that women were inherently different from men in their anatomy, physiology, temperament, and intellect. . . . Even as adults, they remained childlike in body and mind. . . . The great principle of division of labor was here brought to bear: men produced, women reproduced." A basic premise of the dominant ideology concerning women was the belief in fixed gender identities and in the existence of major differences between men and women. For women in the nineteenth century, fashionable clothing had elements of social control, since it exemplified the dominant and very restrictive conception of women's roles.

The ideal role of the upper-class woman, who was not expected to work either inside or outside the home, was reflected in the ornamental and impractical nature of fashionable clothing styles. For other women, who occupied different positions in the social structure, fashionable clothing was problematic in various ways. Middle-class wives may have attempted to emulate the fashionable clothes of the upper class, but with fewer economic resources for doing so. Less is known about how the appearance of working-class wives, whose budgets for clothing were often smaller than those of their husbands, indicated their confinement in the home and their exclusion from public space. Middle- and working-class employed single women occupied roles that contradicted the fashionable ideal gender role, because they worked and often had some financial independence. How did they respond to fashionable clothes? Did they exhibit a greater sense of agency than wives were able or willing to use? To what extent did they seek to dress in ways that subverted the gender values expressed in fashionable clothes?

For the most part, these possibilities are neglected in Simmel's analysis of fashion. He viewed fashion as affecting "externals — clothing, social conduct, amusements," areas which do not involve "really vital motives of human action." Fashion is viewed by Simmel (1957:548) as "an ideal field for individuals with dependent natures, whose self-consciousness, however, requires a certain amount of prominence, attention, and singularity. Fashion raises even the unimportant individual by making him the representative of a class, the embodiment of a joint spirit." In his view, women were most likely to exemplify this category of "dependent natures" and were in general likely to exhibit "a stricter adherence to the social average" (550). For Simmel, fashion was an outlet that satisfied women's desires for prominence that was unavailable to them in other fields. Simmel missed the fact that clothes are important for both genders, because they constitute a major factor in the presentation of self in public space.[9]

Fashion historians often claim that nineteenth-century men eschewed fashion in favor of an intentionally drab and conservative appearance. In fact, men's fashions changed regularly, and there were numerous types of jackets, trousers, cravats, ties, and hats that provided plenty of material for asserting or maintaining social status (Delpierre 1990). Traditional forms of working-class clothing were in use throughout the nineteenth century, along with new forms of working-class clothing such as denim overalls and jeans that appeared during the period. Regional costumes that had existed in England and France gradually disappeared.

By the late twentieth century, nineteenth-century notions of fixed gender identities and intolerance of gender ambiguity were gradually disappearing. Foucault's (1979) assertion that perceptions of gender are not fixed but the effects of medical and psychiatric discourses represents a change in worldview that has been occurring throughout the twentieth century. Butler (1990) theorizes that gender is communicated through social performances involving, for example, the adoption of certain styles of dress and types of accessories and makeup, but the self is not inherently masculine or feminine.

However, at the end of the twentieth century, hegemonic ideals of appropriate gender behavior and appearance still remain very different for each gender. Central to the concept of hegemony is the idea that hegemonic definitions of reality, norms, and standards appear "natural" rather than contestable. Hegemonic masculinity, transmitted through the media, demands that men attempt to exemplify in their behavior ideal conceptions of physical power and control, heterosexuality, occupational achievement, and patriarchal family roles (Trujillo 1991). It seems likely that these ideals are translated in very different ways in clothing that originates in and for different segments of the "fragmented" society. Leisure clothing would be expected to exemplify a more lenient interpretation of hegemonic masculinity than clothes for the workplace, while clothing styles that originate in certain types of subcultures, homosexual as compared with heterosexual, would be likely to engage in creative reinterpretations of hegemonic masculinity. Recently, Kellner (1990b) has argued that contemporary American media and popular culture can more accurately be understood in terms of the concept of conflicted hegemony. Kellner argues that no single elite dominates American society and that the media provide a site for conflicts, debates, and negotiations between different interpretations of the dominant culture.

Fashion for women as a form of media culture fits the definition of conflicted hegemony. In contrast to the character of hegemonic femininity in the nineteenth century, hegemonic femininity as presented in fashion and media images of fashion is conflicted rather than monolithic. Women are confronted with very different conceptions of female identities, ranging from the expression of blatant and marginal sexuality to feminine empowerment and dominance (Rabine 1994). Some images are conservative, while others are attempting to expand the definition of acceptable sexuality and sexual orientations. Feminists view hegemonic femininity as a conception of femininity based on masculine standards for female appearances that emphasize physical attributes and sexuality and that encourage women to look at themselves and other women as men would look at them (Davis 1997). However, attitudes of younger women toward media images identified with hegemonic femininity are said to be moving toward a conception of such images as indications of power rather than passivity (Skeggs 1993).

An analysis of women's images in fashion magazine advertising shows that they are indications of an "internally contradictory hegemonic process — an ongoing dialectic between dominant and oppositional discourses" (Goldman, Heath, and Smith 1991:71). Advertisers have been forced to incorporate oppositional elements into their advertising in order to hold the attention of increasingly sophisticated consumers. Diverse images in fashion magazines associated with clothing styles for women can be seen as an indication of the struggle to define women's identities in the late twentieth century.

If a woman views her personal appearance and her personal identity as an evolving "project" (Giddens 1991), then her choices of consumer goods become a complex form of negotiation between conflicting hegemonic norms, conveyed through images in the media, and her own understandings of gender differences. Wilson (1987:246) speaks of "the enormous psychological work . . . that goes into the production of the social self, of which clothes are an indispensable part." This type of activity becomes a way of overcoming the potentially overwhelming influence of commodities and the "prefabricated identities" they imply (Thompson and Haytko 1997:27). It also becomes a means for a person to resolve ambivalent feelings toward the expression of "master statuses" such as class, gender, and race through clothing (Davis 1992:26). Kaiser, Nagasawa, and Hutton (1991:172) emphasize the role of "appearance management" and the manipulation of symbols in "constructing and negotiating a sense of self." They state (173): "Through an active manipulation of symbols, individuals can strive to construct an identity that enables them to organize a personal sense of existence and to invest it with meaning."

Fashion has always had a social agenda for women, and clothing behavior is always socially motivated. In the nineteenth century, its agenda was conservative, based on a conception of women's roles that was widely shared. In the 1920s and 1960s, fashion's agenda was more progressive, reshaping the appearance of women in keeping with changes in their social roles and in the rest of society (Roberts 1994). Today, fashion has several diverse and inconsistent agendas, ranging from representations that echo sadomasochism and pornography to portrayals of women as empowered and androgynous. This raises the question whether and how women perceive the various social agendas attached to clothing in the fashion press and the extent to which they accept or reject these images as meaningful for the construction of their own appearances.

TRACKING THE EPHEMERAL:
Sources for the Study of Clothing

This study examines fashion and clothing choices in three countries—France, the United States, and England—over a period of 150 years. France and England are examples of class societies in the nineteenth century, but the case of the United States is ambiguous: it was widely believed to offer more opportunities for upward mobility than the other two countries, but the extent of its egalitarianism appears to have been exaggerated. France had the most conservative definition of gender roles, while England and the United States were more liberal. Today, because of its highly developed media cultures, the United States corresponds more closely to the characteristics of a postmodern, postindustrial society than either England or France, although the cultures of each of those countries contain elements of postmodernism. Material from different countries permits comparisons among styles of clothing behavior within the same period and between different systems of organizing the production of fashion and clothing styles.

Four sets of data are central to the study. The first two were collected by researchers during the nineteenth and early twentieth centuries. One consists of case studies by Frédéric Le Play and his collaborators of eighty-one French families drawn from different strata of the working class in the second half of the nineteenth century. Since information was used for both husbands and wives, the total number of people in this sample is 158 (four families were female-headed households). This group of studies includes all studies of French families conducted before 1910 and published by Le Play and his associates (Le Play 1877–79; La Société Internationale des Etudes Pratiques d'Economie Sociale 1857–1928).[10] Because the studies were conducted over a period of sixty years, it was possible to compare earlier studies with later ones. I chose to compare studies before and after 1875 on the grounds that major events in France in the early 1870s (France's defeat in the Franco-Prussian War in 1870 and the workers' rebellion known as the Commune shortly afterward) influenced the subsequent character of French society. The Le Play data are a unique resource for studying French working-class life in the nineteenth century. Aside from occasional references to a few of the case studies, this archive has never been thoroughly exploited. To date, no one has attempted to examine these materials systematically and quantitatively. Because of the wealth of information in these studies about the social context in which clothing was worn, these studies are an excellent source of information for understanding the ways in which the use of different types of clothing was influenced by the position of different working-class strata in French society and the extent to which fashionable clothing was adopted by members of the working class.

The second set of data consists of several studies of family budgets in the United States that were conducted in the late nineteenth and early twentieth centuries. These studies included information about expenditures by husbands and wives for clothing and details about types of clothing purchased. In the United States, Carroll Wright organized surveys of working-class family budgets and living standards in several American states and European countries. These studies were conducted in the 1870s and the 1890s and provide information about incomes and expenditures for food, clothing, housing, health, and other items for American and immigrant workers in the United States and for European workers. Similar studies by Wright and his colleagues provide information about the clothing behavior of young women and poor families (Wright 1969; Worcester and Worcester 1911). While not representative of the population at the time, these studies nevertheless provide virtually the only quantitative information about these types of behavior in the United States during the late nineteenth century.

A third set of data consists of my own case studies of fashion worlds in Paris, London, and New York based on analyses of the careers of national samples of fashion designers, obtained from the following studies: Benaïm (1988), Delbourg-Delphis (1984), Déslandres and Müller (1986), McDowell (1987), Stegemeyer (1988), Walz and Morris, 1978), and the *Journal du Textile*, a newspaper published for the fashion industry in Paris. These samples included luxury fashion designers who were established or who had received some recognition. The sizes of the samples were as follows: France, 146; Britain, 74; United States, 80. About 100 interviews were conducted with fashion designers, fashion magazine editors, fashion public relations staff, and fashion forecasting experts in the United States and France. By examining the evolution of fashion organizations in France, the United States, and England, I show how changes in the relationships between fashion organizations and their publics have affected the nature of fashion itself. Fashion no longer projects cultural ideals of gendered appearance and behavior but targets certain groups and lifestyles with specific types of products.

A fourth set of data consists of women's responses in focus groups to fashion photographs and clothing advertisements, which reveal their perceptions of media images of gender, sexuality, and sexual orientation. Focus groups were conducted with white and black undergraduates at universities in an East Coast city, with middle-aged women living in the same city, and with undergraduates at an international university in Paris. A total of forty-five women participated. They also completed a short questionnaire that elicited their attitudes toward fashion and clothing behavior. This study was intended to show to what extent women identify with images that represent contemporary fashion's conflicting hegemonic ideals for women's appearance.

These sets of data were useful but necessarily incomplete. The types of questions I was asking required additional types of information about the nature of clothing, the ways in which it was worn, and the social contexts in which styles of clothing were used. Since items of information about clothing practices are generally based on observation, historical documents, photographs, and artworks, they need to be cross-checked in different sources for reliability. Costume histories indicate what people of different social classes, occupations, regions, and countries typically wore in different periods. Costume histories and photographs were particularly useful in providing information about the role of accessories, such as hats, ties, gold watches, canes, parasols, and corsets in crossing or maintaining class boundaries.[11] Photographs appearing in costume histories and in collections devoted to the history of a particular city, region, industry, or occupation were revealing in the same sense that data from qualitative field studies are useful: not as representative samples of behavior but as illustrations of different types of behavior, particularly when comparable photographs of similar social situations could be located in the three countries.[12] The usefulness of photographs depends on the availability of information on the social backgrounds, environments, and histories of the subjects.

Histories of clothing that focused more on the context in which clothing was worn than on the styles of the clothing themselves were also useful.[13] Brew's (1945) study, which documented the extent to which fashionable styles were being used in different social strata in the United States in 1879 and 1909 was invaluable.[14]

Numerous histories of workers, servants, women, feminism, and shopping provided background information that was necessary for interpreting changes in clothing behavior (see references). In order to understand the relationship between the luxury fashion industry and street styles in the twentieth century, I consulted various fashion histories,[15] as well as books on street cultures and popular music costume design.[16] Trade journals for the garment industry were also useful, especially the *Journal du Textile*, published in Paris. Finally, recent studies of clothing wardrobes, expenditures for clothing, and attitudes toward clothing offered insights into the public's responses to contemporary clothing.[17] Use of a wide variety of materials about fashion and clothing choices, collected in various time periods and about various time periods, was intended to elucidate differences in the nature of the societies in which these types of behavior occurred, as discussed in the following section.

FASHION AND ITS SOCIAL AGENDAS:
A Research Program

The manner in which people perceive the social structure and conceptualize their identities within it has changed in the course of the twentieth century. These differences can be expressed by contrasting two ideal types representing "class" and "fragmented" societies. In class societies, class status was more salient than affiliation with a lifestyle. People perceived their social identities as relatively fixed, but those with less status sought to emulate the styles and behavior of those with higher status. By contrast, in fragmented societies, occupational settings are status hierarchies, but, outside the workplace, social distinctions are based on criteria that vary within as well as between social classes.

In this book, I treat clothing as a strategic site for studying changes in the meanings of cultural goods in relation to changes in social structures, in the character of cultural organizations, and in other forms of culture. For the study of class societies in the nineteenth century, models of class inequality and fashion diffusion suggest several questions related to the significance of clothing among members of different social classes: (1) Given their relatively limited resources, how did working-class men and women use clothing to express and negotiate their social positions in the nineteenth century? Were their clothing practices circumscribed by class and regional cultures, as Bourdieu's theory predicts? (2) To what extent did fashionable styles diffuse to the working class and under what circumstances? To what extent did the democratization of clothing occur in these countries? (3) How did economic and social changes affect clothing choices in the working class? Were clothes a new form of popular culture used by some segments of the working class to indicate changes in their relationship to the public sphere and public space?

Other examples of nineteenth-century clothing behavior cannot be understood with these models and require other approaches, such as theories of nonverbal communication and symbolic subversion (Goffman 1966; Cassell 1974) and hypotheses about the relationships between different types of public space. These perspectives suggest additional questions: (1) How did the powerful, hegemonic gender coding of clothes affect the use of clothing by women who were marginal according to the gender ideals of nineteenth century societies, such as middle-class and working-class women who were employed? (2) How did "secluded" public spaces, specifically those that were used exclusively by certain types of people (such as the American frontier, coal mines, and educational institutions for women) or used exclusively for leisure pursuits (such as beaches and areas set aside for certain types of sports) facilitate the wearing of clothing styles that were unacceptable on city streets? (3) How important were uniforms and dress codes as a form of social control?

In the late twentieth century, questions posed by models of class inequality and diffusion are less relevant. Various forms of fashionable clothing are worn by some members of all social classes, but the characteristics of social classes have changed, and patterns of fashion dissemination are much more complex than models of fashion diffusion suggest. Here it is necessary to rely on alternative models to explain the role of clothing in contemporary fragmented societies, such as Bell's (1976) model of postindustrial society, the complex concept of postmodernism (Kellner 1990a), including postmodernist theories of gender (Butler 1990), the role of cultural organizations and the media in the production and dissemination of cultural meanings (Peterson 1994), and theories of cultural reception (Press 1994). These approaches suggest the importance of the following questions: (1) What do patterns of diffusion of fashionable clothing by age and lifestyle indicate about the fragmentation of contemporary society? (2) How do the characteristics of organizations in which clothing is designed and manufactured influence the meanings and diffusion of clothing styles? (3) To what extent do men's clothing and the ways in which it is used by men confirm predictions based on theories of postindustrial societies? (4) How do clothes for work and leisure express the disjunction between economic and noneconomic roles? (5) How do leisure clothes exemplify the increasing complexity of cultural codes in fragmented societies? (6) To what extent do women's responses to images of fashionable clothing in the media indicate that they perceive themselves as postmodernist role players who enjoy using clothing to project heterogeneous and contradictory identities or that they view themselves as modernists who prefer clothing that expresses coherent and stable identities? (7) What does this analysis of women's interpretations of fashion and media culture reveal about the nature of hegemonic femininity as expressed in clothing?

Clothes and fashionable clothing styles are "carriers" of a wide range of ideological meanings or "social agendas." In this book, they will be used to trace changes in the nature of the relationships between social classes and lifestyles and between men and women, and to expand our understanding of material culture and its codes from the nineteenth century to the present.

NOTES

1. The major difference between the United States and Europe was in the level of upward mobility of unskilled workers, which was higher in the United States. In all three societies, the social structure gradually became more rigid during the nineteenth century, and the rate of upward mobility declined.

2. Exceptions to this statement include designer clothing sold at auction and antique clothing. Secondhand clothing is a relatively minor economic activity, although secondhand clothing stores exist in most major cities. Huge quantities of old clothes are regularly shipped to Third World countries, where clothes retain their traditional attributes of scarcity and as barter (McKinley 1996) and the poorest inhabitants are willing to wear ill-fitting, inappropriate castoffs from developing countries.

3. For further information about Le Play and his work, see chapter 2 and appendix 1. See also Kalaora and Savoye (1989).

4. Holt (1997a) defines "lifestyles" as collective patterns of consumption practices based on shared cultural frameworks that exist in specific social contexts.

5. The eight groups defined by this typology constitute the following proportions of the population (Waldrop 1994): Fulfilleds: 12 percent; Believers: 17 percent; Makers:

12 percent; Strugglers: 16 percent; Actualizers: 8 percent; Achievers: 10 percent; Experiencers: 11 percent; and Strivers: 14 percent.

6. Lamont et al. (1996) found that traditional attitudes were associated with specific geographical regions in the United States.

7. Halle (1984), in a study of working-class men in a factory setting and in their suburban homes, found that, in the factory, the men identified with the working class, but in their private lives, they sought to maintain middle-class lifestyles.

8. Smith and Clurman (1997) argue that the second group, the Boomers, are more oriented toward consumption that the two other groups. Weiss (1989) identified forty lifestyles in the United States. For a discussion of lifestyles in France, see Valette-Florence (1994). Studies of lifestyles in France suggest that slightly over one-third of the French population might be likely to engage in some form of postmodernist consumption (269).

9. For other critiques of Simmel, see Blumer (1969) and Davis (1992).

10. Additional studies were done that were not published and have not survived in manuscript form (personal communication from Antoine Savoie, author of two books about Le Play and his school, March 9, 1999).

11. See, e.g., for England: Byrde (1992); Cunnington and Cunnington (1959); Cunnington and Lucas (1967); Cunnington (1974); Ewing (1975); Ewing (1984); Gernsheim (1963); Ginsburg (1988); Lambert (1991); Levitt (1991); de Marly (1986); for the United States, Gorsline (1952); Lee Hall (1992); Kidwell and Christman (1974); Kidwell and Steele (1989); Severa (1995); for France, Blum and Chassé (1931); Delpierre (1990); *Femmes Fin de Siècle, 1885–1895* (1990). For accessories, see, e.g., Gibbings (1990), Robinson (1993), and Wilcox (1945).

12. See, e.g., Borgé and Viasnoff (1993), Hine (1977), Juin (1994), *La Mémoire de Paris, 1919–1939* (1993), and Severa (1995).

13. See, e.g., for England: Wilson (1987); for the United States: Banner (1984); for France: Chaumette (1995); Delbourg-Delphis (1981); Perrot (1981); Roche (1994); and Steele (1989a and 1989b).

14. Brew's sources included photographs, trade literature, newspaper and magazine advertisements, mail-order catalogues, autobiographies and diaries, books of etiquette, accounts by foreign visitors, and novels.

15. See, e.g., Chenoune (1993), Déslandres and Müller (1986), Garnier (1987), Martin and Koda (1989), and Milbank (1985).

16. See, e.g., Jones (1987), Obalk, Soral, and Pasche (1984), Polhemus (1994), and York (1983).

17. See, e.g., Brown (1994), Herpin (1986), and Pujol (1992).

Clothes are never a frivolity; they are always an expression of the fundamental social and economic pressures of the time. Laver (1968:10)

2 WORKING-CLASS CLOTHING AND THE EXPERIENCE OF SOCIAL CLASS IN THE NINETEENTH CENTURY

The classic model of fashion advanced by Simmel (1957) and Veblen (1899) claimed that new styles began with elites and gradually disseminated downward in the social structure. However, this theory offers little information about the categories of people who adopted fashionable styles or who retained traditional styles. Costume historians argue that, at least in cities, men in America, France, and England acquired a type of costume, consisting of a jacket and trousers, that was similar at all social class levels. Steele (1989a: 78) states: "Over the course of the nineteenth century, men of all classes came to wear more or less the same type of clothing." Some costume historians have extended the democratization thesis to include women's clothing (Kidwell and Christman 1974; Severa 1995). While, in a very literal sense, the democratization thesis appears to be correct, it too is silent on the extent of variations in appearance at different social class levels.

From the perspective of Bourdieu's (1984) theory of cultural tastes and class reproduction, one would expect changes in clothing behavior to have been more varied than is suggested by either the classical theory of fashion or the democratization thesis. Bourdieu argues that the consumption of cultural goods associated with the upper and middle classes requires attitudes and knowledge that are not readily accessible to members of the working class. His theory suggests that differences in clothing behavior between social classes would be maintained. The clothing of the working class would be practical, functional, and durable rather than aesthetically pleasing and stylish. Among members of the working class that did adopt middle-class dress, his theory suggests that intensive contacts with the middle class, possibly in certain types of occupations, might be sufficient to overcome lack of family socialization or middle-class education and lead to the adoption of middle-class tastes and clothing styles.

However, Bourdieu's approach is less clear about differences in responses to cultural goods within the working class. In the nineteenth century, the French working class consisted of several distinct strata, with different levels of income and different standards of living. In the fourth quarter of the century, social changes altered the relationships between these different social strata and changed workers' attitudes toward the middle class. France became increasingly industrialized, which led to an improvement in the situation of unskilled workers as compared with skilled workers, since there were more and better-paying jobs in factories. Consequently, Bourdieu's theory of class reproduction needs to be supplemented by an understanding of the effects of changes in the incomes and social relationships of members of different strata of the working class that were bringing them into contact with new forms of culture (Erickson 1996). In the middle of the century, the social environment of Paris was much more "modern" than that of provincial cities and of the farming communities in the countryside. During the last twenty-five years of the century, as the level of literacy increased, followed by expansion in the numbers of newspapers, towns and cities in the provinces became sites for working-class public spheres not unlike the bourgeois public spheres described by Habermas in England in the previous century (Calhoun 1994). Cafes, clubs, circles, and associations in which the working class participated appeared even in small towns. Rural communities were becoming less isolated, bringing certain groups, such as farmers, into contact with new forms of culture and public space. Members of the working class, both in cities and in the countryside, were becoming increasingly aware of styles of behavior at other levels of society.

While, in a very general sense, a new standard costume for men was gradually accepted during the nineteenth century, traditional types of clothing, particularly in the working class, continued to be worn. Trousers had been worn since antiquity but had not been fashionable (de Marly 1986:8, 27; Tarrant 1994:38). In the Middle Ages and subsequent centuries, they had been worn by soldiers, peasants, and probably even by the aristocracy, either as loose or full garments or as tight-fitting "pantaloons." Adopted by workers during the French Revolution, trousers may have contributed to the vogue for less extravagant styles of clothing in the nineteenth century. De Marly (1986:76) states: "Trousers were a craze for the urban young, and were given much political significance by the French Revolution: the revolt of the *sans-culottes* (those without kneebreeches), the trousered peasants, against the aristocratic establishment." By about 1840, they were widely worn for most daily activities in cities in England, France, and the United States, and in many rural areas as well (Tarrant 1994:42–44; Lee Hall 1992).[1] By the middle of the nineteenth century, trousers with jackets in varying styles— suits—were widely accepted (de Marly 1986:114; Blum and Chassé 1931: 111). In general, these clothes were black, in conformity with the norm set by the English dandy Beau Brummell for the clothing of a British duke in the early nineteenth century and followed first by the British aristocracy and soon after by the rest of Europe (de Marly 1985:84).[2] England assumed the role of fashion leader for men's styles, influencing both France and America (Byrde 1992:94).

Men in the nineteenth century are often said to have renounced fashion in favor of a drab, almost severe style of dress. In fact, the upper and middle classes wore several different fashionable styles of jackets and suits, including knee-length frock coats, tailcoats, and lounge coats and used numerous accessories. It was a style of clothing in which the luxury and ostentation of the previous century had been replaced by a deliberate asceticism, but presenting a fashionable appearance required time, taste, and money. Specific types of jackets and trousers were appropriate for different types of activities and times of day (Delpierre 1990). Some outfits were suitable for the city and others for the country. Accessories such as top hats, silk ties, silk and satin waistcoats, gloves, canes, and watches were also important elements in constructing the appearance of the middle- and upper-class man. As Perrot (1981:157) describes the period: "It is in the world of nuances and details that now everything takes place." Meanwhile, other types of clothing that had traditionally been worn by working-class men, such as smocks and wooden shoes, did not disappear until the twentieth century. The smock, a shapeless, sleeved, hip-length garment, had been worn by workers and peasants for several hundred years.

While the democratization thesis is believed to apply to women's clothing as well as men's, Bourdieu's theory is generally silent on gender differences. However, there are reasons to believe that working-class women and particularly working-class wives found it more difficult than working-class men to imitate the clothing of the middle and upper classes. One reason lies in the nature of women's clothing during this period. Because clothing styles for women originated in France, they were heavily coded with a particular set of values about the role of women, specifically the ideal role of the French bourgeois matron. This type of clothing served as an indication that the women who wore it had servants and did not have to perform household tasks or to work outside the home. Aristocratic idleness was seen as the suitable way of life for middle- and upper-class women. Fashionable women's clothing during this period was exceptionally restrictive and ornamental. The impractical construction of this clothing included at various periods tightly laced corsets, wide crinolines, and long trains, impeding even normal activities such as climbing the stairs or walking in the streets, and was detrimental to women's health. Consequently, fashionable clothing was unsuitable for the daily activities of most working-class women.

To what extent were working-class women able to construct a fashionable appearance in order to participate in social and community activities? Married, working-class women were at a disadvantage in this respect compared with employed, single women who had more disposable income. Clothing expenditures were one indication of the extent of working-class wives' involvement in social life outside the household (Smith 1994). Working-class wives generally spent less money on their own clothing than on the clothing of their husbands, daughters, and sons. By contrast, young, single, working-class women, including servants and other types of employees, were able to spend substantial amounts of their incomes on clothing worn outside the workplace as a means of enhancing their social lives and their prospects for upward mobility.

In nineteenth-century industrial societies, fashionable styles were created for the upper class, but diffusion of those styles to the working class depended upon a person's location in different social strata, the relationship between those strata and the public sphere, and the level of resources the individual could command within the family. The democratization thesis proposes that class differences were eliminated by the standardization of clothing, whereas the diffusion theory implies that class differences were maintained by the continual appearance of new styles created for elites. Does the evidence support the hypothesis that men's and women's clothing was democratized during the nineteenth century or that status barriers were difficult or impossible to overcome?

RECONSTRUCTING THE PAST: Frédéric Le Play's Studies of Working-Class Families

In order to study these questions of the diffusion and democratization of clothing, I rely on costume histories and a series of case studies of working-class families conducted by Frédéric Le Play and his associates during the nineteenth century. In his lifetime (1806–82), Le Play was an important figure in French and European social science, both as a theorist and as one of the originators of empirical sociology (Silver 1982). Trained as an engineer and not as a social scientist, he developed a methodology for the collection of qualitative and quantitative information (Le Play 1862). His methodology consisted of a system of categories for classifying information he obtained through case studies. For Le Play, the family was the focal point of social life; the character and organization of the family had enormous repercussions for the individual and for society itself. His goal was to describe and classify different types of working-class families as they existed in various parts of the world. With the assistance of several collaborators who applied his methodological system, he produced over 150 case studies of families, mainly in Europe but also in America and Asia. Beginning in the middle of the century, the project was administered by La Société Internationale des Etudes Pratiques d'Economie Sociale and continued for approximately seventy-five years. Probably the first private research foundation in sociology, the society was supported by 339 contributors, who were scientists, businessmen, lawyers, civil servants, publishers, and elected officials (Silver 1982:11).

Le Play sought to obtain information about the economic and social life of each family and about the social environment or community in which the family resided. Each case study consisted of four parts containing certain types of information which each author was expected to provide. In part 1, the worker was characterized by the nature of his or her employment, which constituted for Le Play an approximate classification of the social stratum the family occupied within the working class (Le Play 1862:21). The second part contained information about the family itself and its social and economic milieu. This section included detailed inventories of clothing and of all other family possessions.

Part 3 of each monograph presented a detailed description of the annual budget of each family, including receipts and expenses. Le Play believed that the family budget was an essential factor in understanding family life and that the day-to-day existence of the family was encoded in its budget. In his instructions on his method (Le Play 1862:31), he stated: "The complete and systematic listing of receipts and expenses of a family is, in fact, the way to verify information obtained through observation and the only means of thoroughly investigating the conditions of the material and moral existence of working class populations."[3]

Consequently, his approach required the collection of a great deal of information about the financial situation of the family, including its expenses and its income. The emphasis on budgets in Le Play's work is consistent both with characteristics of French family life and with French social science. The ideal bourgeois wife in the nineteenth century was expected to maintain meticulous accounts of all her expenditures. French magazines for women during the period published articles instructing women in the techniques of maintaining domestic budgets (Flamant-Paparatti 1984:77). Historical studies suggest that nineteenth-century bourgeois women did in fact maintain such accounts (see Smith 1981; and Perrot 1982). Historians have found household budgets to be important elements in reconstructing and interpreting the life of the French middle class in the nineteenth century. Twentieth-century French social scientists have continued to study family budgets (see, e.g., Herpin and Verger 1988) but generally without attempting to obtain the wealth of additional sociological information that Le Play's approach required.[4] The final section of each monograph was devoted to a discussion of general issues concerning the region, the family, local industry, and social organization. It was the only part of the monograph where the author was permitted to "deviate from the rigorous analysis of facts and to produce his own evaluation" (Le Play 1862:31).

How were materials for these monographs obtained? It appears that they were obtained through a series of visits to the families extending over a period of several months to a year. Both husband and wife were interviewed extensively, the husband providing information about his occupation and work life, and the wife details about the family budget and domestic life. Accuracy is suggested by the enormous amount of detail contained in each case study about, for example, items in the budgets and inventories of possessions such as furniture and clothing.

An important element in evaluating these materials is the question of how the cases were selected. Clearly these cases do not constitute a random sample. In the French population at the end of the century, the percentage of working-class men who were farmers or farm laborers was much higher than the percentage of men employed in other working-class occupations (62 percent vs. 38 percent [Duroselle 1972:85]. In the case studies, these percentages were reversed: 33 vs. 67. Although the process of selection is not very clear, it appears from comments in certain case studies that families were selected because they were believed to be representative of a particular subclass of worker in a particular region. Another criterion which appears to have been used and which is often used in qualitative research is the selection of cases in such a way as to maximize diversity. It appears that cases were chosen so as to represent a wide variety of regions and of occupations at different levels of the working class. The absence of a random sample is compensated for by the extraordinarily rich amount of detail that is available about each family and the fact that comparisons are possible over time (between the third quarter and the fourth quarter of the century).

Among the eighty-one monographs dealing with French families, Le Play produced six (he conducted a substantial proportion of the studies in other countries). The remainder were researched and written by forty-two investigators who were described as lawyers, engineers, and local officials. Eight of these investigators produced more than two reports. Most of them were unpaid, but a few who were not well-to-do were probably funded by Le Play out of his own pocket.[5]

Le Play's entire life was lived in the nineteenth century. The values and worldview of that century were exemplified in his work, which partially explains why his work has been almost totally eclipsed in the twentieth century. The case studies written by Le Play and his followers reveal his concerns about changes that were transforming French society during the nineteenth century in such a way as to decrease the importance of the family. Le Play revered a type of traditional society that he believed had formerly existed in France but was in the process of disappearing as a result of economic and social changes. He was concerned that changes brought about by the Industrial Revolution were destroying a delicately balanced social system in which paternalism on the part of the upper class led them to protect and guide the working class. He believed that the unhealthy influences generated by industrialization could be combated if religious organizations and the traditional family maintained their influence. The advantage of Le Play's methodological system is that it is not necessary to subscribe to his theoretical outlook in order to make use of the information that he and his followers collected.

The case studies include forty-two families that were observed in the third quarter of the century and thirty-nine families that were observed between 1875 and 1909.[6] Six intraclass strata among these eighty-one families represented distinctly different working-class environments: (1) skilled workers in Paris (artisans and craftsmen), (2) farmers who owned or rented land, (3) unskilled workers in Paris, (4) skilled workers in the provinces, (5) unskilled workers in the provinces, (6) unskilled farm laborers (see appendix table 1.1).[7]

These French families represent a situation that seems anomalous in light of the way we view social structure today. Some of these families had incomes comparable to those typical of lower levels of the middle class, but they were considered to be working class by Le Play and his associates on the basis of their occupations and standard of living.[8] Many of the families had the means to adopt middle-class dress, but not all of them did. Among the families studied before 1875, seven (17 percent) had incomes over 3,000 francs per year, the lowest among the middle class. All these families were headed by skilled workers in Paris or by farmers. Goulène (1974:40), speaking of the period before 1875, says: "The lower middle class (office workers, small businessmen, low-ranking civil servants) lead an existence sometimes close to that of the working class. Their major concern is to differentiate themselves as much as possible through external characteristics such as clothing." In the families studied after 1875, almost two-thirds (61 percent) had incomes over 3,000 francs per year. Particularly in the later period, these families were identified as working class on the basis of occupation rather than income.

In each period, there were considerable differences in the standard of living between these French families (see appendix table 1.1).[9] During the third quarter of the century, the skilled workers in Paris and the farmers constituted an elite among the working class; their standard of living was substantially higher than that of the other three groups, approaching that of the lower middle class. Unskilled farm laborers had the lowest standard of living. During the fourth quarter of the century, the situation of unskilled workers relative to skilled workers improved as wages in factories rose, while farmers' incomes increased substantially (see appendix table 1.1). In other words, the relationships between different strata changed significantly during the period in ways that would be expected to influence the types of clothing these men and women chose to wear.

The importance of clothing for these working-class families is suggested by the percentages of their annual incomes that were devoted to purchasing clothing or materials for making clothing: the median was 8 percent for both periods (see appendix table 1.2). Comparable figures for bourgeois families with modest incomes were 8.3 percent to 15 percent (Perrot 1982), indicating that the percentages of their incomes poorer families spent on clothing were similar to the percentages spent by more prosperous families. The median value of the clothing possessed by these families amounted to 13 percent of their total wealth (including property, buildings, equipment, furniture, and household utensils) in the earlier period and 16.5 percent in the later period (see appendix table 1.2), but there was considerable variation between different strata. Among those whose wealth was limited, clothing represented a significant share of their wealth: clothes were often their only valuable possessions.

The case studies specified precisely the types of clothes in each wardrobe (male and female), the numbers of such items a person owned, and the value of each item. The studies also specified whether an item of clothing was worn on Sunday or during the week. There were clearly two types of clothing in different types of materials in every wardrobe (see table 2.1), such as, for men, suits, jackets, and the occasional top hat, as compared with smocks, cotton or linen waistcoats, and vests, accompanied by straw hats, peaked caps, and berets. Middle-class clothing that was in good condition was generally worn on Sundays. At work, men and women wore traditional clothing or worn-out Sunday clothing.

Clothing was obtained in a number of ways. Major items of men's clothing were generally purchased. By the middle of the century, a sizable ready-to-wear clothing industry for men's clothes had developed in Paris that produced relatively inexpensive clothes for sale both in Paris and in the provinces (no. 13 [1856]: 446–47). Alternatively, men's clothes were made to order by tailors. Suits and jackets were often bought when a man married and, particularly in the provinces, were likely to be used for decades. One eighty-year-old tenant farmer was still wearing his wedding suit on Sundays (no. 80 [1892]). Men's work clothes, however, were frequently made by their wives. A water carrier in Paris wore clothes similar to those worn by workers in the region of France from which he had come (no. 17 [1858]: 153). The material for his clothes had been spun and woven in his village and was identical for both sexes except for the color, which was green for men and brown for women. Another worker in Paris, a ragpicker, was so poor that the hats and handkerchiefs in his wardrobe were items he had found on the streets.

Women's clothing was more likely to have been made at home, and again, this was especially true in the provinces. Many of the women were expert dressmakers, having been employed in that capacity before marriage. In some families, women received assistance from local dressmakers. The men and women in these families do not appear to have acquired used clothes and very rarely received gifts of clothing for themselves. Gifts of clothing were limited to children.

The nature of Le Play's materials makes it impossible to generalize about the motivations of workers and their wives in choosing to wear items of middle-class clothing. With a few exceptions, where the case studies provide specific information about the attitudes of a person toward specific items of clothing, it is not known whether workers and their wives perceived themselves as imitating the middle class or whether they were influenced by styles

TABLE 2.1

TYPES OF CLOTHES IN WORKING-CLASS MEN'S WARDROBES,
1850–74 AND 1875–1909 (in percentages)

Types of Clothing	1850–74 (*N* = 41)	1875–1909 (*N* = 36)
Middle Class		
Clothes		
Frock coat	21	19
Tailcoat	0	6
Dress jacket	27	3
Overcoat	39	53
Suit (3-piece)	10	50
Lounge coat	3	38
Suit jacket	34	19
Accessories		
Tie (silk)	46	17
Waistcoat (silk or satin)	17	3
Gloves	5	8
Cane	2	3
Watch with or without chain	12	43
Hats		
Top hat	22	22
Bowler	0	8
Working Class		
Clothes		
Smock	59	36
Waistcoat (knit, cotton, linen, flannel)	98	84
Accessories		
Tie (cotton or linen)	59	58
Apron	18	16
Shoes (wooden)	54	50
Hats		
Peaked cap	51	37
Cap, beret	34	23
Felt	49	47

Note: Based on inventories of working-class men's clothes in case studies conducted by Le Play and his associates, this table shows the percentage of men in each time period who owned specific items of clothing. This table excludes four female-headed households.

of dress being worn by their friends or in their communities. Testing Simmel's model of the diffusion of fashion and costume historians' hypothesis about the democratization of fashion does not require an understanding of people's motives for wearing specific types of clothing. What is important is whether or not they wore items of clothing that were identified with the upper and middle classes.

FASHION DIFFUSION OR DEMOCRATIZATION?
Clothing Owned by French Working-Class Men before and after 1875

Possession of a specific item of dress identified with either the middle or the working class indicates the level of fashion diffusion or, alternatively, of democratization among working-class men (see table 2.1). During the period 1850–74, a few workers owned items identified with the upper and middle classes, such as the knee-length frock coat and the dress jacket, but other items of clothing that became fashionable during this period, such as the tailcoat and the lounge coat were rarely found in their wardrobes. For Sunday use, fourteen workers (34 percent) possessed less stylish types of jackets, but only 10 percent owned suits (trousers, waistcoat, and jacket; see fig. 1). These clothes were generally in black or dark blue so that they could be used, when necessary, as mourning clothes.

During the week, workers were more likely to wear items of clothing that were identified with the working class. Twenty-four (59 percent) of this group possessed smocks of some sort (see fig. 2). Ninety-eight percent of the men owned sleeveless waistcoats, which were worn with trousers and shirts (see fig. 3). More than half the men wore wooden shoes.

Another indication of the diffusion of fashionable items was the use of middle-class accessories, such as top hats, gloves, canes, and watches, which might be interpreted as evidence that people sought to cross class boundaries. Costume historians have observed that since many accessories associated with clothing in the previous century had been abandoned, those that remained—hats, gloves, canes—became even more important as indicators of social rank (Dike and Bezzaz 1988:275; Perrot 1981). Only nine (22 percent) of the men in families studied before 1875 owned top hats, which, according to a costume historian (Delpierre 1990:27) "covered almost all heads" during this period. Another status marker was the black silk or satin tie. Nineteen

(46 percent) owned ties of this sort for Sunday wear. The silk or satin waistcoat or vest was also identified with the middle class: seven workers (17 percent) owned such items. However, certain types of accessories identified with the middle class were apparently not seen as appropriate for the working class, since these workers rarely used them. For example, canes and gloves were indispensable middle-class accessories but were apparently not utilized by workers in this period.

During the last quarter of the century, a number of changes affected social environments in the working class that were noticeable in the resources available to families in the case studies. More than half the families had incomes over 3,000 francs, the minimum income for the middle class. This was reflected in an improvement in the stylishness of the Sunday clothing of some workers. The lounge coat became somewhat more popular (38 percent). Owning a suit (jacket, waistcoat, and trousers) increased substantially (from 10 percent to 50 percent), and it was worn by all types of workers and farmers. The overcoat also increased in popularity. Certain types of clothing identified with the working class and with rural areas were less frequently worn. For example, only 36 percent of the men in the later period wore the smock, as compared with 59 percent of the earlier group, but the number of men wearing wooden shoes remained about the same (see table 2.1).

As in the previous period, there appeared to be certain items of clothing or accessories identified with the middle class that were not seen as appropriate for members of the working class, and consequently most workers hesitated to wear them. The percentage of men wearing frock coats and tailcoats remained small. Canes and gloves, which were essential aspects of bourgeois dress (according to Delpierre [1990:60], "Men never went out without a cane"), were still virtually nonexistent. Watches were the only middle-class accessory that became much more prevalent among the men in these families.

These data suggest that democratization of clothing occurred in a rather limited sense during the last quarter of the nineteenth century. The number of workers owning at least one fashionable item increased from 63 percent in the first period to 92 percent in the second period. However, the diffusion of fashionable styles was limited to certain items (see table 2.1). The proportion of workers owning suits and overcoats increased substantially, but the extent to which they owned other types of fashionable clothing identified with the middle class, such as frock coats, tailcoats, and top hats, changed very little. Consequently, increases in the incomes of these men can explain only part of the changes that occurred.

WHO WAS FASHIONABLE AND WHO WAS UNFASHIONABLE? Variation within the Working Class before and after 1875

According to the theory of fashion diffusion, those at higher levels of the working class should have been better dressed than those at lower levels. In both periods, the authors of some of the case studies included their judgments on whether members of the families dressed in the style of the middle class, usually on Sundays. Eight men (20 percent) studied before 1875 were identified as having a style of dress comparable to that of the middle class. Surprisingly, only two of these men had incomes comparable to the lower levels of the bourgeoisie, which again suggests that income was not the only factor influencing clothing behavior. However, these men were located in the upper-working-class stratum. All but one of these men were skilled workers in Paris or the provinces. Eleven men (27 percent), mainly farmers and farm laborers in the provinces, were specifically described as being dressed in a manner that had "no affinity with the bourgeoisie," "without refinement," or "very simply."

Skilled workers in Paris and, to a lesser extent, in the provinces dressed in the style of the middle class on Sundays by wearing frock coats, silk ties, silk or satin waistcoats, and top hats. Skilled workers were artisans and craftsmen whose work brought them into contact with the middle class.[10] Bourdieu's theory suggests that they might have acquired bourgeois tastes in clothing and the appreciation of fine clothes as a result of these contacts. Their business relationships with the middle class may have constituted, in effect, a form of socialization for these men, learning "on the job" how to emulate the clothing style of the middle class. Artisans had the highest prestige in the working class, particularly those associated with the manufacture of luxury goods. Among the skilled workers in Paris during the third quarter of the century, the tailor was considered by the author of the case study of one family to be exceptionally well dressed. The author commented (no. 13 [1856]: 162, 163): "As customary among tailors in Paris, he wears the clothes of the middle class. . . . Their relations with the practices associated with the bourgeois class oblige the tailors to put on a more elegant appearance than that of other workers and to develop a taste for clothing."

Bourdieu (1984), however, would argue that styles of middle-class taste and behavior acquired by the working class are never identical to those of the middle class. The upwardly mobile person retains certain characteristics from his previous background. This idea is exemplified in the case of the tailors, some of whom wore middle-class clothing but retained other, inelegant tastes of the working class. The author of the case study states (no. 13 [1856]: 163–64): "Association with women who have a bad reputation is habitual among these workers and, in the midst of this debauchery, they develop the taste for wine and strong liquor." But some tailors acquired other bourgeois tastes in addition to clothes. The same case study continues: "Their leisure pursuits are not unlike those of dissipated young men from superior backgrounds, and one notices ordinarily that they seek artistic pleasures, such as parties where people sing, races in canoes on the Seine, and theater parties. . . . Intellectual distractions are also sought by tailors; most of them, especially in the workshops, read a great many inexpensive books on historical topics and these notions, more or less exact, provide the background for their political preoccupations."

An important motive for imitating the clothing of the middle class in Paris — the desire to participate in social activities in the city — is suggested in the account of the leisure activities of a skilled weaver of shawls (no. 7 [1857]: 318–19). One of the major recreations in the nineteenth century was walking in the city and in the surrounding countryside. Because this particular worker was relatively well-to-do, he was able to participate in this type of activity, unlike many of his fellow workers. According to the authors of this case study, "In the shawl-making industry, as in many others, workers rarely go out; in general they would like to take promenades but they are discouraged from doing so by *the shame they experience in showing themselves in public wearing clothes unsuitable for this activity*" (italics added).

This comment suggests the salience of clothes during the period, as well as a perception of public space as one in which a person's appearance is subject to the critical gaze of strangers. On workdays, these workers, and particularly the unskilled ones, wore the distinctive work clothes of their class: smocks, cotton or linen waistcoats, wooden shoes, and peaked caps.

Among the skilled workers in the provinces, only the artisans — a glassmaker, a fan maker, a pottery maker, and a glove maker — attempted to dress like the middle class. On Sundays, these workers wore clothing identified with the middle class such as frock coats, silk waistcoats, and silk ties. The fan maker's wardrobe included another sign of identification with the middle class — trousers and a waistcoat made of materials described as *"fantaisie,"* meaning that they were printed with fancy patterns, in contrast to the almost universal black or dark blue typically worn on Sundays by the working class. Compared with other workers, the fan maker had an unusually large number (ten) of items of Sunday clothes and spent 16 percent of his income on clothing for himself and his family (no. 40 [1863]). The glove maker's Sunday clothes were described as "very elegant and very numerous" (no. 55 [1865]).

During the week, however, these artisans wore working-class clothes. Other workers in the provinces wore working-class clothes, including smocks, on Sundays as well as weekdays.

By contrast, despite their relatively high incomes and levels of wealth, the farmers made little attempt to imitate the middle class. Farmers belonged to a distinctly different cultural milieu, one which was more likely to be anchored in the past. Half of the sixteen farmers and farm laborers were illiterate or semiliterate, or spoke only a local dialect. As a result, they were unable to participate in the national culture by reading newspapers and books or by taking part in political debates. The author of a case study of one of the farmer families commented (no. 59 [1862]: 178): "The ignorance of the family is profound . . . and that absolute ignorance, with which, although proud and rich, they appear to be satisfied, explains their abstention from politics as well as from religion."

The few items of bourgeois clothing among the farmers included one frock coat and four silk ties. There were no silk waistcoats among the farmers or the farm laborers. Those who were attempting to adopt new styles imitated the working class in cities rather than the middle class. Farmers wore smocks, although not as frequently as the workers in Paris and the provinces. Three farmers were still wearing distinctive occupational costumes that had originated centuries before.

The clothing of members of the lowest stratum, the farm laborers, revealed the scarcity of their resources. They were described as wearing clothes that had been repaired until they were completely worn out. Four wore old Sunday clothes at work. Most wore the smock. All six wore felt hats and wooden shoes. The parents' old clothes were used to make clothes for their children.

Before 1875, diffusion of fashionable items was limited to the higher strata of the working class; democratization of clothing was relatively limited. For a broader diffusion of clothing styles to occur, barriers of tradition, poverty, and illiteracy had to be overcome. Because of the expense of clothing, men in the lower strata attempted to make each piece of clothing last as long as possible. Their clothes were often described as having been very frequently repaired. The clothing of many of these workers reflected "the culture of necessity" that Bourdieu attributes to the working class.

After 1875, the relative standing of the working-class strata represented in the case studies changed (see appendix table 1.1). The unskilled workers now had a higher median income than the skilled workers. Some unskilled workers earned higher salaries in factories than some skilled workers earned as artisans. For example, aside from the farmers, the worker who earned the highest income was an unskilled worker in Paris who polished bronze in a factory. In comparison with the median for the entire group, he spent a high proportion of his income on clothes for his family (19 percent; see appendix table 1.2). Another man in Paris had formerly worked as an artisan, making artificial leaves for artificial flowers, which were in great demand by milliners for women's hats, but he had frequently been unemployed. As an unskilled worker in a factory, however, he was much better paid, even though he was performing a task that was entirely mechanical and repetitive, and was never unemployed. There were still unskilled workers in Paris who were too poor to buy decent clothes, such as the ragpicker, who did not go out on Sundays with his family because he was ashamed of the family's clothes (no 41A [1878]:194). Perhaps in response to changes in the situation of unskilled workers, the skilled workers in Paris now spent a substantially higher percentage of their incomes on clothing (11.5) than members of all the other strata (see appendix table 1.2).

After 1875, the percentage of workers who were specifically cited as dressing like the middle class or with refinement was similar to the previous period—19 percent—but now most of these men had lower-middle-class incomes. Unlike in the previous period, more than half of those who were dressing in the style of the middle class were not living in the Paris area. Only five workers (14 percent), mainly in the provinces, were specifically described as being dressed in a manner that had "no affinity with the bourgeoisie," "without refinement," or "very simply."

In the provinces, workers were still less prosperous than those in Paris, as shown by median income (see appendix table 1.1). However, they were now more aware of national events and trends and were said to be anxious to show that they were not inferior to the middle class. Describing the inhabitants of a small town, one author (no. 104 [1904–5]:273) noted "the intense desire of the workers to imitate bourgeois life in all its exterior manifestations. Unsatisfied, this expectation is exaggerated so that clothing, fashion magazines, goods of all kinds absorb almost all their savings."

Accessories that had previously been used exclusively in the top stratum of the working class were now adopted by the less prestigious groups. Watches with or without chains appeared in the clothing inventories of unskilled workers in the provinces.[11] The top hat was now worn by unskilled workers and farmers, even though it was described by a costume historian as the "elegant hat" of the period (Delpierre 1990:39). Another hat that became fashionable among the middle class during this period, the bowler, was adopted by only three members of this group, not, as one might have expected, skilled workers in Paris, but unskilled workers in Paris and in the provinces. However, in the workplace, clear-cut distinctions between workers and employers remained (see. fig. 3).

With the exception of one tenant farmer, all the farmers and tenant farmers had incomes comparable to those of the lower middle class.[12] While the majority of the farmers were still religious and conservative, most were now literate and therefore exposed to external influences. Local languages did not disappear but ceased to be the only language spoken. Farmers were now more likely to read newspapers and were less bound by tradition. Traditional regional costumes had virtually disappeared by the fourth quarter of the century. Only two farmers, both middle-aged, wore the traditional costume or remnants of it. The only one who wore the complete traditional costumes, made in his home, both in the work-day and the Sunday version, worked in the salt marshes on the western coast of France (no. 47 [1883]:22–23).[13] His son wore contemporary clothing. A case study of a farmer's family living in the southwestern part of France found that the clothes worn in the community "were very much like those worn in other parts of France" (no. 44 [1881]:3). The farmers' increasing exposure to national trends was reflected in their adoption of some of the clothing identified with the middle class, particularly among the younger generation. The same extended family might exhibit two distinct sartorial styles, as seen in this vignette from one of the case studies (no. 94 [1897–99]:149): "The family still appears to be completely rustic, without intellectual refinement, when one looks at the mother and father—veritable winegrower of olden times—but it takes on an aspect of the urban lower middle class of the north when one sees it represented by the son, well-dressed, accompanied by his hunting dogs, and by the daughter-in-law, coquettishly dressed in outfits from a department store in Paris. The father . . . is in the center between the past and the future."

As costume historians have documented, during the nineteenth century a new wardrobe of men's clothes replaced the clothing worn in the previous century. However, in France, different social strata in the working class adopted particular items and accessories from this wardrobe to varying degrees. This is revealed through the use of indexes of middle-class and traditional working-class clothing items in which workers were scored on the basis of the numbers of fashionable and traditional items they possessed.[14]

Table 2.2 indicates that before 1875, those who were most likely to have items of middle-class clothing in their wardrobes were skilled and unskilled workers in Paris. Among the skilled workers living in provincial cities, a minority (the artisans) owned such items, while the farmers and farm laborers rarely did. During this period, skilled workers in Paris were beginning to reject traditional items of working-class clothing, although other urban workers

TABLE 2.2
MIDDLE-CLASS AND TRADITIONAL CLOTHES
IN WORKING-CLASS MEN'S WARDROBES,
1850–74 AND 1875–1909

Region and Occupation	Index of Middle-Class Clothing	
	1850–1874 (*N* = 41)	1875–1909 (*N* = 36)
Paris		
Skilled	3.5	2.5
Unskilled	2.6	3.7
Provinces		
Skilled	1.9	1.7
Unskilled[a]	0.6	2.7
Farm owners	1.0	2.0
Farm tenants	—	1.6
Average	1.9	2.4

	Index of Traditional Clothing	
	(*N* = 41)	(*N* = 35)[b]
Paris		
Skilled	2.7	2.0
Unskilled	3.2	1.2
Provinces		
Skilled	3.9	3.2
Unskilled[a]	2.5	2.6
Farm owners	2.9	3.8
Farm tenants	—	3.2
Average	3.0	2.7

Note: The index of middle-class clothing used seven items for
each period. The index of traditional clothing used six items
for each period. Workers in each occupational stratum were
scored on each item in each index, and their total scores were
averaged for the stratum. The table shows the average scores
for each stratum on each index in both periods. For a description of the items of clothing used in the indexes, see n. 14.
[a] Unskilled workers in the provinces were farm laborers during
the period 1850–74. During the later period, they were employed in provincial cities and towns.
[b] Excludes one worker, who wore a military uniform.

were not. Farmers and particularly farm laborers had relatively few clothes, so that their stocks of either middle- or working-class clothing items were small. During this period, they lived in "enclaves" that favored tradition rather than change.

After 1875, scores on the indexes of middle-class and traditional working-class items show that the unskilled workers in Paris were the most fashionably dressed group in the study, but even the unskilled workers in provincial cities were more "fashionable" than the skilled workers in Paris. The farmers wore more middle-class items than in the previous period (fig. 4). The farmers, both owners and tenants, continued to wear traditional clothing, but the skilled and particularly the unskilled workers in Paris had virtually abandoned it.

These changes in clothing preferences cannot readily be explained by the fashion-diffusion model, since lower strata in the later period were sometimes more fashionable than higher strata. They do suggest an uneven and rather incomplete process of democratization, since the diffusion of fashionable items varied considerably within the working class (see fig. 5).

Factors emphasized by Bourdieu such as socialization in the family or even in the workplace are insufficient to explain these changes. Instead, workers' adoption of middle-class clothing seems to have been a response to expanding social horizons in which previously excluded workers had access to expanding social circles that brought them into contact with new, often oppositional political ideas as well as new consumer goods (Erickson 1996). The fact that some men adopted certain aspects of bourgeois clothing, along with, paradoxically, negative political attitudes toward the middle class (see below), is consistent with this thesis.

CLOTHING AND THE EXPERIENCE OF SOCIAL CLASS AFTER 1875

During the fourth quarter of the century, workers' incomes rose, but opportunities for workers to become employers declined. The development of big businesses "accentuated . . . the gulf between managers and workers" (Goulène 1974:43). According to Goulène (57), "The defeat of 1870 [in the Franco-Prussian War of 1870] and the Paris Commune [a workers' revolt in the same year] marked the beginning of working-class participation in political struggle." Strikes became increasingly prevalent, along with workers' clubs and cafes that were centers for political activity.[15] The author of an early case study (no. 59 [1862]:217), describing the provinces during a later visit to the area in 1886, noticed considerable change: "Cafes, concerts, press, inexpensive publications, photographs, circles and associations of all kinds have invaded even the most insignificant hamlet." A case study (no. 107 [1889]:462) described a small town in the central region of France that had 90 cafes and inns for a population of 9,000 inhabitants. These establishments were described as "veritable clubs, where war is openly declared against capitalism," along with lengthy discussions of socialist theories.

What was the relationship between opposition to the social order and sartorial practices? Was there any evidence that resistance to the social order was expressed through clothing styles that violated accepted standards of dress, as has sometimes been the case in the twentieth century? In this period, some of the workers who were well paid and consequently well dressed were also socialists and would-be revolutionaries. The cases of two very prosperous skilled workers in Paris are revealing. One was a carpenter who supervised other employees, earned a relatively high salary, and dressed in the style of the lower middle class. At the same time, he was an important member of a socialist political organization whose goal was "the complete reorganization of society" (no. 70 [1889–90]:341). For this man, "Politics was the principal and even the sole diversion. . . . Each of his hours of leisure is consecrated to the study of the most efficacious means to exacerbate class hatred" (337).

Another skilled worker in Paris with revolutionary opinions was a cabinetmaker (no. 74 [1891]) who worked in ateliers that produced the most expensive and luxurious pieces of furniture of the period. Well-paid and spending a high proportion of his income (17 percent) on clothing (he wore silk ties), he led a lifestyle that was close to that of the middle class. His son was an apprentice sculptor, a middle-class occupation. His leisure pastimes included skating and picnics in the suburbs and attendance at café concerts and theaters. At the same time, he was secretary of a political association and devoted much of his leisure time to reading leftist newspapers and to discussions with fellow workers. Their goal was to overthrow the state. By contrast, an illiterate ragpicker, at the very bottom of the social scale, was described as having no antagonism toward the upper classes. The author of the case study attributed this to "that ignorance which prevents him from reading the newspapers" (no. 41A [1878]:189).

Only one worker, unskilled but earning an income higher than that of many skilled workers in Paris, was sensitive to the contradiction between his clothing and his political opinions. An anarchist, he spent much of his leisure time with men who shared his opinions (no. 115 [1896]:97). Together, they organized a library containing books related to their political views. Before he became an anarchist, he had belonged to a choral society and on Sundays had worn a frock coat and a top hat. He told the author of the case study that he had seen himself as becoming middle class. After becoming an anarchist, he stopped wearing the frock coat and instead adopted a lounge suit, for which he paid less than one-third the price of the frock coat. He also ceased to wear his overcoat on the grounds that it was too pretentious. He replaced it with a long cape with a hood that cost one-third the price of the overcoat.

LE PLAY IN ENGLAND: Gentlemen versus Workers

Costume historians disagree about the level of democratization of clothing in England toward the end of the nineteenth century. Ginsburg (1988:175), a museum curator, claims that in England "visible distinction between classes slowly begins to become less apparent in the last two decades of the century." Alternatively, Levitt (1991:13), who analyzed a national archive of portrait photography in Britain, concludes: "The rigid class system was nowhere more apparent than in clothing, through which power, wealth, and status were expressed. . . . Vulgarity, inferior workmanship, and shoddy materials distinguished the less well-bred, while a poor person's situation was instantly apparent."

A small number of English case studies in the 1850s by Le Play and his associates offer evidence of differences in the quality and quantities of men's clothing in the English working class. The character of the most "fashionable" of these wardrobes can be compared with information from other sources about the wardrobes of typical "gentlemen" of the upper middle class. This type of comparison reveals that fashionable clothing as adopted by the working class was a veneer rather than a way of life.

Le Play's case studies reveal substantial differences in the types and amounts of clothing owned by different families in the English working class. At the lowest end of the social scale, the clothing of a smelter in Derbyshire (no. IV [1850]), with a wife and four children, was almost entirely second-hand and so minimal that the author of the study omitted the inventory that usually accompanied these studies. A cutler in Sheffield (no. II [1851]), with a wife and three children, had a wardrobe which exhibited "a state of habitual penury." It also was not described. However, a somewhat more prosperous cutler (no. I [1851]) in London, with a wife and six children, dressed in blue frock coats, one for Sunday and one for work. A carpenter (no. III [1842–51]) in Sheffield had a Sunday suit of black cloth, a silk waistcoat, and a silk tie, as well as another suit for work. A tenant farmer (no. 8 [1856]) had a cloth suit, a silk waistcoat, and a black silk hat. Finally, a dairy farmer (no. 6 [1857]) had several items of clothing that resembled those of the middle class, including a black frock coat, satin and velvet waistcoats, satin ties, a black silk hat, and a silver watch with a gold chain.

Comparing the wardrobe of the dairy farmer, the largest in this group of mid-century English workers, with that of a typical well-dressed upper-middle-class Englishman of the period indicates that the latter must have included many more items. In 1857, the dairy farmer had a morning coat, a frock coat, four overcoats, six pairs of trousers, and seven waistcoats, but there is no indication that these items were purchased in that year. In fact, some of these items had been given to him at the time of his marriage, several years before. By contrast, in the 1860s, the well-dressed middle-class Englishman was expected to purchase *each year* four morning coats, a frock coat, a dress coat, an overcoat, six pairs of trousers, and five waistcoats (Ginsburg 1988:183).

According to costume historians, by the 1870s, those who belonged to the upper strata of the working class were able to imitate the clothing styles of the middle class, if not the amplitude of their wardrobes, even on very modest salaries (Byrde 1992:88). In the early 1870s, the *Tailor and Cutter*, a trade magazine, claimed: "In these days, the clerk with a very moderate salary can appear on the promenade with all the airs and appearances of those very much his superiors" (quoted in Byrde 1992:88). In the sole case study for 1888 (no. 69 [1888]), the author commented: "The clothing of English workers has lost all local character . . . no external characteristics distinguish well-to-do workers from the lower middle class."

However, the difference between the wardrobe of the subject of the 1888 case study, a tanner, and the wardrobe of a fashionable member of the upper middle class can be seen by comparing the inventories of their clothing. The tanner had three suits of clothing (jacket, waistcoat, and trousers), one for Sundays and holidays, one for the house on days when he was not working, and one for work. By contrast, in 1890, according to the *Tailor and Cutter*, (Cunnington and Cunnington 1959:310): "The smart man has a fresh coat for every day of the week. He will start the season with about twenty suits. . . . Thrice each day does a fashionable man array himself; a tweed suit is his morning wear; in the afternoon, he dons a frock coat, a smarter waistcoat, and a bigger tie. In the evening, he dresses for dinner."

A middle-class man was expected to buy four new suits a year (Ginsburg 1988:183). Middle- and upper-class ties were more difficult to copy in England than in France, since the former were frequently identified with organizations to which workers did not belong: private clubs, private schools, and elite regiments (Gibbings 1990:81). Ties worn by workers at their jobs were an indication of middle-class aspirations. Workers without such aspirations were more likely to wear scarves (Gibbings 1990:84–85; de Marly 1986:118). However, canes, which were virtually never used by French workers, were widely sold on English city streets on Sundays and greatly contributed to an elegant appearance, "no matter what social rank" a person held (Dike and Bezazz 1988:290).

At the end of the century, workers in the upper strata of the English working class were, like many middle-class men, wearing lounge suits, but men at the lowest levels of the working class still dressed mainly in secondhand clothing. Charles Booth (1903, 5:325), in his extensive study of the working class in London at the end of the century, describes the very poor as wearing the "cast-off clothes of the wealthy . . . disreputable in appearance, ill-fitting and unsuitable."

CLOTHING BEHAVIOR AND WORKING-CLASS WOMEN IN FRANCE

Compared with their husbands, the working-class wives in the Le Play case studies had very different relationships to the world outside the family, both that of employment and that of social life. Twenty-nine percent of the working-class wives were employed, but in the majority of the cases, employed wives worked in their homes.[16] Four families were female-headed households. There was little variety in the types of jobs these women held. Clothing was a major aspect of their jobs. Over half performed tasks that were in some way related to the making of cloth or of clothing. For example, these women were employed making lingerie, corsets, gloves, coats, and men's waistcoats or spinning thread for cloth. Several others had worked as dressmakers before marriage.

During this period, the social gap between the French middle-class woman and the working-class woman was probably even greater than that between men in the two classes. Flamant-Paparatti (1984:30) describes the situation of the women in the two classes as one in which, particularly in the cities, each class evolved "in its own sphere, in its own microcosm, without any point of contact."

Within the home, working-class women, like their bourgeois counterparts, were expected to manage the family's assets and socialize the children.[17] Those who had some knowledge of figures were expected to maintain accurate domestic accounts. The authors of one of the case studies comment on the role of one of the wives (no. 1 [1856]: 10): "She is immediately entrusted with the total sum of her husband's monthly pay, and it is she who, each morning, gives to her husband the money required for his meals . . . to her, in a word, *in conformity with the general custom among French workers . . . is confided the entire administration of the internal affairs of the family and the allocation of its resources*" (italics added).

The working-class wife, like middle-class women, was also expected to be concerned about her appearance. In 1873, a writer for a magazine for middle-class women stated (quoted in Flamant-Paparatti 1984: 95): "I have told you this, and I will come back to it often: a woman, even if she is a simple worker, ought always to be a woman, and to take *extraordinary* care of her appearance" (italics added).

While it is not clear to what extent they were aware of these expectations, it would have been difficult for most French working-class wives to conform to expectations of this sort. This was particularly true of women in families studied before 1875. While 20 percent of the men in the pre-1875 families were considered by the authors of the case studies to be dressing in the style of the middle class, only three (7 percent) of the women in this group (all wives of skilled workers) were evaluated in this way. In the later period, six wives (17 percent, compared with 19 percent of husbands) were identified by the authors of the case studies as wearing a style of dress close or identical to that of the middle class.

More likely than men to remain at home, working-class wives may have been less aware of bourgeois styles of dress than their husbands. Another factor that prevented them from dressing like the middle class was their limited financial resources for making or acquiring clothes. Family clothing budgets reveal the inferior position of these working-class wives in comparison with their husbands. Budgets for families studied between 1850 and 1874 show that 29 percent of the families spent more for the worker's clothing than his wife's. In only 21 percent of the families did the wife spend more than the husband. In the remaining families, husbands and wives spent about the same amount per year on clothing. Among the families who were studied during the later period, the husbands were even more likely to spend more on their wardrobes than their wives: 70 percent spent more than their wives. Only one farm family reported that they spent less on the husband's clothing than on the wife's. In actual expenditures, the husbands in French working-class families studied after 1875 spent considerably more than their wives (35 percent more in Paris, 44 percent more in provincial cities, and 20 percent more in the countryside).

Not surprisingly, the head of the family was more likely than his wife to be described as dressing in the style of the middle class; the wife was more likely to be wearing *"le costume populaire."* [18] Variations in the same family were sometimes striking. The husband and wife in a farm family were described as follows (no. 21 [1859]): "The clothes of the worker, purchased ready-made in Marseille, are in the style of the working class of the city. . . . The wife has a costume that is entirely rustic, clean but extremely simple." A similar contrast is seen in figure 1, in which the husband is wearing stylish clothes of the period, but the wife is dressed in traditional clothing. Again, the tenant farmers' wives in figure 4 are more traditionally dressed than their husbands.

A third factor that limited working-class wives in imitating the clothes of the middle class was the nature of the clothes themselves. Cunnington and Cunnington (1959:460), discussing the fashions of the period, which were set in France, state: "The true symbol of ladylike elegance was the correctness of every detail of the costume for each particular occasion." Middle-class dress was signified in several ways: first, by specific details of the style of an outfit, for example, the tight fit of the sleeves or a bustle or train on a skirt (certain details of clothing changed every year and can be dated precisely) (Severa 1995); second, by the use of expensive and fragile fabrics; third, by the use of light and bright colors; and fourth, by accessories, including hats, gloves, shoes, parasols, fans, and handkerchiefs and by lingerie such as corsets and crinolines.

While fashionable clothing was highly unsuitable for the daily activities of most working-class women, they sometimes made a considerable effort to conform to these styles, particularly if they participated in activities outside the home. The distinction between Sunday and weekday clothing was very important in these women's wardrobes. On Sundays, their clothing was likely to be closer to the middle-class ideal than on weekdays. Although information is lacking on the styles of the dresses worn by these women, the clothing inventories provide detailed information about specific items they owned, including different types of apparel and accessories. These data suggest that the level of democratization of clothing styles was very low. With the exception of wives of skilled workers living in Paris, differences between the styles of dress of these working-class wives and those of middle-class women were evident.

In the families studied before 1875, almost all of the wives owned dresses. In most cases, they owned at least one dress that was meant to be worn on Sundays and another for weekdays. Almost two-thirds of the women owned more than two dresses, while 10 percent owned eleven or twelve dresses. Regardless of the style of these dresses, the materials and the colors identified these women as working class. During the daytime, middle-class women wore dresses made of different types of silk, velvet, and muslin (for summer) in the city and cotton in the country (Delpierre 1990:24; Cunnington and Cunnington 1959:450). Only three working-class wives in the group (all living in or near Paris) owned silk dresses. Most of these working-class women wore wool or printed calico, which was easily washed (see fig. 6).

Middle-class women wore light colors that became increasingly vivid during this period as new aniline dyes were introduced that permitted a wider range of hues. Although information about colors of clothing is available for only slightly more than half of this group, it suggests that these working-class women wore black and other dark colors almost exclusively. Black dresses were favored, because they could be used interchangeably for weddings, for mourning, and for Sunday best. Only one woman, the companion of a Parisian tailor (an occupation noted for fashionable attire), had a dress in the most fashionable color of the period, blue-green (Delpierre 1990:24).

Throughout the second half of the nineteenth century, women's lingerie gave a distinctive form to fashionable clothing. The crinoline, a set of hoops placed under the skirt to increase its fullness, was one of the most noticeable aspects of fashionable dresses during the third quarter of the century. According to a French costume historian (Delpierre 1990:19), "The crinoline, worn between 1845 and 1869, is the most characteristic element of clothing styles of the second Empire." Worn at all times of the day, the crinoline was a highly impractical garment that impeded physical activity, particularly outdoors. Only two of the women in the pre-1875 group owned crinolines, one the wife of a skilled worker in Paris, the other the wife of a skilled worker in the provinces. The latter was described by the author of the case study as having "a pronounced taste for clothing" (no. 55 [1865]:182).

The other distinctive undergarment that remained fashionable until the beginning of the twentieth century was the corset, "an essential element of feminine clothing among the rich" (Guiral 1976:177). Tightly laced around the chest, waist, and hips, it impeded breathing and physical activity generally. One-third of the wives in the pre-1875 group owned corsets (see table 2.3). All but one of the wives of skilled workers in Paris owned this type of undergarment. Its expense was probably one factor inhibiting its use by other women in these families (Guiral 1976:177). Another factor was certainly the limitations it placed on physical activity.

The character of a woman's wardrobe was influenced considerably by the types of accessories she was able to use. A stylish appearance was the result of adding items, such as shawls, scarves, hats, gloves, umbrellas, and handkerchiefs, each of which expressed varying degrees of stylishness. Even

TABLE 2.3

TYPES OF CLOTHES IN WORKING-CLASS WIVES'
WARDROBES, 1850–74 AND 1875–1909 (in percentages)

Types of Clothing	1850–74 (*N* = 42)	1875–1909 (*N* = 39)
Middle Class		
Clothes		
Dress (silk)	7	10
Suit	2	31
Visite	0	8
Matinée	0	8
Underwear		
Corset	33	44
Crinoline	5	—ᵃ
Accessories		
Collars	17	13
Shawl (cashmere)	5	3
Gloves	10	23
Sunshade	0	15
Umbrella	2	23
Watch	10	40
Jewelry	38	33
Handkerchief	60	56
Ankle boots	17	36
Head coverings		
Bonnet (with ribbons or lace)	26	5
Hat	2	44
Working Class		
Clothes		
Dress (calico)ᵇ	57	13
Dress (wool)	66	28
Accessories		
Aprons		
weekday	62	59
Sunday	55	18
Shawl	48	44
Fichu	48	21
Neckerchief	17	5
Shoes (wooden)	64	49
Head coverings		
Head scarf	28	13
Coiffe	24	13

Note: Based on inventories of working-class women's clothes contained in case studies of working-class families conducted by Le Play and his associates, this table shows the percentage of women in each time period who owned specific items of clothing.

ᵃThe crinoline was not in fashion during this period.

ᵇOver one-third of the women in the later period did not own dresses, having replaced that type of garment with the newly fashionable suit (jacket plus skirt).

middle-class women rarely wore overcoats during this period, using various types of capes and shawls as well as numerous petticoats for warmth. During much of the period, the most elegant shawls were made of cashmere (Galéries nationales 1987:240–41), but only two women in the group owned such items.

In every social class, it was considered inappropriate for a woman to leave her home without a hat (Guiral 1976:175). Only the very poorest women went out *"en cheveux"* (bareheaded). Only two of the working-class wives did not own any type of headdress. The fashionable hat style of the period was a special type of bonnet called a *"capote"* (Cunnington and Cunnington 1959: 457; Delpierre 1990:22). The exact form of bonnet worn by working-class women in the group was not specified in the inventories, but eleven (26 percent) owned bonnets decorated with ribbons or lace, usually for Sunday wear.

Other accessories identified with middle-class dress such as gloves, sunshades made of silk and lace (Delpierre 1990:25), and umbrellas, appear to have been considered inappropriate for their own use by most of these women. None of these women owned a sunshade; there was one umbrella. Most middle-class women owned and used fans, but there were no fans in this group. Gloves were particularly important during this period. Ladies were expected to wear gloves at all times except at meals (Gernsheim 1963: 35). Most middle-class women would have owned numerous pairs of gloves, but only four (10 percent) of the women in the families studied before 1875 owned gloves. Three were wives of skilled workers; one was the wife of a farmer.

The Le Play case studies indicate that the clothing of most of these working-class wives clearly identified them as belonging to the working class. Instead of gloves and sunshades, these working-class wives used relatively inexpensive accessories, such as handkerchiefs and collars. Ladies were expected to carry handkerchiefs (often embroidered with lace trim) (Delpierre 1990:25). Sixty percent of these working-class wives owned handkerchiefs, including some of the poorest women in the group, suggesting that these women wished to conform to middle-class standards and were able to do so when the expense was minimal. Another way in which these women attempted to add touches of fashion and respectability to their clothing was through the use of detachable collars, decorated with lace or embroidery (17 percent owned such items). Another 17 percent used a simpler version of the collar—handkerchiefs wound around the neck (see table 2.3).

About half the working-class wives owned shawls. In addition to shawls or, alternatively, as a substitute for shawls, about half these women owned small shawls, called *fichus*. Instead of bonnets, about a quarter of the women simply wore scarves on their heads, and another quarter, mainly wives of farmers and farm laborers, were still wearing the traditional *"coiffe,"* or head-dress, associated with regional costumes. The traditional symbol of the working-class woman is the apron. Twenty-six (62 percent) of the wives in the pre-1875 families wore aprons during the week, and twenty-three (55 percent) wore them on Sundays. Women in the countryside (wives of farmers and farm laborers) were most likely to wear aprons on Sundays.

In the fourth quarter of the century, fashions changed, and some of the wives in the Le Play studies adopted the new styles. A sizable number of the women adopted a new style, the *costume complet* (a jacket with a skirt), which had partially replaced the dress. A larger proportion of the later group owned corsets, which remained an essential element of dress for bourgeois women (see table 2.3). However, only a small number of these women adopted two new styles among the middle class — *la visite* and *la matinée*. The former, because of the special cut of its sleeves, which permitted only very limited movement above the elbow, was "very typical of the restraints imposed at that time on women" (Delpierre 1990:33). The latter was daring for middle-class women, because it was a relatively shapeless garment that was intended to be worn without a corset.

Women as well as men used watches as a sign of their prosperity. Watches, suspended on gold or silver chains around the neck, appeared in these women's wardrobes frequently after 1875 (10 percent of the earlier group owned watches, compared with 40 percent of the later group). About a third of the women in each period owned at least two or three small pieces of jewelry, usually earrings or a necklace.

More of these women in the later period used fashionable accessories, such as gloves, sunshades, and umbrellas, although the relatively small numbers in these categories suggest that these items still remained out of reach for most of these women (see table 2.3). The use of outerwear and head coverings identified with the working class, such as the *fichu*, the head scarf, and the traditional headdress (*coiffe*), declined, but almost half of this group adopted the hat, which now replaced the bonnet as a fashionable head covering. Shoes showed similar changes. The use of wooden shoes declined, while the use of boots and slippers increased. Most of these women wore aprons during the week, although the use of the apron on Sundays declined sharply.

That there was some increase in the democratization of fashionable clothing in the later period is suggested by the fact that 93 percent of the post-1875 group had at least one fashionable item of clothing, compared with 69 percent of the pre-1875 group. The use of traditional clothing declined:

1. Working-class couple in Sunday clothes sitting for a photographer (France), ca. 1857–60. As was often the case, the husband is more stylishly dressed than the wife. His dark suit is worn with the checked vest in vogue during the late 1850s and the winged collar that began to be worn during this period. His wife wears a light-colored dress with a suggestion of the bishop sleeve characteristic of the same decade, but her fichu and particularly her black apron, probably of wool, would not have been included in fashionable outfits of the period and are indicative of her social class. She also wears a lace-trimmed white bonnet in a style that dates from the beginning of the century. Courtesy of the Bibliothèque nationale de France, Paris

2. Working-class men wearing long, full traditional smocks and peaked caps (France), 1862. Courtesy of the Bibliothèque nationale de France, Paris

3. Workers and boss at metal foundry in a small provincial town (France), ca. 1875. In sharp contrast to his employees, the boss wears a loose-fitting jacket with wide lapels, which was in style in the 1870s, and a wide necktie in a loose knot. Most of the workers are not wearing neckties or suit jackets. Five men are wearing collarless jackets. Most wear vests, including five with shawl-collared vests. Almost all wear either peaked caps or hats in a variety of styles.
Courtesy of Collection Sirot/Angel, Paris

4. *Tenant farmers in their Sunday clothes (France), ca. 1890. The men are not wearing suit jackets or hats (two are holding their hats), but several wear neckties. Their shirts have the small pointed collars often seen in this period. However, the women's clothes are made in styles typical of the 1880s, including tight-fitting bodices with buttons in front and tight sleeves without puffs and rather short at the wrist. Several of the women wear aprons and head scarves. One woman is wearing a fichu. Courtesy of Jacques Borgé, Paris*

5. *Parisian workers (France), ca. 1900. All three wear collarless shirts without ties. The man on the left wears a short jacket, typically worn by workers of the period. The man in the center wears a shirt without cuffs, a waistcoat, and cotton trousers. The man on the right wears a rather worn lounge suit or sack suit with matching waistcoat and a bowler. Courtesy of Jacques Borgé, Paris*

6. *Peasant woman near Grasse (France), 1852, wearing a calico dress with an apron and a bonnet with ribbons in a style that would have been worn only in the home by middle-class women. Courtesy of Collection André Jammes. Photograph by Charles Nègre; print by Patrice Schmidt, Musée d'Orsay, Paris*

7. A farmer's wife with middle-class visitors in Villiers (northeastern France), 1904. The farmer's wife is wearing her Sunday clothes, including a black skirt and a blouse with sleeves in a style that had been fashionable in 1890. She wears a traditional coiffe. Three of her visitors are wearing the fashionable dresses and hats of the period, including the light colors characteristic of the upper and middle classes. The woman on the left is dressed in the style fashionable in 1895. Photo by Jenny de Vasson. Courtesy of Gilles Wolkowitsch, Paris

8. *Midwestern farmers in black sack suits, with farmhand in trousers, vest, and long-sleeved shirt (United States), 1873. The woman in the center is fashionably dressed; the costumes of the two others reflect styles of the last years of the previous decade. Courtesy of the State Historical Society of Wisconsin (neg. WHi [D31] 395)*

9. Rustlers in New Mexico, wearing "businesslike clothing—dark, patterned shirts, vests, sack jackets, and wool trousers . . . that would have been seen anywhere in the country" (Severa 1995:355) (United States), 1878–79. Photo by Bennett and Burrall. Courtesy of the Museum of New Mexico, Santa Fe (neg. 14264)

10. Factory workers at the San Francisco Stove Works in shirtsleeves, suspenders, and no ties. They wear several different styles of hats, including bowlers. Their boss in the center wears a three-piece suit, silk necktie, and bowler (United States), 1892. Courtesy of the California History Room, California State Library, Sacramento

11. Young man wearing a cheap, ready-made, seersucker jacket, widely available at the time (United States), 1885–92. He has added a middle-class accessory, a watch and chain. Photo by J. C. Burge. Courtesy of the Museum of New Mexico, Santa Fe (neg. 76778)

12. At Rosedale Ranch, near Bakersfield: farmer's wife in a remote area in fashionable dress (United States), 1892. Courtesy of Kern County Museum, Bakersfield, CA. Used by permission

13. *Ragpickers wearing different styles of hats, including peaked caps but also one bowler (France), ca. 1900.* © Collection Roger-Viollet, Paris

14. Foremen wearing different styles of high hats (England), 1861

15. Road repairmen in bowler hats (England), 1892

16. *Ironmongers' Picnic. Workers at leisure wearing middle-class clothing and hats, including bowlers (United States), 1890. Courtesy of the California Historical Society, FN-28402*

17. *Railroad workers in uniforms (France), ca. 1890. The staff of the station at Suresnes (near Paris) wear uniforms that indicate their rank. Those of higher rank are wearing jackets and shirt collars. The men second from left and second from right wear short smocks. The man on the far right appears to have removed his smock for the photograph (he is holding it in his hand) and put on a more stylish jacket. Courtesy of the Bibliothèque nationale de France, Paris*

18. *Chimney sweep in one-piece overall (England), ca. 1900. Courtesy of the Rural History Centre, University of Reading, UK*

19. *Servants of the Countess of Warwick, wearing uniforms indicating different positions in the household (England), 1898*

20. *Group portrait of servants (France), ca. 1890. Their costumes indicate their positions in the hierarchy of the household. As is frequently seen in photographs of the period, they display the "tools" they use in their work. The gardener wears a long apron and wooden shoes. Courtesy of the Bibliothèque nationale de France, Paris*

83 percent of the earlier group had at least one traditional item of clothing, compared with 63 percent of the later group. However, the diffusion of fashionable items was very selective. Only one item of fashionable clothing, the suit, was adopted to any great extent; the use of fashionable accessories, with the exception of watches, remained low. Again, this suggests, as in the case of their husbands, that many of these women perceived certain types of fashionable styles and accessories as inappropriate for their own use. Figure 7 illustrates the contrast between middle- and working-class women's attire.

VARIATION IN FRENCH WORKING-CLASS WIVES' CLOTHING: Paris versus the Provinces

Whether these working-class wives dressed traditionally or in the style of middle-class women depended on where they lived—in Paris or the provinces, in cities or in the countryside—and on the occupations of their husbands. In order to examine the diffusion of fashionable items among different strata of the working class and the persistence of traditional styles, I constructed indexes of women's middle class and traditional dress.[19] Women in each stratum were scored on the numbers of such items they possessed. The average scores for each stratum are shown in table 2.4. Although the index includes items that were fashionable during that period, it would not be accurate to say that working-class women with high scores were "fashionable," since it is very unlikely that they met the complicated standards for a fashionable appearance that existed at the time.

Among the families in the earlier period, Parisian women owned more middle-class items than women living in cities in the provinces, and the latter owned more middle-class items than women living in the countryside. In each setting, wives of skilled workers owned more middle-class items than wives of unskilled workers. The scores on the index show that, in this period, the diffusion of fashionable items to lower-working-class strata was minimal.

Among the families in the later period, the wives of skilled workers in Paris were again the ones who were most likely to own items of middle-class clothing. Presumably reflecting the increased incomes of their husbands, as well as changes in attitudes and lifestyles, the wives of unskilled workers in the provinces now had more middle-class items than the wives of skilled workers in the provinces and the wives of farmers. The latter were still the most traditional, but all groups owned fewer traditional items.

Among the families studied before 1875, the most "fashionable" woman (no. 55 [1865]:466) was the wife of a glove maker in Grenoble, who herself

TABLE 2.4
MIDDLE-CLASS AND TRADITIONAL CLOTHES
IN WORKING-CLASS WIVES' WARDROBES,
1850–74 AND 1875–1909

Region and Husband's Occupation	Index of Middle-Class Clothing	
	1850–1874 (*N* = 42)	1875–1909 (*N* = 39)
Paris		
Skilled	3.8	4.1
Unskilled	1.8	2.7
Provinces		
Skilled	1.5	1.7
Unskilled^a	0.7	2.3
Farm owners	0.7	1.2
Farm tenants	—	1.6
Average	1.6	2.3

	Index of Traditional Clothing	
	1850–74	1875–1909
Paris		
Skilled	1.7	0.9
Unskilled	2.2	0.2
Provinces		
Skilled	2.6	1.7
Unskilled^a	4.0	1.0
Farm owners	2.9	3.0
Farm tenants	—	2.0
Average	2.6	1.4

Note: The index of middle-class clothing used seven items of clothing for both periods. The index of traditional clothing used six items of traditional working-class clothing for both periods. Women in each occupational stratum were scored on each item in each index, and their total scores were averaged for the stratum. The table shows the average scores for each stratum on each index in both periods. For a description of the items of clothing used in the indexes, see n. 19.

^aUnskilled workers were farm laborers during the period 1850–74. During the later period, they were employed in provincial cities and towns.

did some sewing and glove making.[20] At twenty-one, she was one of the youngest women in the group. She had received some education and was described as spending the evenings and Sundays reading books from the local library before the birth of her child. Because her husband was well paid and the couple received gifts and other types of support from family and relatives, the young woman was able to acquire a substantial quantity of clothing. She was one of only two women in the pre-1875 group who wore a crinoline. She owned two crinolines and two corsets, as well as eleven dresses and several bonnets and collars trimmed with lace. However, during the week, she dressed in a more traditional manner, including wooden shoes and aprons made out of printed calico.

For many working-class women, Sunday dress often included a few bourgeois items, while weekday dress largely comprised traditional items. The contrast between the two types of outfits worn by working-class women was often quite marked, as in the case of the wife of a skilled worker who worked in her husband's laundry business (no. XI [1852]:263). During the week she wore a blouse, an unfitted jacket, and a petticoat, but on the rare occasions when she went out, she liked to dress fashionably. For this purpose, she had eight dresses, a corset, an expensive collar, six expensive bonnets with ribbons and lace whose style varied according to the latest fashion, a large shawl (*façon cachemire*), a watch with a gold chain, and gloves.

The following inventory of clothing described as "*costume des paysannes*" gives an idea of the appearance of many working-class wives in the countryside in the middle of the nineteenth century (no. 26 [1860]:338): "1 brown wool dress, 1 small shawl (*fichu*), 1 wool apron and 1 raised white bonnet [in the countryside, women wore a colored handkerchief around their heads on week days] . . . 1 complete set of everyday clothing composed of old Sunday clothing . . . 1 petticoat made from an old dress, 6 linen undershirts, 6 pocket handkerchiefs, 6 pairs of cotton stockings, 1 pair of wooden shoes, 1 pair of shoes."

The women whose clothing corresponded most closely to that of the middle class in the families studied after 1875 were two Parisian women, both of whom were employed. The first was a woman living with her young sons and working at a craft: making figurines for a luxury market. Even though her income was substantially below the median for skilled workers in Paris in that period, her clothing was described as an exact copy of that worn by the lower middle class (no. 76 [1892]). She possessed several items of bourgeois clothing, including a jacket, a suit, a hat, gloves, an umbrella, a corset, and a sunshade.

The other woman in this category was the wife of another artisan, who was making high-quality furniture for a luxury market. She herself had a successful business as a tailor, working for the middle class. Her wardrobe included a number of bourgeois items, such as black silk dresses, cashmere suits, a *visite*, four *matinées*, embroidered petticoats, and satin shoes. Nevertheless, she shared her husband's political opinions; they saw themselves as revolutionaries (no. 74 [1891]:61).[21]

By contrast, the woman with the most traditional clothing in the post-1875 group was the wife of a farmer living in a large extended family in the southwestern part of France (no. 65 [1888]). Her clothing was made of heavy, rough material (*drugget*) and was not abundant. It included two styles of *coiffe* that were traditional in the region, as well as the familiar headkerchief.

In comparison with the men in these families, women in both periods who dressed in the style of the middle class were wives of skilled workers who were located primarily in Paris. Parisian women were more likely than women in the provinces to become artisans and consequently to have personal contacts with the middle class that exposed them to middle-class tastes. Even without personal contacts, Paris presumably provided more opportunities for women interested in fashionable clothing to observe well-dressed women. In the later period, wives of unskilled workers in Paris and in the provinces wore more middle-class items than previously, responding to changes in levels of income in these groups and to changes taking place in regions outside Paris. However, the scores in table 2.4 suggest that considerable differences in the diffusion of fashionable items to different strata of the working class remained and that the overall level of diffusion was relatively low.

THE BEGINNING OF CONSUMER CULTURE:
Servants, Employed Working-Class Women, and Fashion

Since fashionable items did not diffuse widely among members of the lower strata of the working class, why did Simmel, who was writing at the end of this period, believe that the working class adopted these styles, even belatedly. It seems likely that Simmel drew his conclusions from the types of clothing worn by members of the working class who were most likely to have contacts with the middle class and who tended to be visible on city streets. Two categories of workers fit these criteria: (1) male and female artisans and other skilled workers, (2) unmarried working-class women who were employed in offices and department stores or as servants. The clothing of artisans and skilled workers probably influenced middle-class perceptions of working-class dress. The clothing of unmarried, employed women also tended to be seen as representative of the clothing behavior of working-class women, leading some observers at the time to declare that social class differences in clothing had been erased (Ginsburg 1988:175). Confined to their homes, working-class wives in their drab clothing were less noticeable than young, unmarried, employed women, who frequently engaged in leisure activities outside their homes. Under what circumstances did these women adopt fashionable clothing styles?

In France, the United States, and England, maidservants were frequently accused of attempting to dress fashionably like their employers. It was even said that it was difficult to distinguish between the maid in her leisure clothes and her mistress (Banner 1984:20; Guiral and Thuillier 1978:48–49). Servant women's clothing behavior on and off the job was often criticized in articles in women's magazines or in books on etiquette, where it was seen as an inappropriate attempt to claim social equality (Helvenston 1980:35; Dudden 1983:120; McBride 1976:95).

Alternatively, the maidservant's fascination with fashionable clothes, particularly those worn when she was not in the household, can be seen as a response to the unpleasant conditions under which she worked. The servant's isolation from peers and relatives, due to the exceptionally long hours domestic service required, was one of the most difficult aspects of her job. The perception of being in a household but not part of it — in other words, being excluded from the social life of the family — was especially difficult for very young women who had left their families for their first jobs (Dudden 1983: 238). Housework had to be performed when the employer and his family were not using the rooms being cleaned: "The maintenance of the house was to be a clockwork function and the separation of master and servant complete" (Burnett 1974:173). Servants who wore uniforms deeply resented them as the badge of a low-status job and as a kind of infringement on their personal identities (Clark-Lewis 1994:113–17).

For female servants, wearing attractive and fashionable clothing was a means of participating in and feeling part of the community outside the employer's household. Fashionable clothing was virtually the only form of popular culture that was readily accessible to servants in this period, and they used it to affirm their personal identities as much as claim a higher social status.[22]

Other young, unmarried working-class women who were employed outside the family economy (Scott and Tilly 1975) were also reported as having an enormous interest in clothing and in dressing well. These women were generally young and unmarried or widowed.[23] Most of them performed jobs that were identified as women's: making clothing, making textiles, and selling goods in department stores. In the workplace, young working-class women dressed elegantly, even in dirty factories, performing menial tasks in corsets, tight-fitting sleeves, elegant silk bows, and gold watch chains. They attempted to follow the latest styles. For example, in the mid-nineteenth century, young English and American women working in textile mills wore crinolines to work despite the danger of getting them caught in the machinery (de Marly 1986:123–24; Severa 1995:263). Clothing was the principal consumer good that was available to working-class female employees, and they spent substantial proportions of their incomes on it (Wright 1969:128; Cross and Shergold 1986:261; Stearns 1972:110). They were often able to afford fashionable items, probably of rather inferior quality, that transformed their appearance in comparison with that of married working-class women. For these women, dressing fashionably was seen as necessary for participating in social activities and for upward mobility (Smith 1994:14).

In their leisure lives, young employed working-class women tended to emulate bourgeois clothing in an exaggerated manner. Describing the style of dress of young working-class women who participated in the Bowery subculture in New York City in the middle of the nineteenth century, Stansell (1987:93–94) contrasted it with that of the bourgeois "lady": "They were distinguished by their self-conscious 'airs,' a style of dress and manner which was a studied departure from ladyhood, an implicit rejection of bourgeois female decorum. Genteel rules of gender dictated that 'womanly' women minimize what they saw in public of others and what others saw of them. The respectable woman on the street deflected rather than drew attention to her physical appearance. . . . Muted colors, a costume that covered the flesh except for the face (including obligatory gloves and hat), and an aloof manner were the hallmarks of the lady. . . . Bowery fashions . . . repudiated genteel principles of harmonious dress for their own internal logic of color, pattern, and accessories. Women wore startling combinations of colors, a sharp contrast to the modest pastels, grays and browns of ladies' street wear."

Contemporaries (Brew 1945:435) described the attire of Chicago office girls at the turn of the century as follows: "feathers, garlands of flowers, masses of trimming weight down their broad-brimmed picture hats, fancy veils, kid gloves, silver side-bags, embroidered blouses and elaborate belt buckles. . . ." Young Jewish immigrant women living in New York City and working in the garment business exemplified a similar pattern. For these women, dressing in fashionable clothes was a way of showing their knowledge of American culture, of rejecting their traditional ethnic culture, and of expressing their own identities. Although they had little money, they competed with fellow workers to emulate the latest styles, particularly favoring brash, brightly colored outfits and preferring to be "intentionally overdressed to 'put on style'" (Schreier 1994:132). Deliberately breaking the rules of "genteel femininity" in order to be noticed, "they sampled, mixed, and reassembled the decorative with the practical to create a range of hybrid styles. . . . Asserting their cultural agency, working-class young women actively created their own standards of dress" (132, 110).

In France, young women who moved into jobs as salesclerks in newly created department stores were described as "the queens of the urban prole-tariat" because of their lavish dress, including leather boots and stylish hats (McBride 1978:680–81). Working-class employed women were expected to adopt new styles. A poorly paid telephone operator in Paris is said to have refused to visit her parents during her vacation because her entire wardrobe was at least two years old (Riot-Sarcey and Zylberberg-Hocquard 1987). By the beginning of the twentieth century, the image of the working-class woman who was employed had clearly become that of someone "who wore a hat, gloves, and who could be confused with a lower middle class woman of leisure."

Servants and young female employees can be seen as "pioneers" of an emerging consumer culture, of which clothes were a major element. Unlike working-class wives, their attitudes and behavior toward clothing were similar to those of young working-class women and men in the late twentieth century (de la Haye and Dingwall 1996) — clothes as a means of expressing identities related to leisure pursuits, dreams, and ambitions rather than those conferred by their menial occupations.

CONCLUSION: Diffusion, Democratization, and Symbolic Boundaries

Several theories have been invoked in this chapter to interpret and explain the clothing choices of French working-class men and women in the second half of the nineteenth century. Simmel's theory of fashion diffusion from the upper to the lower class suggests that fashionable clothing would eventually be adopted by the working class. In fact, French workers and their wives adopted fashionable clothing selectively; certain styles were not adopted. His theory would also predict that within the working class, fashionable styles would be adopted first by higher strata and later by lower strata. In the third quarter of the century, this appeared to be the case, although the existence of cultural barriers in the form of illiteracy and the use of languages other than French impeded the diffusion of fashionable styles in farming communities.

However, particularly in the last quarter of the century, fashionable styles were most likely to be adopted not by the more prestigious skilled workers but by unskilled workers in Paris and the provinces. These data suggest that Simmel's model needs to be qualified by information about the likelihood that members of different class strata did or did not adopt fashionable styles and an understanding of the factors that encouraged or inhibited adoption.

The democratization thesis proposed by costume historians implies an eventual standardization of clothing in which social class differences would be less visible or nonexistent. In fact, although social class distinctions grew subtler during the period in comparison with those expressed by clothing in the previous century, they did not disappear. Data from Le Play's case studies in England reveal the disparities between the wardrobes of even the most fashionable working-class men and the type of wardrobe considered suitable for fashionable members of the upper-middle class. The numbers of items in these wardrobes and the frequencies with which new items were added to them are strikingly different.

Differences in clothing behavior among different class strata during the earlier period can be explained in part using Bourdieu's theory of cultural tastes and class reproduction. Before 1875, French working-class men who were most likely to adopt items of middle-class clothing were artisans and craftsmen whose work brought them into frequent contact with the middle class. These contacts may have constituted a form of socialization in middle-class sartorial practices that substituted for the kind of socialization that middle-class families provide, according to Bourdieu's theory. In this period, influences associated with occupational status as opposed to level of income were the major factors affecting clothing behavior.

In both periods, workers behaved as if they considered some types of fashionable items, such as gloves, canes, top hats and bowlers, as inappropriate for their own use. The reluctance to use these items cannot be explained entirely by their expense. Workers' incomes were rising throughout this period (Goulène 1974:71). Instead, the explanation may lie in the fact that these items required a greater understanding of standards of middle-class etiquette than other items. In this sense, these sartorial signs were effective in distinguishing between those who knew the "rules" and were able to follow them and those who did not. This interpretation is consistent with Bourdieu's theory of symbolic boundaries.

After 1875, in Paris and the provinces, unskilled workers in lower strata were more likely to adopt fashionable items than skilled workers in higher strata in the same settings. In this period, the theories proposed by Simmel and Bourdieu are less applicable, because they assume a linear rank-ordering of social classes in which each stratum was clearly higher than the one immediately below. During the later period, lower working-class strata acquired economic resources that outweighed the levels of their skills and craftsmanship and changed their status relative to higher strata, whose economic resources were now lower than theirs. In each setting, Paris and the provinces, unskilled workers as a group had a higher median income than skilled workers in the same setting, with whom they would have been likely to compare themselves (see appendix table 1.1). As a result, a set of sartorial signs which had previously ranked each class and each stratum within the working-class in terms of their relative occupational prestige became less predictable as these signs were adopted by those for whom economic resources substituted for lack of occupational prestige.

During this period, the clothing behavior of French working-class men can also be explained by social and economic changes that were breaking down traditional enclaves, exposing workers to new cultural influences and creating social and political tensions. These changes increased the workers' awareness of the standards of behavior of other social classes. Social tensions led to increasing identification with their own class. Their enthusiasm for consumer goods can be seen not only as a striving for status but also as a desire to participate in their own social communities. The adoption of middle-class clothing did not necessarily imply the acceptance of a middle-class worldview. Some workers whose clothing and lifestyles were virtually identical to those of the middle class were strongly opposed to the political system. Other workers adopted the clothing but rejected other aspects of the middle class lifestyle.

Working-class wives were in general more isolated than their husbands from social life outside the home. In spite of enormous efforts at sewing—making new clothes and repairing old ones—for all members of the family, working-class wives in these families often remained least well served by their own efforts. In general they spent less on clothing than did their husbands. Only the Parisian wives of skilled workers, some of whom were themselves artisans, could be defined as "fashionable." Wives of unskilled workers in Paris and the provinces were somewhat more fashionable after 1875, but less so than their husbands. However, with the exception of farmers' wives, the women who were studied after 1875 were much less traditional in appearance than wives in the earlier group. In this sense, the clothing of these working-class women was democratized, although it lacked the elegance of clothing worn by the middle class. On the whole, the appearance of working-class wives was an indicator of their positions in their families, their confinement in the home, and their relative exclusion from public space.

The data derived from these case studies provide a valuable corrective to a widespread tendency to generalize about the extent to which fashionable clothing was adopted on the basis of categories of people who were most visible in public space and particularly to middle-class observers. From the perspective of such observers, those who were most visible appeared to be representative of the entire working class. Consequently, there was a tendency to assume that working-class men and women dressed in fashionable clothing because fashionable styles were adopted by men and women whose occupations brought them into contact with the middle class such as artisans and unmarried, employed women. The drab, unfashionable clothing of many working-class people was less likely to be noticed.

NOTES

1. Breeches remained in use for horseback riding, court dress, and servants' livery (Tarrant 1994: 42–44).

2. In 1829, Balzac observed: "We all go about dressed in black like people who are in mourning for something" (quoted in Robb 1994: 170).

3. All translations from the French, unless otherwise noted, are my own.

4. These types of studies will be discussed in chapters 3 and 6.

5. Personal communication from Antoine Savoye, March 9, 1999.

6. The sources for the case studies cited in the text are Le Play (1877–79) and La Société Internationale des Etudes Pratiques d'Economie Sociale (1857–1928). A complete list of the cases, with their bibliographic sources, appears in appendix 1. In the text, the cases are identified by number and year, as indicated in this list. For further information about the case studies and for additional tables, see appendix 1. There were four female-headed households which are not included in appendix tables 1.1 and 1.2 or in tables 2.1 and 2.2 below; one family was in the pre-1875 group and three in the post-1875 group (see chap. 1).

7. The farmers included two groups: (1) those who owned land and who were relatively prosperous, and (2) tenant farmers who rented land and who were generally less well-to-do. Farm laborers earned their livelihoods primarily by working for other farmers. They were equivalent to unskilled laborers. The group of farmers before 1875 included two tenant farmers. Because their incomes were comparable to those of the farm owners, they were included with the farmers. After 1875, the farmer-owners were substantially more prosperous than the tenant farmers. Therefore, the two groups were examined separately.

8. A study of family budgets of French bourgeois families during the period 1873–1913 allows useful comparisons (Perrot 1982). Three strata in the French bourgeoisie were identified by Perrot: bourgeois families with "modest" annual incomes of 3,000–

12,000 francs per year; families with "comfortable" incomes of 13,000–19,000 francs; and "rich" families with incomes of 20,000–28,000 francs.

9. Medians rather than means were used to calculate the statistics in appendix table 1.1 because the ranges were large.

10. For example, "technicians making delicate adjustments in clocks, carvers in the Marais [a district in Paris], craftsmen making inlaid furniture or illustrators in the faubourg Saint-Antoine" (no. 89 [1895]:373).

11. In this period, the unskilled workers in the provinces were no longer farm laborers but unskilled workers in provincial cities.

12. A French historian (Duroselle 1972:84) explained that farmers at the end of the nineteenth century, even when they were rich, were not considered middle class, because they remained primarily peasants. Their horizons were very limited.

13. The complexity of the costume is suggested by the following description of the Sunday costume (no. 47 [1883]:22–23): "For Sunday, there were two outfits, one with a blue fitted jacket with sleeves, the other with a white fitted jacket. Each outfit had a waistcoat and a loose brown jacket as well as white puffed breeches, wool stockings, and suede shoes. The outfits were worn with a large hat with a silver buckle." Many farmers were unable to afford these elaborate costumes by the middle of the nineteenth century.

14. The index of middle-class clothing used seven items for the first period, 1850–74: frock coat, overcoat, three-piece suit, dress jacket, silk or satin waistcoat, silk tie, and top hat. For the second period, the waistcoat was replaced by the watch. The index of traditional clothing used six items for both periods: smock frock; wool, cotton, or knit waistcoat; cotton or linen tie; wooden shoes; cap; and peaked cap. Workers in each occupational stratum were scored on each item in each index, and their total scores were averaged for the stratum. The average scores for each stratum on each index in both periods appear in table 2.2.

15. For example, Goulène (1974:65) reports that there were 313 strikes and 118,300 strikers in 1890, and 523 strikes and 212,700 strikers in 1901.

16. Thirty-five percent of wives in the families studied before 1875 and 23 percent of wives in the families studied after 1875 were employed.

17. All the women in these families had children. The average family in the study had 3.6 children.

18. The total value of the husband's clothing was not necessarily greater than that of the wife. In families of skilled and unskilled workers in Paris after 1875, the husbands' clothes were worth only 3 percent more than their wives'. For skilled and unskilled workers in the provinces, the figure was 29 percent, but the clothes of farmers' wives were worth 19 percent more their husbands'.

19. The index of middle-class clothing used seven items: (before 1875) corset, crinoline, collar with lace or embroidery, bonnet with ribbons, gloves, ankle boots, and the absence of an apron on Sundays; (after 1875) corset, jacket with skirt (*costume complet*), hat, gloves, ankle boots, umbrella, and no apron on Sunday. The index of traditional items included six items: (before 1875) dresses in printed calico, *coiffe* (traditional headdress),

kerchief worn on the head, *fichu*, wooden shoes, and apron worn on Sunday; (after 1875) bonnet, kerchief worn on the head, *coiffe*, *fichu*, wooden shoes, and apron worn on Sunday.

20. During this period, Grenoble was a major center for the glove industry in France.

21. For a discussion of her husband, see p. 45.

22. For examples of fashionable aspects of maids' clothing in the home, see Severa (1995:218, 281, and 451).

23. Wright (1969:127), in his study of working girls in Boston in 1880, found that 89 percent of them were unmarried. The average length of time they were employed was 7.49 years.

*Don't take any clothing, because when you get here we will not
let you wear those clothes.* Letter from American immigrant to relative
emigrating from Romania, quoted in Schreier (1994:4)

Tell me how you spend your money, and I will tell you what you are.
American economist, quoted in Smith (1994:3)

3 FASHION, DEMOCRATIZATION, AND SOCIAL CONTROL

The most visible forms of fashion often have a ludicrous aspect that contributes to the erroneous assumption that neither fashion nor clothing has any social importance. Consequently, the significance of clothing, both as an instrument of self-enhancement for the individual and as a form of social control by organizations, both public and private, tends to be ignored. In the late nineteenth century, clothing appears to have had a special significance as one of the first consumer goods to become widely available. Clothing was useful for "blurring" social standing, as a means of breaking away from social constraints and of appearing to have more social or economic resources than was actually the case. The seductiveness of fashion, then as now, lay in the fact that it seemed to offer a person the possibility of becoming in some way different, more attractive, or more powerful. At the same time, clothing was primarily used as a means of indicating social status in the sense of claiming the status that one had actually attained and of reinforcing affiliations with specific social groups that dressed in a characteristic manner. Certain types of apparel, such as hats, were particularly useful for this purpose. Clothing was also used as a form of social control: people were often required to dress in a certain manner that indicated particular aspects of their social identities. During the nineteenth century, this aspect of clothing was increasingly

67

evident, as new types of uniforms and occupational clothing replaced traditional forms of clothing that had disappeared.

Clothing was particularly important in the United States, where studies
show that the higher the income, the more people spent on clothing. Since
the United States was believed to be more democratic than European countries, the attention devoted to clothing appears incongruous. Clothing as a
means of indicating differences in social rank should not have mattered, but
in fact it did. Because it was a society characterized by a great deal of mobility
from one region to another, as well as a continual influx of immigrants from
different countries, claiming, indicating, and blurring one's social identity
was especially important.

This chapter will examine these two contradictory aspects of clothing,
clothing as a means of expanding a person's social capital and clothing as a
form of social control, reinforcing the significance of economic or occupational identities. How did American society exemplify these aspects of clothing in the nineteenth century? What is the evidence that clothes were more
important in America than in Europe? As we will see, both in the United
States and Europe, certain types of apparel, such as hats and uniforms, were
used in similar ways to indicate or reinforce certain aspects of social identity.

CLOTHING BEHAVIOR AND DEMOCRATIZATION IN THE UNITED STATES

The country that is believed to be the best example of the thesis that clothing
was democratized in the nineteenth century is the United States. Lee Hall
(1992:73) claims that in the United States, during the nineteenth century,
men at all social levels attempted to eliminate status distinctions based on
clothing. She says: "To dress in the style of the rich—whether possessing
wealth or not—made personal worth apparent. And those men who were not
actually successful nonetheless sought to appear that way."

Was nineteenth-century America a classless society, as indicated by the
clothing of its citizens? In the absence of case studies, it is necessary to rely
on various types of aggregate data: descriptions by historians of class structures, clothing historians' reconstruction of patterns of clothing behavior,
photographs (Lee Hall 1992; Kidwell and Christman 1974; Severa 1995),
Brew's (1945) study of the adoption of fashionable clothing styles by different
social classes in 1879 and 1909, and studies of family expenditures for clothing contained in budgets of families both in America and Europe, such as
Carroll Wright's studies in 1875 and 1890.

In nineteenth-century America, there were three distinct regions in which the drama of class relations was performed in different ways. In the hierarchical social order of the South, clothing was particularly important in marking the social positions of slaves, slave owners, and non-slave-owning whites before the Civil War (Lee Hall 1992:87). In the early 1850s, a journalist from the North described members of the upper-middle class as wearing black cloth coats, black cravats, and satin or embroidered silk waistcoats, while poor whites went barefoot in the winter despite several inches of snow (87, 89). These distinctions remained after the Civil War.

By contrast, farming communities in the West and Middle West were less stratified than those either in the South or in Europe, because land ownership was more widespread. Farm tenants and farm laborers were less numerous (Fishlow 1973:76). This relatively classless society represented a majority of the labor force in the region until 1890 (74). To a greater extent than among the farmers and farm laborers described in the French case studies, farmers in the Middle West appear to have emulated the clothing of middle class. Photographs of the period show the suit as the Sunday dress of a large proportion of the male population in rural areas in the 1870s and 1880s, with regional variations (see figs. 8 and 9). According to Gorsline (1952:206, 213): "The businessmen's world, represented by the East, continued to be the model toward which each person tried to orient himself. . . . Men in the most remote, dangerous, and wild country wore the clerk's suit of the East, complete with fedora, starched shirt and even a Prince Albert."[1]

The aspirations of farm families in this period are documented by numerous photographs, commissioned by members of these families, in which they were depicted in stylish clothes. According to Severa (1995:317), a costume historian, conformity to fashion guidelines "reached even the poorest farm, if sometimes in a naive interpretation." On Sundays, farmers wore lounge suits (known as sack suits in America), striped trousers, and silk ties.

Laborers on farms and in factories or mines wore simpler clothing. The costume of farm laborers generally consisted of long-sleeved cotton shirts, vests, denim trousers, and felt hats. Although the smock frock was occasionally worn, it had been largely replaced by denim trousers by the second half of the century. The farm laborer's vest was actually an expression of conformity to the styles of period. Severa states (1995:314): "Wearing a vest was the rule even for the most casual attire." At work, the farmers themselves wore similar outfits as well as worn-out black Sunday clothing.

Class gradations may have been less pronounced than in cities on the East Coast, even in nonfarm occupations. The author of the one of the two case studies in the Le Play archive that dealt with the United States (no. 22

[1859]:153) commented on the clothing of a miner in California in 1895: "It is impossible to assign any rank to this individual. In France, where social ranks are very clearly marked, he would be a worker and nothing more. In California, it was otherwise."

The third region consisted of industrial cities, mainly on the East Coast. In the second half of the century, these cities were characterized by substantial opportunities for social mobility (Archer and Blau 1993:30) but also by widespread industrial conflict (Ehrenreich 1989:133; Vanneman and Cannon 1987:13) and by wage levels, in real terms, that had been lower than those of European workers for several decades (Vanneman and Cannon 1987:274).[2] Here social strata in the working class tended to correlate with immigrant status, immigrants from non-English-speaking countries having substantially lower incomes than American-born workers and immigrants from English-speaking countries (Williamson 1967:108). In Eastern cities, families at lower levels of the working class struggled to get by (Shergold 1982:204). Particularly in this region, poverty remained a fact of life for most working class families (Shergold 1982:7).

As in France, class differences were revealed by the choices of different styles of suits by members of different classes. Upper- and middle-class men adopted dark, knee-length frock coats, with trousers of the same or a lighter color. Businessmen wore dark suits, with jackets that buttoned high on the chest, shirts with soft or hard collars, and soft fedoras (Lee Hall 1992:133) or bowler hats, which were called derbies in America (Byrde 1979:185). On Sundays and occasions when formal wear was required, laborers, shop assistants, and other city workers wore ready-to-wear versions of the lounge suit. Some degree of democratization is evident in the fact that, by the 1870s, according to Brew (1945:444), "Men living in the city, even of the lowest wage-earning class, had a suit." At work, class differences were more apparent. Workers wore shirts, vests, and trousers or overalls, but bosses wore suits with vests, ties, watch chains, and bowler hats (Lee Hall 1992:53; Severa 1995:493) (see fig. 10).

By the middle of the century, American men benefited from the availability of ready-made clothing as sewing machines expanded the output of clothing factories (Severa 1995:2, 19, 85–86).[3] However, at the beginning of the twentieth century, this advantage had disappeared. Shergold (1982:225), who compared the clothing of working-class men in Pittsburgh and in Birmingham and Sheffield (England) between 1900 and 1910, found that clothing of equivalent quality was considerably more expensive in America. Differences in the quality of clothing in the working class, often falling along ethnic and racial lines, were far more pronounced in Pittsburgh than in

Birmingham or Sheffield. A relatively small number of American skilled workers earned substantially more than their English counterparts, but the majority of workers received incomes similar to those of unskilled workers in England. Skilled workers were generally white, native-born Americans, while unskilled workers were either African Americans or new immigrants. Shergold (1982:225) concluded: "There were two worlds among Pittsburgh's manual workers: a world of $10 Chesterfield suits and $5 Elton jackets, Red Cross shoes and embroidered antimacassars, and a world of collarless shirts and patched overalls, made-up flannelette and paste jewelry."

As was the case with French workers, accessories offered important clues about the aspirations of the American working class. A photograph taken in 1900 of a local doctor in Maine portrays the costume and the major accessories of the conservative upper-middle class: top hat, frock coat, vest, tie, gloves, watch with chain, and cane (Toner 1994). Skilled workers and those who were emulating the middle class wore ties; most unskilled workers did not (Lee Hall 1992:55, 63, 141). According to Brew (1945:293), "Gloves had social values and were used for street and dress wear by men of the middle and wealthier classes." Rigid customs had developed about what types of gloves were to be worn and for what types of functions. As in France, few American workers owned gloves, either in the 1870s or even by the first decade of the twentieth century (Brew 1945:518, 520). Since working-class wives did not generally own gloves either (see below), lack of money rather than the perception of gloves as "unmasculine" would seem to be the explanation. Canes were also not widely used by the working class. However, watches with chains were widespread. In America, a watch with a gold chain was the accessory that was most frequently acquired by workers aspiring to higher social status, as suggested by photographs reproduced in Severa (1995). Its importance is indicated by the fact that watch chains were sometimes provided as props by photographers to add momentary prestige to their customers' appearance (Heinze 1990:89).

While some degree of democratization of men's styles occurred in nineteenth-century America, particularly in some regions, the effects were offset by the ways in which certain items of clothing became the prerogative of one class rather than another and by the scarcity and poor quality of clothing available at the lowest levels of the working class (Shergold 1982). Figure 11 shows a young man wearing cheap, ready-made, seersucker clothing of a type that was available everywhere in the United States in the 1880s (Severa 1995:441). Shergold (1982:205–6) states that American workers often appeared to be better dressed than their European counterparts because of the variety and flamboyance of their clothes but that their clothes tended to be of poor quality. Brew (1945:276), commenting on the United States in the last quarter of the century, states: "All evidence points to the fact that men's clothing was less democratic than today." Class distinctions were played out in subtle combinations of styles and accessories to reproduce the social structure.

CLOTHING BEHAVIOR AND WORKING-CLASS WIVES IN AMERICA

Some writers claim that the clothing of American women was democratized in the nineteenth century (Kidwell and Christman 1974; Severa 1995). Other authors (Jensen 1984:8) argue that democratization of clothing occurred during this period only in the sense that fashionable clothing became available to middle-class rather than working-class American women. Smith (1994) argues that clothes became less important "as markers of individuality or status" during the twentieth century rather than the nineteenth. In order for this change to occur, clothes themselves had to become simpler and easier to produce, developments that occurred during the twentieth century. In the nineteenth century, fashionable clothes remained complicated but gradually became easier to make.

Like their husbands, American women participated in different sartorial worlds, some of which were democratized, while others were not. Nineteenth-century American women obtained their clothing from three sources (Walsh 1979:300–301). The most fashionable clothing was copied from the latest European styles by skilled dressmakers and was available to wealthy customers in a few major East Coast cities. During most of the second half of the nineteenth century, fashionable clothing worn by rich American women was exceptionally decorative and extravagant, requiring enormous amounts of fabric and trimmings (Brew 1945:161). One observer, writing in 1870 (Brew 1945:432), claimed that it was not unusual for New York society women to wear outfits, including jewelry, then costing $30,000 to $50,000.[4]

A second level of fashionable clothing was represented by the work of dressmakers in other towns and cities, who reproduced styles appearing in women's magazines. However, most American women did not have access to either of these sources of clothing and were obliged to make their own clothes (Walsh 1979). Photographs reveal (Severa 1995) that these women were able to assimilate fashionable details into their clothing, such as the shape of sleeves or the use of crinolines, but the overall effect was sometimes amateurish. Walsh states (1979:300): "More often than not, homemade dresses ranged not from good to passable, but from poor to bad." As Severa's photographs show, working-class American women often made new dresses out of old dresses by adding a new type of sleeve to an existing dress or a new bodice to an old skirt. Women spent enormous amounts of time redoing outdated clothing to conform to new styles, an indication of their interest in having a fashionable appearance (Severa 1995:374). Working-class women relied heavily on cheap materials, particularly calico, rather than silks and other expensive materials that were considered fashionable (Brew 1945:180; Severa 1995). However, when posing for a photograph, they were generally able to present a remarkably fashionable appearance even in very isolated areas (see fig. 12).

At the upper levels of the working class, the style and quality of women's clothing improved during the second half of the nineteenth century owing to the increasing availability of sewing machines, which facilitated the production of fashionable clothing both at home and in factories. Brew (1945:180) concluded that in 1879, "the general silhouette, although not the light colors and gorgeous fabrics, was adopted by the women in rural districts and those of lower economic status. Hard-working homeworkers dispensed with the train and probably also limited the amount of drapery at the back and the fullness of the skirt."

Skillful use of hairstyles and accessories, such as watches with chains, broaches, and cameo pins, improved the overall result. Not surprisingly, working-class women possessed smaller quantities of specific items of clothing (Brew 1945:180, 419). While rich women owned large numbers of dresses, fifty to sixty according to one observer at the time (Brew 1945:431–32), Carroll Wright's Massachusetts survey (Massachusetts Bureau of Labor Statistics 1875) estimated in 1875 that a reasonable annual expenditure for clothing for a working-class woman was for four dresses, three in calico and one for Sunday. Similar estimates were given at the beginning of the century (Brew 1945:438), although, as in France, there must have been substantial variation. Over three-quarters of the wives of northern and southern mill workers studied at the beginning of the twentieth century did not meet these standards (Worcester and Worcester 1911), although many of their older daughters did.[5] Virtually none of these women had purchased corsets, an item considered essential for a fashionable figure, but again many of their daughters had.

There was a similar disparity in the numbers of hats, gloves, and shawls owned by working-class women as compared with middle-class women. The number of hats considered appropriate for rich women substantially increased between 1879 and 1909 from two to three new ones per year to a dozen. Working-class women were likely to own one or two hats, although some older, foreign-born women were still wearing shawls in place of hats in the early 1900s. In 1879 and 1909, working-class women were expected to own at least one shawl and often also owned a coat or a cloak. By comparison, rich women were likely to own as many as twenty-five jackets, shawls, capes, and cloaks (Brew 1945:429, 437, 508, 510–11).

Gloves were another item that was acquired in large quantities by the well-to-do, particularly in the earlier period. Gloves were required for all social occasions and were not removed for eating or dancing. Brew estimates that fashionable women would have owned a pair of gloves to match each of their dresses. Wright's minimum standards for working-class women's clothing included a single pair (cited in Brew 1945:518), but Worcester and Worcester (1911:235), in their study of northern and southern mill workers, did not include gloves as a necessary annual expenditure for wives. Over 90 percent of the wives had not purchased gloves in the year of the study, although many of their older daughters had.[6] Gloves had considerable symbolic value as fashionable items. A young Jewish immigrant reported in her diary that her first pair of white silk gloves, for which she had saved for several weeks, were "the real treasure of my life" (Schreier 1994:134). Rich women wore kid or lambskin gloves in winter and silk or cashmere gloves in summer, while those of limited means used cotton gloves.

There is, however, some indication that the desire to dress well was more widespread among working-class women in America than in France or England. Photographs of Americans in rural areas and small towns (Severa 1995), as well as diaries and letters from the period, suggest that even in remote areas Americans were concerned about meeting middle-class standards (see figs. 8 and 12). Their preoccupation with clothing suggests that clothes may have represented for them a form of popular culture, specifically a link to urban culture that was unavailable to them in isolated regions. Many of these women had migrated from the East and left behind a way of life, including cultural resources, that was difficult or impossible to duplicate in small towns and villages in the Middle and Far West. Making and wearing fashionable clothing became a way of participating in cultural life outside their homes. The absence of traditional clothing, which immigrants generally discarded when they arrived, as well as higher levels of literacy early in the century, may have made these American women more susceptible than European women in similar regions to social pressures to establish their social status.

The transition from handmade to machine-made clothing for women occurred at an earlier date in America than in Europe. The major elements in this transformation were the sewing machine, patterns for specific clothing items, and the development of an accurate system of body measurements. These developments greatly simplified the production of complicated items of clothing at home and in factories. Invented in Europe and in the United States, the sewing machine was successfully marketed at an earlier date in the United States than in Europe. Beginning in the 1860s, the machines were mass produced by American firms and were widely used both commercially and in the home. Commercial use of these machines was enhanced by the development of a system of proportional measurements and subsequently of proportional sizes, making feasible ready-made clothing on a mass scale. Purchase of these machines for use in the home was made easier by a system of installment payments (Baron and Klepp 1984:30, 35). In 1875, Carroll Wright's survey of families of skilled and unskilled workers in Massachusetts revealed that one-third owned sewing machines (Massachusetts Bureau of Labor Statistics 1875:436). By the late nineteenth century, the sewing machine was in use throughout the country (Jensen 1984).

During the 1860s, an American company began to distribute clothing patterns on a wide scale (Walsh 1979). Patterns were the necessary accompaniment to the sewing machine, enabling women at home to make fashionable clothes of higher quality. By the 1870s, the company was selling six million patterns per year (the American population in 1870 was 38.5 million). Patterns were available even in small towns throughout the country (Jensen 1984:12). Production of machine-made clothing expanded during the Civil War. Afterward, the industry turned out large quantities of widely available ready-made clothing for women (Baron and Klepp 1984:28). Information about ready-made clothing was disseminated by mail-order catalogues.[7] The expansion of ready-made clothing encouraged simpler styles of clothing that were easier and cheaper to produce, foreshadowing twentieth-century clothing styles. Examples for women included unfitted cotton wrappers and the Mother Hubbard dress, a very full, shapeless smock that women wore while working at home.

In France, similar developments occurred, but with different results. Sewing machines were marketed to the French female consumer through advertising campaigns and were recommended by women's magazines (Coffin 1996a:136), but the objective appears to have been to enable the working-class housewife to save money or to make money rather than to make fashionable attire for herself. According to Coffin (137), working-class women purchased these machines mainly for the purpose of earning money by doing piecework at home. She claims that French working-class women rarely made their own clothes, relying on used clothes and by the end of the century on inexpensive ready-made clothes. French ready-made clothing was aimed at the working-class and was generally of inferior quality. It was scorned by middle-class women. However, the majority of women in the families studied by Le Play and his associates did make at least some of their clothing at home, whether or not they owned sewing machines. After 1875, sewing machines appeared in the inventories of family possessions. A quarter of the families had purchased sewing machines, generally families in which the wives were sewing as a livelihood.

French working-class wives may also have been less likely than American working-class wives to buy sewing machines because the machines were more expensive in France than in the United States, and credit was more difficult to obtain in France until the 1890s. Still another factor seems to have been the absence of one of the crucial elements in the sewing machine's success in America: the widespread availability of clothing patterns in specific sizes. Patterns were published in French women's magazines, but like similar patterns in American magazines, they were difficult to implement because of the necessity of adapting them to the size of the consumer. Most of these patterns were used by seamstresses rather than by housewives (Coffin 1996b: 79, 114; 1994: 180). Although American manufacturers sold patterns in various sizes in Europe in the late nineteenth century (Walsh 1979: 312–13), French working-class women were not inclined to use them to enhance their own wardrobes. All of these factors reinforced rather than reduced social class differences in clothing and appearance.

CLOTHING EXPENDITURES, FAMILY BUDGETS, AND STATUS SEEKING

One of the most frequently used measures for comparing clothing behavior in different countries is the percentage of family income spent on clothing. Nineteenth-century economic theory hypothesized that this percentage would be approximately the same, regardless of income (Williamson 1967: 107). As other studies have demonstrated, this is not the case, either in a particular period or over time (e.g., More 1907: 263). In fact, there were differences in the percentages of income allocated to clothing in family budgets from one country to another, as well as between different social strata in the same country. Even within the same family, men, women, and children benefited in different degrees from the family's budget for clothing. During the past one hundred years, the percentages of family income spent on clothing have steadily declined.

How can one explain such differences among working-class families in different countries? One interpretation is that higher percentages signify "status seeking," attempts to display or acquire social status. Higher percentages might also indicate a greater concern for involvement in social life outside the household. From this perspective, expenditures on clothing are a means of achieving a form of social integration (Smith 1994): dress as an important factor in establishing a person's identity as a member of a social group.

The greater importance of clothing for Americans is indicated by information about the percentages of income allocated for clothing by Americans, by immigrants to America from European countries, and by workers living in the same European countries.[8] Workers living in America allocated greater percentages of their incomes to clothing than workers living in Europe. Carroll Wright's study (Massachusetts Bureau of Labor Statistics 1875) of 397 skilled and unskilled workers, including Americans and immigrants, in Massachusetts in 1875 can be compared with Le Play's studies of French working-class families between 1850 and 1875. Families of skilled and unskilled workers in Le Play's case studies spent an average of 8.6 percent of their incomes for clothing. American families in Massachusetts spent 14.8 percent, and English and Irish immigrants spent 14.6 percent and 11.7 percent, respectively (Williamson 1967:121).

One indication that clothing was being used to enhance social status was that percentages of income allocated to clothing were higher among workers with larger incomes. In other words, disposable income tended to be used for clothing, an indication of its significance at the time. In the 1875 study, there was a pronounced relationship between income and expenditure for clothing, ranging from 7 percent of their incomes among those in the lowest income category to 19 percent among those in the highest income category (Massachusetts Bureau of Statistics of Labor 1875:441). In the same study, unskilled workers spent 12 percent of their incomes on clothing, while skilled workers spent 14 percent and overseers spent 18 percent.[9] A reanalysis of Wright's data showed that workers spent more on clothing than would be expected on the basis of their incomes (Williamson 1967:115–16), another indication of its importance.[10]

Wright's 1890 study (U. S. Commissioner of Labor 1891) permits further comparisons.[11] This study of American-born workers, immigrant workers in America, and European workers in Europe revealed that American-born workers, whose incomes were higher than those of the other groups, spent 52 percent more per year on their own clothing than the Europeans who had the lowest incomes, while immigrants, whose incomes were slightly less than those of the American workers, spent 61 percent more than the Europeans.[12]

In the Le Play studies, working-class families with lower incomes spent larger percentages of their incomes on clothing. Owing to the high cost of clothing, its burden on smaller budgets was greater. However, after 1875, skilled workers in Paris spent higher percentages of their incomes on clothing than workers in the provinces, who had lower incomes, suggesting that the former were using clothing as a form of status seeking (see appendix table 1.2). At the same time, farmers who had the highest incomes spent less than the median for the entire group, suggesting that status striving was not important for them. The farmers, living in the countryside, were less exposed than the Parisian workers to the clothing behavior of the middle class.

Unlike the farmers, the more affluent middle-class French families devoted higher percentages of their income to clothing than those who were less affluent. Perrot's (1982:167, 170) analysis of budgets kept by French middle-class women from 1873 to 1913 shows that families at the lowest level of the middle class spent the least on clothing (8.3 percent of their incomes), while families in the middle and upper levels of the middle class spent 14 percent and 15 percent, respectively.[13] When these expenditures were controlled for the number of people in these households, the families at the lower levels of the bourgeoisie were spending 10 percent of their incomes, and those at the upper levels were spending 18 percent, suggesting that clothing was being used to display social status (171–75).

American workers, both native born and immigrants, appeared to attach a greater significance to clothing than most European workers. This may have reflected the attainment of a standard of living in some regions that permitted them to spend more money on clothing, as well as an environment that encouraged such expenditures.[14] The middle class in both the United States and France apparently considered clothing an important asset in their claims for social standing.

In both Europe and America, the use of clothing to enhance social status seems to have peaked at the end of the nineteenth and the beginning of the twentieth century and declined during subsequent decades. The percentage of family income allocated to clothing declined, along with social class differences in these percentages. Brown (1994) examined household expenditure data from Consumer Expenditure Surveys conducted by the American government at five intervals from 1918 to 1988.[15] She found that in 1918 those in the lowest social class category spent 13.3 percent of their incomes for clothing, compared with 18.7 percent of those in the highest category. By 1935, social class differences in the percentages of incomes allocated for clothing had virtually disappeared; the percentages had declined to 9 percent in the lowest social class and 10 percent in the highest. By 1950, Brown (1994:203) notes that "clothing became a less important status marker between salaried and working-classes as the quality and availability of store-bought clothing improved." By 1973, the proportions allocated had declined by almost 50 percent and were virtually identical in the lowest and highest categories (5.7 percent and 6 percent). In 1988, the comparable figures were 4.2 percent and 4.8 percent.

Studies of clothing budgets in France (Herpin 1986:73) showed similar declines, although the proportions of incomes allocated were slightly higher in the later period than in the American data (see table 3.1).[16] Perrot's (1982) study of bourgeois families in France revealed similar changes.[17] Perrot (1982:217) argues that, in the earlier periods, middle-class families put their additional income into clothing but concludes that more recently "the French attach less importance than previously to sartorial elegance once their basic needs have been largely satisfied."

These diverse studies suggest that clothing had a special significance in the nineteenth century as one of the first consumer goods to become widely available and as a particularly visible means for expressing status differentials. The fact that American working-class families spent more than European working-class families suggests the greater salience of clothing in America, but by the late twentieth century, American families were spending lower percentages of their incomes on clothing than French families. Rather than

TABLE 3.1

MEAN ANNUAL PERCENTAGES OF INCOME SPENT ON CLOTHES, FRANCE, 1850–1984

	Agricultural Laborer	Farmer	Skilled and Unskilled Workers	Middle Class
Pre–1875	10.3	8.1	8.6	—
Post–1875	—	6.6	9.8	8.3–15.1
1956	12.0	10.5	12.3	11.9
1972	10.4	9.7	9.8	10.1
1979	7.4	7.4	7.7	7.7
1984	6.3	8.0	6.8	9.0

Note: Figures for the working class in the nineteenth century are based on data contained in the Le Play case studies. Figures for the middle class in the nineteenth century are drawn from Perrot (1982:167, 170). Figures for the twentieth century are taken from Herpin (1986:73).

indicating that French families attached greater importance to clothing than the American families, these data may simply reflect the lower cost of clothing in the United States and greater access to other types of goods as consumer items.

WORKING-CLASS WIVES AND FAMILY CLOTHING BUDGETS

Family clothing budgets reveal both the tendency of American working-class women to spend more on clothing than European women and the inferior position of working-class wives in general in comparison with other members of working-class families. Carroll Wright's studies of workers in America, both native born and immigrants, and in Europe indicate that workers' wives living in America spent substantially higher percentages of family income on clothing than their counterparts in Europe (U.S. Commissioner of Labor 1891). American wives spent 41 percent more per year than European wives, while wives of immigrants spent 47 percent more.[18]

Nevertheless, the same study indicates the relative deprivation of both American and European working-class wives in comparison with their husbands. In actual expenditures, American men were spending 46 percent more than their wives, and immigrant men were spending 47 percent more. European workers in the study spent an average of 27 percent more than their wives (see table 3.2).

TABLE 3.2
PERCENTAGE OF INCOME ALLOCATED FOR CLOTHING AMONG AMERICAN-BORN WORKERS, AMERICAN IMMIGRANT WORKERS AND EUROPEAN WORKERS, 1890

	Family Income Allocated for Clothing		Husbands' Compared with Wives' Expenditures
	Husbands	Wives	
American-born workers	6	4	+46
American immigrant workers	6	4	+47
European workers	5	4	+27

Note: Calculated from data contained in United States Commissioner of Labor (1891).

As we have seen, in the French working-class families, the head of the family was more likely than his wife to be described as dressing in the style of the middle class. A smaller proportion of the family budget was generally allocated to the wife's clothes as compared with the husband's. By contrast, in a group of twenty-two middle-class families during the same period (1873–1913), 62 percent of the families spent more on the *wife's* clothing than the husband's (Perrot 1982:88). French middle-class women engaged in numerous social activities outside their homes that required different types of costumes, depending upon the time of day (Delbourg-Delphis 1981).

American studies suggest that the situation of American working-class wives on the East Coast was not that different from that of French working-class wives. In both environments, working-class wives were less likely to participate in activities outside their homes that required more elaborate clothing than they typically wore at home. In poor American working-class families, wives were also less likely to spend money on clothing than their adolescent daughters. The studies of families of American-born cotton-mill workers in the South and immigrant cotton-mill workers in the North in 1908–9 reveal differences in clothing expenditures by mothers and daughters.[19] In the southern cotton-mill families, wives spent substantially less on their clothing than their husbands and their daughters over seventeen years of age. Husbands spent 128 percent more than their wives, while older daughters spent 436 percent more and older sons 157 percent more. According to the authors of the study (Worcester and Worcester 1911:26): "The mothers, as a rule, spent less for their clothing than did the older daughters. In some instances the amount spent by them for clothing was wholly inadequate. In these cases their clothing was either supplemented by that left over from former years or by the cast-off clothing of the daughters."

All the northern mill families were immigrants, about half from England, Ireland, and Quebec and the remainder, more recent arrivals, from Italy, Poland, and Portugal. Again, the wives spent less than their husbands and their older children. Husbands spent 50 percent more than their wives; older daughters in families from northern countries spent 105 percent more than their mothers, but those in families from the remaining countries appear to have been relatively cloistered and spent only 5 percent more. In general, the wives in these studies purchased only essentials such as materials, shoes, and hats, but their daughters often purchased corsets, gloves, ribbons, jewelry, and handkerchiefs.

Only about 25 percent of the families in the Le Play case studies had teenage daughters who were living at home. Daughters in these families were less likely than American daughters to spend more on clothing than their mothers. In the families studied before 1875, daughters spent only 12 percent more than their mothers, but in the families studied after 1875, mothers spent 5 percent more than their daughters. The attitudes that existed in some of these families are suggested by the comment in one study that the daughter's taste for elegant clothes was sharply reprimanded by her parents.

Differences in clothing expenditures for husbands and wives changed during the twentieth century as incomes rose and as married women became less confined to the household. Using data from Consumer Expenditure Surveys conducted by the American government, Brown (1994:51) found that in 1918, laborers' wives were spending 20 percent less than their husbands, while there was virtually no disparity in middle-class families. By 1950, American women at all social class levels were spending substantially more of the family income for their clothes than men (200–201). In France, this transition did not occur until the early seventies (Herpin 1986:67).[20] In 1972, French wives were spending 10 percent more than men, and by 1984, they were spending 30 percent more. By 1988, American wives were spending 66 percent more on clothing than husbands were (Brown 1994:384).

These figures suggest that clothing is an important indicator of women's position in the family and in the community. In the nineteenth century, the middle-class wife represented her family in the community, but the working-class wife generally lacked the resources to participate in social life outside the family. The family's meager resources for clothing were reserved for husbands and children. Even daughters, because they were more likely to be working outside the home and seeking husbands, had greater claim than their mothers to these funds.

THE SOCIAL MEANING OF HATS

Until the 1960s, the article of clothing that played the most important role in indicating social distinctions among men was the hat. The fact that it ceased to fulfill this role in the 1960s suggests that in the nineteenth-century, hats, which continued to be worn during the first half of the twentieth century, were particularly suitable for the social environment of the period. Several new types of hats appeared during the nineteenth century and were rapidly adopted at different social levels. Exactly what roles did hats perform? Because hats represented a more modest expense than jackets and coats, they provided an ideal opportunity for "blurring and transforming . . . traditional class boundaries" (Robinson 1993:39). Men's hats were also used to claim and maintain, rather than to confuse, social status, as seen in the fact that specific types of hats became closely identified with particular social strata. Elaborate customs of "hat tipping" as a means of expressing deference to a man's superiors reflect the importance of the hat in marking class boundaries (McCannell 1973). Since men represented their families in public space, men's hats, rather than women's, were used to indicate the status of the family. Women's head coverings during this period were more varied and more individualized than men's (Wilcox 1945). Women's hats exemplified conspicuous consumption instead of relaying coded signals referring to social rank.

In the nineteenth and early twentieth centuries, hats were worn by members of all social classes, including the lowest strata. In a photograph taken in Paris around 1900 of a group of ragpickers, twenty out of twenty-three wear hats or caps (see fig. 13). In the same period, photographs of workers leaving factories (Borgé and Viasnoff 1993:113) and of workers' demonstrations in Boston (Robinson 1993:6) show virtually everyone wearing a hat or a cap.

Head coverings were worn in situations which now seem inappropriate. Not only was it unacceptable to go into the street without a hat (La Mémoire de Paris 1993:128; Guiral 1976:175; Brew 1945:507–8), regardless of one's social status, but in the nineteenth century, some form of head covering was often worn indoors. For example, Englishmen wore hats all day in their offices (Ginsburg 1990:104). Sonenscher (1987:14–15) argues that hats in previous centuries were worn in what we would now call the public sphere but that the public sphere was defined differently to include activities indoors as well as outdoors: "Possession of a hat was an acknowledgment of the codes that governed admission to the particular sphere of public life in question."

The social significance of men's head coverings is indicated by the fact that, since the early nineteenth century, there has been a great deal of uniformity in what American and European men put on their heads. At any one time, there were less than a dozen types of hats, each of which might be sold with slight variations in color, size, shape of brim, and material that were not sufficient to prevent its being recognized as belonging to one of the major categories (Wilcox 1945). When a new type of hat was first introduced, there was often a period when it was worn by members of different social classes, but, eventually, it found its "niche" and became the prerogative of a particular social class.

The histories of several types of hats introduced in England in the early and mid-nineteenth century and widely adopted in other countries illustrate this principle. The top hat, which appeared in England at the beginning of the nineteenth century, was worn first by the middle and upper classes.

During the century, it spread downward, possibly because it was adopted by coachmen in the 1820s and for policemen's uniforms in the same period (de Marly 1986:123, 98). In 1839, workers in London were wearing them with their Sunday clothes, and a potter from Staffordshire, the subject of a drawing in the same year, was wearing one with a smock frock (86). In the 1840s and 1850s, unskilled laborers and fishermen were photographed wearing these hats (Ginsburg 1988:148, 152). At mid-century, they were being worn by all social classes (Ewing 1984:112).[21] Head coverings worn by a group of foremen, who represented the upper stratum of the working class, illustrate the use of hats to express their aspirations for social status (Ginsburg 1988:124). In an 1861 photograph, most of the men were wearing the newly fashionable lounge jacket, and seven out of ten were wearing top hats (see fig. 14). The older men were wearing top hats, in a slightly outdated style, but the younger ones were wearing the latest model. Only one man in the photograph was wearing a peaked cap. By the end of the century, the use of the top hat had reverted to the middle and upper classes.

The bowler was invented in England in 1850 as an occupational hat for gamekeepers and hunters but was rapidly adopted by the upper class for sports (Robinson 1993:14, 18). Within a decade it had spread to the city, where it was widely adopted by the middle and lower-middle classes (Lister 1972:163) and by members of the working class, particularly in cities (see fig. 15). According to Robinson (1993:46), "They were worn by men doing road repairs, newshawkers, milkmen, knife grinders, rabbit sellers, and sherbet and water vendors—all manner of working folk who seemed to wear their bowlers as badges of the city street."

The working-class man's attempt to blur class boundaries by wearing the bowler was satirized in the early films of Charlie Chaplin. Eventually, the bowler became an icon of the bourgeoisie, as immortalized in Magritte's famous painting of a middle-class man wearing a bowler (Robinson 1993:166) and, after the Second World War, was worn mainly by middle-class businessmen.

The cap with visor, which, like the top hat, appeared at the beginning of the nineteenth century, was first worn by military officers (Wilcox 1945:212). By mid-century, the peaked cap was identified with the working class; it was "the most usual head covering for the working man" (Ginsburg 1988:124). At the beginning of the twentieth century, cloth caps, without visors, were mainly worn by the working class and particularly by younger workers (de Marly 1986:130), while members of the middle and upper classes wore peaked or cloth caps only for sports or in the countryside (Wilcox 1945:212).

When worn by politicians, cloth caps were thought to indicate "radical tendencies" (Ginsburg 1988:138).

The straw boater had a different history. Straw hats had been widely worn by working-class men during the nineteenth century, but following the invention in 1870 of a machine for sewing straw, a new form of straw hat, the boater, became extremely popular with all social classes for about five decades (Wilcox 1945:245; Berendt 1988:24; Cunnington and Cunnington 1959:341). Afterward the boater ceased to be worn except as a form of costume for musical entertainment.

The patterns of diffusion of these types of hats were different in France and the United States. In France, each social class used hats differently. In mid-century, the upper and middle classes wore top hats; in the last quarter of the century, they wore the top hat for formal occasions and the bowler for business and less formal occasions. By the end of the century, they were still wearing the top hat and bowler, along with felt hats and, in summer, straw hats, straw boaters, and panamas (Delpierre 1990).

The case studies in the Le Play archive give an idea of how the French working class used hats (see table 3.3). Virtually every worker owned hats. Before 1875, the workers in these case studies had an average of 2.2 hats; after

TABLE 3.3

HATS AND SOCIAL CLASS BY TIME PERIOD AND REGION IN THE LE PLAY CASE STUDIES (in percentages)

	1850–1874			1875–1909		
		Provinces			Provinces	
	Paris	Urban	Rural	Paris	Urban	Rural
Middle Class						
Top hat	55	14	6	30	23	18
Bowler	0	0	0	10	8	0
Working Class						
Peaked cap	73	79	13	50	54	36
Cap, beret	9	7	38	0	8	45
Felt	36	29	62	30	54	36
Straw	0	14	19	50	54	62
N	(11)	(14)	(16)	(10)[a]	(13)	(11)

Note: Percentages in each column do not total 100, because most workers owned more than one type of hat.
[a] Two cases for which information about hats was not available are excluded from this category.

1875, they had an average of 3.2 hats. The top hat (also known in France at the black silk hat) was used on Sundays and holidays by about one-quarter of these workers, primarily by workers in Paris in the 1850s and 1860s, and also by unskilled workers and farmers after 1875. Unlike workers in England, French workers did not adopt the bowler. Only three workers owned a bowler (after 1875).

Rather than wearing the workday hat of the French middle class during the week, French workers in cities wore peaked caps, which were almost invariably designated in the case studies as hats to be worn with work clothes. Farmers and laborers in the countryside wore felt hats on Sundays and caps without visors and berets on workdays. Before 1875, straw hats were only worn in the provinces. After 1875, straw hats worn in Paris were probably boaters, which were stylish, unlike the straws hats worn in the earlier period.[22] Hats had regional as well as class connotations. In the late twentieth century, the beret has become an icon that symbolizes the Frenchman in advertising and films, but in fact the beret was primarily associated with rural life in France.[23]

While about one-quarter of the workers who were studied by Le Play and his associates owned middle-class hats (top hats or bowlers), almost all (97 percent) owned working-class hats. Only 23 percent owned both types. None of the workers owned middle-class hats without also having working-class hats. These figures indicate that the primary use of hats for these working-class men was to indicate their social status rather than to blur social class distinctions by wearing middle-class hats.

In the different American sartorial worlds of city and countryside, wearing a hat was equally important (Brew 1945:507). According to Severa (1995:210), "A hatless man was an anomaly" in the 1860s; in the 1890s, the hat was described as being "almost always in place, even when the coat and necktie have been laid aside because of the heat." Brew (1945:508, 511) estimates that, in the 1880s, the average American bought a hat every year or two and, in the first decade of this century, probably owned two hats.

As in France, there were both regional and class differences in the types of hats men selected. In the middle decades of the nineteenth century, top hats were required in cities and were sometimes worn by workers with their work clothes (Severa 1995:106, 225). During this period, the "wide-awake" (a black hat with a broad, stiff brim) was very popular in the western states (106). By the 1870s, top hats made of silk were worn in cities by prosperous businessmen but were not worn in the countryside (Brew 1945:291), where the soft felt hat was popular with railroad workers and farmers (Severa 1995: 210, 472). Straw hats were worn in the fields by farmers (Brew 1945:507). Bowlers (derbies) were worn by businessmen, particularly when they visited the countryside, and by some workmen in the cities, although caps were more "typical of the laborer" (Brew 1945:506).

By the early 1900s, the middle class was using silk top hats in the cities mainly for formal occasions, such as weddings and church services. Straw boaters were being widely worn by both the middle and the working class in the summer months. Broad-brimmed felt hats remained popular among ranchers and farmers (Brew 1945:311). Bowlers were being widely worn by both the middle and the working class (Brew 1945:311, 506–7, 510), although peaked caps were generally worn in the workplace by workers.

Two photographs of workers at work and leisure illustrate the use of the bowler to blur status boundaries. A photograph of workers at leisure, an "ironmongers' picnic" in 1890, shows most of the workers wearing bowlers (see fig. 16), but a photograph of workers in 1892 (at the San Francisco Stove Works) shows most of them wearing peaked caps or felt hats (see fig. 10). Only two workers, and the owner of the business, wear bowlers.

The use of hats to blur class boundaries appears to have occurred most frequently in England, to a lesser extent in the United States (particularly outside the workplace), and least in France. However, this type of use generally occurred during the early stages in the history of a particular style of hat. A more common practice in all three countries was the use of particular styles of hats to indicate social class status as well as affiliation with a specific region, either city or countryside.

UNIFORMS, OCCUPATIONAL CLOTHING, AND CLASS DIFFERENTIATION

By the middle of the nineteenth century, status boundaries represented by some aspects of upper- and middle-class clothing were beginning to disappear. In comparison with the eighteenth century, upper- and middle-class clothing had been simplified, but new types of clothing, such as uniforms for workers and servants, proliferated in the second half of the nineteenth century. This clothing made it easier to identify members of the working class and facilitated their differentiation from other social classes. Uniforms and occupational clothing were used to express social distinctions that could no longer be expressed as blatantly in regular attire. Three major categories of uniforms can be identified during this period: (1) uniforms of public servants such as police, postmen, firemen, and employees of railroads, (2) occupational clothing of employees of private concerns, such as shops, department stores, and factories, and (3) uniforms of domestic servants.[24]

In England and France, before the Industrial Revolution, skilled workers sometimes wore costumes that were honorific (Cunnington and Lucas 1967: 370–71). Often worn mainly for ceremonial occasions rather than for work itself, these costumes symbolized competence in specific occupations. In a few occupations, workers continued during the nineteenth century to wear their traditional costumes, some of which were quite elaborate.[25] Uniforms, as opposed to occupational costumes, were purposely developed to meet the needs of organizations for distinguishing between different levels and grades of employees and reflected the image of its employees that an organization's management wished to project, such as, for example, an analogy to servants' livery or to military dress. Uniforms based on styles from the previous century, like servants' livery, guaranteed that employees' appearance was unfashionable. The police in mid-century New York at first refused to wear uniforms because they identified such costumes with servants' livery, which they viewed as degrading (Joseph 1986:112).

In England in the 1840s, directors of railroad companies wore black frock coats and top hats, while station staff wore colorful liveries (de Marly 1986: 125). The uniforms of railroad employees recalled the elaborate liveries of eighteenth-century servants, implying that their roles were analogous to those of servants.[26] For example, in one company, foremen porters and ticket collectors at urban stations wore green frock coats, waistcoats with silver buttons, and green trousers, but brakemen, guards, and ordinary porters wore jackets and trousers in simpler styles and cheaper materials (126). When uniforms for postmen were first devised in England early in the nineteenth century, their colors also recalled eighteenth-century clothing styles: red coats with blue facing and beige knee breeches (88).

Uniforms proliferated in France in the nineteenth century for police, prison guards, and postmen, among others (Musée de la Mode et du Costume 1983). During the nineteenth and twentieth centuries, they were continually revised in ways that appeared to reflect changes in the perceived status of these workers. For example, at the beginning of the century, postmen were dressed in frock coats, waistcoats, and round hats. In 1830, postmen in cities were dressed in royal blue dress jackets with a coat of arms, yellow metal buttons, a red neckband with blue ornaments, gray trousers, and top hats in polished felt; but postmen in rural areas wore the blue smock of the working class, suggesting a lower level of prestige. In 1862, city postmen were assigned tunics with yellow metal buttons and military caps; rural postmen remained in blue smocks, with either Russian caps in winter or straw hats in the summer. By the early 1890s, both town and country postmen were expected to wear a type of smock.

Uniforms for French railway employees copied the dress styles of different social classes, with higher level employees wearing frock coats, dress jackets, and overcoats, while lower-level employees, such as ticket punchers and porters, wore canvas smocks (Musée de la Mode et du Costume 1983:75) (see fig. 17). Employees on horse-drawn buses wore different types of coats depending on their rank, with inspectors wearing long frock coats, drivers wearing hip-length jackets, and conductors wearing jackets that reached just below the waist (77).

In businesses, toward the end of the century, standardized clothing appeared for the lowest strata, manual workers, both skilled and unskilled. For other types of employees, such as department-store salespeople, dress codes appeared during this period. Overalls consisting of a long white jacket and trousers were first used in England in the 1870s as a type of protective clothing designed to meet requirements mandated by government legislation (de Marly 1986:110). Among the first types of workers to wear them were street cleaners and milk deliverymen, while their supervisors wore "professional black." The one-piece overall in denim appeared in England at the end of the century (ibid.:144) (see fig. 18) along with American-style, bib-and-brace overalls (Williams-Mitchell 1982:113), but the old white overalls also continued to be worn (de Marly 1986:162).

In the United States, denim overalls were widely available from mail-order catalogues by the end of the century and were worn by farmers as well as factory workers (Lee Hall 1992:133). The outfit was standard and mass produced and provided a kind of undifferentiated anonymity. It was in general use in factories by the end of the first decade of the twentieth century (Hall 1992:141). Hine's (1977) photographs of workers during this period show that overalls were worn in a wide variety of skilled and unskilled occupations. Many farmers, however, could not afford them and wore worn-out Sunday clothing instead, as they had done throughout the nineteenth century. Department-store catalogues in France showed these types of clothing (Debrosse 1994), as well as loose blue smocks which became standard occupational dress for many types of workers.

Industrial societies developed complex systems of sartorial signs that replaced the equally complex but different systems used in pre-industrial societies. In these systems, uniforms and standardized clothing performed a role opposite that of fashionable clothing, with its implications of self-enhancement. Uniforms worn by those at the upper levels of organizations often had honorific connotations, but uniforms worn by employees in the lower ranks of organizations generally lacked such connotations and represented a form of social control. Required to dress in a specific manner, the individual was identified with an organization and constrained to behave according to its rules and regulations.

Uniforms and other types of standardized clothing and dress codes in the workplace are still widely used, particularly in large corporations, at the end of the twentieth century. Airlines are perhaps the most assiduous in attempting to monitor the appearance of their employees, particularly female employees, but other corporations also view their employees' adherence to dress codes as an indication of their commitment to the organization (Hochschild 1983, 1997). Hotels and restaurants use dress codes to exercise control over the selection of their clienteles. Other types of organizations such as schools and churches attempt to influence the behavior of their clienteles with various types of uniforms and dress codes. Servants' uniforms, worn in private homes, represent a different version of this phenomenon.

BEING A SERVANT: Uniforms and Symbolic Boundaries

Servants' uniforms were comparable to uniforms for other types of workers: they indicated status boundaries. Their clothing expressed the relationships between social classes in domestic settings — how it felt to be a servant — and, like other types of uniforms, exhibited the increasing tendency to make social differences between employers and employees explicit and visible. Since the nature of their clothing was determined largely by their employers, servants' clothing is an excellent indicator of the degree of hierarchy in the class system. If servants dressed like their employers, class hierarchy was minimized; if they dressed differently, this indicated class differentiation. During the nineteenth century, servants in upper- and middle-class households were increasingly required to adopt a form of dress that distinguished them from their employers. In France, England, and America, there was a trend toward increasing standardization of servant's clothing, specifically the widespread adoption of uniforms.

Domestic service as an occupation was important in Europe and America in the nineteenth century, because it was a major source of employment, particularly for women (see table 3.4). Working-class women who were employed were likely to be maids, nursemaids, cooks, or housekeepers. For example, in the United States, domestic service represented 50 percent of female employment in 1870 (Katzman 1978:53) and was still the most common occupation of working women at the end of the century (Dudden 1983:1). In France the proportion of male servants was substantially higher (31 percent at mid-century and 18 percent in 1901) than in the other two countries, but

TABLE 3.4

DOMESTIC SERVANTS AND THE LABOR FORCE IN ENGLAND,
FRANCE, AND THE UNITED STATES, 1850–1901

	England	France	United States
Servants as percentage			
of total labor force			
Mid-nineteenth century	11	6	7 (1860)
1900	14	5 (1901)	8
Percentage of servants			
who were female			
1851	87	69	90
1901	92	82	90
Servants as percentage			
of female labor force			
Mid-nineteenth century	32 (1851)	29 (1866)	50 (1870)
1900	40	12 (1901)	26

Sources: England, Burnett (1974:48, 136, 140), McBride (1976:36, 45, 118). France, Guiral
and Thuillier (1978:11), Martin-Fugier (1979:36), Service Nationale de la Statistique (1906).
United States, Katzman (1978:53), Sutherland (1981:45), U.S. Census Office (1902).

domestic service was the largest nonagricultural occupation for women in the
nineteenth century. About one out of three women was employed as a servant
at some point during her lifetime (McBride 1986:929). In all three countries,
the number of servants declined steadily during the twentieth century.[27]

Changes in servants' clothing in the nineteenth century corresponded to
changes in the nature of the relationship between middle- and upper-class
wives and their servants, which became less intimate and more authoritarian.
In the eighteenth and early nineteenth centuries, middle-class housewives
performed substantial amounts of the work necessary to maintain a household. During the second half of the nineteenth century, middle- and upper-
class housewives participated only minimally in household activities. The
ideal wife (and her daughters) had no domestic functions and were free to
pursue social activities (Burnett 1974:144). Changes in servants' clothing occurred as middle-class women sought to create visible status boundaries between themselves and their maidservants.

The precise nature of these changes varied in each country, but the basic
pattern of increasing social differentiation was evident. In England, in the
eighteenth century, house servants such as butlers, valets, chambermaids, and
waiting women sometimes dressed in clothing so similar to the clothing of
their employers that visitors had difficulty distinguishing between guests and

servants (de Marly 1986:70–73). During the nineteenth century, rules about clothing, headdress, and physical appearance developed that served to maintain status boundaries between employer and servant. For example, in England, in the first decades of the nineteenth century, unmarried maids wore mob cops in the house to distinguish them from unmarried daughters, who did not wear headdress indoors (104). By 1860, there was a standard uniform: "a cotton print dress for the morning, with black dresses, white aprons and caps for the afternoon" (Burnett 1974:171–72). At the end of the century, maids were still wearing black dresses, white aprons, and caps, sometimes with streamers (Cunnington 1974:126–27). However, those who were least visible, such as scullery maids, were often as poorly dressed as unskilled laborers (de Marly 1986:136). Male servants whose activities brought them into contact with visitors were often well or even elaborately dressed, but their clothing was usually slightly or even considerably out of fashion.[28] In large upper-class households, the costumes worn by different types of servants reflected a rigid status hierarchy among them that mirrored the hierarchy of English society. This is exemplified in a photograph taken in 1898 of the servants of an English countess (see fig. 19). The photograph shows eight maids who were at the bottom of the hierarchy in print dresses, starched caps, collars, and aprons, two parlor maids with higher and more frilly caps, three footmen in white ties and brass-buttoned livery tail coats, the cook in a bibbed apron, the butler in formal clothes with a black bow tie, and the housekeeper in dark silk and no apron.

Typical middle-class homes had only two or three servants but "aimed at being a microcosm of the great estate, . . . sharing many of the same attitudes, assumptions and beliefs" (Burnett 1974:146). Toward the end of the century, eighteenth-century livery for male servants disappeared in England (Cunnington and Lucas 1967), but maids' uniforms became increasingly elaborate (Levitt 1986:178). In the twentieth century, the class differences between English housewife and maidservant have been described as "unbridgeable in anything but the most superficial way . . . the social differences between women made any kind of friendly or informal relationship between mistress and servant impossible" (Giles 1995:132).

A similar change in the relationship between housewife and servant occurred in the United States, epitomized in a change of vocabulary from the use of the word "help" to describe servant women to the word "domestic" (Dudden 1983:6). Before the middle of the nineteenth century, young local girls were hired to work alongside the housewife and were treated as companions rather than as employees. These girls did not perceive themselves as servants and refused to wear uniforms. Even caps were considered "an infringement upon their natural liberty" (Sutherland 1981:129) and were accepted only by those who were employed in wealthy households.

With the increase in the number of immigrants in the East at mid-century, local girls were replaced by immigrant girls and women who served as domestics and were treated as employees, serving longer hours and doing the great majority of the housework as housewives retreated into "genteel idleness." Maids' uniforms seem to have developed later in the United States than in England. Certain types of materials were considered appropriate for their clothing, such as dark chintz, as well as items such as the *fichu*, the cap, and in the South, the turban (Severa 1995:218, 509, 536). By the early twentieth century, female servants were wearing "an assortment of uniforms on different occasions and at various times of the day," suggesting an increasing level of status differentiation in American society (Sutherland 1981:130). According to Clark-Lewis (1994:113), after 1900 "the uniformed servant became one of the most visible and valued signs of a white person's social arrival" in Washington, D.C. Uniforms remained the norm for domestic service for another half century. By the 1920s, the occupation had been abandoned by native-born and foreign-born whites; most servants were African American (147). The persistence of servants' uniforms in the United States in the twentieth century can be explained by race and ethnic differences as well as by social class.

Duroselle (1972:80) calls French servants "a class apart that we can place neither among the workers, nor among the farmers, nor among the middle classes." According to Le Play, servants occupied the lowest strata of French society in the nineteenth century and were generally poorly treated. The authors of a book about the daily lives of servants in France in the nineteenth century admit that they are very poorly informed about the nature of servants' clothing (Guiral and Thuillier 1978:46). They rely for the most part on books of etiquette, which in turn recommend that their readers follow the example of the English. Guiral and Thuillier (46) suggest that French servants were not as elaborately dressed as English ones. For the period 1852–79, Guiral (1976:173) states that, except in "*les grandes maisons*," servants frequently wore their employers' old clothes. Very few of the households described in the Le Play studies had domestic servants, and their clothing is generally not described. The author of a study written in 1856 (no. 3:451) comments: "The servant himself is lodged, fed, and dressed exactly as a member of the family: his situation, which is evidently the result of tradition, forms a striking contrast with that which is now done with servants in most classes in French society."

This comment suggests that in France, as in the United States and

England, the relationships between servants and employers in an earlier period had been more egalitarian, but photographs toward the end of the century show servants and nursemaids dressed in uniforms similar to those in England and the United States (see fig. 20).

CONCLUSION

Fashionable clothing, which could be used to enhance the individual's social capital, was mainly accessible to the middle and upper class during the nineteenth century, while uniforms that represented instruments of social control were imposed primarily on employees drawn from the working class. Even in the United States, which represented a somewhat less hierarchical society than either France or England, fashionable clothing was primarily worn by members of the middle and upper classes. The availability of fashionable clothing to the working class varied by region, ethnicity, race, and gender. In general, working-class men had greater access than women to family resources for purchasing clothes, but working-class wives in the more democratic communities of the Middle West appear to have been better dressed than working-class wives on the East Coast. Technologies for simplifying the production of clothing, both at home and in factories, were first widely commercialized in the United States and contributed to the eventual democratization of clothing.

As the first widely accessible consumer good, clothes had a symbolic importance that is less salient in late twentieth-century consumer economies. The tendency for American workers to increase their levels of expenditure on clothing as their incomes rose and the high "elasticity" of the amounts they were willing to pay for clothes are indications of the symbolic importance of clothing during this period.

Some writers stress the existence of an American clothing norm that Americans were implicitly following and that immigrants rapidly assimilated (e.g., Severa 1995:109). The American clothing norm seems to have been based on the idea that being well dressed was an indication of respectability (294). Regional differences in clothing styles were surprisingly small, but class differences remained. Fashion was treated selectively; exaggerated styles were toned down or rejected. There appears to have been considerable uniformity in the styles that were worn in different parts of the country, but different versions of these styles existed at different class levels (283, 507).[29] In some regions, such as the Middle West, it seems to have been easier for the working class to adopt the clothing styles of the middle class than in others.

African Americans and immigrants, when they had the means to do so, spent considerable time, effort, and money emulating dominant clothing styles.[30]

As the populations of industrial societies expanded in size, the numbers of contacts between strangers increased, but relations between people in different social classes decreased. Uniforms served as useful reminders that the content of interpersonal communication in settings where uniforms were worn was expected to be limited to information about the task being performed, thus reinforcing the separation between social classes, and even between employer and servant in the household. Dress codes were a subtler means of reminding higher status employees of the necessity of conforming to the norms and values of organizational cultures. In these highly class-conscious industrial societies, hats were enormously important as signals that claimed and maintained social status. The ubiquity of hats suggests the importance attached to having one's status recognized immediately by others and being able to identify instantly the social status of others. At times, hats provided a means of blurring status differences, but their primary function seems to have been that of claiming or signaling social status.

Industrial societies in the nineteenth century were undergoing changes that were producing hegemonic national cultures in which regional and ethnic cultures were disappearing or, in some cases, being suppressed (Schudson 1994). The emergence of national educational systems, rising levels of literacy, and the expansion of the press contributed to this phenomenon. The development of fashionable clothing from being the exclusive prerogative of the upper class to being a form of popular culture for all social classes was part of the same process of cultural unification. As other forms of popular culture expanded to unprecedented levels in the late twentieth century, the importance of clothing in national cultures, as indicated by family expenditures, declined.

NOTES

1. A Prince Albert is a double-breasted frock coat. Severa (1995:283) states: "What may seem remarkable . . . is the almost universal adherence to coat, vest, tie, and hat in a situation far from urban refinements. The prevalence of this custom is borne out by all American photographs of men throughout this decade [1860s]."

2. The real wages of American workers rose less than those of Swedish, German, British, or French workers between 1860 and 1913 (Vanneman and Cannon 1987:274).

3. Sewing machines were not widely used in the French ready-made clothing industry until the 1860s and were not produced in France until 1870 (Coffin 1996b).

4. Approximately $897,000 to $1,495,000 in 1989 dollars (Derko 1994). Using the value of the dollar in 1867 as a baseline, Derko estimates the value of the 1867 dollar in 1879 as $0.94 and in 1989 as $30.84. Comparisons of prices across such large intervals of time are inevitably imprecise.

5. Worcester and Worcester (1911:10) studied family budgets of cotton-mill workers in the North and the South in 1909. These workers had a very low standard of living (133). Fourteen families were studied in Fall River, Massachusetts, and twenty-one families in three locations in Georgia (Atlanta) and North Carolina (Greensboro and Burlington). The survey included detailed information about the quantities and costs of clothing owned by the families. Only 21 percent of the southern and northern mothers had purchased four or more dresses in the year of the study, while 77 percent of the southern daughters over nine years old met the standard. Only 25 percent of northern daughters met the standard.

6. Five percent of southern mothers and 7 percent of northern mothers had purchased gloves, compared with 19 percent of the southern daughters and 50 percent of the northern daughters.

7. The negative side of these developments was that they reduced the wages of women employed in the garment industry, particularly of women doing piecework at home (Baron and Klepp 1984).

8. Budget information was collected from the families of American workers and English and Irish immigrants in Massachusetts in 1875 (Massachusetts Bureau of Labor Statistics 1875) and in the United States, Britain, and Western Europe in 1889 and 1890 (U.S. Commissioner of Labor 1891). The second study included immigrants from the following countries: England, France, Germany, Ireland, Scotland, and Wales. It also included samples of workers living in the following European countries: Belgium, England, France, Germany, Scotland, and Wales. In both the earlier and the later study, workers were approached at specific work sites. Response rates were low, possibly because many workers were unwilling or unable to provide the types of information requested. For example, in the 1875 study, the response rate was less than 40 percent (Massachusetts Bureau of Labor Statistics 1875:202; see also Williamson 1967; Modell 1978; and Smith 1994).

9. Computed on the basis of information contained in Massachusetts Bureau of Labor Statistics (1875:368 and 429). Unfortunately, the number of overseers was very small ($N = 4$).

10. This represents income elasticity, which measures the extent to which people spend more or less for a particular item than would be expected on the basis of their income.

11. These comparisons are restricted to groups of immigrants containing at least sixty workers. In the 1890 study, there was a slight relationship between income and clothing expenditure among American-born workers and immigrants in America and a slight inverse relationship between the two variables in the European samples. It is possible that income differences between the groups were too small to reveal differences among them on these variables.

12. Average annual expenditures for working-class men in dollars:

		Percentage more than expenditures by Europeans
American-born workers	$35	52 percent
Immigrant workers	$37	61 percent

Note: Average expenditure by Europeans was $23 per year. Data computed from U.S. Commissioner of Labor (1891).

13. Perrot's study (1982:3) is based on budgets of French families that were solicited in a newspaper article. Out of 1,100 budgets received, 547 were usable (5). Indicative of the importance attached to budgets in French families, these budgets had been preserved by later generations. They were produced in three different time periods: the last quarter of the nineteenth century and the beginning of the twentieth century, the period between the two world wars, and an eight-year period following the second World War.

14. Shergold (1982:204) argues that workers in America spent more for their clothing than European workers at the beginning of the twentieth century because comparable clothing was more expensive in America.

15. Brown (1994) used three occupational groups: salaried (managers and professionals), wage earners (skilled and semiskilled workers), and laborers (unskilled workers), and two residual categories consisting of the poor or underclass and seniors (families with household heads over sixty-four years old). Her findings regarding the proportion of income spent on clothing in the United States may be summarized as follows:

Year	Low	Laborers	Wage earners	Salaried
1918	13.3	14.5	15.9	18.7
1935	9.0	8.8	9.5	10.1
1950	11.9	9.2	9.7	10.4
1973	5.7	5.4	5.4	6.0
1988	4.2	4.6	4.7	4.8

Source: From Brown (1994:43, 106, 188, 270, 367).

16. Herpin's data are drawn from several surveys of household expenditures, using random samples of French households (1986:72).

17. Perrot (1982:216) shows that the income elasticity of expenditures by French middle-class families for clothing declined to 1.05 in 1945–53 (in comparison with 1.24 in 1873–1913 and 1.36 in 1920–39).

18. Computed from data contained in U.S. Commissioner of Labor (1891:1364, 1370).

19. For a description of these studies, see note 5.

20. Using national surveys of family clothing expenditures, Herpin (1986:67) shows that French women spent 23 percent less than men in 1953. Brown's (1994) study shows that American women were spending 28 percent more on clothing than men in 1950.

21. Ginsburg (1990:86) says that by mid-century, "photography, the new visual record of the period, shows them on the heads of everyman [sic]."

22. The inventories do not indicate whether the straw hats were boaters; therefore it is not possible to trace the usage of this particular type of hat.

23. Until recently, the proportion of French people working in agriculture was exceptionally high for an advanced industrial country. This may explain why the beret attained the status of a "national" hat.

24. Military uniforms were an additional category, which will not be discussed here. Since public officials were generally middle or upper class, their uniforms will also not be discussed here. Uniforms of professional workers such as doctors and nurses will not be discussed for the same reason.

25. Duveau (1946:364) cites the example of men employed in the 1830s at Saint-Gobain in the manufacture of mirrors, who wore large felt hats, white shirts, blue breeches, and white gaiters.

26. Joseph (1986:112) differentiates between livery and uniforms: livery is clothing that symbolizes a personal tie between the wearer and another person, but a uniform symbolizes membership in an impersonal organization.

27. At the end of the twentieth century, the proportion of the labor force working as servants in private homes was less than 1 percent in the United States and the United Kingdom and less than 2 percent in France (U.S. Department of Labor 1990; Statistical Office of the European Communities 1993).

28. Livery was most widely used for servants employed by the aristocracy and the newly rich middle class in England. Male servants in upper-class English households were required to wear wigs long after they ceased to be fashionable. They were permitted to wear top hats but only with a cockade at the side to denote servant status (de Marly 1986: 103, 104). Facial hair was another means of delineating status boundaries. In the period between the two World Wars, the French bourgeoisie wore mustaches, beards, and goatees but required their male servants to be clean shaven (*La Mémoire de Paris* 1993:133). Joseph (1986:42) argues that a male servant's fashionable appearance could have been perceived as a threat to the dominance of the male head of the household, while fashionable details in the uniform of maidservants were not.

29. For example, the clothing norm for the middle-class male consisted of coat, vest, tie, and hat (Severa 1995:283). A typical outfit of the working class included "unironed cotton shirts, denim or wool trousers, vests, suspenders, and felt hats" (507).

30. Severa (1995) includes numerous examples of working-class African Americans wearing stylish clothing. Schreier (1994) documents the elegant clothing of young Jewish immigrant women at the end of the century. See White and White (1998) for a discussion of differences between African-American and white clothing styles and negative reactions of southern whites to well-dressed African Americans.

A woman's dress is a permanent revelation of her most secret thoughts, a language, and a symbol. Balzac, Une fille d'Eve (1839)

4 WOMEN'S CLOTHING BEHAVIOR AS NONVERBAL RESISTANCE

Symbolic Boundaries, Alternative Dress, and Public Space

Had a nineteenth-century social scientist set out to predict how women would dress at the beginning of the twenty-first century, it would only have been by considering the clothing of the most marginal women in Europe and America that an accurate assessment would have been obtained. Women's clothing today descends in part from the clothing styles of both middle- and working-class women, whose behavior did not correspond to that of the ideal Victorian woman. Social theorists from Marx to Foucault tend to emphasize the ways in which dominant discourses concerning, for example, class and sexuality influence behavior and attitudes. Foucault (1978) argued that Victorian discourse about sexuality constituted a "technology" for exerting power over the individual and the family. What such theories tend to neglect are the ways in which marginal discourses survive and continue to exert an influence alongside hegemonic discourses, which they may eventually modify or displace. Clothing and clothing choices in the nineteenth century are valuable sites for examining the relationships between marginal and hegemonic discourses. While histories of fashionable clothing give the impression of consensus, clothing actually involved a great deal of debate and controversy.

99

In any period, the set of clothing discourses always includes those that support conformity to dominant conceptions of social roles and those that express social tensions that are pushing widely accepted conceptions of social roles in new directions (Smith 1988). The latter include the perspectives of marginal groups that are seeking acceptance for clothing behavior that is deviant or marginal according to dominant conceptions of status or gender roles. Each discourse is supported by different social groups. It has its constituency, its leaders and followers, as well as its visual language expressed in clothing behavior. Discourses that express dominant cultural norms and values are supported by more powerful groups, while those that express subcultural or marginal norms are supported by minorities and by groups that are in different ways socially marginal, such as intellectuals, artists, and entertainers. Over time, the social impact of each discourse shifts as social and economic changes create a more or less favorable environment for it. The influence of these discourses often depends on factors over which their proponents have little control, such as changes in levels of social mobility, availability of employment for women, and the relative importance attached to work as compared with leisure activities.

Clothing as a form of symbolic communication was enormously important in the nineteenth century as a means of conveying information about the wearer's social role, social standing, and personal character. Upper- and middle-class women devoted enormous amounts of time and money to creating elaborate wardrobes in order to present themselves appropriately to members of their social milieus (Smith 1981). Lacking other forms of power, they used nonverbal symbols as a means of self-expression. Fashionable clothing exemplified the doctrine of separate spheres that was supported by other social institutions. It suited the subordinate and passive social roles women were expected to perform. Industrialization had removed most middle- and upper-middle-class married women in Europe and America from active participation in the economy. Aristocratic idleness was considered the suitable activity for middle- and upper-class wives. Effectively denied anything but very limited participation in the public sphere, women were frequently identified according to their clothing. Political cartoons, satire, and commentary tended to refer to women as "petticoats" (Rolley 1990a:48).[1]

Fashionable styles originating in Paris were adopted by women in other parts of Europe and America. Dresses were composed of several separate garments and enormous quantities of fabric (Brew 1945:160–61). Trimmings were elaborate and complicated. These clothes constricted the body and made any form of movement difficult. Each occasion required a specific type of dress, necessitating constant wardrobe changes.[2] These styles symbolized women's exclusion from male occupations and their economic dependence on husbands and male relatives.

The subject of this chapter is a puzzle: there were in fact two distinct styles of dress for women in the second half of the nineteenth century. Photographs reveal that, coexisting with the fashionable style, was another style, which I will call the alternative style. It was widely worn but has seldom been discussed. This style incorporated items from men's clothing, such as ties, men's hats, suit jackets, waistcoats, and men's shirts, sometimes singly, sometimes in combination with one another, but always associated with items of fashionable female clothing. Trousers were not part of this alternative style, probably because trousers, when worn by women, constituted a greater symbolic challenge to the system than most middle-class women were prepared to make. Women who were considered to be behaving in defiance of the social order were sometimes represented as wearing trousers by satirists and cartoonists (Moses 1984:123–26; Rolley 1990a).

The significance of the alternative style is difficult to assess. Unlike the styles proposed by dress reformers, it appears frequently in photographs of the period but is generally ignored in fashion histories, presumably because the style was worn primarily, although not exclusively, by employed women, who were considered marginal. I will argue that this type of clothing constituted a form of nonverbal communication that appealed to women whose roles were conflicted or constrained. At the same time, while some items in this style were widely adopted, they did not displace the fashionable style. That style remained dominant. In this chapter, I will first give a more detailed description of the alternative style of dress and then suggest some tentative explanations for its origins and influence. How did certain types of clothing as a form of nonverbal communication support discourses that challenged dominant conceptions of women's roles in the nineteenth century? How did the use of these garments vary in different countries and in different types of public space? Why were conventional norms for suitable apparel frequently violated in certain types of public and institutional settings?

COMPONENTS OF ALTERNATIVE DRESS

While the fashionable style originated in France, the English influence on the alternative style was unmistakable, particularly in clothing worn for sports and in the design of the tailored suit jacket, suggesting a receptiveness in English culture to alternative images of women. This may have been the effect of a tradition of British female rulers, embodied in the nineteenth century by Queen Victoria. In 1837, the first year of her reign, Victoria reviewed her troops at Windsor wearing a masculine military cap and a blue cloth military coat (Ewing 1975:62).

The alternative style can be understood as a set of signs, borrowed from male clothing and consisting of items that were used separately or together, that subtly changed the overall effect of female clothing. One of the most frequently worn items of alternative dress was the man's tie. The significance of the tie in the alternative style was related to its function in the male wardrobe. Gibbings (1990:64) states that in Victorian society: "The neckwear of each man proclaimed his current position in society . . . and his aspirations." As nineteenth-century male clothing became increasingly somber and formulaic, the tie was used to encode information about the wearer's background, "regimental, club, sporting or educational" (81). The tie when worn by a woman was in the most general sense an expression of independence, but various alternative lifestyles were invoked. Elizabeth Gaskell in her novel *Cranford*, set in an English provincial town in the 1840s, describes one of her unmarried female characters, who was the essence of propriety, as wearing "a cravat and a little bonnet like a jockey-cap" (Gaskell 1994:17). In 1851, dress reformer Amelia Bloomer's daughter was described as wearing a crimson silk necktie with a lavender-colored tunic and white trousers (Gibbings 1990:71). Photographs of middle- and upper-class women that began to appear more frequently during this period are useful as an indication of different meanings the tie conveyed. A young woman whose picture was taken by an anonymous photographer in 1855 had four types of neckwear as accessories to the fashionable dress of the period: "a lace collar, a choker held in place with a butterfly broach, and . . . stylized man's sharp-ended bow tie," in addition to a necklace (Gibbings 1990:67). Cunnington and Cunnington (1959:475) mention that cravats and neckties for women "were conspicuous in 1861." Photographed in front of a seaside backdrop in 1864, an Englishwoman wore a tie with a very full skirt, a jacket whose style was adapted from men's jackets of the period, and a straw sailor's hat (fig. 21). Significantly, a photograph of the University of Wisconsin class of 1876 (which contained almost as many women as men) shows all the young women wearing some version of a necktie (see fig. 22).

Beginning in the 1870s, many young women wore black velvet neck ribbons (Severa 1995:305, 495). Worn in widths from a quarter to a half inch, the neck ribbon closely resembled the inch-wide black ties worn by men during this period (Severa 1995:388, 396; Gibbings 1990:88; Duroselle 1972:109). At the end of the century, ribbon ties were worn by members of all social classes, including upper-class women, although their presence is

21. *Middle-class woman in "alternative" dress (England), 1864, including a loose-fitting jacket, imitating men's jackets, a straw sailor's hat, and a tie (England), 1864. Courtesy of the National Portrait Gallery, London*

22. *Female college students wearing neckties (United States), 1876. Courtesy of the State Historical Society of Wisconsin (neg. WHi [D31] 590)*

23. *Cotton-mill worker wearing ribbon tie (United States), 1879–80. Courtesy of the Photo-graphic History Collection, National Museum of American History, Smithsonian Institution, Washington, DC*

24. *Middle-class woman in "alternative" dress, including straw hat, tie, suit jacket, and match-ing vest (England), 1893. Courtesy of Manchester City Art Galleries, Manchester, UK*

25. *Upper-class woman in fashionable dress with friends in "alternative" dress (England), 1897. Reproduced by permission of Birmingham Library Services, Birmingham, UK*

26. Self-portrait of French woman photographer in fashionable dress (France), 1895. Photo by Amélie Galup.© Ministère de la Culture, France

27. Self-portrait of French woman photographer in "alternative" dress, ca. 1911. Photo by Agathe Coutemoine. Courtesy of Collection Rameaux, F-39300

28. Dress reform: bloomer dress (United States), 1862–67. Homemade version of the bloomer dress, using brocaded silk for dress and pants. Collection of Deborah Fontana Cooney

29. *Dress reformer in an adaptation of reform dress that anticipates the pant suit a century later (United States), 1866–70. Collection of Deborah Fontana Cooney*

30. On a San Francisco beach, young women wading in the ocean reveal their bare legs but are fully dressed, including bustle poufs and hats (United States), 1886. The body of the woman in the foreground is completely covered by a dark tailored suit with a bustle back and a full-length skirt. Courtesy of the California History Room, California State Library, Sacramento

31. Schoolgirls in sports costumes: knee-length, belted tunics that anticipate styles in the late twentieth century (Scotland), 1888. Reproduced with permission of St. Leonards School, St. Andrews, Scotland

32. Young women wearing ankle-length skirts for an exercise class in a teacher-training school (France), ca. 1900. Courtesy of Musée national de l'Education, I.N.R.P, Rouen

33. Bicycle outfit (knee-length bloomers or knickerbockers), as represented in an advertisement (England), 1897

34. A French woman bicyclist had her photograph taken in a photographer's studio with her bicycle and her bicycling outfit, including a knee-length divided skirt, a straw boater, and a blouse with fashionably wide sleeves (France), ca. 1895. Courtesy of the Bibliothèque nationale de France, Paris

35. *Wigan collier girl (England), 1873, wearing a wadded hood bonnet, patched men's trousers, brass-tipped clogs, and a rolled-up petticoat as a "symbol of sex" (Ginsburg 1988:150). Courtesy of the Masters and Fellows of Trinity College, Cambridge, UK*

36. *Women munitions workers in trousers during the First World War (England), 1916. Courtesy of the Imperial War Museum, London*

37. *Adaptation of reform dress on a frontier farm (United States), 1867. Courtesy of the State Historical Society of Wisconsin (neg. WHi [X3] 37029).*

38. *Actresses bound for the Klondike, wearing men's trousers, suspenders, boots, and men's hats, including, in some cases, corsets and wide sleeves (United States), 1897. The length of the skirt worn by the woman in the background would have been unacceptable in American cities of the period.* Courtesy of Special Collections Division, University of Washington Libraries, Seattle (neg. LaR 2049)

39. Munitions workers in loose-fitting overalls (United States), 1916. Courtesy of the Engineering and Industrial History Collection, National Museum of American History, Smithsonian Institution

40. Female railway porter in "masculine" uniform (England), 1954. Courtesy of the National Railway Museum/Science and Society Picture Library, London.

41. *Parody of the tie, as a statement of feminine independence, with the female model's tie worn askew in contrast to those of her male counterparts. Ralph Lauren advertisement, 1995.*

barely hinted at in French fashion histories (Delpierre 1990). Middle-class women wore them with business dress, school uniforms (Ewing 1975) and nurses' uniforms (Juin 1994:168); working-class women wore them with servants' and nursemaids' uniforms (Lister 1972) and in factories (see fig. 23). Ties, in various styles, were frequently a part of costumes for sports, particularly bicycling, which became popular in the last decade of the century (Gibbings 1990:88–89; Delpierre 1990:43). Photographs of women wearing ties increased in frequency in all three countries toward the end of the century. Women wearing ties began to appear in paintings (Hollander 1994: 130), a sign of increased social acceptability, since painting a portrait was a much more formal occasion than taking a photograph.

Ginsburg (1988:114) identifies the tie as being central to the "feminist uniform" of the 1890s, as worn by a young woman who is described as follows: "The very high, stiff, stud-fastened collar and plain tie secured by a small pearl pin are uncompromising assertions of a claim to sex equality and mark an assault on masculine privilege." At the same time, Ginsburg notes that the young woman "hedges her bets" by emphasizing her small waist with a wide belt and wearing a large bow in her long hair. She conforms to fashionable trends of the period by wearing a blouse with wide sleeves and a smoothly fitted skirt. That wearing a tie constituted a social statement is also seen in the example of the French novelist Colette. Photographed with her husband in 1900, Colette was wearing the conventional costume of the middle-class matron—huge hat trimmed with daisies, a lace blouse, and a necklace. A few years later, separated from her husband, she was photographed wearing a long tie and without a hat.

Hats were also potent symbols of masculine identity and were coopted by women during this period. Top hats were worn with riding habits beginning in the 1830s and right through the century; bowler hats for riding appeared toward the end of the century (Wilcox 1945; Schreier 1989). The use of men's hats by women for other types of activities began in the middle of the century. Sailors' straw hats were first adopted as a fashionable style for children before becoming fashionable for women in the 1860s (Lambert 1991:55). According to Brew (1945:209–10), a popular hat in the 1870s was the derby (bowler), "made almost exactly like those used by men." Alexandra, then Princess of Wales, was photographed in afternoon dress wearing a round cloth hat with narrow brim, reminiscent of a man's bowler. Felt fedoras identical to those worn by men appeared in the 1880s (Severa 1995:417). Men's jockey caps, hunting caps, and peaked yachting caps were worn by women for sports during this period (Wilcox 1945).

In the 1880s the hard straw hat, or boater, became very fashionable as a man's hat (Wilcox 1945:254) and was also widely worn by women for the next three decades (Severa 1995:470, 510). It was so popular with both sexes that it could be described as a "unisex" accessory (Ginsburg 1988:94). This very simple hat, with its geometrically precise lines, offered a stark contrast to the typical hat worn by women during this period, which was often worn with a veil and generally piled high with flowers, ribbon, lace, feathers, stuffed birds, and sometimes reptiles, shellfish, and insects (Brew 1945:210; Cunnington and Cunnington 1959:564). Combined with a tie and a suit jacket, the boater expressed the independence of young women in new occupations such as office work. Worn with a bow tie and a man's jacket in the costume of a nursemaid, it became a gesture suggesting defiance (Juin 1994:89).

The suit jacket has been called "the symbol of the emancipated woman in the nineteenth century" (Chaumette 1995:9). The simplicity of the woman's suit jacket contrasted with the increasing complexity of fashionable dresses as the century progressed. In the seventeenth century, upper-class women had worn jackets as part of their riding habits and for walking in the countryside (Ewing 1984:82). In the first half of the nineteenth century, the dress dominated fashion, but, in the middle of the century, the jacket again appeared for use in the countryside or by the sea. Loose-fitting jackets, imitating men's jackets, were worn with blouses with masculine shirt collars, bow ties, and straw hats (Byrde 1992:162). These styles originated in England, which was already the leader in styles for men's clothes. In the 1860s, "double-breasted almost man-tailored jackets" were fashionable but not entirely respectable (Ginsburg 1988:129). In 1874, Princess Alexandra was photographed wearing a feminine version of a naval officer's uniform (Newton 1974). In 1877, an imitation of the masculine Norfolk jacket became fashionable in England (Cunnington and Cunnington 1959:488). In the United States, women's participation in the Civil War provided the impetus for the development of a mannish suit, "with dark jacket, shortened skirt, and a plain blouse" (Banner 1984:98). Women continued to wear these suits in later decades.

In the 1870s, an English fashion designer, Redfern, produced jackets for women that were made from materials used for men's clothes and included details from men's garments such as lapels and buttons on the sleeves. They were to be worn with matching skirts, a blouse, and a tie (Chaumette 1995:45). Figure 24 shows a similar outfit twenty years later. The inclusion of such an outfit in the trousseau of a British princess (granddaughter of Queen Victoria), whose contents were widely publicized, led to its widespread adoption (Davray-Piekolek 1990:45).

A French costume historian (Davray-Piekolek 1990:44) called the suit "the only piece of feminine clothing not launched in France."[3] Preferably made by tailors rather than dressmakers, "the tailor-made gown was seen as essentially an English garment, both in make and origin" (Byrde 1992:81). To the French it signaled a new style of female behavior: a woman who moved very freely was called "*l'anglaise*" (Chaumette 1995:46). Nevertheless, French women adopted the *tailleur* (tailored suit), including middle-class women who engaged in sports or travel and working-class women in offices and shops. Even women living in the countryside adopted the suit jacket (51).

In the United States, ready-made tailored suits, consisting of jacket, skirt, and vest, were available in the 1880s and more widely in the 1890s. They were made of heavy materials and included details, such as the collar, associated with men's suits (Kidwell and Christman 1974:143). According to Brew (1945:226), "The suit, especially the tailored suit, was an extremely important article in a women's wardrobe of 1909." Like the tie and the boater, it was worn by women at all social class levels. The suit influenced the styles of dresses during the period, particularly in the selection of fabrics previously used for men's suits. Ginsburg (1988:82) describes a woman photographed in the mid-1880s as wearing "a trim check wool bodice and skirt. Her bustle . . . is as feminine as her neat, starched, stud-fastening cuffs are masculine." Waistcoats for women with distinctly masculine connotations appeared in 1846 and were fashionable for about a decade (Byrde 1992:55). They became fashionable again between 1880 and 1895 as suits began to be widely worn.

The final element in the costume for the independent woman appeared in the United States in the seventies in the form of the shirtwaist, a man's shirt adapted for women, with a stand-up or turn-down collar, often ornamented with a small black tie or bow tie (Brew 1945:165; Lee Hall 1992:55). A similar type of garment, referred to as a shirt, was popular in England in the 1880s (Byrde 1992:85). In the 1890s, it was virtually a uniform for middle- and working-class American women. Appearing in the drawings of Charles Dana Gibson, the Gibson girl blouse became an icon representing the emancipated young woman (Banner 1984).

In the course of the century, the alternative style of clothing incorporated an increasing number of items, and the individual items themselves evolved, particularly the suit jacket. Even at the end of the century, however, women used the style selectively. Wearing a bow tie and a straw boater represented a relatively weak statement. Wearing a four-in-hand tie, a shirtwaist, a waistcoat, a tailored jacket, and a boater or another masculine hat style was a strong statement (Byrde 1992:168). The style was seen at different social class levels, including society women (Bradfield 1981:291) and the working class.[4]

The alternative and the dominant styles of clothing provided a notable contrast in photographs (Bradfield 1981:383; Ginsburg 1988:94) (see fig. 25).

Self-portraits of two amateur French women photographers (Condé 1992:115) illustrate the connection between clothing and self-image. The first woman, who entitled her photograph "Amateur Photographer," is dressed in the dominant feminine style of the 1890s (see fig. 26). The second woman, photographed a decade and a half later, is dressed in the alternative style: a shirtwaist with a bow tie (see fig. 27). Significantly, she posed herself with a copy of a professional photography magazine, presumably to indicate her identification with her craft. A working woman, she was the director of a private boarding school.

What is significant is the way in which these items of masculine dress were invariably combined with items of feminine dress and the lack of social ostracism attached to this mode of dress (Brew 1945:161). It was not until the beginning of the twentieth century, and particularly in the 1920s, that the suit jacket worn by women acquired lesbian connotations (Chaumette 1995: 68). By contrast, Dr. Mary Edwards Walker, a physician who became the first female commissioned assistant surgeon in the Union Army, adopted men's trousers and frock coats but encountered considerable hostility owing to her style of dress. Congress passed a special decree that granted Walker the right to wear trousers (Lee Hall 1992:238).[5]

How were these items of masculine clothing understood by the women who adopted them in the nineteenth century? Were these items "emptied of their original meaning," as Perrot (1981:343) suggests?[6] The frequency with which women incorporated items from men's clothing into their costumes, the fact that the borrowed items did not lose their masculine connotations, and the way in which this type of clothing behavior transcended social class lines suggest that these items constituted a symbolic statement about women's status and the debates over their status that raged throughout the nineteenth century.

After the First World War, the alternative style, with its ties, men's hats, men's jackets, and vests, was no longer such a dramatic contrast to the dominant style. The dominant feminine ideal of the nineteenth century, the voluptuous matron, had been replaced by the flapper (whom the French called "la garçonne," implying a female boy), an independent yet childish young woman with a boyish figure who combined some of the qualities of both the dominant and the alternative female images of the previous century, specifically, the femininity and helplessness of the former and the assertiveness and athleticism of the latter. The alternative style was no longer an oppositional style (Gibbings 1990:109). Elements of it, particularly the suit jacket, were now part of the dominant style. After the First World War, a new type of alternative style emerged which was associated with lesbian subcultures in New York, London, and Paris but not widely adopted outside these circles (Rolley 1990b; Weiss 1995). Instead of combining a few items of masculine dress with feminine dress, this style was much closer to "cross-dressing."

CLOTHING STYLES AND WOMEN'S ROLES:
France, England, and the United States

At the turn of the century, French fashion designers responded slowly to changes that were taking place in the lifestyles of middle- and upper-class women. Their clothing styles expressed French conceptions of how bourgeois women should behave. The predominant fashionable style in Paris was a statuesque, corseted silhouette suitable for a bosomy matron rather than for a young athletic woman (Steele 1985:224). The mature woman was still the fashion leader for whom fashions were created (222). In Paris, the fashion icon of the period was the courtesan, whose lavish clothes were virtually a parody of fashionable clothing. According to the son of the leading fashion designer of the period (Worth 1928:102), "It was the day when fashionable and fast women were veritable queens." By contrast, in the United States in the 1890s, the young, athletic woman in short skirts or gym suit became a popular icon along with the Gibson girl in shirtwaist, tie, and long skirts.

Although a surprisingly similar ideology of domesticity was shared by middle-class women in France, the United States, and Britain (Rendall 1985: 206–7), consensus on this ideal of feminine behavior was much lower in England and the United States than in France. French women had received an enormous setback from legislation that derived from the French Revolution. A strong feminist movement emerged during the revolution, but women did not prevail. The revolution enhanced the rights of men but excluded women: "The Revolution and its ideals were those of men" (Ribeiro 1988: 141). The Civil Code of 1804, enacted under Napoleon's regime, incorporated attitudes toward women that represented the legacy of the revolution (Nye 1993:54–55). The code deprived women of virtually all civil rights.

While the ideal French bourgeois matron was a powerful figure in her own home, outside her home she was powerless and had virtually no legal rights over property or children until almost the end of the century (Flamant-Paparatti 1984:27) and no political rights until the middle of the twentieth century.[7] Her capacities for functioning outside her home were limited by a minimal level of education and by the fact that only a few occupations were open to her, at salary levels that remained approximately 50 percent of those of men throughout the century (Goulène 1974).[8] Major French intellectuals of the period, such as P. J. Proudhon, Jules Michelet, and Auguste Comte, were strongly committed to the belief that women were inferior to men (physically, morally, and intellectually) and suitable only for marriage (Rendall 1985:296–97).[9] What American feminists have referred to as "the ideology of separate spheres" was taken for granted for middle-class women. Women were expected to devote themselves entirely to their domestic roles. Because of an exaggerated concern with safeguarding their "virtue," young, unmarried, middle-class women in France were not allowed to go out unescorted by female relatives or even to associate with female peers. Women who remained unmarried, usually because of the lack of a dowry, had very limited resources and endured marginal existences on small incomes or meager salaries with minimal social contact (Moses 1984:33; McMillan 1980:19, 12).

The fact that fashionable styles emanating from Paris were actually injurious to women's physical well-being and therefore not appropriate costumes for child-bearing women seems surprising. One explanation is that maternity was less central to women's activities in France than in other Northern European countries. By the 1860s, France had the lowest fertility levels in Europe. While the population of England and Wales almost doubled between 1851 and 1901, the French population increased by only 9.5 percent during the same period (Offen 1984:651).

In both England and America, women and particularly single women had greater freedom and many more options outside domestic space. In the middle of the century, single women in America were much more independent than their French counterparts. Banner (1984:78–85) describes the "bold and provocative" behavior of young American women in public and the absence of chaperones when young women went out with male friends. Some middle-class Englishwomen were not shy and retiring with men and adopted male pastimes such as smoking and playing billiards (Crowe 1971: 331–32). Not dependent on dowries in order to marry, American women were free to select their husbands and to engage in activities that interested them. By contrast, the Frenchwomen of the period were described by a French historian (in Moses 1984:36) as follows: "Brought up to be married, locked within the confines of the family, not being permitted the collective responsibilities of civic life or even professional life, most women could have had only limited horizons."

The surplus of unmarried women in Britain and America influenced the way women were perceived in those countries. In England, this fact became a subject of controversy at mid-century, when it was revealed by the census of 1851. A result of the greater tendency of men than women to emigrate, the surplus of unmarried women increased during the second half of the century and was more evident in the middle than in the working class. A similar problem occurred in America in sixteen eastern and southern states, as men rather than women settled in the West (Massey 1994:350). The absence of men from home and work during the Civil War had a similar effect. Women replaced men in many occupations. The American Civil War has been described as hastening women's emancipation by fifty years (339).

The necessity for increasing numbers of middle-class women to work had the effect of changing their images of themselves. Significantly, most of the women in the first organized women's movement in Britain in the 1850s were unmarried (Rendall 1985:314). At mid-century, the choice of occupations for English middle-class women consisted largely of governess, companion, and seamstress (Vicinus 1985:3). By the end of the century, middle-class women were working as teachers, nurses, civil servants, saleswomen, and clerks (Holcombe 1973:197). In the United States, substantial numbers of women physicians and lawyers were practicing (Crowe 1978:138). According to Freeman and Klaus (1984:394): "Much of the movement to improve women's education and employment in both countries developed in response to the plight of the impoverished gentlewoman."

In France, by the end of the century, positions as teachers, clerks, and sales personnel were the only middle-class careers open to women (they were not legally permitted to practice law and encountered enormous prejudice in the medical profession) (Shaffer 1978:66). Although the proportion of unmarried women who were employed was about the same as in England (54 percent), a much larger percentage of married women, mainly working class, were employed in France (38 percent, compared with 10 percent) (Holcombe 1973:217). However, the negative status accorded to women workers in general in France is indicated by the fact that their wages relative to those of men remained at the same level throughout the century (Reberioux 1980; Rendall 1985), while the wages of Englishwomen workers during the same period increased along with men's wages but more rapidly and more consistently (Wood 1903:282–84, 308). Frenchwomen's wages were deliberately kept at minimal levels. French intellectuals, concerned about the declining birth rate, argued that women should not work but rather devote themselves to raising families, ignoring the fact that many women lacked husbands to support them. All these factors meant that, in France, women's participation in the labor force did not contribute to their emancipation. Shaffer (1978: 75) concludes: "Limited career opportunities for women, the stereotyping of sex roles, limited family resources, and even schooling itself contributed to render women's work primarily a means to supplement the incomes of families, whether of their parents or of their own."

Higher education was important in developing awareness of women's political and social rights and the skills that were necessary to fight for them. Until the middle of the nineteenth century, women in all three countries had little access to education of any sort (see Graham 1978; Holcombe 1973; Massey 1994; and Moses 1984). Secondary education was not widespread in these countries until after 1870. A few colleges were open to American women early in the century, but women's colleges proliferated in the 1870s and 1880s, including two women's medical colleges and twenty-two nursing schools.[10] By 1880, one-third of all American college students were women, although college students represented a small proportion of women and of the entire population. Two colleges for women appeared in England before the middle of the century, but Englishwomen's advancement in the university system was slower than that of American women. Frenchwomen were admitted to universities in the 1860s, but again the numbers of university-educated women remained very small throughout the century. According to Moses (1984:32), "For nineteenth century French women, education was mediocre, if it existed at all." This was true for both middle- and working-class women.

The status and role of women in these three countries was also influenced by their involvement in religious and philanthropic activities that provided English and particularly American women with important skills in running organizations and in communicating with the public. Through women's organizations, American women exerted considerable influence on the practice of social welfare (Ryan 1994:279). At the end of the century they launched an effective national drive for social reform (Fuchs 1995: 183). Frenchwomen remained the most constrained; they had "limited autonomy and roles in public policy formulation" (185).[11] The majority of French middle-class women, as seen in their activities in women's organizations, acquiesced to a system that accorded them a very limited and very subordinate position outside their families. Ironically, as the French birthrate declined steadily throughout the century, public policy and public culture increasingly defined the French women's role as that of motherhood. The feminist movement was seen as a potential threat to the welfare of the country, because it appeared to turn women away from marriage and maternity. French feminists countered by including in their demands for political change measures that would ameliorate the condition of mothers rather than asserting the importance for women of an expanded role in the public sphere (Offen 1984).

By the end of the century, in England and America, the "strong, independent woman" had become the "New Woman," who was "visible in education, in athletics, in reform, in the work force" (Banner 1984:175). In France, significant changes in the legal rights and employment opportunities for middle-class women had only begun in the 1890s; relatively few women had been able to take advantage of them (Silverman 1991:148).

Given the Victorian ideal of domesticity and motherhood, the role of the middle-class spinster was marginal. However, some women in the United States, particularly those who were educated and urban, deliberately chose spinsterhood as a form of revolt and as an escape from the demands and restrictions of middle-class marriage (Freeman and Klaus 1984:395). Between 1885 and 1910, marriage rates for female college graduates in the United States were distinctly lower than for female college graduates before or after that period. In the 1890s only about half of these college graduates married, in comparison with 90 percent of all native-born white women (Cookingham 1984:350–51). In the white female labor force as a whole in this decade, 75 percent were single (Goldin 1980:81). Goldin (88) concluded: "Work in the labor force for women from 1870 to 1920 was the realm of the unmarried." At the same time, this "new" spinster was seen as a threat to the institutions of marriage and motherhood. By the 1890s, educated, employed spinsters were viewed as rebels but also as having distinct advantages in terms of material goods and independence (Freeman and Klaus 1984:409).

Since these middle-class women who worked outside the home represented a set of values in opposition to the Victorian ideal, it is not surprising that, in various ways, their clothing behavior set them apart from married women. Less controversial than dress reform but more widely adopted, the subtly masculine clothing behavior of the single, employed middle-class woman signified another form of resistance to the dominant culture.

ALTERNATIVE DRESS AND CLOTHING REFORM

At the center of much of the debate about women's clothing in the nineteenth century were members of women's movements who attempted to bring about dress reform in the direction of practical, healthy, and comfortable clothing. They deplored the use of corsets and excessively heavy sets of garments.

Unlike the alternative style, which was not advocated by any particular group, dress reformers centered their proposals on the adoption of trousers.

Trousers were particularly controversial in the nineteenth century, because nineteenth-century ideology prescribed fixed gender identities, enormous differences — physical, psychological, and intellectual — between men and women. The dominant point of view allowed for no ambiguity about sexual identification and no possibility for evolution or change in the prescribed behaviors and attitudes of members of each gender. Throughout the second half of the nineteenth century, dress reforms proposed by women's movements were inconsistent with this point of view and, consequently, were unable to win the support of substantial numbers of women outside these groups.

The first and best-known proposal for dress reform was also the most notorious — the costume proposed by Mrs. Amelia Bloomer in America in the 1850s — because it subverted gender differences.[12] This costume consisted of a short skirt over a pair of full Turkish trousers. Bloomer, a women's activist, and a few of her fellow activists wore the costume because it was "comfortable, convenient, safe and tidy — with no thought of introducing a fashion" (Russell 1892: 326–27). The enormous amount of attention and controversy the costume generated points to the salience of gender differentiation (Fatout 1952: 365). When Bloomer, who published a women's temperance magazine, wrote an article in 1851 describing her new costume (Russell 1892), the information was reprinted in a leading New York newspaper and subsequently in newspapers all over the country and abroad. Numerous articles described the costume's appearance in different cities and at various types of social events. It was said to be spreading throughout the nation "like wildfire" and to be generating "furious excitement" wherever it was seen (Lauer and Lauer 1981: 252). Women who wore the costume attracted huge crowds, which were generally male and often hostile. The level of public harassment was so severe that most women stopped wearing it in public after a few months, but the costume was supported by women's activists and others on the grounds that it was healthy, fostered women's independence from men by increasing their capacity for physical movement, represented independence from fashion, and fitted the values of American society — economy, utility, and comfort (Lauer and Lauer 1981). However, the majority response was negative. The Bloomer costume was interpreted as threat to the ideology of separate spheres on the grounds that it would erase all distinctions between the sexes (Lauer and Lauer 1981: 257). Victorian clothing was a form of social control which contributed to the maintenance of women in dependent, subservient roles.

According to her own account (reprinted in Russell 1892:326), Bloomer herself was "praised and censured, glorified and ridiculed." Owing to the amount of ridicule and censure that the costume engendered, she and her friends ceased to wear it after a few years. However, adaptations of the Bloomer costume continued to be worn in the private sphere of the home, particularly on the frontier (Foote 1980; Severa 1995:88, 239). By the 1860s, some women had replaced the Turkish-style trousers with masculine trousers, creating costumes that prefigured the late twentieth-century pants suit (Severa 1995:257, 275) (see figs. 28 and 29). Later in the century, dress-reform patterns were available, and dress-reform styles were sold in stores (Banner 1984:148).

Members of the American women's movement continued throughout the century to lobby for dress reform, forming associations, holding conventions, writing books and articles, and seeking to popularize simpler, healthier styles of dress (Riegel 1963). In 1892 and 1893, dress reformers organized a "Symposium on Dress," at which they presented three designs that included either a divided skirt or trousers (Sims 1991:139). The response when members of the symposium wore these clothes on the street was much more favorable than it had been forty years before, but eventually the women ceased to wear them, too. These dress reforms were still too radical for many middle-class women and tended to alienate potential supporters of the women's rights movement, which was the principal interest of these dress reformers (141).

Dress-reform movements were less evident in England and France. In 1881, a Rational Dress Society was founded in England to promote a knee-length, divided skirt (McCrone 1988:220–21; Gernsheim 1963:72). Dress reform was absent in France until 1887, when a society was formed with the goal of eliminating the corset (Déslandres and Müller 1986:18). From the beginning of the century, pants were forbidden by law in France; special permission from the police was required to wear them (Toussaint-Samat 1990:376). Legislation forbidding women to wear pants was a reaction to the behavior of French feminists who had worn trousers with riding habits during the revolution. Their clothing and their political views were unacceptable to the men who wielded power. The leaders of the revolution considered dress "a statement of freedom and an expression of individuality" but not for women (Ribeiro 1988:141).

At the end of the century, the French legislative body (the Chamber of Deputies) received several petitions requesting a change in the law. They were refused. The few middle-class Frenchwomen (or women leading a middle-class style of life) who wore pants during the nineteenth century did so from personal preference and not in order to advance an agenda of dress reform. In various ways, these women were atypical or marginal.[13]

SPORTS, ALTERNATIVE DRESS, AND MARGINAL PUBLIC SPACE

Both in Europe and America, women in the nineteenth century were required to dress according to the dominant fashion on the streets and in other people's homes, but in certain types of public spaces they were able to blur symbolic boundaries by adopting alternative costumes. During the last three decades of the century, there was an increasing number of settings, such as schools, colleges, and resorts, in which women could escape the dominant dress code and discover alternative identities through dress. When American dress reformers wore a skirt over trousers on the street and proposed the costume for general wear, they were widely criticized, but a very similar costume, used in the same period as an exercise uniform in schools, colleges, and sanitariums, was acceptable, apparently because it was not worn on city streets (Warner 1993:144–47). Rules governing clothing behavior in public space were characterized by subtle differences depending on location, class, and gender. For example, trousered costumes for women were permitted when swimming in the ocean but not for promenades on the beach. The introduction of new sports, particularly bicycling, during the second half of the century produced a redefinition of the way in which symbolic boundaries were expressed in public space. In a sense, alternative dress worn in public spaces was a manifestation of more radical changes that were occurring in more secluded spaces.

Until the twentieth century, sports and physical exercise as a leisure activity for women were reserved almost exclusively for the upper and upper-middle classes (McCrone 1987:119, 121; Bulger 1982:10). What women wore while engaging in these sports depended largely upon the nature of the public spaces in which they were performed. When sports were performed near the home or in social clubs, conformity to middle-class standards of feminine dress was generally required. Tennis, croquet, ice skating, and golf were perceived as social rather than sports activities (Bulger 1982:6). Consequently, in the 1870s, women were expected to dress for these sports as they dressed for other social occasions: long skirts with trains, tight corsets, bustles, and large hats (McCrone 1988:219, 232). When sports were played in institutions or in the countryside, sports costumes were more likely to include items of masculine clothing. Women's colleges provided settings where women could play men's sports, such as baseball, without being seen. Sports were considered a "male preserve," a means by which men proved their masculinity (Mrozek 1987:283). Women who played men's sports in public were considered vulgar and possibly immoral (Bulger 1982:4).

Riding was one of the earliest recreations in which upper-class women engaged. In the middle of the seventeenth century, the riding habit worn by women in the countryside for riding, walking, and traveling included (Ewing 1984:82) "an imitation of the wide-skirted coat then worn by men, with a similar cravat at the neck, a periwig and cocked hat on the head." Significantly, these masculine items of clothing were worn with full skirts and numerous petticoats. In the nineteenth century, women continued to wear riding habits derived from masculine clothing, but primarily for riding. Made by tailors rather than dressmakers, the sidesaddle riding habit in 1850 imitated a man's formal suit from the waist up but incorporated full and long skirts below (Schreier 1989:107). By the 1880s, most women wore long, straight, dark trousers underneath the skirts (Byrde 1992:164; Albrecht, Farrell-Beck, and Winakor 1988:59). They were also wearing high silk top hats, similar to those worn by men, as well as jockey caps and straw hats (59). By 1890, the costume from the waist up bore an even closer resemblance to male styles (Schreier 1989): "The hip-length jacket featured an open collar and lapels that revealed a hunting shirt and stock tie underneath.... A bowler hat or a straight hat, 'like a man's, with the addition of a veil.'" The costume still included a voluminous skirt. A new type of costume originating in London included an ankle-length frock coat over breeches. This costume was controversial because it implied that the rider rode astride rather than sidesaddle. Riding astride was not considered appropriate until after the First World War. Made in the style of men's breeches by specialized tailors (Albrecht, Farrell-Beck, and Winakor 1988:63), breeches were more frequently worn by women after 1900. The evolution of riding costume reveals the extent to which upper-class women wore items of masculine clothing, including various forms of trousers, which were considered totally inappropriate in other contexts.

Swimming costume was another area in which upper- and middle-class women were permitted to engage in otherwise inappropriate clothing behavior. Lencek and Bosker (1989:27) describe summer resorts as "fashion laboratories where the well-to-do came to experiment with new styles of dress and behavior." As early as the 1860s, short trousers or bloomers, which were not acceptable in other public places, were adopted for bathing suits for women

(Byrde 1992:163, 170; Cunnington and Cunnington 1959:474; Brew 1945: 350) and were worn with a belted jacket, for example. Byrde quotes a magazine of the period saying that young women in this costume resembled "pretty boys." In the United States, a knee-length or ankle-length skirt was worn over the trousers. Stockings were optional. By 1909, women's bathing suits had changed very little. Corsets were recommended, although the type of corset generally used was much smaller than for land wear (Brew 1945: 364; Lencek and Bosker 1989:27).

Throughout this period, women were expected to wear their regular clothes—long-sleeved blouses, floor-length skirts, corsets, enormous hats, and gloves—on the beach itself, and photographs suggest that most of them did (Lencek and Bosker 1989:26–27; Severa 1995:415). The sea itself was defined as a liminal space in which normal sartorial (and moral) standards did not apply. The sharp segregation between land and sea was emphasized by the use of wooden huts on wheels at the water's edge, in which women changed into bathing suits and from which they entered the sea (Adburgham 1987:127). Photographs suggest that it was not unusual for women, when wading in the ocean or in rivers fully dressed, to show bare legs, in contrast to norms that skirts should always cover the ankles (Severa 1995:415, 538; Roberts 1984:162) (see fig. 30).

Uniforms that young women wore at school or college but not in the street supplied an alternative clothing discourse that was more effective than that of dress reformers, because these clothes were probably worn by a larger number of women. During the middle decades of the century, the opening of American colleges for women coincided with a popular health and exercise movement. The colleges adopted exercise programs and appropriate costumes, which students were required to obtain and probably made for themselves (Warner 1993). One type of costume used in these schools was the gym suit, a knee-length divided skirt, worn with black cotton stockings (Brew 1945:349). It is significant that these exercise costumes were intended to be worn for exercise only and were not permitted in public. When there was a possibility that the students could be seen by the public, skirts were required (Warner 1993:157). However, leading fashion magazines of the period wrote about gym suits and explained how they were made. At the end of the century, a gym suit pattern was available (Warner 1993:153–54).

School uniforms for athletics also played a role in introducing nonrestrictive dress into England (Ewing 1975:68). Principals of girls' schools were very conscious of their roles as dress reformers. In 1877, a school in Scotland, which was "the model for many future girls' schools in England," introduced a uniform consisting of "a blue knee-length belted tunic, with knickerbockers [knee-length bloomers] or trousers underneath" (71–72), an outfit that anticipated fashionable dresses in the 1920s (see fig. 31).

The practice of sports by women in France was more controversial than in either England or the United States. Women were advised in popular magazines that their athletic activities would provoke less criticism if they dressed elegantly and fashionably and did not lose their femininity (Flamant-Paparatti 1984:182). A law passed in 1880 required the teaching of gymnastics in public schools for boys but made it optional for girls' schools. A Paris department-store catalogue advertised knee-length pants to be worn by adolescent girls for fencing and gymnastics, but at the end of the century, women at a training school for teachers in Paris were photographed during their exercise class wearing long, full, black skirts that covered their ankles (see fig. 32).

The impact of the bicycle on clothing behavior in the 1890s derived from its being a completely new sport and therefore not identified as a male activity. It was also an activity that was difficult to perform in privacy; it required space and public roads, although early upper-class female riders attempted to seclude themselves in public parks. The first female bicycle riders in England were society women who were driven in carriages to London parks to ride (Rubinstein 1977:49). Bicycling also differed from previous recreations in that it was virtually impossible to ride bicycles in the fashionable clothing of the period.

The most suitable costumes for bicycling were the divided skirt, which looked like a skirt but was actually a pair of very full knee-length pants, and knickerbockers (see fig. 33). In America, the latter were widely used for about two years (1895–97) as bicycling became increasingly popular but disappeared rapidly afterward. For the most part, bloomers were worn with skirts. When women wore them without skirts, they were "jeered and scorned" (Sims 1991:134). The solution that was accepted by the end of the decade was shorter skirts. Women had already begun to wear shorter skirts at summer resorts in the 1890s, but the first women who wore ankle-length skirts in the city in the mid-1890s attracted hostile, shrieking crowds (Banner 1983:149). In England, a few women wore bloomers; others wore a special type of skirt that could be buttoned around each leg in the form of trousers when on the machine (Gernsheim 1963:80–81). Outside city parks and in the countryside there was considerable resistance to the use of such costumes, particularly among the working class (Gernsheim 1963:81; McCrone 1988:238): "Women cyclists in 'rationals' met jeering crowds wherever they went and sometimes encountered violence, especially in urban areas . . . the poorer the district, the more incensed . . . the people" (Rubinstein 1977:64–65).

Curiously, in France, where the gym suit was unknown and women had participated relatively little in sports before the advent of the bicycle, the divided skirt for women bicyclists was accepted very rapidly. In 1892, only four years after the invention of a safety bicycle that could be widely used, the minister of the interior decreed that the law against women wearing trousers could be lifted for bicycling only (Davray-Piekolek 1990:46). A French department store sold bicycling costumes with divided skirts or pants concealed by skirts as early as 1893 (Falluel 1990:85–86). Most women wore skirts over bloomers or wore divided skirts (Déslandres and Müller 1986:72–73) (see fig. 34). The controversy over the use of these costumes was much less heated than in the United States. The explanation appears to be that the activity was adopted mostly by a relatively small number of upper-class women (bicycles were too expensive for other women) (Chaumette 1995:53) and that they practiced it in parks, such as the Bois de Boulogne, on the edge of Paris (a liminal space), or at the seaside rather than on city streets (Davray-Piekolek 1990:46; Delpierre 1990:43–44).[14]

According to a French costume historian (Monier 1990:121, 125), the bicycle became "one of the symbols of emancipation" that definitively changed people's attitudes toward sports clothes for women.[15] She claims (127): "This famous bike in effect still appears as an object that determined the moment when one evokes a modern conception of clothing, pants worn by women, the emancipation and physical freedom of women. . . ." However, in 1911, French designers were still able to provoke controversy by proposing a trouser skirt for regular activities. It attracted very negative reactions when worn at the races (Gernsheim 1963:92; Steele 1985:232). Trousers were unacceptable on the street for the average woman.[16]

WORKING-CLASS WOMEN AND PUBLIC SPACE

Sports and exercise programs were virtually unavailable to working-class women, but these women violated Victorian norms for clothing behavior in other types of public spaces. Frequently, the public spaces in which they worked or were employed were relatively "invisible" to the middle class, such as coal mines and remote sites in the countryside or by the sea, permitting these women to wear trousers and other items of masculine clothing.[17] At the same time, working-class women were not expected to meet the same standards of propriety as middle-class women.

Costume historians have documented the use of trousers and knee breeches, as well as men's hats and jackets, by working-class Englishwomen for centuries. Englishwomen who worked in coal mines adopted knee breeches in the sixteenth century. In the seventeenth century, women who gathered shellfish by the sea "breeched" their skirts to simulate trousers. In the nineteenth century, this practice continued as others wore "kneebreeches under their short skirts, along with a sailor's jacket and a headscarf knotted under the chin." In the same period, working-class women wore knee breeches, trousers, and overalls in coal mines, ironworks and brickworks (de Marly 1986:15, 67, 100, 126–27). Most of these cases attracted little attention, with the exception of women working in British coal mines.

In 1841, there were approximately 5,000–6,000 women working in or at the top of coal mines in Britain (John 1980:25). Women in some districts wore a distinctive costume that included trousers, aprons or petticoats of striped cotton rolled up around their waists, open-necked shirts, waistcoats, and clogs. In cold weather, they wore either the traditional countrywoman's jacket, known as the "bed gown," or short coats obtained from male relatives (181) (see fig. 35). They conformed to the Victorian norm requiring head covering by wearing bonnets of padded cotton or scarves. For decoration, the women often added earrings, necklaces, flowers, and feathers (182–83). On Sundays, however, most of the women wore dresses typical of the period. Located in close proximity to the mines, mining communities provided settings isolated from the rest of English working-class society in which such an unorthodox work costume could develop. Neither marrying nor interacting with other English workers, both men and women were viewed as "outcasts" and "savages" who were potentially dangerous to property owners (26–27).

These women's costumes attracted attention in the press in connection with attempts by their male co-workers to ban women's employment in order to safeguard their own jobs. In 1842, a sensational government report, documenting the nature of work performed by women, the conditions under which it was performed, and the characteristics of their clothing, led to a ban on the employment of women inside the mines but not above them. In 1865 and 1887, unsuccessful attempts were made, instigated by male miners, to ban women's work at the entrance to mines.

Some newspaper accounts portrayed the women as the antithesis of the Victorian ideal: their clothing, particularly their trousers, was seen as "unsexing" them. Inappropriately dressed, they had ceased to be women and had become indecent, immoral, repulsive "creatures" (John 1980:180). The purpose of most of the newspaper articles was to argue in favor of banning their work altogether. At the same time, there was a substantial market for photographs of these women, often in the form of the *cartes de visite* popular during the period. Several photographers specialized in producing and selling such photographs, suggesting that public opinion toward them was not unfavorable.

In the 1880s, middle-class dress reformers began to defend the pit-brow women's costume. By this time, sports were bringing about changes in upper-class dress that made their costume seem less deviant. In one region, in the late 1880s, the costume was manufactured for the pit-brow women and included "a dark-blue flannel jacket, serge trousers, and a long apron" (John 1980:181, 182).

During the First World War, other types of public spaces offered settings in which working-class women were exempted from the usual norms concerning clothing behavior. Englishwomen served in the armed forces, wearing men's uniforms, including jackets, ties, and caps, with long skirts. In civilian life, they took over a variety of men's jobs, often with the uniforms that went with the jobs. Women, who worked in munitions factories in large numbers, wore overall suits — canvas trousers and smocks (Ewing 1975:94–95) (see fig. 36). British farm women wore dungarees, trousers, or skirts with tight jodhpurs underneath (de Marly 1986:141). De Marly (151) comments: "Officialdom preferred women not to wear trousers, so lady inspectors on railways were mannish as far as hat and jacket were concerned but wore skirts below that."

THE AMERICAN FRONTIER AND PUBLIC SPACE

In the United States, the "secluded" space in which working-class women engaged in deviant clothing behavior was the frontier. The bloomer dress was frequently worn for work in isolated areas (Severa 1995:88). After most middle-class women had abandoned it under social pressure, working-class women continued to wear it on farms. The outfit, often created from standard dresses, consisted of knee-length skirts, with tubular trouser legs made of the same material (205) (see fig. 37).

Even further removed from "civilized" public spaces was the wilderness in Alaska. Photographs taken at the end of the century reveal that women who made long treks on foot in the area adopted men's trousers and hats, which they wore with feminine blouses and corsets (Severa 1995:519) (see fig. 38). The appearance of these women, who may have been prostitutes, is astonishing in its resemblance to contemporary styles. By contrast, when working-class American women performed heavy industrial work during the First World War, they were required to wear "special 'feminine' trousered uniforms" (Steele 1989a:80) (see fig. 39) or long, full knickers based on the bloomer costume (Lee Hall 1992:242).[18]

"INVISIBLE" SPACES:
Illegal Clothing Behavior in France

Although Frenchwomen in the nineteenth century were not legally permitted to wear trousers, this did not prevent working-class women from doing so. Instead the prohibition made this type of behavior virtually invisible.[19] To what extent did Frenchwomen perform jobs for which men's clothing would have been appropriate? Underground work by women in coal mines was forbidden in 1810, but the law was not enforced (Riot-Sarcey and Zylberberg-Hocquard 1987).[20] Frenchwomen worked as haulers at the entrance to mines in the northern part of France, but they represented a very small percentage of employees, and their numbers steadily declined after 1860. Women appear to have been working in mining and other areas of heavy industry, but pictorial records do not exist, in contrast to England.[21] That some of these women wore trousers is suggested by photographs of women dressed in this manner who were hauling coal in neighboring Belgian mines (Hiley 1979:101–2). Significantly, Zola, who researched his novels thoroughly, described the heroine of *Germinal*, a novel set in French coal mines and published in 1885, as wearing men's clothes, including trousers.

Working-class women who entered very visible occupations, such as post-office employee and coach driver, and who adopted feminine versions (i.e., without trousers) of the uniforms worn by their male counterparts were often photographed.[22] The first women coach drivers in Paris in 1907 became the subjects of postcards, wearing men's hats and overcoats (Papayanis 1993). By contrast, in the First World War, almost half a million Frenchwomen worked in the defense industry — *les munitionettes* — many of them wearing smocks over wide trousers or overalls (Thébaud 1986:172; Déslandres and Müller 1986:110), but they remained "invisible." According to Robert (1988:265), "Not a single illustration of the *munitionette* . . . appeared in the popular press during the war." Déslandres and Müller (110) state that this costume "had no success with the bourgeoisie; consequently trousers remained a phenomenon limited to the interior of the factory."

GENDER, CLOTHING, AND PUBLIC SPACE
IN THE TWENTIETH CENTURY

In general, in all three countries, upper- and middle-class women were expected to conform more closely to cultural norms about the expression of gender in clothing and physical appearance than working-class women. The role of trousers in female clothing during the nineteenth century exemplifies differences in attitudes toward the clothing of middle- and working-class women. The culture of the Victorian era associated trousers with male authority. Dress reformers attempted to convince upper- and middle-class women to wear trousers, but on the whole they were unsuccessful, probably because women who wore trousers were seen as attempting to usurp male authority (McCrone 1988:221). During the nineteenth century, even in "secluded" public spaces, upper-class women wore trousers only when covered by skirts. Working-class women adopted trousers more readily.

While there was increasing acceptance of men's clothing for the upper body for women from the middle to the end of the nineteenth century, the taboo against the use of trousers by women was overcome only during the twentieth. This shift in clothing norms was pioneered in secluded public spaces associated with leisure and among working-class women in the workplace. Working-class women who became artists' and photographers' models in Montparnasse and Montmartre began wearing pants toward the end of the First World War, although apparently not in Paris streets and cafés. These women belonged to an urban bohemian subculture in which some of them functioned as "fashion leaders" (Klüver and Martin 1989:78, 145, 158). In the twenties, the French designer Chanel attempted to popularize trousers as a style for middle- and upper-class women but was unsuccessful (Delbourg-Delphis 1981:121). Rather than moving in the direction of incorporating masculine clothing into feminine dress, French women preferred to "masculinize" the female body: bustlines and waistlines were suppressed and hair was cut short. Women went to men's barbershops for very short, masculine haircuts such as the bob, the shingle, and the Eton crop (Sichel 1978:56). The public's response to these changes was very negative (Roberts 1994). Since other types of changes were taking place very slowly, short hair became a focal point for intense controversies over Frenchwomen's sexual and personal identity.

During the 1930s in France, rich women wore pants at resorts (Déslandres and Müller 1986:165), but they were seldom worn in cities. Norms concerning appropriate attire on city streets were strict. Oral histories (*La*

Memoire de Paris 1993:23, 128) indicate that it was not correct to go out without a hat, gloves, or stockings, even in the summer. There were no women in pants on the streets.[23] During the Second World War, pants were frequently worn because of the scarcity of all types of new clothing (Déslandres and Müller 1986:179), but it was not until the middle 1950s (Delpierre 1991:41) that they began to be acceptable for urban life.

In England, the use of slacks was accelerated by the Second World War both for work and leisure. The Women's Land Army was given uniforms that included ties and knee breeches or denim dungarees (de Marly 1986:147). De Marly (155) quotes Evelyn Waugh's description of London in 1943: "girls with film star hairdos, slacks and high heels going out with soldiers." Trousers were accepted by working-class women during the war and only much later in the sixties by middle-class women after pants began to appear in the collections of French fashion designers (Wilson 1987:164–65).[24]

In the United States, between the wars, upper- and middle-class women wore pants primarily in secluded public spaces, such as ranches and resorts. Several seemingly contradictory trends came together in the 1930s that led to trousers' being worn with greater frequency for leisure activities. Dude ranches became popular vacation spots for the middle class, and this in turn led to the introduction of dungarees for women. At the same time, Hollywood films, which were then an important influence on clothing fashions, depicted numerous strong, "masculine" heroines (Banner 1984:282). Marlene Dietrich's heroines, who engaged in "cross-dressing," were probably the most powerful of these characterizations. Fisher (1987:4) argues that the Depression in the 1930s was a social as well as an economic crisis and produced profound anxiety about personal identity and particularly gender identity. She claims that prevailing ideas of masculinity and femininity were in flux during this period.

However, working-class women gradually assimilated trousers into their daily lives. Evidence from Sears catalogues in the 1940s and from photographs suggest that widespread acceptance of pants began among working-class women in the West, particularly California, and gradually spread to the East and the middle classes in the fifties, reversing the usual direction of fashion change, which was from east to west.[25] Olian (1992:2) states: "Steadily increasing numbers of sportswear pages featured slacks. Originating in California, as befitting the informality of the West Coast lifestyle, they enjoyed great popularity for work as well as for recreation." The Second World War, with its images of working-class women in heavy industry, reinforced this trend in its early stages. More women worked in industry than ever before and were frequently provided with uniforms consisting of "slacks, blouse, and visor-cap of matching material" (Steele 1989a:82). Others wore jeans and overalls (Gorguet-Ballesteros 1994:65).

As they had been in the nineteenth century, feminists during the late 1960s and the 1970s were resolutely opposed to fashionable clothing. French feminist Simone de Beauvoir performed an important role in shaping feminists' views of fashion. Unlike their predecessors, they were more critical of the "manipulative discourses" of femininity underlying clothing styles than of the clothes themselves. In the United States, the first mass women's liberation movement demonstration was directed against the Miss America beauty contest in 1968, and specifically against the stereotype of the female body as sexual object that the contest represented (Evans and Thornton 1989:3).

Again like their predecessors in the nineteenth century, feminists in the 1970s proposed alternative modes of dress to substitute for fashionable styles, specifically various forms of trousers, worn with other simple and casual clothes, such as T-shirts and low-heeled shoes. In the United States, lesbian feminists were the most committed to rejecting any attempt at personal adornment or body display. They wore loose-fitting jeans or baggy workmen's denim overalls, with men's T-shirts or work shirts and men's work boots or sneakers, and avoided cosmetics, jewelry, or conventional haircuts (Cassell 1974:87). Less extreme versions of this costume permitted fitted jeans with matching accessories, which produced a more "becoming" look. Many non-lesbian feminists wore dresses and long skirts or, at resorts, tight fitting pants and shirts; their appearance was very similar to nonfeminist middle-class women. Although the level of hostility and ridicule toward the clothing of the lesbian-feminists in the early 1970s was very high (Cassell 1974:90), within a decade, variations on the lesbian-feminist "style," ranging from austere to flattering, had become the typical leisure costume of young middle-class women. The widespread acceptance of pants by middle-class women appears to have been pioneered by marginal groups within that class, specifically lesbian feminists.

In the late twentieth century, middle-class professional and business-women have not been permitted to don a totally mannish look but are still expected to retain elements of femininity in their office clothes. The short-skirted business suit appeared in the 1920s and has changed relatively little in subsequent decades (Steele 1989a). In middle-class corporate workplaces, taboos against the use of trousers by women executives remain, although these women typically wear jeans and other types of trousers for leisure

activities. In accordance with corporate dress codes that may or may not be explicitly defined, they are likely to wear contemporary versions of nineteenth-
century alternative dress, including suit jackets and skirts, with shirts styled
like men's or with silk blouses, the entire outfit in neutral, conservative colors
(McDowell 1997:146; Hochschild 1997:74). Now, however, these types of
outfits are considered conservative rather than subversive (Kimle and Damhorst 1997). A fashionably feminine or seductive appearance is considered
demeaning.

The contrast with working-class female employees is striking. They frequently wear uniforms that are virtually identical to those of men (Ewing
1975; Steele 1989a:70–71). In the postwar period, masculine uniforms for
women gradually appeared in occupations where women were performing
work similar to that of men. Englishwomen transport workers were wearing
masculine uniforms in the 1940s (see fig. 40). American police departments
adopted masculine uniforms for women after Congress amended the Civil
Rights Act in 1972 to prohibit state and local governments from discriminating on the basis of gender. Beginning in 1973, police departments all
over the country gave women the same assignments as men, along with suitable clothing. Skirts were replaced by trousers, creating uniforms very similar
to those of men, including ties, visored caps, and trousers.[26] Subsequently,
railroad conductors, nurses, and airline stewardesses, among other occupations, were assigned unisex uniforms.[27] Similar changes have occurred in
France, and the earlier restrictions on trousers for women have disappeared.
Nevertheless, in the higher ranks of these occupations, one finds the same
ambivalence toward the use of trousers that occurs in middle-class corporate
workplaces. At work, women adapt to male cultures that vary in the extent to
which women are permitted or required to "assimilate."

In the late twentieth century, the tie, which was a symbol of feminine
emancipation and willingness to challenge the social status of men in the
nineteenth century, now has different meanings depending upon where and
by whom it is worn. It has remained a symbol of female independence in
advertising, fashion magazines, and films. In luxury fashion-designer clothes
aimed at upper-class women, ties are occasionally used either to signify female authority or to parody it. In a Ralph Lauren advertisement (see fig. 41),
the woman's tie is worn askew, in contrast to that of her two male companions.
It is not treated seriously. In the early 1980s, bow ties for executive women
were very popular (Kiechel 1983), presumably as an unthreatening assertion
of feminine power. By contrast, ties that frequently appear in uniforms for
working-class women, both public (the military) and private (airlines, rail-

roads), have lost these connotations and appear to reflect the routine assimilation of women into certain types of bureaucratic and corporate hierarchies.

CONCLUSION: Alternative Dress as Symbolic Subversion

Victorian culture, in the form of literature and women's magazines (Ballaster et al. 1991), generally stressed domestic ideology, but clothing was curiously ambivalent. One reason why clothing, as opposed to written culture, was able to express tensions has to do with the differences between verbal and non-verbal culture. Nonverbal culture is more susceptible to different interpretations than verbal culture. Those who do not wish to receive a message can refuse to perceive it. Those who send subversive messages by means of non-verbal culture may deny their subversive intentions or, in some cases, not be fully aware of them (Goffman 1966; Cassell 1974). The alternative style of dress, a style that associated items of masculine clothing with feminine apparel, represented, consciously or unconsciously, a form of resistance to the dominant style of dress. Distinctly different from cross-dressing (which often seems to have been motivated in part by severe economic discrimination), this style of dressing represented a kind of symbolic inversion of the dominant message of feminine clothing by associating it with masculine clothing. Through a process of symbolic inversion, items associated with masculine costume were given new meanings, specifically, feminine independence, that challenged gender boundaries. Oppositional styles of clothing such as those that emerged in the nineteenth century disrupt existing boundaries and create new ones. The dominant style was designed to maintain existing social class boundaries and was relatively inaccessible to the lower-middle and working classes. It was also very effective at marking gender boundaries. The alternative style, relatively inexpensive and uncomplicated to reproduce, crossed class boundaries.

The alternative style of dress illustrates a process that precedes and accompanies social change whereby the meanings of symbols gradually adapt to changing definitions of social roles and structures (Cassell 1974). Nonverbal symbols are the least stable, and therefore manipulation of these symbols is likely to precede manipulation of verbal symbols. Nonverbal behavior is a powerful means of conveying social status, particularly because it is often performed on the basis of habit rather than conscious decisions.

The alternative dress style was worn by many women who had no connection with the feminist movement. There were sufficient indications of alienation among middle-class women during the period that the desire to affirm their identity as members of a new social category, the middle-class working woman, cannot have been entirely absent. On the other hand, the level of social control in the form of hostility and ridicule that they encountered in public spaces made a mild form of symbolic inversion, jackets and ties combined with skirts instead of trousers, preferable.

To what extent were the women who wore alternative styles conscious of their symbolic significance? Cassell (1974:92), who interviewed feminists in the early stages of the postwar American feminist movement, found them to be relatively unaware of the symbolic meanings of their unorthodox clothing. She argues that personal appearance is a powerful force because "it operates below the level of words."

However, the fact that the militant English suffragette movement, the Women's Social and Political Union, pointedly rejected the alternative style of clothing is an indication of its symbolic power. In pursuit of their cause, the suffragettes were forced to "invade" public space, conducting demonstrations, disrupting political meetings, and sometimes destroying property. These confrontational invasions of male public space "presented a fundamental challenge to dominant definitions of what women were and what they could do" (Rolley 1990a:50). Since the dominant culture identified women with their clothing and expected femininity to be "written on the body," the issue of clothing was central to the public image of the suffragettes. One tactic used by their opponents and the press was to represent the suffragettes as women who had lost their femininity, as indicated by their masculine style of clothing, and who had ceased to be women as a result of their unwomanly behavior. The opposition attempted to discredit the movement by presenting the suffragettes as unfeminine freaks and therefore as not representing the "women and mothers of England" (Rolley 1990a:63; Tickner 1988). In order to counteract these attempts to marginalize them and their activities, the leaders of the WSPU developed what was in effect a dress code for their members, an emphasis on feminine dress and avoidance of tailor-made suits, shirts, and ties. According to a member of the organization (quoted in Rolley 1990a:47), "In the WSPU . . . all suggestion of the masculine was carefully avoided, and the outfit of a militant setting forth to smash windows would probably include a picture hat." Both the suffragettes' rejection of clothing with masculine connotations and its use by their opponents to discredit them suggest that masculine items of clothing did not lose their symbolic meaning in the process of being adapted for women's wear. They represented an alternative image of women which challenged the dominant ideal of femininity.

In the nineteenth century, changes in clothing and physical appearance that were consistent with dominant cultural norms about the expression of sexuality and personal identity followed the classic model of fashion change (Simmel 1957): they were proposed by fashion designers, popularized by leading entertainers, and adopted first by upper-class women or those aspiring to enter that class. Fashionable clothing which originated in France reflected the dominance of traditional feminine roles in that country.

By contrast, changes in clothing and physical appearance that represented modifications of upper- and middle-class norms were likely to begin among marginal women, both middle and working class, often in secluded public spaces. Both middle- and working-class women took advantage of these public spaces to adopt masculine items of clothing, not to express their rebellion against the dominant culture, but to facilitate certain types of activities, either work or pleasure. England and the United States provided more favorable environments than France for the development of alternative feminine roles and alternative clothing behavior suitable for those roles. Ironically, types of clothing that were relatively or entirely unfashionable in the nineteenth century became the dominant style in the twentieth century.

The history of alternative dress in the nineteenth century suggests that marginal discourses about gender are not maintained entirely through verbal communication; nonverbal communication involving symbolic inversion performs an important role, affecting people both consciously and unconsciously. In the nineteenth century, the alternative dress style, as it added new items to form a complete costume and attracted increasing numbers of women, was an important element in bringing about changes in attitudes that were essential preconditions for structural changes.

NOTES

1. For example, a suffragette demonstration was a "procession of petticoats," a cabinet that supported votes for women was a "petticoat-elected cabinet" (Rolley 1990a:48).

2. Brew (1945:162) lists the following types of dresses: traveling, morning, carriage, opera, ball, occasional, housekeeping, house, tea gowns, and summer. See also Flamant-Paparatti (1984:105).

3. The English perspective is different. At the end of the century, an English periodical, *The London Tailor*, claimed that "the only really new dress development which has taken place during the last half century has been the evolution of the tailor-made gown."

4. Le Play's studies of working-class families suggest that the alternative clothing style was adopted by working-class women who were employed rather than by working-class housewives. Slightly over half the working-class women in French families studied after

1875 had at least one item of alternative dress in their wardrobes. Significantly, seven (77 percent) out of the nine women in the group who were employed owned such items as compared with fourteen (45 percent) of the women who were not employed. The women who were employed were more likely than the others to have two or more of these items. Thirty-three percent of these women owned a suit jacket or tailored jacket. Seven (18 percent) owned waistcoats, but only two owned ties. One woman, a widow, who was employed as a painter of porcelain, owned a blue smock which she wore in her workshop. She also owned a suit, a jacket, and a waistcoat. Four of the employed women in the group had daughters over sixteen whose clothing behavior suggests that younger working-class women were adopting the style. The painter of porcelain had three daughters who were employed in the same occupation. Each daughter owned a tweed dress, a jacket, and a tie. The two daughters of a widow who made corsets each had a jacket and a suit.

5. Dr. Walker also wore a tunic with trousers, reminiscent of the original bloomer costume (Gernsheim 1963:11).

6. Perrot (1981:343) states, "The soft collar, the rolled collar, the blazer, the cap, more recently, the vest, the overall, and the boots are elements borrowed by the bourgeoisie from the wardrobes of sailors, workers or peasants. But . . . emptied of their original meaning." Perrot's argument is that "borrowed" items are transformed by color changes or changes in form or material that turn the copy into a parody or an ironic comment on the original version. However, the items that are being discussed here have not undergone these types of changes but appear to have been copied faithfully from male wardrobes.

7. French women obtained the right to vote in 1944, approximately twenty-five years after English and American women, who obtained the vote in 1918 and 1920, respectively. American wives obtained control over their wages and property in 1860, English wives in 1882, and French wives in 1907 (Hause and Kenney 1981:781).

8. Secondary school education became available to French girls in 1880 (Flamant-Paparatti 1984:30).

9. Englishwomen had the advantage of having at least one major male scholar, John Stuart Mill, who actively espoused and wrote about women's rights.

10. The first American women's college, Troy Female Seminary, was founded in 1821. Oberlin College admitted women in 1833. Mount Holyoke College for women was founded in 1837 (Warner 1993:147).

11. Frenchwomen involved in charitable activities sponsored by the Catholic church were given little freedom in the management of those activities, which were controlled by the male leadership of the church (Moses 1984:38; Rendall 1985:323).

12. Amelia Bloomer did not originate the costume, but copied it from a friend (Russell 1892). Similar costumes were worn by religious communities in America during the early nineteenth century (Lauer and Lauer 1981).

13. These women were artists, writers, and courtesans such as the early nineteenth-century novelist George Sand, the mid-century artist Rosa Bonheur, several courtesans during the Second Empire (1845–70), including the emperor's mistress (Richardson 1967), the novelist Colette, the actress Sarah Bernhardt, and the radical feminist and physician Madeleine Pelletier (McMillan 1980:91). All of these women were single or

divorced. Some marginal women, attempting to escape a conventional existence, used masculine clothing as an alternative to clothing that would have pegged them to a particular social class background. At the turn of the century, the designer Chanel preferred to attend the races, a showplace for high fashion at the time, wearing her lover's clothes (a tie and a man's coat that was much too big for her) rather than the exaggerated finery of the courtesan (Evans and Thornton 1989:122).

14. A photograph shows women wearing cycling bloomers on the pier in Boulogne in 1897 (Gernsheim 1963:illus.175).

15. The importance of the bicycle as an instrument of liberation has not disappeared. During a recent period of right-wing backlash against liberalizing influences in Iran, bicycle riding by women became controversial and was forbidden in Teheran except in specific locations under police surveillance (MacFarquhar 1996).

16. According to Behling and Dickey (1980), costumes of this sort were worn only by a few avant-garde women in Paris.

17. Cross-dressing (wearing costumes composed *entirely* of items associated with the opposite sex) seems to have been a means of coping with prejudices against employing women in men's occupations. De Marly (1986:120) cites several examples in England, including women dressing as vegetable sellers and construction workers in the nineteenth century. Some cases of women who pretended to be men were taken to court (Hiley 1979:41–42).

18. Between the wars, American working-class women in factories reverted to skirts, but, during the Second World War, they again adopted masculine clothing.

19. One exception was a group of working-class women who wore pants as an expression of rebellion. Known as the *"premières journalistes,"* they were active between 1830 and 1850 (Adler 1979; Riot-Sarcey and Zylberberg-Hocquard 1987). These women who dressed in men's clothes campaigned for women's suffrage and equality with men by writing and publishing newspapers.

20. For example, in 1867, there were seventy-six young girls working underground in the mines in the Pas-de-Calais region (Riot-Sarcey and Zylberberg-Hocquard 1987).

21. Statistics for 1901 for extractive industries, manufacturing, and construction indicate that the numbers of women working in these industries in France and England were very similar (Mitchell 1981:163, 171). Figures for earlier years are not comparable because of understatement of the numbers of women working in such occupations in England and the inclusion of other types of workers in these categories in France.

22. France also had its counterparts to English short-skirted fisherwomen — the Boulogne fisher girls (Hiley 1979:37).

23. *La Mémoire de Paris* (a collection of photographs of ordinary people engaged in a wide range of daily activities) (1993:75) contains only one example of women wearing pants: nurses in hospital operating rooms.

24. Wilson (1987:164) cites a passage from a novel by the British writer Nancy Mitford which suggests that in 1945 pants were considered daring by the middle class but "every suburban shopgirl" was wearing them.

25. Hochswender (1993:13) states that in the 1930s the usual direction in which fashion for men traveled was from east to west: "from London to New York, from New York and Palm Beach onward."

26. In England, the response by the police force to legislation forbidding discrimination on the basis of gender was much more ambivalent. Trousers for women police officers were still controversial in the 1980s, although a masculine uniform from the waist up had been use since the 1920s (Young 1992:273, 276).

27. Controversy did not entirely disappear. In the United States, one state enacted sumptuary legislation in 1986 to enforce a norm against pants for women. The South Carolina Legislative Assembly passed a rule requiring its male staff to wear jackets and ties and women to wear skirts (Steele 1989a:63). According to Steele, "Only a few legislators argued that women should be allowed to wear trousers."

Paris reigns but does not rule. Benaïm (1997)

Haute couture has escaped from fashion. Christian Lacroix (television interview, 1998)

5 FASHION WORLDS AND GLOBAL MARKETS
From "Class" to "Consumer" Fashion

In the late twentieth century, fashion no longer originated exclusively in Paris or London or even in the fashion industry. Thousands of organizations in numerous countries produced a wide variety of choices for the consumer. The development of powerful electronic media with enormous audience penetration and postmodern imagery changed the diffusion of fashion and redefined issues of democratization. Social and economic changes that have produced postindustrial societies have altered the significance of fashionable clothing and consumer goods generally.

In the preceding chapters, I examined the reception of fashionable and alternative styles in the nineteenth century. In this chapter, I turn to the production of fashion, mainly in the twentieth century.[1] How does the nature of fashion organizations affect what is available to consumers and how, in turn, do certain types of consumers influence what is defined as fashion? Until the 1960s, the creation of fashionable clothing styles was a highly centralized process in which, with few exceptions, styles originating in Paris predominated. Other centers of style were not nearly as influential as Paris and generally followed its dictates. Popular stereotypes of how fashion operates are drawn from this period and persist today, although fashion now functions very differently.

Since the 1960s, the diversification of fashion genres has increased the numbers and visibility of luxury fashion designers in other countries, with the result that Paris fashion has become less dominant while other fashion centers have increased in importance.[2] In order to provide a background for a discussion of these changes, I will begin by describing the elite-oriented fashion system that produced fashionable clothing in the late nineteenth and early twentieth centuries.

Since then, changes in the nature of fashion organizations and a huge increase in the numbers of organizations participating in these markets have produced increasingly turbulent conditions that affect the nature of fashion innovation and change. The characteristics of cultural products, including consumer goods, are shaped by the organizational environments in which culture creators perform their work and by the nature of the markets in which organizations sell their wares.

As studies of other types of culture organizations have shown, the size of a fashion organization has an influence on the level of innovation in its products (Peterson 1994). Very large fashion organizations are likely to be controlled by managers whose major concern is profits rather than aesthetic quality and innovation. Small fashion organizations tend to be controlled by creators rather than by managers and therefore are more likely to take risks in producing and distributing innovative products. On the other hand, the size of an organization is associated with its survival, particularly in global markets. The standard interpretation of the fashion organization as a small, short-lived firm with few employees that requires little capital investment, because of rapid changes in products (Brittain and Freeman 1980:313), does not apply to luxury fashion organizations that require stable management and sizable investments to operate in a large number of countries.

Changes in the environment in which fashion organizations operate have led designers to develop new strategies for framing their products for presentation to the consumer. Two frames that have frequently been used in the past are those of "fashion as craft" and "fashion as art." According to Becker (1982), craftsmen value utility in their creations, while artist-craftsmen stress their beauty and aesthetic qualities. Most luxury fashion designers are artist-craftsmen. Artists use the skills of the craftsman, but the objects they make are often neither useful nor beautiful. Instead, they are deliberately created so as to subvert these values. Their goal is to produce a work that is unique — totally different from other objects. These roles are ideal types; actual designers rarely specialize entirely in one of them but, more typically, move from one to another during the course of their careers or even combine them in different aspects of their businesses.

Following Bourdieu (1993), McRobbie (1998:64–65) argues that associating fashion design with art is a way of conferring meaning on fashion products and of acquiring cultural capital for the occupation. Designers attempt to acquire prestige by demonstrating their associations, either aesthetic or social, with members of art worlds. I will argue that whether and how designers engage in these activities reflect the designer's position in the market. Changes in the fashion marketplace are leading to changes in the way designers frame their work as art. Under pressure to establish themselves in very competitive markets, they sometimes project images that are avant-garde or postmodern, but the consequences of these strategies vary in different environments. In the final section, I will examine how these changes have affected the diffusion and reception of luxury fashion.

FROM "CLASS" TO "CONSUMER" FASHION

The fashion system in the nineteenth and early twentieth centuries produced clothing styles that expressed the social position of the women who wore them or the position to which they aspired. It differed from the system that has emerged since then in several ways: in the level of consensus among designers, the nature of stylistic change, the process of dissemination of new styles, the emphasis on conformity, the type of motivation it elicited from consumers, and the selection of role models. "Class" fashion necessitated a centralized system of fashion creation and production in which there was a high level of consensus among designers. A small number of designers defined a specific style that evolved in a consistent manner from year to year. Class fashion was expressed in strict rules about how certain items of dress, such as shoes and gloves, were to be used ("Each occasion, each ensemble, had only possible, one correct glove" [Melinkoff 1984:31]). Rules also specified exactly which colors were permissible and in which seasons. Lengths of hemlines were dictated by Paris and generally accepted unquestioningly by the public. Implicit in these rules were widely accepted norms about sexual identity, femininity, and behavior (Melinkoff 1984). Fashion expressed social ideals of feminine attitudes and behavior (Barber and Lobel 1952). Underlying acceptance of this type of fashion was fear of exclusion on the basis of nonconformity, signifying that a woman was not aware of the correct mode of behavior.

In "consumer" fashion, which has replaced class fashion, there is much more stylistic diversity and much less consensus about what is "in fashion" at a particular time. Instead of being oriented toward the tastes of social elites, consumer fashion incorporates tastes and concerns of social groups at all so-cial class levels. A single fashion genre, haute couture, has been replaced by three major categories of styles, each with its own genres: luxury fashion de-sign, industrial fashion, and street styles. Luxury designer fashion is created by designers in several countries, as will be discussed in this chapter. Indus-trial fashion is created by manufacturers, which sell similar products to simi-lar social groups in many different countries, as well as by smaller companies that confine themselves to a particular country or continent. These compa-nies advertise extensively in the media, in elaborate catalogues, and even on the clothes themselves. Here the selling point is not style itself but an image that can compete in the world of mass-disseminated images that constitutes media culture. Industrial fashion is a form of media culture in the sense that its values and attractiveness to the consumer are largely created by advertis-ing. Street styles are created by urban subcultures and supply many of the ideas for fads and trends (see chap. 6). Different styles have different publics; there are no precise rules about what is to be worn and no agreement about a fashion ideal that represents contemporary culture.

In each of the three categories, the process of stylistic change and dis-semination varies. Both designers and clothing firms offer a wide range of choices from which the consumer is expected to put together a "look" that is compatible with her identity. A variety of inconsistent and contradictory looks, often influenced directly or indirectly by street styles, are available at any particular time. Motivation for adopting a style is based on identification with social groups through consumer goods rather than on fear of being pe-nalized for nonconformity. Role models are drawn from media culture, spe-cifically, entertainers from television, popular music, film, and sports.

On the basis of his observations of fashion designers in Paris in the late 1950s, Blumer (1969:280) concluded that the designers "created indepen-dently of each other . . . remarkably similar designs," because they derived their ideas from scrutinizing similar materials such as old fashion plates, cur-rent and recent works in the arts, and the media. By the late 1960s, the in-creasing decentralization and complexity of the fashion system necessitated the development of fashion forecasting. Fashion bureaus play a major role in predicting future trends and what types of clothing will sell. In consultation with fabric designers, fashion forecasters predict colors and fabrics two years before styles for a particular season are marketed. In the months preceding the creation of styles for a particular season, forecasters gather information worldwide: in advanced and advancing countries and in different milieus and different social classes within a particular country (Pujol 1989).

Today, major fashion worlds, in the sense that their products influence styles in other regions and countries, exist in a few major cities, such as Paris, New York, London, Tokyo, and Milan. Since the clientele for these clothes is defined as an international luxury market, the clothes are marketed in major cities all over the world, but in each case to a very small proportion of the population. The cost of haute couture clothes, which are made to order for each client, is such that they are said to be within the reach of no more than a thousand women in the entire world. Luxury ready-to-wear clothes have a substantially larger market, but, owing to the cost of materials and their labor-intensive production, they are also beyond the reach of all but a privileged few.

CLASS FASHION AND THE DOMINANCE OF THE FRENCH FASHION WORLD

Among fashion worlds, the position of Paris is unique, reflecting the high value placed on the decorative arts in France for many centuries. In the nineteenth and early twentieth centuries, the fashion designer achieved a high level of autonomy and fashion leadership. In the middle of the nineteenth century, the role of fashion designer was considerably enhanced by the activities of Charles Frederick Worth, an Englishman. French designers creating haute couture for elite clients influenced styles all over the Western world for 100 years (de Marly 1980, 1990b). Worth's position was above that of a dressmaker or tailor in that he was not expected to copy designs created by others. He hired artisans and helpers to assist in the creation and realization of his styles. He sold designs that epitomized the fashionable styles of the period. He invented the idea of seasonal collections containing his latest ideas and displayed in the couture house by models. Highly successful both artistically and financially, he clothed many members of European royalty and the aristocracy, as well as the French upper class and the demimonde of courtesans and actresses, who in turn served as fashion leaders. He also had a large American clientele.

Fashion design as haute couture emphasized style and technique: style, such as the dominant silhouette, supplied a unifying theme, while technical details created diversity. Clothes for the elite had to be perfectly executed, since customers knew that their clothing would be carefully scrutinized at social gatherings by friends and acquaintances. Fashionable women changed their clothes several times a day and participated in a great many social events. The enormous demand for clothes in Paris is indicated by statistics published in 1887: 200 first- or second-rank couturiers, 1,800 dressmakers,

500 clothing stores, and a half a dozen major department stores (Delbourg-Delphis 1981:45, 60). Department stores attracted large clienteles, but ready-to-wear clothing was not considered sufficiently stylish or elegant for middle- and upper-class women, whose dressmakers copied couturiers' styles if they were unable to afford originals. Fashions were adopted rapidly by the upper class and by women with working-class origins who participated in the social life of the upper class, such as actresses and courtesans, and more gradually by the middle class (63). Disseminated by numerous fashion magazines, the influence of Paris designers, and particularly Worth, extended to other countries, including the United States, where information about French fashions continued to be transmitted even during the Civil War (Severa 1995:189, 293; Barbera 1990).

French fashion influenced English and American clothing styles during this period, because these countries produced virtually no fashion designers who were able to acquire international or even national reputations. One exception was Redfern, an English designer, who developed a style of cloth-ing—suits in plain materials with little decoration—that was suitable for em-ployed middle-class women, whose lifestyle was not represented in the collec-tions of the Parisian designers (see chap. 4). More generally, women who called themselves court dressmakers in England or simply dressmakers in America, whose reputations were entirely local, created clothes for their cli-ents on the basis of styles emanating from Paris (Adburgham 1987; Jerde 1980). A case study of a successful dressmaker in this category, who worked in Minneapolis at the end of the nineteenth century, illustrates how much these artisans depended upon Paris for fashion ideas and materials (Traut-mann and DeLong 1997). This particular designer assumed the title of "Ma-dame Boyd" (born Rosanna Crelley, of Irish extraction) and traveled twice a year to Europe to obtain sketches from famous fashion houses and to pur-chase fabrics. Like the French designers of the period, she created unique garments in the dominant style, using ornamentation such as jet beading, sequins, feathers, lace, and embroidery. Madame Boyd headed a business consisting of about 100 employees, including seamstresses, cutters, and fit-ters.[3] Much more numerous were dressmakers who simply followed the or-ders of their clients, sometimes making only the more complicated portions of a piece of clothing, which their customers completed. More numerous still were thousands of underpaid seamstresses, who did most of the work entailed in making these garments.

In both England and the United States, women's ready-to-wear clothing industries developed more rapidly than in France and were more readily ac-cepted (Green 1997). These industries began with the production of cloaks and other loose-fitting garments and with partially finished dresses, which were completed by the customer at home. In England, ready-to-wear dresses were available by the late 1860s (Adburgham 1987:125–26). In the United States, the production of ready-made clothes for women was a sizable industry by the 1870s (Severa 1995:297). While the very rich in both countries continued to have their dresses made to order by the top tier of dressmakers, the middle class gradually shifted to ready-to-wear clothing and garments that were a combination of ready-to-wear elements and items sewn at home or by a dressmaker.[4] Despite the expansion of ready-to-wear clothing, the influence of Paris styles remained very important, particularly in the United States (375). In the 1890s, the more practical English styles began to compete with French styles, but the richest women continued to purchase their clothing in Paris (Coleman 1990).

Most French designers were trained as apprentices in the houses of established designers. Among the French designers who created fashion houses from the late nineteenth to the late twentieth century, there was a sizable network of masters and apprentices that linked most of the major fashion houses and many of the minor ones. Young designers began their careers in the houses of established designers. The result was a relatively cohesive group with shared norms and values that helped new trends to be diffused and accepted.[5] The nature of the socialization that French designers received contributed to the increasing success and prestige of the occupation of couturier in the twentieth century.

Unlike that of the French designers, the prestige of English and American fashion designers did not substantially increase in the early twentieth century. Few English designers acquired the glamorous aura of artistic genius that surrounded the most successful designers in Paris. The English designer continued to be viewed as an artisan rather than as an artist and was generally an employee rather than self-employed. In England, the clientele for couture clothes was primarily composed of royalty and members of the British upper class, whose tastes were extremely conservative. Constrained to produce clothes for ceremonial occasions and appearances, the designer had much less freedom to express his or her artistry. Not until the 1960s did small designer firms appear in substantial numbers, creating less conventional and more original clothing (de la Haye 1997). One of the first and best-known of these designers was Mary Quant, who took her cues from what young women were wearing on "the street" and, in doing so, redefined the fashionable styles of the period (Quant 1965).

In the United States, ready-to-wear clothing displaced made-to-order clothing almost entirely. Most American designers worked anonymously for large clothing manufacturers (Walz and Morris 1978; Diamonstein 1985:47). They had little autonomy or job security, although they were paid well by the standards of the time when they were working. Designers were paid to create, but their employers did not hesitate to change their creations without their consent to fit the employers' perceptions of the market.

An alternative career for the American designer was costume design for the Hollywood film industry. Among the generation of leading American designers born before 1920, one-fourth had careers in the film industry. Film designers in Hollywood produced clothes that rivaled those of the French couturiers in quality, expense, and glamour and that had an enormous influence on the public. The styles of these clothes were influenced in part by styles set in Paris, and, in turn, Hollywood increasingly influenced Paris designers (Delbourg-Delphis 1981:167).

Much of the time, American designers working for clothing manufacturers were required to adapt designs created in Paris for the American market. They produced clothes that resembled Paris styles very closely, although they were made with less expensive materials. Possibly because the influence of French fashion on the American clothing industry was disrupted during the Second World War, female designers, such as Claire McCardell and Bonnie Cashin, working for mass-market manufacturers, were able to escape the influence of French couture, in which they had been trained (Martin 1998). They challenged many of the accepted practices of the clothing industry of the period and created a more informal style of clothing for the average woman — sportswear. These clothes were intended for a mass market (for example, clothes for doing housework, to be sold for $6.95) and manufactured in inexpensive fabrics, such as denim, corduroy, seersucker, and calico (Milbank 1985:352).

The styles created by these women designers were exactly the opposite of the dominant French fashionable style of dressing of the period. Rather than imposing forms upon female bodies, their designs allowed for agency on the part of the wearer, who could modify certain aspects of a costume or choose exactly how it was to be worn. Their garments were wrapped or tied around the body, giving the wearer control over the way the garment fitted her body. Waistlines were adjustable. Collars and bows could be tied or placed in a variety of ways, again creating options for the wearer. Years later, the philosophy underlying this type of clothing was expressed by another American designer, Halston, who asserted that women, not designers, make clothing, meaning that individual expression is more important than style (Martin 1998:23, 87).

However, the influence of French couture resumed after the war. From the late 1940s to the 1960s, many American manufacturers engaged in "line for line" copying of French models (Ziegert 1991). New styles created by Paris couturiers were copied exactly, first in small quantities at high prices and then, within a few weeks or months, in successively larger quantities at lower prices.

The influence of fashionable styles originating in France declined in the 1960s as a result of the media visibility and popularity of a variety of styles emanating from the streets rather than from leading designers. For example, the hippy style provided the fashion industry, both in America and Europe, with a powerful competitor for the public's imagination. The success of this style with the public indicated that totally different clothing styles could co-exist and, by extension, that rigid rules about apparel were no longer appropriate. People were free to choose from a variety of possibilities the type of clothing they preferred. In doing so, they identified with a subgroup or life-style, as exemplified by a particular look, rather than with the middle class as a whole. Television, whose audiences expanded rapidly during the 1950s, prepared the way for this transformation by reinforcing people's identification with social groups on the basis of attitudes and behavior (culture classes) rather than on socioeconomic groups (Meyrowitz 1985).

THE GLOBALIZATION OF THE FRENCH FASHION MARKET: From Fashion House to Corporate Subsidiary

In the prewar period, French fashion designers' businesses were relatively small, stable organizations, functioning primarily in local urban markets. In the postwar period, and particularly in the past three decades, two factors have become increasingly important in the fashion industry: (1) ownership of culture organizations by conglomerates, companies whose major activity consists in buying and selling other companies, and (2) the globalization of markets for their products. The presence of conglomerates is associated with the emergence of oligopolies, in which a small number of large firms control the market for a specific type of cultural product (Bagdikian 1997). Particularly in global markets, a few very large firms are likely to dominate, to the detriment of small firms. Members of oligopolies aim for profits rather than innovation. Large firms generally prefer to avoid the risks associated with sty-listic innovation and to capitalize on stylistic innovations developed by small firms (Peterson 1994; Crane 1997b). Globalization has exacerbated the nega-tive consequences for small firms of sharing markets with large firms, because it greatly increases the costs to new firms of entering markets for cultural products and decreases their chances of survival. How these changes have affected fashion organizations and their products will be shown through an analysis of two types of French luxury fashion organizations: haute couture and luxury ready-to-wear.

In the prewar period, French couture firms were usually owned at least partially by the designer. The sums invested to start these firms were generally small; the principal activity was the production of made-to-order clothes for clients. Couturiers between the two world wars had substantial numbers of employees engaged in making and selling clothing, produced large numbers of models for their biannual collections, and had large numbers of clients. For example, Patou and Lelong each had 1,200 employees in the 1920s; Chanel had 4,000 employees in 1935 (Grumbach 1993:36, 168). The prewar firms served relatively stable and homogenous clienteles, mainly French, drawn from the conservative upper-middle class, the aristocracy, and wealthy bohemians, such as actresses and successful artists and writers.

The most prestigious firms belonged to the Chambre Syndicale de la Haute Couture and were required to obey regulations about the number of employees, the number of models in their seasonal collections, and the number of presentations of their seasonal collections (Henin 1990; Crane 1997b). Many other firms called themselves couture houses, unofficially, but they were less influential.

Before 1945, clothing was the major product of couture houses. Subsidiary lines of products to offset the uncertainties of the market for fashionable clothing were first used by Poiret before the First World War (Grumbach 1993:23). The principal subsidiary product developed by these designers was perfume. Between the two world wars, almost one-third of the haute couture firms developed lines of perfume, which produced substantial additional revenue. Chanel also created costume jewelry to be worn with her clothes (Mackrell 1992).

In the postwar period, most of the prewar firms, both haute couture and others, gradually disappeared. They were unable either to compete with a new style of designer firm or to adapt themselves to the new model. Postwar French haute couture firms represented a different type of fashion organization, which relied on financial expertise, a substantial financial investment, and licensing of many additional types of products as major sources of income. The first example of the new type of postwar firm was one created by a French textile business magnate for Dior in 1946 (de Marly 1990a). Dior's business was unique at that time, because he was associated with a financial partner who provided him with 10 million francs (approximately 2.75 million 1998 francs) to start a business and also with a business manager (de Marly 1990a : 17–18).[6] Dior was the manager, not the owner, although he was allotted a share of the profits (Grumbach 1993 : 46).

The most important innovation in business strategy that the Dior firm introduced was product licensing.[7] The major source of income for prewar firms that survived and new firms that entered the market after the war became the royalties obtained from licensing a great many types of products, ranging from clothing to household goods. By the 1970s, product licensing and perfumes were the major sources of profit for these firms. Clothing styles, including ready-to-wear, were primarily used to create a prestigious image for the company, which enhanced the salability of other products, particularly perfume. Leading French designers became global celebrities, selling their clothes in many other markets. With a worldwide structure of licenses and exports, the designer could no longer run his own business and supervise the creation of designs at the same time. The fashion houses that developed in the postwar period were run by business executives, often close friends or relatives of the designer.

After 1970, the escalating costs of made-to-order clothes made them accessible mainly to older, wealthy clients, generally residing outside France. Increasingly, couturiers were designing clothes for social milieus in which they no longer participated. In 1955, the Dior firm had over 25,000 clients (Grumbach 1993 : 44). In 1989, the Dior firm and the Yves Saint-Laurent firm were said to have more couture clients than any other couture house — about 200 (Menkes 1989; Samet 1989). The majority of clients were foreign (Menkes 1992), primarily Americans and Arabs. By the 1980s, most couture firms had less than 100 employees making clothes.

The enormous cost of creating an haute couture firm meant that only four new couture houses opened between 1970 and 1995.[8] Costs of entering the business escalated owing in part to increasing globalization of the fashion industry. These costs included the initial investment to set up the business, as well as the costs of creating a collection, opening a boutique on a fashionable street in Paris, showing collections twice a year in prestigious settings, and starting and advertising a perfume. Shops in several other countries were also required. By the late 1980s, the amount of money required to set up a couture business in Paris could only be afforded by a conglomerate. In the mid-1990s, one conglomerate owned three couture houses. It became virtually impossible for young designers to raise sufficient capital to enter the couture business unless they did so as employees of large firms, often owned by conglomerates.

In response to this situation, the Chambre Syndicale de la Haute Couture relaxed its rules in 1997 to permit new design firms to present smaller collections and to allow the participation of a few luxury ready-to-wear designers (Sepulchre 1997 : 3–4). These developments raised the level of interest by the media in the couture presentations, which benefited established couturiers with conventional collections (Menkes 1999). As a result, a number of young French and foreign designers, who were not recognized by the Chambre Syndicale, presented small collections reflecting very personal and sometimes very experimental perspectives on clothing (Quilleriet 1999). These changes did not, however, resolve the problems surrounding the long-run growth and survival of new couture firms.

By the late 1980s, within the entire group of couturiers, there were two types of designers. One group included older designers, working for companies that had existed for several decades, who produced collections that often consisted of restatements of ideas and motifs from the history of designer fashion. These clothes changed relatively little from year to year. In the late 1980s, this group was exemplified by a few large haute couture houses run by aging designers. Studies of other types of organizations have found that conglomerate ownership protects subsidiaries from financial pressures that might lead to failure (Freeman 1990 : 74). This appeared to be the case in this sector. In 1992, 75 percent of the couturiers were over fifty; four were over seventy. Journalists described many couturiers as taking few risks, varying their collections just enough to keep in step with the times, but not enough to make their middle-aged and conservative clients feel uncomfortable (Benaïm 1994).[9] Even in France, their influence on fashion had greatly diminished.

The second group of designers working for these firms was younger; their work was less conventional. Like culture-producing organizations in other fields, which coopt innovators from other firms (Lopes 1992), conglomerate owners of couture firms, whose designers died or retired, hired designers from small ready-to-wear firms who were recruited especially for the originality or the entertainment value of their designs. Designers working for large French couture firms, which depended upon the sale of auxiliary products for profits and on clothing design for the construction of the firm's image in the global marketplace, were able to concentrate on creating beautiful clothing or clothing that subverted conventional values. At first, the designers who were recruited in this way were already established. In the late 1990s, they were recruited because of their skill in attracting the attention of the media.

GLOBALIZATION, INNOVATION, AND FRENCH LUXURY READY-TO-WEAR FIRMS

In the 1960s, a second group of designers, who were called *créateurs*, began selling low-cost, original, ready-to-wear clothing. However, in the 1970s, they entered the luxury clothing business, where they designed clothes for clients from a different social milieu than that served by the couture firms (Bourdieu and Delsaut 1975). In the 1960s and 1970s, *créateurs* were able to start businesses with small investments from personal funds and to expand on the basis of profits. During this period, costs of entering the business were relatively low, and designers with new small firms were able to develop reputations as innovators.[10] In the 1980s, a few of these firms grew in size and profitability.

However, by the mid-1980s, new designers entering the luxury ready-to-wear business had difficulty locating venture capital as the cost of starting their firms in a global market escalated. Generally, *créateurs'* firms expanded by signing license agreements with industrial clothing firms or by finding sponsors willing to invest in them (Pasquet 1990). In most cases, growth was achieved by obtaining a financial sponsor, usually Japanese but occasionally Italian. French clothing manufacturers were reluctant to invest in young French designers. Financial sponsorship entailed a risk of losing control over the business if it became profitable.

Young *créateurs* were often unable to find sponsors and had to finance themselves (Piganeau 1998). Many firms began with very small investments, much less than the sum of $250,000 which experts considered necessary to start such a business in the 1990s (Lecompte-Boinet 1991). This usually meant that they lacked funds to expand their businesses. Costs were high, because it was necessary to use expensive fabrics in order to compete in the luxury market and also because their knowledge of the production side of the clothing business was often limited. One designer explained (Godard 1993): "I have practically no mark-up, but I produce in small quantities. The press follows my work, buyers come and they order one blouse in size 6, another in size 8, and then the same thing in another color. I lose money on practically every piece of clothing. I make my living as a stylist for a manufacturer."

In the early 1990s, most *créateur* firms were small, with few employees and having annual sales of less than $10 million. Two of the three most successful *créateur* firms in annual sales were owned by conglomerates and were very similar in character to the large couture firms that were also owned by conglomerates. Even new firms were selling as much as 80 percent of their merchandise outside France (Guyot 1993). According to the president of a clothing firm that manufactured lines of designer clothing (Pujol 1995:46), "Today one only talks about a global market. But who can undertake the very heavy global investment necessary to introduce a designer firm simultaneously in Europe, South-East Asia, and in the United States? The investments required to start a new firm are out of proportion with the short-term profits."

Those that survived often did so by designing other firms' collections in addition to their own, including relatively banal collections of industrial ready-to-wear firms. A designer said in an interview: "When you're a stylist for somebody else, you have to conform. You must respect their product and their image. Each time I wanted to do something new, my clients would automatically reject it." Other designers admitted in interviews that their own firms provided them with artistic satisfaction rather than profits. In some cases, when a small firm was deluged with orders as a result of the sudden success of a collection, it was unable to meet its financial obligations and went, at least temporarily, into receivership.

In this financial climate, it was difficult for young designers working in small firms to attempt the type of unconventional designs that had established the careers of major *créateurs* in the 1970s and early 1980s. The smallest companies tended to be pushed toward "wearability," which in fact meant a relatively homogenous product. The relationship between the age of designer firms and the extent to which these firms were perceived as innovative was examined through an analysis of rankings of designers by fashion journalists and managers of stores selling fashionable clothes. These rankings were obtained by a trade paper for the clothing industry in Paris, the *Journal du Textile*.

During an eighteen-year period (1978–95), a few firms appeared in these rankings much more frequently than others. Out of a total of 128 French *créateur* firms, only 22 (17 percent) appeared in the top 10 ranks at any time between 1978 (when the lists of rankings began) and 1995 (see table 5.1). Firms that appeared on the lists during the first period (1978–83) represented the majority of firms that ever appeared on the lists (see table 5.2). Seventeen (77 percent) of the twenty-two French firms that ever reached the top-ten ranks on these lists appeared on the lists during the first six-year period. Four firms, all of which started between 1978 and 1983, appeared eleven or more times on the list. One of these firms remained in the number one position in the rankings by boutique managers for twelve years. New firms that appeared in the 1980s and 1990s faced increasing difficulty in achieving recognition by fashion experts (table 5.1). Small firms that entered the business after 1984

TABLE 5.1

AGE OF FIRM BY RECOGNITION: DATE OF ORIGIN OF FRENCH *CRÉATEUR* FIRMS BY
APPEARANCE ON BIANNUAL LISTS OF TOP TWENTY *CRÉATEURS*

	Date of Origin of Firm						
	1960–69	1970–74	1975–79	1980–84	1985–89	1990–95	Total
Top ten	3	2	11	3	2	1	22
Top twenty	2	0	4	6	3	0	15
Neither	4	1	15	32	20	19	91
Total	9	3	30	41	25	20	128

Note: Computed on the basis of information appearing in *Journal du Textile,* 1978–95.

were less likely to be perceived as innovative by fashion experts and may actually have been less innovative, since their precarious financial situations precluded experimentation.

During the 1980s and 1990s, the environment in which both couturiers and *créateurs* worked had become increasingly turbulent. Paris had become a major center for the display of biannual collections by designers from many different countries—the place where young designers must display their work in order to obtain both recognition as innovators and a foothold in the global market (Cabasset 1989). Since the goal of luxury fashion design was now to attract publicity that would benefit sales of other products rather than to sell clothes, fashion shows became public events covered by the media and attended by large numbers of people. Until 1976, collections were generally shown in the fashion houses themselves. The traditional *defilé* was a staid event in which the models paraded in silence and were expected to be as expressionless as mannequins in department store windows but at the same time to embody upper-class elegance and propriety. In 1976, designers began to show their collections in more visible locations in Paris, such as museums, theaters, and luxury hotels, an indication that they were no longer relying on local clients but needed publicity to reach clients in many other countries. During the 1980s, the shows became theatrical spectacles, ranging from imitations of musical comedy to performance art, featuring eccentric or avant-garde clothes, music (sometimes composed especially for the event), and highly paid models who were often expected to be performers as well as clotheshorses. In the 1990s, the cost of shows in the most prestigious locations was over $1 million (Vettraino-Soulard 1998).

French designers no longer dominated this increasingly competitive

TABLE 5.2
AGE OF FIRM BY RECOGNITION: DATE OF FRENCH
CRÉATEUR FIRMS' FIRST APPEARANCE ON BIANNUAL
LISTS OF TOP TEN *CRÉATEURS* BY NUMBER OF TIMES
THEY EVER APPEARED ON THESE LISTS

Number of Times on Top Ten Lists	Date of First Appearance on Top Ten Lists			
	1978–83	1984–89	1990–95	Total
1–2	6	1	3	10
3–5	3	0	0	3
6–10	4	1	0	5
Over 10	4	0	0	4
Total	17	2	3	22

Note: Includes all French *créateur* firms ever ranked on biannual lists of top ten *créateurs* between 1978 and 1995. Computed on the basis of information appearing in *Journal du Textile*, 1978–95.

marketplace. Foreign designers, including Japanese, Italians, Spaniards, Britons, and Belgians, represented approximately one-third of the luxury fashion designers showing their collections in Paris. Large French couture firms favored foreigners when hiring designers to replace in-house talent. According to a fashion journalist, Paris "reigns but does not rule" (Benaïm 1997).

LUXURY FASHION DESIGN IN NEW YORK:
Differences between Large and Small Firms

While the French luxury fashion world continued to produce clothing styles for social elites, the styles produced by many post-1960s American designers were intended to be worn by a larger segment of the population: people who saw their identities in terms of lifestyles. In the late 1950s, opportunities available to American fashion designers improved. Clothing firms began to sell a designer's line, with his name on the label. A few designers bought the firms for which they had worked. Others started their own businesses, some of which were highly successful. By the 1970s, the increased prestige of the designer meant that designers' names could be licensed to other firms which produced a wide range of consumer products. Some designers headed fashion conglomerates composed of their firms and their licensees worth hundreds of millions of dollars. A few wealthy and successful firms were able to dominate the American fashion press as a result of their ability to purchase advertising, which led, in turn, to editorial coverage.

These firms succeeded not by attempting to define a single annual style that would be marketed to a mass public but by creating clothing for fictional lifestyles that matched the aspirations of certain segments of the middle and upper-middle class to differentiate themselves from the rest of the public. One of the most successful firms, Ralph Lauren, marketed a very conservative, traditional rendition of upper- class American and British life to a huge public (Brubach 1987). On a less expensive level, this approach permeated hundreds of mail-order catalogues that described and photographed clothing as very specifically defined lifestyles, which were often fictional amalgamations of items drawn from American and especially British traditions, from popular culture, and to a limited extent from designer fashion (Brubach 1993). A fashion journalist (Brubach 1987:72) identified the rationale underlying these sales strategies: "The crux of a person's identity, the experience of being that person — resides in the trappings, not in the person himself . . . *one can seem to be whoever one wants to be*" (italics added).

The orientation toward "lifestyle specialist" meant that American designers emphasized leisure clothes that were worn by millions of people, not only in America but also all over the world, rather than the relatively formal clothes for upper-class women that preoccupied the attention of their European counterparts. However, a small group of American designers, while not making clothes to order, attempted to create pieces of clothing that were exceptional in the quality of their fabrics, designs, or both. In some cases, these clothes have become collectors' items and have been displayed at museums of contemporary crafts. Others have been the subject of retrospective exhibitions.[11]

In the postwar period, this type of career was possible in the United States only when the market was defined as consisting of people with a specific lifestyle rather than as members of an elite setting trends for the general public. Designers who headed successful small firms were adept at making and maintaining relationships with clients in different cities, understanding their way of life and their social milieu. Their clientele consisted of socialites in cities all over the country, film stars, wives of political figures, and successful businesswomen. To reach these groups, these designers and their staffs took their collections to department stores in areas of the country with the largest concentrations of wealth: New York, Dallas, Houston, San Francisco, and Chicago (Diamonstein 1985:83).[12] As one designer said (Diamonstein 1985: 190): "It's important to go to places where the clothes are sold in order to reach the public and communicate and learn what their lifestyle is and what the social structure is." These contacts were invaluable, because, in America, the rich led relatively secluded lives in country estates and private clubs, as is suggested by this comment by a successful designer in the 1970s, Halston (Walz and Morris 1978:95): "In private homes, yachts, or resorts, people still want to dress up. In a way, it is an *underground society because you don't see it so much in public*" (emphasis in original). The public relations director for one of these designers said in an interview: "He knows his customers all across America. He's been to their homes and been entertained at their country clubs. . . . The kind of women who are his customers are very similar all across America. He understands their lifestyle."

Some of them were described as having the same kind of lifestyle as many of their clients. One member of this group, Pauline Trigère, was said to move "in the company of the most accomplished people of her time" (Walz and Morris 1978:209). Another woman designer said in an interview: "I live the lifestyle of my customers. . . . I am my ideal customer."

Because they target a very specific clientele, these designers are not well known among the general public. Young designers attempting to create small firms of this type in the 1980s and 1990s faced the same problems of survival as their European counterparts, and their numbers have dwindled in the late 1990s (King 1998; White 1998). Some of these designers survived by designing for a few large firms that increasingly dominate the American fashion industry and for large French firms.

THE ARTS AS A MARKET STRATEGY:
Designers as Patrons of the Arts

In order to attract clienteles who are able and willing to purchase the clothes they design, designers find it necessary to frame their work using categories that are meaningful to and understandable by these groups. Suitable frames increase designers' cultural capital, leading to their inclusion in the social activities of their clients, and expand sales of clothes and licensed products. One strategy for winning acceptance in elite social circles was contributing to the art world as patrons and collectors. Another means of acquiring status in these circles was by emphasizing the aesthetic value of their designs and by claiming the status of artist or artist-craftsman.

In the nineteenth and early twentieth centuries, designers were considered artisans or tradesmen (White 1986:91). Worth did not become an art collector and did not normally participate in the social activities of his clients, although he met them frequently in his shop. However, by the end of the nineteenth century, designers such as Jacques Doucet were being recognized for their connoisseurship as outstanding collectors of artworks and were beginning to aspire to a more elevated lifestyle (McDowell 1987: 133).

After the First World War, French designers' social status steadily increased. A French fashion curator (Garnier 1987: 100) states: "Between 1919 and 1930, the couturiers accomplished a spectacular social advancement, becoming, little by little, a sort of aristocracy of taste, and managing to secure an appreciable amount of aesthetic authority, intellectual prestige, and economic standing." During this period, one of the designers who invested most heavily in the role of patron was Chanel.

Unlike most of her peers, Chanel did not undergo years of apprenticeship in a fashion house and was later criticized for her lack of technical knowledge. Perhaps because of her lack of technical experience in dressmaking, her designs were stripped of superfluous detail and decoration. She popularized inexpensive materials such as jersey, formerly used for workmen's clothes (Mackrell 1992: 23). Since her clothes were easy to copy, her designs were quickly made available to a very diverse clientele. Her styles were suitable for women of all social ranks, although only the rich could afford to buy the clothes she actually sold. On the one hand, she sought to create a nonelitist image by claiming that her success as a designer was the result of her capacity to understand the experiences of the women of her generation: "I set fashions precisely because I went out, because I was the first woman to live fully the life of her times" (Mackrell 1992: 9). She presented her clothes as suitable for a new lifestyle that was being adopted by young women during and after the First World War, one that was more physically active and less socially constrained than had been possible in the early years of the century.

On the other hand, since the role of artist or artist-craftsman was unsuitable as a frame for these types of clothes, she developed the role of patron of the arts. She devoted a great deal of time to making and maintaining social contacts with wealthy elites and with celebrated artists. She designed costumes for plays written by major playwrights and provided financial backing for dancers. Her lavish dinner parties at her townhouse in the center of Paris were attended by the most important writers and artists of the period and were considered "the highlight of every social season in Paris" (Mackrell 1992: 65).

The social and artistic ascent of the designer during this period is particularly impressive considering the social backgrounds from which many of them came. During the late nineteenth and early twentieth centuries, the social origins of fashion designers were generally working or lower-middle class. Chanel was the daughter of an itinerant trader (Mackrell 1992: 18); her contemporary Vionnet was the daughter of a toll taker (Bertin 1956:164). Other designers were sons or daughters of craftsmen or shopkeepers in the dry-goods industry. However, an analysis of the biographies of men who became fashion designers after the Second World War shows that they had frequently been designated by their families for professional careers, such as law, medicine, or architecture, suggesting that they came from relatively affluent families. Others had attempted careers in the arts. The increased prestige of those who entered the occupation in that period was a result of the prestige the occupation had acquired in the prewar period.

After 1945, many successful couturiers and luxury fashion designers continued to cultivate images of themselves as exemplars of taste who identified with the upper class. In their personal lives, they maintained luxurious lifestyles, with lavishly decorated homes, frequent travel, and celebrity friends, exemplifying the ideal consumer of their products. In some cases, they practiced other arts, such as photography, painting, and literature, but were more likely to be art collectors and patrons, in keeping with their new positions in the upper class (LaBalme 1984). The status of the fashion designer continued to rise as fashion museums were created in Paris and in other French cities. Auction houses held sales of designer clothes which had become collectors' items.

THE ARTS AS A MARKET STRATEGY:
Designers as Artist-Craftsmen and Artists

During the period between the two wars, the designer in France managed to acquire some of the charisma of the artist because his or her creations were seen as being uniquely the product of his or her genius.[13] As a consequence, ever since, designers' biographies and personalities have been analyzed for clues to the sources of their aesthetic inspiration. While established designers invariably produce their collections with the collaboration of numerous assistants, their designs are presented in the press as if they were the creations of a single individual working alone in the studio.

Designers' strategies in framing the aesthetic qualities of their designs are derived from their perceptions of themselves as artists or as artist-craftsmen. At the beginning of his career, Worth made a considerable effort to distinguish his activities from those of his predecessors, emphasizing his autonomy as a creator and the quality of his craftsmanship. After he became successful, Worth began to consider himself an artist rather than a dressmaker. He believed that he was applying "the standards and principles of fine art to dress design" (Marly 1990b:110). He studied paintings and drawings assiduously in museums and developed an aesthetic of which "the history of art and the history of costume were the twin foundations" (112). Painters consulted him about posing their subjects when they painted portraits of women wearing his designs. In midcareer, he began dressing like an artist, modeling his costume on that of Rembrandt, including a velvet beret, full, shapeless jacket, and a silk scarf instead of a cravat.

In framing their work, artist-craftsmen emphasize continuity, predictability, and elegance. Balenciaga, one of the leading designers in Paris in the postwar period, whose work epitomized the tradition of haute couture, has been described in terms that fit the concept of artist-craftsman (Herreros 1985:41): "Armed with a very elaborate technique that he had himself invented, he did not cease to develop and perfect it without abandoning the canons which constituted his style: rigor, unremitting effort, elegance, and beauty."

This approach to fashion design was characteristic of the tradition of haute couture and is still used by many fashion designers. Changes in fashion tend to be interpreted as evolving from previous styles or as involving cyclical changes in which the same type of style recurs at regular intervals. From the point of view of the naïve public, fashion change appears to be linear. Each season new fashion innovations are presented and appear to be entirely novel. In fact, in the past, the process of fashion has usually corresponded to both the evolutionary and the cyclical model.[14] The evolutionary model is exemplified by the appearance of major fashion innovations that generate a succession of smaller, derivative changes, as seen in the work of Balenciaga and Dior in the 1950s. According to Milbank (1985:320): "Balenciaga's whole work was thematic, each collection growing out of the last." As an example of the nature of his creative style, when he invented the three-quarter sleeve, he experimented with numerous variations (Delbourg-Delphis 1985). Dior devised a series of new silhouettes, to which he gave names taken from the letters of the alphabet: the H line, the A line, the Y line, and the S line. These lines were created by systematically varying the basic components of a dress: the width of the shoulders and the fullness or narrowness of the skirt (Sichel 1979:30). Trained in this tradition, Givenchy was still faithful to its precepts forty years later. His last collection was described by a fashion critic (Benaïm 1995:16) as "a manifesto of balance, clarity, rigor, the grammar of French taste applied to couture. . . . Each detail conformed to an absolute order of lines, of perfect diagonals, of silk jackets that never creased against the body but still clung to it."

Artist-craftsmen seek to project a distinct image that customers understand and expect to find again each season. In order to maintain a distinctive image, many designers deliberately avoided fads and trends. In interviews, some American designers described their collections as evolving from year to year without radical changes. Derived from themes in previous collections, the basic elements of a collection remain the same. One designer said in an interview: "My look never totally changes; the collection always unfolds into the next collection. You have to stick to an image but let it change." Some claimed their clothes were timeless and could be worn for many years. Customers were said to be unable to identify the year in which a piece of clothing was produced. A few designers were claimed to be reproducing in their collections specific designs that other well-known designers had created one or two decades before. One designer identified three distinct categories of clothing in his collection: "Thirty percent present a strong fashion statement, sixty percent are signature clothes in our style, and ten percent are more classic pieces."

Another type of fashion change is cyclical, in other words, the variation and rearrangement of elements that had been used successfully in the past (Milbank 1985; Déslandres and Müller 1986). In an interview, one young French designer described her selection of such details as based on the notion that "a piece of clothing is like a record. One plays it because it brings back a memory." Some designers whom I interviewed said that everything had already been done and that their work consisted entirely of recombining elements from the past. One of the most successful young French designers of haute couture, Christian Lacroix, has been quoted as saying (Thim 1987:66): "I revive what I feel like reviving and what I think women want. Every one of my dresses possesses a detail that can be clearly connected to something historic, something from a past culture. We don't invent anything."

This process of recombination is not random but is always based on what was done immediately before. Any particular fashion tendency, such as shoulder size, skirt length, and shape, is eventually replaced by its opposite. Some trends recur frequently, others after a considerable lapse of time. The "genius" or "luck" of the successful designer using this approach lies in determining exactly when the cycle should be reversed and in producing dramatic examples of the countertendency.

Artist-craftsmen vary in their commitment to the role of artist or craftsman, although their actual designs may not be very different from one another. Zandra Rhodes, a British designer, at one time attached a label to her garments that read: "This is one of my special dresses: I think of it as an art work that you will treasure forever" (McDowell 1987:229). By contrast, Bill Blass has been quoted as saying: "Fashion is a craft, and an expression of a period of time, but it is not an art" (Milbank 1985:306). In general, designers in this category, both men and women, produces clothes that express their personal interpretations of current styles but rarely exhibit "the shock of the new."

A second set of market strategies are oriented toward disrupting the orderly evolution of fashion change, often using techniques associated with the avant-garde or with postmodernism. The emergence of a group of designers espousing an avant-garde or postmodernist approach is the result of a very competitive market position that requires radical innovation to establish an image and of a highly fragmented public that includes subgroups willing to pick up on new trends.

The reliance on avant-garde and postmodernist techniques is a result of the impact of the electronic media on all forms of culture. Holding the attention of audiences that are increasingly sophisticated at interpreting complex visual and verbal imagery requires the use of more varied techniques than were necessary before the emergence of the electronic media, which, in the past fifteen years, have appropriated many of the images and tactics of the avant-garde and postmodernism.[15]

The term "avant-garde," which implies a phenomenon that is difficult to understand because it challenges the public's preconceptions and consequently is not immediately accepted, seems incongruous when applied to fashions in clothing. Fashion is generally thought to refer to phenomena that are new but that are rapidly and widely accepted, implying that their acceptance does not require a major shift in worldview on the part of the public. In fact, many fashionable styles are not immediately accepted and may be accepted ultimately by only a fraction of the public.

In the context of clothing, the term "avant-garde" often involves changing the usual meanings attributed to specific items of clothing (such as the use of a type of costume associated with one activity for another, very different purpose) or changing the meanings associated with other types of objects in order to redefine them as being appropriate as apparel (such as the use of jam jar lids as bracelets or a chain intended for flushing a toilet as a belt) (Delbourg-Delphis 1983:154, 159).

Alternatively, the avant-gardist violates the expectations of the audience. As part of the presentation of a recent collection, a French designer, Jean-Paul Gaultier, recently showed an outfit whose front was an elegant Balenciaga-style sculpted white dress but whose back was completely bare except for fishnet hose and a flower (Menkes 1996). Artworks that are considered avant-garde sometimes have political or social connotations that are critical of or different from those of the dominant culture (Crane 1987). Similarly, avant-garde clothing designers try to reveal and comment on the implications of luxury fashion by proposing clothes that deliberately defy the perfect craftsmanship of haute couture.

In the 1980s and 1990s, as the level of competition greatly increased in the Paris fashion world, several foreign designers used avant-garde strategies to launch themselves and to obtain recognition in Paris. In the early 1980s, a Japanese designer, Rei Kawakubo, who was based in Japan but showed her collections in Paris, attracted a great deal of attention by adopting such an approach.[16] Specifically, she produced clothes that expressed the antithesis of values created in the tradition of haute couture. Perfection of craftsmanship is the hallmark of couture clothes. The stitching is expected to be perfect, the cut impeccable. Kawakubo designed sweaters full of holes and dresses with unfinished ragged hems. Machines for making her clothes were deliberately manipulated so that what they produced was flawed (Sudjic 1990:80). Almost invariably black, her designs were viewed as social statements, as oblique references to the clothes of homeless women and as veiled attacks on the decadence of Western fashion. A second major characteristic of Western clothing as epitomized by haute couture is symmetry. Kawakubo produced dresses that had three sleeves and jackets with one side longer than the other. In Paris and other fashion capitals, Kawakubo's styles in the early 1980s were perceived as both outrageous and important. The success of her strategy is indicated by a comment by her biographer (Sudjic 1990: 79), "Some of her garments were interpreted as an out-and-out assault on the very idea of fashion."

Later in the decade, a group of Belgian designers, all graduates of the same fashion school in Antwerp, used a similar avant-gardist strategy to establish themselves in the Paris fashion world. In the work of some of these designers and some French designers who were also attempting to launch new firms, the deliberate avoidance of craftsmanship and luxury became a "pauperist" style, using trousers that were too small, rumpled jackets and dresses, partially unraveled sweaters, torn materials, and jackets attached in the middle of the back with a large safety pin or with buttons and buttonholes that did not align (Sepulchre 1992:61) (see fig. 42). Even more iconoclastic, because it constituted a threat to the economic basis of fashion, was the project of one member of the group, Martin Margiela, which created new styles from cut-up pieces of secondhand garments (62). The simulation of poverty in luxury fashion design is intended to be perceived as a commentary on the opulence of haute couture, exemplified by embroidery that requires hundreds of hours of labor for a single garment and the reappearance of trains with evening dresses.[17] In the early 1990s, a Viennese designer, Helmut Lang, challenged the opulence and vivid colors of haute couture with very simple, drab clothes in unexpected combinations of materials, such as a dress made of rubber and lace which was described as "a perfect marriage of the classic and the illicit" (Hirschberg 1997:28).

Postmodernism as an element of fashion design is difficult to characterize in part because such works exhibit ambiguity and contradiction.[18] While the avant-gardist attempts to subvert aesthetic conventions by taking an oppositional stance, the postmodernist oscillates between conventional and unconventional codes, creating ambiguous effects or engaging in parody. Postmodernist works are polysemic, having no fixed meanings or multiple meanings. Authoritative interpretations are neither expected nor possible. In place of the modernist artist-craftsman's commitment to the development and elaboration of a particular style, the postmodernist fashion artist is interested not in style conceived as a consistent, integrated set of aesthetic elements but in pastiche, bringing together disparate elements from many previous texts, regardless of whether they produce a coherent entity. While other designers draw on previous styles to create new work, postmodernists recreate them in order to juxtapose different periods and ambiences.

The differences between these approaches to the past can be seen in Dior's adaptation of an early twentieth-century style. Rather than produce a copy, he used elements from the older style to create what is probably the most famous twentieth-century style, the New Look (Sichel 1979:30). By contrast, a postmodernist, John Galliano, duplicates styles from different periods, often juxtaposing them in the same collection, or mixes elements of styles from past and present in the same costume (see fig. 43). It is typical for designers in the same season to revive clothing styles identified with several different decades of the twentieth century or with historical periods from previous centuries. While Wilson (1990) has argued that designers were drawing on past styles long before the period that is generally defined as postmodernist, referencing the past appears to have escalated and become increasingly anarchic. Incorporating details from contemporary ethnic cultures is an equivalent strategy, since ethnic cultures are remnants from earlier periods: it has provided an additional source of ambiguity based on cultural fusion. Africa, India, China, and Islam were frequently evoked in these collections.

An analogue to the postmodernist art project of repudiating the modernist cult of originality by creating and selling identical copies of famous paintings (Connor 1989) is found in the work of Belgian designer Martin Margiela, who dedicated one of his collections to producing exact copies of collections of clothing that had been created decades before. What he chose to copy, however, were collections that had no prestige whatsoever in the history of fashion: the complete wardrobe of a doll in the 1960s, ceremonial robes from the turn of the century, and black school uniforms (Sepulchre 1994a).

Another postmodernist, Vivienne Westwood, emphasizes parody and ambiguity. An example from a 1989 menswear collection was an outfit entitled "Half-dressed City Gent," which consisted of a man's large shirt with a loose collar and tie, worn with pink knickers, on which was a graffito of an enormous penis. Another item from this collection was a pair of tights, intended for women, with a fig-leaf covering the genital area. The tights were shown with a man's shirt and traditional female attire on the feet, the intention being to suggest gender ambiguity (Ash 1992: 174–75). According to Goldman (1992: 214), the meaning of postmodernist texts cannot be discerned from analyzing the texts themselves but only by asking where the elements in the text came from. While in some cases these types of clothes have the effect of expressing the attitudes and preoccupations of a new generation, at other times they can deteriorate into "a kind of esoteric performance art for a very particular group of insiders that is so obscure as to block out its relevance to anyone else" (Buckley 1997: 19). This phenomenon is often evident at fashion shows.

Designers who use avant-garde or postmodernist strategies sometimes also present clothes which imply antihegemonic interpretations of women's roles unlike those that dominate the collections of more conventional designers. Many design clothes for women who are likely to conform to traditional cultural expectations of women's roles and whose clothing fits men's expectations of the way femininity and sexuality should be expressed in dress. By contrast, avant-garde and postmodernist clothes sometimes appear to be either redefining the significance of overt expressions of sexuality or denying sexuality altogether.[19]

For example, some of these designers appeared to be interpreting expressions of sexuality as a form of female power and control, as seen in the emphasis on bodily exposure in many of the collections shown in Paris in the 1990s. Year after year, collections included outfits in which breasts and midriffs were bare or, alternatively, covered with transparent materials that revealed as much as they concealed (see fig. 44). The tailored suit jacket worn over a naked torso became virtually a cliché. In one collection, a bridal costume consisted of nothing more than a bouquet of flowers and a piece of string. While in the past female nudity evoked powerlessness and subordination, it may now be interpreted as female empowerment. Displaying the nude female body is not intended to imply sexual availability. Sexual fetishism appears in the form of brassieres and corsets as outerwear. Madonna, for example, defends her use of explicit pornographic imagery in videos by claiming that she remains in control of her image and that she is not a passive sex object (Skeggs 1993).

Other designers were challenging traditional images of femininity through the expression of sexual orientations and sexual deviance that are typically viewed as marginal by the general public, specifically bisexuality and androgyny. Sexual ambiguity appeared year after year in designer collections. One form it took was the juxtaposition of clothing items identified with masculine and feminine clothing (see fig. 45). In 1991, the Paris collections for summer 1992 included the following: men's jackets in dark colors worn over a brassiere or a bustier of thin strips of plastic, oversized men's jackets over tops made out of material that resembled a coarse fisherman's net, neckties worn with skirts with seams open to the hip, severe men's jackets worn over bodysuits in leather (*Journal du Textile* 1991). While in some collections, masculine and feminine themes were combined in the same costume, in others, they were mixed in the collection as a whole: men's jackets, vests, and trousers alternating with nudity, transparency, and cutouts. While women have incorporated elements of masculine clothing into their outfits for centuries, the extent of gender blurring in these collections is peculiar to the contemporary period. It has been suggested that androgyny in women's fashion is an indication that the younger generation is "genderless"; the expression of gender differences is not important to them (Horyn 1996). The idea of assuming the sexual identity of the opposite sex is widely accepted on the internet (Bassett 1997).

By contrast, Rei Kawakubo's designs were antihegemonic in a different sense. She emphasized concealment rather than enhancement of female sexual attributes. She has been described as suppressing sexuality and sensuality: "Every seduction of flesh is forsaken, every indication of eros is sublimated" (Martin 1987a:65). Kawakubo has explained her point of view (Sudjic 1990:81): "We must break away from conventional forms of dress for the new woman of today. We need a strong new image, not to revisit the past."

Few fashion designers have a strong commitment to avant-gardist and postmodernist approaches; they are adopted for specific purposes and often abandoned later but do not necessarily lead to financial success. The overall effect of these collections was one of enormous variety and apparent change, because different elements in the repertoire were evoked each season. In fact, however, the underlying themes remained very similar. Each piece of clothing could be deciphered as a complex set of allusions to the past and to various sexual identities. Young designers working for major firms in the French luxury fashion industry have been encouraged to produce clothes that will attract attention in the media. Many designer firms from other countries find it necessary to engage in similar stylistic experiments to draw attention in an increasingly chaotic and competitive atmosphere. This has led to a great deal of erratic innovation—wide-ranging, often flamboyant experiments in style—that disrupts the normal patterns of fashion change and production. Paris has been in the past, and remains today, a location for the display of highly innovative designs, many of which will never be widely adopted and others perhaps not till decades from now.[20]

THE ROLE OF THE FASHION DESIGNER AS ARTIST IN ENGLAND

In England, fashion designers were largely excluded during recent decades from the kinds of changes that transformed the fashion industries in France and the United States. In the postwar period, the British clothing industry was dominated by an oligopoly consisting of a few giant manufacturers (Wilson 1987:82). The retailing business was controlled by a small number of chains, which exercised tight control over their suppliers (Morokvasic, Waldinger, and Phizacklea 1990). Large manufacturers and large retailers had a conservative influence on styles, preferring standardized clothing that could be sold to a mass market. Until the 1960s, clothing manufacturers in Britain were said to have hired pattern cutters, rather than designers, to copy ideas from magazines instead of creating new designs (Kemeny 1984). Even though opportunities in the British clothing industry improved in the 1990s, many young designers found it necessary to take jobs in other countries or to create small businesses, most of which failed owing to lack of capital and insufficient knowledge of the technical details of manufacturing clothing (McRobbie 1998).

Young British designers developed highly unconventional clothing, not as a market strategy per se but in response to the nature of the environment in which they were trained. The character of their designs can be attributed partly to the steeply hierarchical British social structure, in which

working-class youth, denied other outlets, expressed its frustrations by invent-
ing unconventional styles of clothing, and partly to the atmosphere of the art
schools in which fashion design was usually taught (Frith 1987). Careers in
the arts and design in general attracted lower middle-class and working-class
students who did not qualify for entrance to university or professional schools
but were unwilling to settle for routine working-class occupations. While students at French design schools produced clothes showing the influence of
leading designers, the work of British design students was more likely to be
influenced by working-class street culture. British art schools provided an in-
terface between fashion, street cultures, and rebellious music, whose creators
often started their careers performing in these settings (Frith 1987).[21] Fashion
designers were part of this community, along with popular music performers
and creators, video and filmmakers, and dancers and actors.

In the 1970s, this large pool of art school graduates in London constituted an unusually sophisticated audience for experiments with style of all
sorts. Young urbanites were described as being "excessively literate in the language of style . . . people who will make the supreme sacrifice to look inter-
esting rather than sexy" (York 1983: 114). Their goal was "the *confusion* of
the usual rules of consistency and good taste." Art students and other inhabitants of London's bohemian enclaves dressed to attract attention to themselves. Clothing took on exceptional importance as a means of making a
statement about oneself, not as an expression of social status, but as an indication that the person understood how to subvert the rules of fashionable
clothing (Frith 1987: 141–42). Each choice of a garment or an accessory was
seen as a creative act, as part of a practice of subversive consumption. Street
fashion in London is said to be "world-renowned, probably more innovative,
and certainly more versatile than in any other country" (Labovitch and Tesler
1984: 108).

The interaction between street culture and young fashion designers was
reinforced by the institution of urban street-stall markets (McRobbie 1988).
The street-stall markets were the primary source of secondhand clothes for
members of youth street subcultures, art students, and other members of
fringe communities. Young fashion designers who did not want to work for
clothing chains attempted to market their designs in these settings. Putting
up a stall was a way of obtaining a certain amount of artistic autonomy. Street-
stall designers who were close to the "street" were said to have played more
important roles in setting fashion trends — by locating "redeemable" pieces,
which then reentered the fashion system — than successful fashion designers
who picked up these trends at a later stage in their development. Major fashion labels were said to "rework the already recycled goods found in the street

markets" by producing more expensive versions of these styles in cheaper materials, which were marketed to a wider audience (McRobbie 1988:28).

Consequently, a number of factors worked together in England to create a situation where the young designer had an affinity with oppositional dress rather than with upper-class styles: the atmosphere of the art and design schools, the richness of urban street cultures, the ideology of dress as a personal statement of subversion rather than conformity, as well as the scarcity of opportunities for young designers in the British clothing industry. Unlike older designers who continued to create clothes for an establishment that was dominated by conservative tastes and personal appearance, younger designers perceived themselves as rebels and as artists rather than as entrepreneurs. In France, where the decorative arts have been greatly esteemed by elites, designers could position themselves both as artists and as people producing highly valued objects for elite publics. In England, the status of artist has been used by educators to justify training fashion designers in art school and by the designers themselves to explain the type of designs they create and to rationalize their failures in the marketplace (McRobbie 1998).

RECONCEPTUALIZING THE DIFFUSION OF FASHION

In the past, class fashion consisted of a single style which was widely disseminated. Today, the diffusion of fashion is highly complex because of the geographical dispersion of the fashion system, the number of actors involved, and the enormous variety of products. In principle, luxury fashion which is created for upper-class elites should diffuse downward to less privileged classes. However, although luxury fashion designers are still presented in the media as setting fashion each season, there is often little consensus about the direction in which fashion is moving; instead, designers produce a large number of "propositions" — a grab bag of ideas. Industrial fashion adopts some trends from luxury fashion but also conforms to the "bottom-up" model, coopting innovations from working-class and other subcultures which it sells to more privileged groups

In the French luxury fashion world, one speaks of *"tendances"* (tendencies) rather than fashions, suggesting subtle changes that will exert a discreet influence on the public rather than produce powerful bandwagon effects. The clothes shown by designers in their seasonal collections are generally so varied that detecting tendencies requires considerable skill and experience. A fashion reporter explained the problem (Spindler 1995:B10): "Looking for trends at the runway shows of Jean-Paul Gaultier, Vivienne Westwood, John

Galliano and Karl Lagerfeld is a bit like going to the Museum of Modern Art and doggedly seeking paintings with flowers and trees. . . . What makes these designers great is not the trends they create but how they have no use for them. . . . What has become more important is to show work so distinctive that what is appropriated is as valuable as a lump of lead."

The extent to which the ideas of many of these designers are actually disseminated to a larger public is relatively slight. There are a number of reasons for this. Many pieces of designer clothing are sumptuous, luxurious, and virtually unwearable on the street or in the workplace. The clothes created by some designers, particularly the younger ones, are often so highly coded that they are not easily understood by the general public. As one observer states (Swartz 1998:94): "Clothes have become more difficult to understand and far more expensive to acquire." In general, in luxury design collections, each piece of clothing in the collection tends to fit with the rest as a totality. It is often difficult to extract specific details to copy on a mass basis. When this is done, such details often lose their original meanings and impact. As an informant who had worked for a leading designer in the industry for many years put it: "It never looks the same . . . because they are not going to be using expensive fabrics, so they are never going to get it to look like the real thing."

Second, the luxury fashion market reflects increasing differentiation between lifestyles in social classes, as seen in, specifically, levels of disposable income and standard of living. As a result, diverse clothing styles created by luxury fashion designers are directed toward different segments of the middle and upper classes. Luxury fashion represents not a type of style adopted by the upper class and disseminated downward but a set of styles adopted primarily by certain segments in the upper and upper-middle classes. The perspective of some of the women who make no attempt whatsoever to follow fashionable styles was described by a woman executive in a fashion forecasting bureau: "I recently went to a wedding in Queens, for example. I've never seen a grosser selection of dresses in my life. Coming from the fashion industry, you look at this and you say: These people come from New York City? . . . These people are completely out of tune with what's happening. They go to a store and they try on something that looks nice. They don't know whether it's fashionable or not. They don't care. Who cares?"

Wearing fashionable clothes is the prerogative of certain social groups including the young (ages fifteen to twenty-five), celebrities (rock and film stars), successful or rising professionals and executives in fields where it is important to exhibit taste, and the very rich. But for each group, being in fashion has a different meaning. The young have their own clothing "traditions," many of which are very recent in origin and heavily influenced by American sportswear and subcultural styles associated with rock bands (see chap. 6). Rich women tend to prefer the creations of relatively conservative designers but media celebrities opt for styles created by younger, more daring avant-garde or postmodernist designers. When asked about their clienteles in interviews, designers frequently mentioned very specific segments of the population such as "artists, intellectuals, and professionals," "people in the publishing industry," "women working in advertising, art galleries, and museums," and "wives of corporate executives." In large cities, clients often belong to specific subcultures whose members know one another. Some designers belong to social circles that include theatrical and nightclub personalities. Certain fashion designers have virtually a cult following among artists and intellectuals or jet-set celebrities.

In these milieus, women seek clothes that come close to being unique objects that express their individuality as well as their social identity. Prada customers in New York have been described (Swartz 1998:98) as working in "art galleries or advertising, in the movies or television, in fashion or beauty—and what they wore had to communicate silently all sorts of messages about their sophistication and their taste." In some types of businesses in Paris, women were said to be criticized if they wore clothes from the previous season.

Designer clothes are generally sold in stores whose interior decoration is deliberately created to convey an image of high culture, not unlike an art gallery. Enormous sums are spent on architects' and decorators' fees to produce settings that enhance and underline the aesthetic message of the designer. These stores have been described as having the effect of "filtering" the public. This type of shop demands "a certain confidence from the customer—those who would not feel comfortable with the clothes would be unlikely to brave the shop" (Sudjic 1990:114). As in art galleries, the exchange of the commodity takes place through a personal relationship in which the seller explains and interprets the clothes to the knowledgeable client (Swartz 1998).

These styles are perceived by designers as being relatively inaccessible to people outside the social groups for which they are intended. One designer in Paris said that articles in the press sometimes brought people to his store who were unable to understand the clothing. Other French designers stated: "My clientele knows fashion; in order to like my clothes, it is necessary to have a certain education in fashion." "My clothes create an atmosphere not only for the body but also for the mind. On a hanger they don't say anything. The customer has to dare to try them on."

The fashion adopter who was once perceived as a "fashion victim," following fashion automatically without reinterpreting it in terms of her own personality and lifestyle, is now viewed as a discriminating consumer. Fashion designers in interviews frequently stated that each woman is expected to create her own style of dress, one that is uniquely appropriate for her, assembling it from a variety of elements rather than automatically purchasing and consuming a total look. One young designer described fashion as a dialogue, a process of making images with which women could identify and interpret for themselves.

Another tenet of this philosophy is that the same piece of clothing creates a different effect depending upon the physical characteristics and personality of the woman who wears it. The same dress will look different when worn by different women. Similarly, the same piece of clothing worn by the same woman can project different meanings when it is seen in the context of different accessories and other clothes.

Some American designers emphasized their customers' independence: "They are assertive, self-assured women with a strong sense of how they want to look." "They don't listen to the magazines; they read them and take it all in. They don't listen to me. They know what they're all about and that's what's exciting about the customer. They have a strong individual sense about them. They know what works for them and feel great about it." A French designer said: "My ideal customer is in her thirties. Very sure of herself. She uses clothes to project a certain image of herself. Her outfits project seriousness, sensuality, and femininity."

Young designers were often less precise than experienced designers in their conceptions of their customers. Those who had been working longest in the business were skilled at communicating with their clients and were influenced by their attitudes. These designers made an effort to talk to their customers in their stores and to design clothes that met their needs. One designer spoke of the importance of watching how his faithful clients actually wore the clothes he designed in different situations.

Some American designers suggested that their clients influenced their styles: "It's important to listen to your customer. Their input adds something." "I don't just sit down and draw a sketch. I approach it in a much more intellectual way. I think about my own needs. I think about the women I meet when I travel all over the country." By contrast, one of the more avant-garde designers said: "I don't need to see how the customers react to the clothes. You have to be ahead of the customer; you want to be able to show her something she hasn't thought of. You are always behind if you listen to the customer."

Both American and French designers mentioned frequently the influence on their work of people on the street or in clubs. What they appeared to be looking for was, in part, indications of emerging street styles, but also outfits worn by people with a special talent for manipulating sartorial signs. An American designer said: "The people you see day in and day out influence you. All over the place: SoHo, nightclubs, restaurants. Certain people who dress in their own way, for themselves, influence you the most." A French designer recalled that her point of departure was sometimes certain details, such as a collar or a sleeve, that she saw in clothing worn on the street.

For luxury fashion, the hypothesis that a particular fashion will saturate the public is no longer useful. The role of luxury fashion designers is not to set trends but to produce ideas for trends. From these collections, fashion editors and fashion forecasters select items that will be promoted as trends. One forecaster described the process in an interview: "We take from what we see happening with some key designers. There are five or six designers who come to the fore and who really set the trend. The more you do this, the more it becomes a science; you know who to watch by going to the collections. . . . And then as a forecaster, I go back to that original inspiration, to see what was turning him on and how that relates to the present moment in time and why he might have connected to it, what stimulated him, and why that's meaningful."

Another forecaster was skeptical about the extent to which designer fashion was incorporated into clothing manufactured for the general public: "A very small percentage of all clothing that is made is fashionable, and then there's graduating levels from bridge to better to contemporary to moderate. A lot of the ideas are being appropriated into those areas, but the more they become interpreted, the more they become watered down. And that's intentional, because the people who make the clothing know that even though 'newness' is going to sell the goods, if it is too fashionable, people won't buy it, because it's going to be too foreign for them."

A marketing expert defined the American market as consisting of three major groups: women under twenty-five and particularly under twenty, women twenty-five and up, and affluent women between thirty-five and fifty. As fashion designers stated in interviews, affluent women of all ages are interested in and likely to wear fashionable clothes, leading some of them to the erroneous conclusion that age is unimportant in the selection of clothing. In fact, clothes worn by the average woman over twenty-five are likely to be very conservative and to reflect distinct regional differences. Since the average American woman is now over forty, older women now constitute a substantial portion of the market for clothing. According to market researchers, these women are spending less money on clothing and now prefer other activities to shopping (Steinhauer and White 1996). Companies that target middle-aged women avoid fads and trends in favor of a wide variety of relatively simple clothes that are developed on the basis of extensive market research on tastes and preferences.

By contrast, luxury fashion styles are marketed to clienteles with distinct lifestyles within the upper and upper-middle class who appreciate clothing that is not easily interpreted by the average person. The diffusion of luxury fashion seems to consist of many relatively short trajectories, in which a particular style diffuses upward from urban subcultures or downward to certain segments of the population but not to others.

CONCLUSION

In the past three decades, fashion has evolved in the direction of increasing variety, which parallels the fragmentation of contemporary societies, the greater complexity of relationships between social groups, and the expansion of contacts between different societies. Until the 1960s, the creation and dissemination of fashionable styles was highly centralized. Changes in the dominant style were rapidly transmitted to members of different classes. In this process, highly visible members of the upper class acted as role models. Class fashion was expressed in rules about what should be worn and how it should be worn. Conformity to rules signified that a person belonged to or aspired to belong to the middle class.

The fragmentation of the public within and across social classes, combined with changes in the character of fashion organizations, many of which now make their profits from products other than clothing, has led to the development of three distinct categories of fashion—luxury designer fashion, industrial fashion, and street styles. These three categories of fashion are weakly interconnected: street fashion has some influence on luxury fashion and vice versa (see chap. 6) and both have some influence on industrial fashion. Huge clothing manufacturers play major roles that conform to the bottom-up model of fashion diffusion, coopting innovations from working-class and other subcultures and studying consumer tastes in order to market styles that will reflect the preferences of consumers. These styles are most likely to be adopted first by the young and only later by older cohorts. To the extent that role models exist, they are drawn from media culture.

The relative importance of the three categories varies in different countries depending upon the nature of fashion organizations and their relationships with consumers. Designer fashion businesses everywhere face similar constraints in the high costs of investment required to start and expand a business in global markets. These constraints mean that large firms, particularly those backed by conglomerate ownership, tend to remain in business and to be profitable. The same factors tend to discourage potentially innovative small firms. As a relatively weak "semiprofession," faced with economic dependence on powerful clothing firms and high status clienteles, designers tend to find themselves captives of one or the other: dominated by managers and financial experts or dependent on the whims of capricious clienteles whose tastes they endeavor to discern by "infiltrating" their social circles.

The same conditions that have made it difficult for new firms to enter the industry have created a situation in which it is very difficult for new, small firms to receive recognition for their designs by fashion experts, whose judgments affect the reception of styles through their selection of clothes for sale in trendy boutiques and for the editorial pages of fashion magazines. The reception which small fashion firms receive depends upon the environment they face when they enter the business. When costs of entry are relatively low and the number of competitors is relatively small, new small firms are able to attract the attention they need to develop their reputations. When they are competing with larger firms in a market where costs of entry are high, they are less likely to be perceived as trendsetters. As in other types of cultural organizations, a few designers with small firms are coopted to create styles under contract for large firms, where their work tends to receive a great deal of attention.

Each of the three major fashion worlds — Paris, New York, and London — has a distinctly different emphasis. In each setting, fashion designers have developed a unique constellation of roles, as seen in the ways in which they identify themselves as artists, artist-craftsmen, or entrepreneurs. In each environment, characteristics of the market influence designers' strategies for coping with turbulence and competition, leading them to frame their work for the consumer so as to enhance its connections with other forms of culture. Some designers showing their collections in Paris use their connections with the arts to enhance the prestige of their occupation. Others have turned to the use of avant-garde and postmodernist imagery to improve their positions in highly competitive markets.

In the United States, a few designers working as artist-craftsmen serve upper-class elites, but the majority are oriented toward various segments of an increasingly fragmented mass market in which success depends upon being able to identify lifestyles that resonate with the public regardless of whether they actually exist. Major New York designers are lifestyle specialists, adept at creating clothes that express specific lifestyles, real or imaginary. In London, older designers, whose clients belong to the upper class, are generally artist-craftsmen, while younger designers, who are excluded both from this milieu and from the mass market, are likely to adopt the role of artist under the influence of oppositional street cultures and art school environments. Designers in London are in close touch with youth cultures and with creators in other forms of popular culture that influence clothing styles; their environment favors outrageous, subversive, and often impractical designs rather than profit.

In general, the sources of fashion have diversified and the nature of fashion change has become more complex. Fads and trends are drawn from many different sources. In some fashion worlds, fashion change occurs erratically; in others, primarily through the gradual evolution of styles or recurrence of cycles. Consumer fashion is oriented toward distinct lifestyles and "tribes" in social classes. A variety of looks, often inconsistent and contradictory, are in fashion at any particular time. Instead of dictating fashion, both designers and clothing firms offer a wide range of choices from which the consumer is expected to put together a look that is compatible with his or her identity, in keeping with the emphasis on the importance of personal identity in postindustrial societies with postmodern media cultures (Giddens 1991).

Some lifestyles are seldom targeted, while, in the population as a whole, the percentage of women who are interested in fashionable styles has steadily declined. The disappearance of fashion that incorporated widely accepted social and cultural ideals in favor of a pluralistic set of fashions representing conflicting and sometimes deviant values and symbols identified with specific segments of the public appears to have alienated a large segment of the public and raises the question whether fashion in the true sense of the word still exists.

NOTES

1. For a description of the data on which this chapter is based, see chap. 1. For additional data, see Crane (1997b).

2. Fashion centers or "fashon worlds" include designers, their clienteles, shopkeepers, magazine editors, and department store buyers.

3. A similar designer in London during the same period is described as follows (Hardy Amies, quoted in Adburgham 1987:252): "Miss Gray did not set herself up as a

dress designer. She bought some models in Paris, and made others to her own design, which she never pretended were anything other than adaptations of Paris models, which she had either seen in reality or in the fashion newspapers."

4. The number of female dressmakers in the United States continued to increase annually until 1900. In the first two decades of the twentieth century, the numbers of women in the occupation declined rapidly (Trautman 1979:84). A similar decline in the numbers of female dressmakers occurred in London after 1910 (Phizacklea 1990:28).

5. Among the twenty-two designers who created their own couture houses in the decades after the Second World War, 65 percent had begun their careers working for at least one other couturier and 30 percent had worked for two or more. Twenty-five percent had worked for the Dior firm alone.

6. Approximately $525,000 in 1998 dollars.

7. Schiaparelli was the first couturier to license an item of clothing (in 1940), but Dior was the first to make extensive use of this practice (Grumbach 1993:76).

8. From 1891 to 1944 (a period of fifty-three years), thirty-three firms entered the haute couture business. By 1945, one-third of the prewar firms had failed. By 1965, two-thirds had failed. By 1995, only nine survived. Several of these firms had eliminated haute couture itself but remained in other segments of the business. From 1945 to 1995 (a period of fifty years), only twenty-two firms entered the business. Eighteen of these firms existed in 1995. For further details, see Crane (1997b:402).

9. Another indication of the absence of innovation among couture firms in the past twenty years is the fact that only four couture firms appeared at any time in rankings of fashion innovation by fashion experts (buyers and editors), published twice a year in a leading trade paper in the clothing industry in Paris (see below; and Crane 1997b). Only three couture firms appeared in the top ten on these lists between 1978 and 1995, and one appeared in ranks eleven through twenty in the early 1980s.

10. Four members of this early group of *créateurs* were the only ones to appear over ten times on the ranked lists of biannual collections.

11. For example, Geoffrey Beene, Arnold Scaasi, and James Galanos (McDowell 1987).

12. American designers who target elites use the "trunk show," in which designer, staff, and clothes go on tour to stores in major cities. Clients who are known to store personnel are invited to view the collection in this context and to place orders for specific models.

13. In the period between the First and Second World Wars, only one American designer aspired to the role of artist: Charles James. Much admired by other designers but financially unsuccessful, he treated his customers as patrons. Buying a dress from him was compared to commissioning a painting (Walz and Morris 1978).

14. Proof of the role of cycles in fashion change is found in Young's (1937) exhaustive study of changes in the contours of skirts — tubular, bell shaped, and back fullness — which were found to succeed one another at regular intervals of about thirty-five to forty years in the nineteenth and early twentieth centuries.

15. Caldwell (1995:viii) claims that "every framework of the avant-garde . . . had

become highly visible in some form in the corporate world of the new television." Kaplan (1987:55), in an attempt to classify music videos in the mid-1980s, found that all the categories she identified used avant-garde strategies. One of her video categories was postmodernist. Some advertisements, particularly for clothing manufacturers, have been identified as postmodernist, when the connection between the product and the images in the advertisement is not obvious (Goldman 1992).

16. The first fashion designer whose work can truly be characterized as avant-garde was Elsa Schiaparelli, an Italian, who worked first in Paris in the 1920s and 1930s and in the United States after the war. A close friend of leading avant-garde artists, Schiaparelli believed that fashion was an art (White 1986:94) and attempted to translate the ideas behind Dada and Surrealism into clothing design (Martin 1987b). With Salvador Dali, Schiaparelli collaborated on the creation of the Tear Illusion Dress, a dress with pictures of tears on its fabric, which was paired with a cape in which the tears were real, thus violating the norm of perfection inherent in designer clothing and suggesting associations between expensive clothing and the dilapidated clothing of the poor (Martin 1987b:114). This design was a forerunner of recent avant-garde experiments with clothing.

17. A dress that appeared in a fashion show for Chanel in the mid-1990s was overlaid with tiny black beads known as "pearls of caviar." The beading represented 400 hours of handwork, although the results were not evident to most members of the audience (Menkes 1995).

18. Postmodernism, defined in a somewhat different way, is also an aspect of fashion consumption (see Kaiser, Nagasawa, and Hutton 1991; and chap. 7).

19. These observations are based on articles covering fashion collections shown in Paris that appeared in the *Journal du Textile*, from 1987 to 1998. See also Horyn (1996), Spindler (1996a and 1996b), and Steele (1996).

20. Behling and Dickey (1980) note that some designs shown in Paris before the First World War were so far ahead of fashion that women did not wear comparable costumes until the 1920s.

21. Fifty-five percent of the English designers whose careers were examined for this study received their training in art schools. In fact, 44 percent of the British designers had attended just two art schools: St. Martin's School of Art and the Royal College of Art. This pattern begins with the cohort of fashion designers who were born between 1920 and 1940. Among all designers born in 1920 or after, 70 percent had attended an art school. The remainder were largely self-trained. Only 4 percent of the sample had attended a fashion school instead of an art school.

Any crack in the social consensus demands a new set of sartorial codes. Spencer (1992:41)

We make our living from a myth. French importer of men's jeans, quoted in Piganeau (1991:73)

6 MEN'S CLOTHING AND THE CONSTRUCTION OF MASCULINE IDENTITIES
Class, Lifestyle, and Popular Culture

In the nineteenth and early twentieth centuries, identification with a social class was the primary factor affecting the way men perceived their identities and their relationships in their social environments. With the transition to a postindustrial society at the end of the 1960s, as Bell (1976) argued, people were less constrained than in the past by their occupational identities. According to this theory, the construction of personal identity outside the workplace became increasingly important. These changes are likely to affect certain types of men more than others, specifically those whose social statuses are marginal, ambiguous, or conflicted. Clothes are a major tool in the construction of identity, offering a wide range of choices for the expression of lifestyles or subcultural identities.

While theorists agree that the meanings of consumer goods are "open, flexible, and malleable" (Kotarba 1994:157; see also Hetzel 1995), exactly how new meanings are conferred on consumer goods is not clear. As Featherstone (1991:11) points out, part of the appeal of postmodernism is that "it . . . purports to illuminate changes in the day-to-day experiences and cultural practices of broader groups in society. It is here that the evidence is weakest . . . we possess little systematic evidence about day-to-day practices." In contrast to Baudrillard's postmodernist interpretation of media images as "meaningless noise" and the public's response as "a flat, one-dimensional experience . . . a passive absorption of images" (Kellner 1989:70), the public's responses are highly differentiated depending upon age and lifestyle. Meaning is not, as Baudrillard claims, disappearing from media texts and consumer goods such as fashion; instead they are interpreted in contradictory ways by increasingly fragmented publics.

During the twentieth century, two parallel developments have occurred: the public has become increasingly adept at "reading" culture, and culture itself has become increasingly complex. Popular culture constantly redefines social phenomena and social identities; artifacts continually acquire new meanings. In this chapter, I will show how the transition to postindustrial society has affected the meanings of items of masculine clothing in different contexts—business and leisure settings. I will argue that the meanings of clothes worn for economic activities have been relatively fixed, while the meanings of clothes worn for leisure activities have been subject to continual redefinition. In order to understand the ways in which new meanings are conferred on items of clothing and the role of popular culture in this process, I will draw on theories that argue that the meanings of some items of popular culture, including clothing, are "open," because they are frequently redefined by culture creators and consumers alike (Fiske 1984). Film and music media are important elements in this process. By associating salient images with specific types of garments, they alter the meanings of those garments and their symbolic power for the public. To be successful, leisure clothes for men have to be synchronized with media culture as it is expressed in television, film, and popular music.

Since men are more closely identified with the occupational sphere than women, who still remain to some extent "outsiders" whose presence is tolerated owing to economic necessity or government legislation, the postindustrial thesis is particularly pertinent to the nature of men's identities. My emphasis will be on men's use of workplace and leisure clothing, although ironically many of the types of clothing I will discuss are now also worn by women. As I will show in this chapter, meanings of clothing are perceived in various ways by different categories of men, some of whom merely consume clothing, while others both consume and create clothing styles. In general, those who belong to minorities, based on race, ethnicity, or sexual orientation, tend to use style as a means of expressing their identities and their resistance to the dominant culture (Janus, Kaiser, and Gray 1999). Members of youth subcultures produce styles that are eventually assimilated by "consumer" fashion, appropriating icons from media culture and engaging in various forms of fantasy, aesthetic expression, and bricolage. Another category consists of "sophisticated poachers," men who attempt to extend the normative boundaries of acceptable male attire. Although I will draw primarily upon American examples, the changes I am describing are taking place in other Western countries. The American case is particularly relevant, because much of the stylistic innovation in leisure apparel in recent years has come from American ethnic, minority, and sexual subcultures, in what a French observer has called the "*hyperaméricanisation*" of clothing (Valmont 1994:22).

WORK AND LEISURE: Two Clothing Cultures

In the late twentieth century, the business suit is the epitome of a style that expresses social class distinctions. Since it achieved its present form at the end of the nineteenth century, there have been strict rules about exactly how a business suit is to be made and worn.[1] Precise specifications still govern "the shape and proper proportions of . . . details, such as lapels, collars, and trouser length and width" (Flusser 1989:7).[2] A very narrow range of colors is permissible for business suits (primarily navy blue and charcoal gray). These rules enhance the usefulness of the business suit as an indicator of social class. Knowledge of subtle changes in the basic style of the garment is more likely to be available to those who have access to the best tailors. According to Martin and Koda (1989:151): "The cut, fabrication, and accessories of the suit . . . betray the social background . . . of the wearer. . . . The suit is a nuanced and varied garment."

Observance of the rules about how suits are to be worn is thought to have a direct influence on success in business, politics, and the professions, as suggested by the slogan in an advertisement by Hart, Schaffner, and Marx (*New York Times* Magazine 1986): "The right suit might not get you to places of power. But the wrong suit might not get you anywhere at all." In conservative political circles, flouting this "uniform" can appear scandalous, as when the French minister of culture, Jack Lang, wore a suit with a mandarin collar and no tie to a meeting of the French National Assembly in 1985 (Déslandres and Müller 1986:327). A French menswear designer stated in 1999 (Middleton 1999): "There is still the situation that changing the number of buttons on a jacket can create a scandal."

Styles of clothing for middle-class men are described as tradition bound, stable, and oriented toward the past (Martin and Koda 1989:9). Not surprisingly, designers of men's business suits find inspiration in the prewar period, particularly the British suit of the early 1930s (Flusser 1989:3). Flusser quotes Yves Saint Laurent, the French fashion designer, as saying that a handful of basic shapes created in the early 1930s still prevail (6). Flusser states: "The thirties could really be considered the time when the American style of dress reached its pinnacle . . . an era during which the foundations of good taste in men's wear were laid" (3).

In the 1980s and 1990s, role models for middle-class men's clothing were film stars of the 1930s and British royalty, most notably Fred Astaire and the Duke of Windsor. Armani, one of the most influential designers of men's wear, considers Fred Astaire to be "the supreme reference of elegance" (Fitoussi 1991). As a salesman at a leading New York men's store commented in 1988: "The past is what's happening" (Hochswender 1988:75).

Recently, the rising cost of the suit and changes in attitudes toward the expression of social class distinctions have restricted its use to a narrow range of upper-middle-class occupations, such as law, finance, and management. Sales of suits declined precipitously in the 1990s (Saporito 1993). Significantly, only 3 percent of American households purchase suits in a given year (American Demographics 1993). In the United States, the most conservative attitudes toward clothing are to be found in investment-banking houses on Wall Street, where the traditional suit is still required as an indication of a man's commitment to his profession (Hochswender 1989). The business suit is beginning to be perceived as a uniform which conceals a person's identity, rather than as a costume which reveals it (Barringer 1990). According to Joseph (1986:66–68), one of the distinguishing characteristics of a uniform is that it suppresses individuality. The tie, conservative or flashy, serves as a indication of the wearer's level of commitment to the message conveyed by the suit.

Until recently, constrained by the clothing norms set by the organizations that employed them, most men were unable to deviate very much from a standard masculine look during the day. The largest share of the clothing budget was likely to be reserved for clothes that were worn at work. While individuals in high status positions wore business suits, clothes for working-class or lower-middle-class occupations were frequently uniforms that indicated the wearer's status instantly, and unambiguously, as, for example, a policeman, a waiter, or an airline steward.

Although classic suit styles based on clothes worn by movie stars and trendsetters in the 1930s through the 1950s remain popular (New York Times 1995; Yardley 1996), changes in the types of clothing preferred by businessmen suggest that the values embodied in leisure activities and expressed in popular culture are beginning to take precedence over the values of the industrial workplace. The increasing tendency of the leisure sphere to encroach on the business sphere, signifying the growth in the symbolic significance of leisure, is suggested by the trend in the 1990s for businessmen in America and Europe to dress less formally, particularly on Fridays (Mathews 1993; Janus, Kaiser, and Gray 1999). This trend was most pronounced in computer and electronic companies on the West Coast but gradually spread to other regions and other occupations (Bondi 1995), producing a variety of costumes reflecting different social milieus within the upper and middle class (Nabers 1995 : 132): "What we have today are many types, often quite distinctive and varying by industry, profession, and region . . . business folk really do dress differently, even when dressing down, depending on whether they work in the Northeast or Northwest, Silicon Valley or the Motor City, not to mention whether they are proprietors, bankers, or lobbyists."

Men's costumes also change as their position in an organization changes or as their employers change. Men who deal with the public outside their companies alter their clothing styles depending upon the social characteristics of the individuals they expect to meet on a particular day. The director of a French banking firm reported: "I try to adopt the image that my associates or my clients expect. I wear a gray suit for a meeting of the board of directors, a more up-to-date get-up for a visit to a construction site, and a shabby old jacket to convince a communist mayor" (Villacampa 1989 : 98).

What differentiates middle-class men's clothing styles today from their counterparts in the second half of the nineteenth century is that styles worn in the workplace coexist with a completely different set of styles for masculine clothing.[3] Leisure activities tend to shape people's perceptions of themselves and are more meaningful than work for many people.[4] These changes are most noticeable in the clothing behavior of youth. Until the 1960s, college and high school students routinely wore suits to their classes (Lee Hall 1992). By the 1960s, these formal outfits had been replaced by the antithesis of the business suit, the blue jean, which became "the uniform of college youth" (O'Donnol 1982). The values expressed by the business suit no longer matched those of the typical college student. During the same period, artists and writers also deserted the values embodied in the business suit and adopted leisure clothing as their work attire. For example, in 1951, when America's leading avant-garde painters, the Abstract Expressionists, were photographed for *Life* magazine, all fourteen wore some version of the business suit (Sandler 1976:frontispiece). Forty-two years later, when art dealer Arnold Glimcher assembled a comparable group for a cover for the *New York Times* magazine, only one of the twelve artists wore a business suit (Schwartzman

1993). Diane Arbus's photographs (Arbus and Israel 1984) of young artists and writers in the 1960s suggest that the transformation in clothing choices was under way in these groups during that period.[5]

In contrast to the business suit, there are no set rules for how most leisure clothes should be worn. These clothes may be modified or even mutilated by the wearer in order to express his personal identity. The meanings of leisure clothes continually change, as can be seen with blue jeans, the most universally worn and widely accepted item of clothing ever made. In the nineteenth and early twentieth centuries, jeans signified physical labor and ruggedness; they were a uniform in which physical labor was performed. Between the 1930s and 1960s, they were adopted by the middle class for vacations on ranches in western states (Foote and Kidwell 1994:74), by working-class women for work and leisure (Olian 1992), and by members of various marginal groups such as motorcycle gangs, artists and painters, leftist activists, and hippies (Gordon 1991:32–34). In this period jeans signified leisure as well as work, but for different social groups. For the middle class, jeans became "an icon for American values of individualism and honesty" (Foote and Kidwell 1994:77). At the same time, jeans acquired connotations of revolt—freedom, equality, and classlessness—against the dominant cultural values. By the 1970s, jeans were widely accepted by both sexes and had become a fashion item whose characteristics changed slightly each year in order to increase sales. Designers altered their shape to highlight their erotic connotations and turned them into a luxury item by increasing their price.

The ease with which new meanings could be attributed to jeans eventually led to a decline in their significance as an icon. As Fiske (1989:2) shows, by the 1980s jeans had ceased to represent a particular class or sex or a particular location, city, or country, although they retained some of their connotations related to the American West (strength, physical labor, sports). There were indications that the myths from the 1950s that had endowed jeans with a special appeal to adolescents were fading. By the late 1980s, a new generation of teenagers was seeking new myths, new identities, and new types of clothing not identified with their parents (Friedmann 1987; Leroy 1994; Normand 1999). Sales of jeans dropped in the late 1990s in favor of other types of apparel, including khakis, chinos, cargo pants, and sweat pants (Tredre 1999).

Like the blue jean, the meanings of another leisure clothing item, the T-shirt, are open; it has been used to convey both rebellion and conformity, depending upon the context and the types of messages that may be inscribed on the front or back. Unlike the blue jean, the T-shirt decorated with lettering or a design appeared in the 1940s (Nelton 1991) and now epitomizes post-modern media culture. Printing on shirts as a means of identifying the wearer with an organization, such as a sports team, appeared in the middle of the nineteenth century and was being used by universities in the 1930s (Giovan-nini 1984:16–17). The use of a specific type of clothing—the T-shirt—to communicate other types of information began in the late 1940s, when faces and political slogans appeared on T-shirts and, in the 1960s, with commercial logos and other designs.[6] Technical developments in the 1950s and 1960s, such as plastic inks, plastic transfers, and spray paint, led to the use of colored designs and increased the possibilities of the T-shirt as a means of communication. Approximately one billion T-shirts are now purchased annually in the United States (McGraw 1996).[7]

The T-shirt performs a function formerly associated with the hat, that of identifying an individual's social location instantly. Unlike the hat in the nineteenth century, which signaled (or concealed) social class status, the T-shirt speaks to issues related to ideology, difference, and myth: politics, race, gender, and leisure. The variety of slogans and logos that appear on T-shirts is enormous (see fig. 46). Much of the time, people consent to being coopted for "unpaid advertising" for global corporations selling clothes, music, sports, and entertainment in exchange for the social cachet of being associated with certain products (McGraw 1996). Some of the time, people use T-shirts to indicate their support for social and political causes, groups, or organizations to which they have made a commitment. Occasionally, the T-shirt becomes a medium for grass-roots resistance. Bootlegged T-shirts representing characters on the television show *The Simpsons* appeared in response to T-shirts marketed by the network that produced the show (Parisi 1993). The bootlegged T-shirts represented the Simpson family as African Americans. Bart Simpson was shown as Rastabart, with dreadlocks and a red, green, and gold headband, as Rasta-dude Bart Marley, and as Black Bart, paired with Nelson Mandela. Using clothing behavior as a means of making a statement, the T-shirts appeared to be intended as an affirmation of African Americans as an ethnic group and as a commentary on the narrow range of roles for black characters in the show. Victims of gender-related violence, such as rape, incest, battering, and sexual harassment, have used T-shirts as venues for statements about their experiences that are exhibited in clotheslines in public plazas (Ostrowski 1996). By contrast, some young men use T-shirts to express hostile, aggressive, or obscene sentiments denigrating women or to display pictures of guns and pistols (Cose 1993; *Time* 1992). Teens of both sexes use them as a means of expressing their cynicism about the dominant culture, particularly global advertising (Sepulchre 1994b).

The significance of the T-shirt in Western culture, as a means of social and political expression, is seen by comparing its roles in Western countries with the response to it in a nondemocratic country, the People's Republic of China (Barmé 1993). In 1991, a young Chinese artist created T-shirts bearing humorous statements, some of which could be interpreted as having mild political implications. The T-shirts were enormously successful with the public but were perceived as "a serious political incident" by the Chinese authorities. The artist was arrested and interrogated, and the T shirts were officially banned. Thousands of them were confiscated and destroyed, although many Chinese continued to wear them.

Despite recent changes in executive dress codes, two very different clothing cultures remain in effect, one representing the world of work and the other representing the world of leisure. Clothes worn in the workplace mark social class hierarchies very precisely. Leisure clothing, by contrast, tends to blur social class differences. Specific garments cannot be neatly ranked according to social class distinctions and have often been derived from working-class occupations, such as the farmer, the factory worker, and the cowboy (Martin and Koda 1989:45). Rich and poor participate in the same stylistic world, which is dominated by images from popular culture and the entertainment media. Leisure clothes are a means of expressing personal identity; they point to a wide variety of concerns, including race, ethnicity, sexual orientation, and gender. Many styles derive from popular music and are often highly androgynous. Leisure styles that originated in the 1950s and 1960s resonate with more traditional macho mythologies, generally American but sometimes with Latin influences, that are associated with male sports and leisure pursuits, such as riding, driving cars or motorcycles, and hunting. A French importer of clothes manufactured by companies such as Go West, Timberland, and Redskins, said: "We make our living from a myth" (Piganeau 1991: 73). Still another set of styles, that appeal to the current generation of adolescents, are based on costumes for newer and more spectacular sports, such as surfing, snowboarding, and sky surfing (Valmont 1994). They are manufactured in new types of synthetic materials that are sometimes recycled or decorated with graphics created by computers.

Worn in conventional workplaces with steep status hierarchies, leisure clothes are anomalous; the absence of clear-cut norms in situations where statuses need to be clearly differentiated leads to confusion and engenders ad hoc solutions that, according to a corporate image consultant, vary "from industry to industry, company to company—even department to department" (Casey 1997; see also Janus, Kaiser, and Gray 1999).

MEN'S CLOTHING BEHAVIOR: A Typology

Are men using clothing codes to create or adopt identities other than those associated with their occupations, in keeping with Bell's argument that outside the workplace contemporary identities are very fluid? A major constraint on the expression of masculine identity in American society is hegemonic norms about masculinity. Contemporary masculinity as expressed in the American media has four principal features (Trujillo 1991): (1) physical power and control that are identified with the male body, (2) heterosexuality, defined by social relationships with men and sexual relations with women, (3) occupational achievement in jobs that are identified as "men's work," and (4) a patriarchal family role. Many men are reluctant to project an image that deviates from these norms. In the popular mind, masculine identity is often perceived as fixed and innate rather than socially constructed. Therefore, attempts to construct an identity through clothing behavior are regarded as suspect, particularly by older men. Being interested in fashion and clothing behavior tends to be interpreted as effeminate (Gladwell 1997b:62). A man who is considered masculine does not need to care about his appearance, because masculinity is not considered to be a function of appearance. However, the young, both male and female, are more fashion conscious and more active consumers of clothing than the middle-aged. An American stylist said: "It's the young who are interested in fashion and stimulate fashion change. The people on the street who influence me most are young people under twenty-five. Older people are most consistent in the way they dress. Their friends expect them to dress in a certain way." Young people respond very rapidly to fads and trends. A fashion forecaster stated: "They're going through a lot of personality changes. They're trying to find themselves and they focus a lot of their personal expression on clothing." Clothes worn by adolescents and postadolescents tend to be more heavily coded than clothes worn by older people.

On the basis of market research and studies of men's clothing behavior, I have identified four types of male clothing behavior that are related to the construction of nonoccupational identities. Most men are likely to use a particular type of behavior most of the time but might occasionally use another type. The primary types of clothing behavior are: (1) "conventional poaching" of items from different sources without altering them and without a conscious commitment to a particular look identified with a subculture, a genre of popular culture, a lifestyle, or fashion trend, (2) "affiliation with a lifestyle," such as a distinctive style of clothing marketed by clothing firms,

(3) "affiliation with a subculture," which puts together its own style of clothing by assembling existing items in a new way that changes their meanings, or by adopting clothing associated with a subvariant of a genre of popular culture, and (4) "sophisticated poaching" of items from different sources, with a conscious commitment to the construction of a particular personal look and to one or more of the roles of egocentric, dandy, and fashion addict.[8]

Conventional poaching is the most prevalent type of clothing behavior for adult men, and sophisticated poaching the least. Adoption of street styles and of clothing behavior that apes that of rock musicians tends to disappear as young men join the workforce and acquire adult responsibilities. Approximately 55 percent of a sample of the French male population (Pujol 1992) were characterized as dressing in a conservative, "classical" manner, in which the expression of personal identity was minimal.[9] The men in this category were mostly middle-aged and had both high and low incomes. Another 23 percent of the sample were young (under thirty), hostile to fashion, preferring clothes that identified them with a clique, a gang, or a group of friends. Men in this category would be likely to follow street styles or, alternatively, styles set by genres of popular music. Twenty-two percent of the sample fit the description of sophisticated poachers. More than half of these men were relatively young and followed assiduously the avant-garde and postmodernist fashions of French luxury fashion designers. The remaining sophisticated poachers were described as "egocentric" and "anticonformist," older than the previous group with relatively high incomes. Their goal was not to follow fashion but to use clothing to express their personalities, sometimes incorporating items that were highly original and avant-garde.

An American typology of shoppers identified three quite similar categories that apply to male shoppers: (1) "fashion foregoers" (= conventional poachers), men who did not care about their appearance, (2) "progressive patrons" (= lifestyle affiliates), who were young or middle-aged couples and wore clothing identified with yuppie lifestyles, and (3) "power purchasers" (= sophisticated poachers), with substantial incomes, who took fashion risks (Piirto 1990). The percentage of men who are interested in fashion is smaller than the comparable figure for women. The French study estimated the percentage of true male customers for fashion as 12.5 percent (Pujol 1992).

A second French study of young men aged twenty-five to thirty-four found three types of clothing behavior that were used together or separately (Piganeau 1994). All of the men purchased clothes for practical reasons, looking for items that were useful and convenient. A second type of behavior was influenced by the men's desire to be part of a group and to be recognized by their peers. For this purpose, they relied on clothing identified with well-known brand names that represented a lifestyle rather than the latest fashion. Their role models were television stars and anchormen rather than rock musicians or film stars. Finally, the study also identified a desire on the part of some of these men to use clothing to express their personal selves, as reflected in items of clothing that had special significance for them and that were not influenced by media role models or fashion.[10]

No matter which type of clothing behavior men adopt, clothes they wear for leisure activities have been influenced by changes during the past half-century in the relationship between leisure, social class, gender, and popular culture. During this period, wearing certain types of clothes became a means of expressing rebellion and of rejecting middle-class values in favor of values and social identities that had not previously been expressed in middle-class clothing. Popular culture provided role models, often identified with the working class, and endowed them with mythical qualities. This is a very different phenomenon from the situation in the nineteenth century, when the clothing of the middle and upper classes represented the norm, which the working class attempted to follow on Sundays. During the same period, women's wardrobes steadily assimilated items of men's clothing, creating new tensions and dilemmas in the construction of gender identity that were experienced differently by each gender (see chap. 7).

POPULAR CULTURE AND THE EXPRESSION OF IDENTITY IN CLOTHING

Over a period of time, through a process that has been called "semiotic layering" (Turim 1985), items of clothing accumulate connotations from many different contexts. This contributes to their usefulness for both creators and consumers of clothing, who can manipulate different meanings in the same garment. Items of clothing whose meanings are relatively "open" are likely to be associated with antonyms, such as work and leisure, or rebellion and conformity, while items of clothing whose images are relatively closed tend to connote a specific meaning, either work or leisure, rebellion or conformity. Blue jeans and T-shirts exemplify the former, while the black leather motorcycle jacket exemplifies the latter.

Items of clothing that were worn in films, on television, or in concerts by popular musicians have acquired meanings associated with these forms of popular culture. In the 1950s, a series of Hollywood films presented a new conception of adolescent identity that millions of teenagers sought to emulate: the myth of the working class rebel.[11] In these films, actors adopted a costume consisting of blue jeans, black leather jackets, and T-shirts. These films expressed adolescent frustrations with working-class existence in such a powerful manner that viewers identified with the actors and adopted their clothing as a statement of defiance. Chenoune (1993:239) commented: "Adolescents . . . were translating these . . . garments, totally devoid of fashion vocabulary or grammar, into the direct expression of their identity crisis."

In this context, blue jeans and T-shirts acquired negative or rebellious connotations associated with the black leather jacket. First used by German military personnel in the First World War (Farren 1985) and later by military personnel on both sides in World War II, the leather jacket was also adopted in the 1940s by adolescent motorcycle gangs in California (Martin and Koda 1989:64) that terrorized small towns. One of the films that later established the leather jacket's significance in popular consciousness — *The Wild One* — recounted a true story involving these gangs. By the 1940s, the jacket had become "a symbol of the road warrior, a man in combat with all positive social forces" (64) Martin and Koda attribute the jacket's symbolic power in part to its color, black, which when worn by men in the twentieth century, has become a symbol of social militancy and rebellion against social norms. Black is worn by rebels of all kinds, political, social, and artistic. The black leather jacket has been adopted by those who wish to express a rebellious stance either aesthetically or politically, but it has not attained the widespread popularity of the blue jean.

In the 1980s and 1990s, advertisers were still using motifs referring to the films and stars of the 1950s that had first given jeans their qualities of resistance to the dominant culture (Foucher 1994:97). The continuing popularity of these clothes and of a particular combination of these clothes (jeans, leather jacket, and T-shirt) suggests that there is something analogous in the adoption of clothes to the ways in which successful films or television series "enable the reader to make a particular kind of sense of his existence." Fiske (1984:194) argues that very popular texts are not simply relaying the dominant culture but allow the audience "to make unproblematic sense of an inherently self-contradictory area of culture."

Popular culture produced an analogous transformation of clothing styles in France in the 1930s (Chenoune 1993:195–98). In an atmosphere in which left-wing governments had been brought to power by an economic crisis and intellectual and artistic circles produced books and films about the working class, the distinctive costumes of the Paris underworld portrayed in French films became the new clothing style of the proletariat. These clothes, as worn by the French actor Jean Gabin, epitomized this style, as Gabin himself epitomized the working-class struggle to define an identity that was not a pale reflection of the middle class. Gabin's films, which glamorized hood-lums, provided the impetus for the acceptance of their clothes by the working class in Paris and, eventually, by other groups of men.

POPULAR MUSIC, URBAN SUBCULTURES, AND THE MEDIA

What is unique about the post–Second World War period is the link between the media and clothing styles, particularly the way in which clothing trends are influenced by street subcultures, whose styles are disseminated through the media. Previously, styles associated with ethnic subcultures were not widely disseminated outside those groups. The zoot suit, worn by African Americans and Chicanos in the 1930s and 1940s (Martin and Koda 1989: 209), and the *zazou* suit, worn by French adolescents during the Second World War, had social and political connotations that were not present in later subcultural styles, because these costumes were restricted at that time to subordinate groups.[12]

According to Martin and Koda (1989:193), "The zoot suit . . . typically consisted of a knee-length coat with broad, square, padded shoulders and peg-top pants that ballooned at the knees and tapered to narrow cuffs." Worn in bright colors (such as sky blue), with matching hat, a long gold watch chain, and monogrammed belt, the zoot suit identified its wearer immediately as part of a nonwhite subculture, because it was available only in black neigh-borhoods and only worn by blacks and Hispanics. The costume was a forceful statement of black identity (Cosgrove 1988); it represented "a subversive re-fusal to be subservient" (Kelley 1992:160) (see fig. 47). The suit "encoded a culture that celebrated a specific racial, class, spatial, gender, and genera-tional identity. East Coast zoot suiters during the war were primarily young black (and Latino) working-class males whose living spaces and social world were confined to northeastern ghettos, and the suit reflected a struggle to negotiate these multiple identities in opposition to the dominant culture."

During the Second World War, race riots erupted as a result of confronta-tions between white soldiers and sailors and nonwhites in zoot suits (Cosgrove 1988); wearing the zoot suit represented resistance to a war that many blacks and Hispanics refused to support. In France, wearing an offshoot of the zoot suit symbolized resistance by French youth to the German occupation (Chenoune 1993:205). Today's subcultural styles carry much less counter-cultural weight, being rapidly coopted by media industries and marketed in a highly developed consumer culture.

By the end of the 1950s, television was a fixture in many American homes, along with a new form of popular music, rock 'n' roll, aimed specifically at adolescents. In later decades, American films, unless bolstered by rock music, gradually lost their power to alter the meanings of specific items of clothing.[13] Instead, a series of youth subcultures centered on popular music transformed the clothing worn by adolescents and young adults. Popular music consists of a great many interrelated genres whose codes are often opaque to outsiders but meaningful to fans, for whom they provide building blocks for the construction of social identities.

Electronic culture worlds, which produce and transmit popular music, have a distinctive structure that is particularly suitable for assimilating information from marginal subcultures and making it available in electronic space, in which regional boundaries do not exist. Unable to produce successful music "in-house," record companies are obliged to monitor audience networks continually in search of new styles and new talent. These companies are loosely linked to social networks that emerge among each generation of adolescents, who seek new styles of music that express their particular mood and point of view (Burnett 1992). Thousands of small bands playing in urban bars and clubs contribute to the development of new styles and the evolution of familiar styles. The same social networks that generate musical improvisation and innovation also produce "street styles" (Polhemus 1994).

Clothing trends derived from popular music come and go very rapidly, transmitted in part by cable television, and spread from the United States to other countries. Huge profits for clothing companies serving the youth market depend on the clothing selections of rap musicians in black neighborhoods (Senes 1997). One firm that started in the early 1990s — Tommy Hilfiger — has become "one of the most successful clothing businesses in the world" (White 1997) by focusing its publicity entirely on the firm's association with popular musicians. Established rock groups rely on fashion designers who specialize in this field to create their clothes and their images, which in some cases become exceedingly elaborate. Jones (1987: 179) offers the following assessment of the fashion designer's role: "Fashion designers refocus and refine rock and art images into precisely marketable products, reinforcing the original sources by echoing them much as the chorus does in a call-and-response gospel song."

However, while music subcultures, both local amateur and professional, often adopt flamboyant or unconventional styles of clothing that draw on a wide range of clothing and theatrical traditions, certain themes as expressed in particular types of garments have continually recurred. The same items that had been popularized in the 1950s films — jeans, T-shirts, and black leather jackets — frequently reappear, either separately or together. The meanings of these garments as established in the 1950s have evolved, but their associations with rebellion or conformity have not changed. Adolescent music subcultures are actually using a visual language that consists of a limited number of "iconic" garments. These garments are used to express rebellion against or affirmation of the dominant culture or, alternatively, symbolic subversion of gender symbols. Contrary to Baudrillard's thesis, it appears that the media have attributed to particular garments specific meanings that are well understood by the teenage public.

In her extensive study of the clothing of rock musicians from its beginnings in the early 1950s to the late 1980s, Jones (1987:11) argues that the meanings of their clothes are necessarily unambiguous: "Fans must know instantly who are the bad boys and girls and who are the good." The clothing of rock stars is a major element in the communication of their musical message. As she shows, black leather with or without blue jeans and T-shirts was almost invariably used by musical groups that assumed the stance of rebels. Blue jeans and T-shirts without black leather were used to signify a group's affirmation of its American identity. These conventions were established by Hollywood films about teenagers in the 1950s even though only one of these films actually used rock music. Using these conventions, rock musicians, such as Elvis Presley, created archetypes of visual presentation in the late 1950s and 1960s that were constantly revived in later decades (Jones 1987: 14, 53). In the 1980s, Bruce Springsteen achieved enormous success using clothing icons from the 1950s: leather coat, western jeans, and T-shirt. Jones (64) states: "The musical heirs have not generally produced new costumes as much as they have worked within the existing types."

According to Jones, only the biggest stars, such as Elvis Presley, were able to alternate between rebel and heroic images. Before they became successful, the Beatles wore jeans and black leather. Success came when they abandoned the rebel look for emasculated Cardin suits and mild sexual subversion in the form of haircuts that were unconventionally long for the period (Jones 1987: 71). Another rock musician who had previously cultivated "an unsavory, demented persona" signaled his shift to a new, more positive image by wearing jeans and a T-shirt (89). Rather than moving from rebel to hero, most rock musicians adopted one image or the other, often paired in the same decade with musicians who had selected the opposite image.[14]

New themes appeared in the 1970s, such as gender subversion and science fiction. David Bowie produced "a radical attack on the way in which dress encodes and prescribes gender" (Evans and Thornton 1989:7). Bowie was the first singer to project a blatantly transvestite image, with dresses, eye makeup, extravagant wigs, and jewelry, providing a new set of visual icons that were copied by many subsequent groups and their fans, sometimes merged with macho themes. In the early 1980s, Bowie's look was revived and extended by trendsetters in London clubs, who in turn influenced the singer Boy George, whose costumes included skirts, a Joan Collins hairstyle, and masses of jewelry. In the late 1980s, a popular look associated with heavy metal combined long hair and jewelry (rings and bracelets) with black leather jackets, tight jeans, boots, and motorcycle helmets (Bischoff 1989).

Punk epitomizes the intricate association that has developed between popular culture, fashion, and adolescent subcultures. In the early 1970s, a highly successful and provocative film about teenagers, A Clockwork Orange, produced in England, popularized images related to science fiction and a look that later became associated with punk. Capitalizing on working-class disillusionment with British society in the early 1970s, designer Vivienne Westwood and music entrepreneur Malcolm McLaren assimilated elements of an emerging street style into a highly rebellious costume associated with punk music. This costume relied in part on the visual language of clothing that had evolved in the previous two decades—the black leather motorcycle jacket, T-shirt, and blue jeans—but added new elements such as metal studs in the jackets, metal-studded belts, safety-pins as earrings and as facial decorations, torn or mutilated jeans, and a distinctive hair style, often worn in bright, unnatural colors (Nordquist 1991). Abuse of the body and clothing expressed derisive and nihilistic attitudes toward establishment values. They used razor-slashed T-shirts, sewn to simulate scars, T-shirts showing the Queen of England with a safety pin through her nose and mouth, and bondage chains (Jones 1987:135–37). In 1975, McLaren organized the first punk band, the Sex Pistols, made up of working-class men from the neighborhood near their clothing store, and dressed them in this style.

Very rapidly, elements of this costume appeared in the collections of luxury fashion designers and in lower-priced lines of clothing. In a process totally different from the history of the zoot suit, a style that began as the expression of extreme nihilism by a small British subculture was adopted worldwide by adolescents as a means of expressing their individual angst. The social and political connotations of the style evaporated; instead, elements of the style continue to be a widely used, free-floating code for the expression of rebellion in clothing that is totally dissociated from the activities and beliefs of contemporary countercultures (Siroto 1993).

By the 1980s, rock groups had thirty years of musical history from which to construct their images of rebellion, transgression, and gender ambiguity. For example, heavy metal groups continued to use the motorcycle leather garb (black leather jackets and jeans), or, alternatively, high heels, leather studded with spikes and nailheads, and sadomasochistic paraphernalia (Jones 1987:115). They assimilated punk music's torn clothing and sadomasochistic elements, along with psychedelic themes represented by headbands, logo T-shirts, and fringes, and Bowie's glam rock mascara, wigs, and jewelry for men (115). In the 1990s, popular music with its huge audience has continued to fractionate, with fashion trends following (Pareles 1993). Each new variation in musical styles engenders new clothing styles, with the result that there are no more universal clothing trends for adolescents and young adults, but instead different styles merge and new ones appear as codes subdivide (Piganeau 1996, 128; Chenoune 1993:301).

STREET STYLES AND YOUTH SUBCULTURES

The clothing behavior of street cultures has been compared to a "magnifying glass," making it possible to observe the fluctuations in people's attitudes and behavior that constitute the character of a particular period of time (Bischoff 1989). Some adolescent subcultures create looks that are so successful at expressing adolescent identity that they are believed to presage the way the average adolescent will dress in later seasons. According to a fashion professional (Valmont 1994:22), "Young people have created their own codes and communicate them to others. They have become the decision makers."

Youth subcultures proliferated in the postwar period, as adolescents and young adults acquired more time and leisure and became a major focus of attention by popular culture industries.[15] Style and appearance are among the most important elements of subcultural identity (Clarke 1976). For adolescents and young adults who do not belong to the workforce, dress is an aspect of their lives that they can control relatively easily and that they can use to make statements about themselves and their attitudes toward their social environment. Borrowing from existing styles and combining them in new ways, they put possessions, clothing, and hairstyles together in such a way as to define an identity that expresses the personal experiences and situation of a particular group. In some cases, the impulse behind the creation of subcultural identities can be interpreted as an expression of resistance to the dominant culture (Hebdige 1979). More frequently, youth subcultures allow a person to experiment with identities, often "prefabricated" and requiring little imagination or effort on his part. Social identities conferred by these subcultures are often transient (Polhemus 1994). Some subcultures are primarily street styles that are little more than fads; some sweep the country; others vary from city to city. In the United States, each city may have its own distinctive version of what is considered "in" or "cool," and this in turn includes numerous subcategories of items worn for different types of activities and in different places. Sometimes distinct age cohorts (fourteen to eighteen, nineteen to twenty-four, twenty-five to thirty) in each city will have their own versions of each style. Street styles are subtle, highly variegated, and constantly changing. As one "cool hunter" put it, "Cool is a set of dialects, not a language" (Gladwell 1997a:86). Youth subcultures exemplify a process of "identity work" that takes place on the individual level during adolescence, in which young people choose or create ways to express their changing understandings of themselves (Brown et al. 1994). Popular music performs an important role in identity creation for contemporary adolescents, because it is the most available and accessible form of media culture for them and, as such, a rich source of cultural meanings and standards to assimilate or resist. The activities of adolescent networks take place in preferred locations, such as specific streets or malls, and are often loosely anchored in organizations, such as specialized clothing shops, clubs, and "fanzines" (newsletters produced by fans) (Chenoune 1993:301). Participants vary in their levels of commitment to a subculture, from those for whom it is a full-time identity to those for whom it is primarily a weekend diversion (Fox 1987).

Because of its ephemeral and transient nature, the "population" of youth subcultures is generally difficult to examine. A museum exhibition in Britain (de la Haye and Dingwall 1996)[16] in 1995 provided a rare opportunity to compare and analyze the themes expressed in the clothing of about fifty groups that appeared in the United States and Britain during the past five decades.[17] The dominant interest of almost half (twenty) of the groups was a style of music, in most cases popular music, but, in a few cases, music identified with an ethnic group. The second-most frequent theme (eight groups) was a sport, including spectacular and sometimes dangerous sports, such as skateboarding, snowboarding, sea surfing, and sky surfing. Fifteen additional themes were each associated with fewer than five groups. These themes included public aspects of identity, such as race, ethnicity, class, political affiliation, and concerns about ecology, and private concerns, such as sexual orientation and drug habits. Cultural influences included technology, the occult, film, and clothing styles themselves, as seen in some of the earliest subcultures, the Mods and the Teddy Boys.

These groups, like most youth subcultures and street styles, used certain types of iconic garments, including jeans, T-shirts, leather jackets, sports clothes, and army surplus clothing, such as military camouflage outfits, and specific types of footwear, including sneakers and boots (see fig. 48). Among the exceptions were the Mods, the Teddy Boys, and the American "preppies," who were models of sartorial elegance in well-tailored suits, frock coats and decorative waistcoats, and blazers with khakis and loafers, respectively. Followers of glam rock and funk favored platform shoes, satin and lamé jumpsuits, jewelry, and heavy makeup. Ethnic groups such as Bhangra from Asia and Caribbean groups preferred bright colors and a mixture of traditional and contemporary styles. Eco groups, devoted to ecological issues, favored recycled, patchwork, and reconstructed clothes.

Subcultural style groups are closely interconnected; new styles typically take their inspiration from several old ones in an intricate and complex chain of influences that resonate with their publics, as suggested by the following descriptions (de la Haye and Dingwell 1996: n.p.):

> The influence came from the late 1960s/early 1970s reggae/yardie scene but also had many other stylistic references, i.e. early sixties Italian, Beatnik, and more subtly, late seventies football casual. This in essence was the reason for its success—*the multitude of meanings to many different types of people.* (italics added)

> The [Techno] style brings together elements of dress from B-boys, Skaters and Rave mixed with army surplus.

> This body-conscious outfit reveals the influences of Cowboy (1940), Rocker (1950), and Glam Disco (1970) styles and appeals to the more glamorous followers of Heavy Metal music. . . . Pseudo-Satanism is featured on logos and jewelry and is worn by a number of subcultures including Glam Rockers, Headbangers and Goths.

Overt political statements are the exception in these groups. Subversion is generally subtle and takes a variety of forms. In many groups, antiestablishment attitudes are expressed by the choice of garments associated with the working class and by the preference for garments that are unclean, unkempt, and disordered. In the 1950s, the Beats' costume (leather jacket with sheepskin lining, cotton plaid shirt, cotton T-shirt, cotton trousers, and army boots) was "perceived . . . as a powerful anti-establishment and antigray-flannel-suit statement" (de la Haye and Dingwell 1996: n.p.). In the late 1970s, the "rockabillies'" "consciously disheveled look . . . borrowed from utilitarian working dress . . . was often adopted in reaction to the overly smart Teddy Boy suit of the previous generation" (n.p.). In the late 1980s, the "travelers" (a "New Age" alternative lifestyle group) wore outfits that combined "secondhand clothing, army surplus and handmade garments. . . . The clothes are threadbare because they are usually worn until they fall apart and their un-washed appearance is the result of an itinerant life spent outdoors" (n.p.).

In other groups, an anti-establishment outlook is expressed through an-drogynist subversion of sexual mores (such as "overt masculinity with femi-nine overtones") or by placing logos of popular consumer items in unfamiliar contexts. In the mid-1960s, "psychedelics" (a counterculture around the hal-lucinogenic drug LSD) "appropriated Establishment attire and irreverently combined it with casual gear to achieve a contemporary peacock look" (n.p.).

A study of how teenagers expressed their identities through the decora-tion of their bedrooms developed a typology of different ways of using mate-rial culture and the media (Brown et al. 1994) that is useful in interpreting how members of youth subcultures use clothing. The first category is "appro-priation" of items of material culture and media images that suit the specific conditions of young people's daily lives. Appropriation is evident in the ways members of subcultures "customize" items they purchase, through the addi-tion of badges, embroidery, and other types of decoration (Gordon 1991:35). A second category is the use of material and media culture to construct im-plausible or unrealistic identities ("fantasy"). A favorite fantasy is pretending to be rock stars by dressing as their "clones" at rock concerts (Bischoff 1989: 95). Third, street stylists engage in various forms of "aesthetic expression." A home-made punk look was achieved "by splattering a man's collarless shirt with paint, slashing the fabric and embellishing it with chains and safety pins. The lower left front was inscribed with 'Sid Vicious'" (de la Haye and Ding-wall 1996: n.p.).

A fourth category is *bricolage*, putting together different items and im-ages to create an original costume that is meaningful to the individual. An additional category that is evident in the behavior of members of youth sub-cultures is "nostalgia." Some teenagers spend hours combing through thrift-shop bins for clothing items from different decades in the recent past, seeking to recreate exactly a style that was popular in previous decades (Polhemus 1994; Bischoff 1989).

The desired appearance is generally the result of a considerable invest-ment of time, effort, and sometimes money. This often generates a strong attachment to specific pieces of clothing, which might be worn for many years or, if not being worn, are carefully preserved for posterity. Sources for clothing include "small specialist retailers, tailors, markets, and mail-order catalogues . . . along with selected large-scale manufacturers whose product is deemed 'authentic'" (de la Haye and Dingwall 1996: n.p.), but many items are homemade. Occasionally clothes are made to order, with clients dictating precise specifications, such as the positions of pockets and buttons.

As a result, clothing within a particular subculture is not uniform. There are numerous variations, depending upon region, time period, and the idiosyncrasies of individual tastes. For many, the goal is to create styles of dress that are different from those of their peers and from the marketing campaigns of manufacturers or the dictates of most fashion professionals (Gladwell 1997a:84). The result is a highly diverse set of styles that mix time periods and genres but require a very practiced eye to identify.

In other situations, the goal is to succeed in the competition to acquire the latest fashionable items being marketed by the fashion industry before their peers or members of rival groups. Not all subcultures reject the dominant culture. Some street clothing is based on the use of prestigious fashion labels, such as Ralph Lauren, Louis Vuitton, Gucci, Chanel, Moschino, Versace, and Armani (de la Haye and Dingwall 1996: n.p.). In the early 1980s, British "Casuals" were "devoted to expensive labels which were changed continually in order that rival factions might 'out cool' each other" (n.p.). In France, brands of "junior" sportswear, emblazoned with trademarks and slogans, became cult objects for working-class adolescents (Chenoune 1993: 308). In London, West Indian teenagers used baggy jeans made by a French sportswear label to imitate an American rap star (309). When the original items are unattainable, members of these types of subcultures sometimes resort to fakes, which are in fact a form of appropriation. Amongst American "hip-hoppers," "brand consciousness and relentless competition . . . eventually led to individual customization. Tailors . . . took the most expensive and conservative designs of coveted labels and added an extra twist of 'street flavor' . . . in what became known as 'ghetto couture'" (n.p.).

In the mid-1990s, black teenagers at a low-income, inner-city high school in Philadelphia were wearing styles of name-brand clothing that were virtually identical to those worn by wealthy undergraduates on the University of Pennsylvania campus in the same city (Akom 1997). Some black inner-city adolescents purchase as many as twelve pairs of sneakers per year (Gladwell 1997a). The children in African-American families have been described as having "a much greater awareness of fashion and being in style" than white children (American Demographics 1993:10). Black adolescents are more likely than white adolescents to define their masculine identities through fashion. They tend to wear clothing styles that are identified with their race and that therefore identify the young men with their race (Wilson and Sparks 1996:417). Black American households spend 75 percent more than white households on boys' clothing (American Demographics 1993:10). The importance of wearing certain types of items or certain brands of clothing is reflected in the problem of theft and violence related to clothing in black public schools (Holloman et al. 1996:267). Since the late nineteenth century, clothes have had a special significance in African-American culture, in part because of the importance attached by both men and women to personal appearance on the streets in black neighborhoods and churches (White and White 1998). A major source of entertainment for both sexes was walking through their neighborhoods, displaying their own clothing and observing that of others. Young men particularly took great pride in being stylishly dressed.

As some street styles draw from fashion, luxury and industrial fashion "borrow" ideas from street styles. Stylistic innovation often begins outside the mainstream among minorities and categories of people who are perceived and who perceive themselves as marginal to the dominant culture. Luxury fashion designers continually recycle themes from styles associated with punk, rap, and grunge (Spindler 1996a; Polhemus 1994). Street looks that have become commonplace in American cities may become leading motifs of a Paris designer's show. A fad for baggy pants that was picked up by many American and French designers originated as a symbol of identification among Los Angeles street gangs and was first marketed by tiny firms whose designers were in their early twenties (Horyn 1992). Fashion innovators often emerge from communities in urban areas that are "seedbeds" for other types of innovation, such as popular music and the arts. In order to be disseminated to a larger audience, their innovations have to be discovered and promoted. "Secondary" innovators tend to be small firms that are created by people who belong to the communities in which the innovations originated (Branch 1993). If the style shows signs of becoming popular, large firms begin to produce their versions of it and to market them aggressively.

Industrial fashion is guided entirely by consumer demand, specifically what consumers in a particular age group want. According to the design director of a major industrial clothing firm, "There is no question of imposing a style on the public. On the contrary, it is necessary to perceive and to anticipate hidden demand" (Piganeau 1989). To find out how young people are responding to fashion, scouts from clothing companies take hundreds of photographs outside elementary and high schools. They comb streets and clubs for ideas and hire adolescents as consultants (Branch 1993:118). Some use "cool hunters," who observe and interview adolescents in suburbs and poor urban neighborhoods (Gladwell 1997a).

Fashion creation must tap into a wide range of clothing styles in its relentless quest for something that is new or can be made to appear new. There is a curious and ironic chain of influences in which some designers of men's wear adapt ideas from the clothes of adolescent audiences, who are in turn aping rock musicians, who off-stage are among the most faithful customers of the leading designers.

SOPHISTICATED POACHING: The Modern Dandy

The fourth category in the men's clothing typology is "sophisticated poaching." Although a minority of the male population engages in sophisticated poaching, it is the most complex form of clothing behavior and has a long history. In the nineteenth century, men with sufficient means devoted themselves to dressing in an eccentric manner which often involved the adoption of fabrics and ornamentation associated with feminine dress. Laver (1968: 51) describes Benjamin Disraeli (later prime minister) around 1830 as wearing "green velvet trousers, a canary-colored waistcoat, low shoes, silver buckles, lace at his wrists . . . a profusion of rings . . . and long black ringlets." Later in the nineteenth century, the American artist James McNeill Whistler wore "white duck trousers . . . patent leather pumps, sometimes with colored bows . . . and in evening dress . . . a salmon-colored handkerchief protruding from his waistcoat (92).

Like his counterparts in the nineteenth century, the contemporary dandy is generally associated with the arts — novelists, poets, and painters — or with popular culture, which now means advertising, film, television, and popular music. The use of "feminine" clothing is confined to a few details in a particular outfit. For example, the dandy adopts colors associated with women such as white and pastels, particularly pink or pale blue. Other examples of feminine details include flowered prints for shirts and ties or as decoration on vests and suit jackets, the use of ruffles, bows, and lace for collars and cuffs, or exceptionally conspicuous handkerchiefs (Martin and Koda 1989:191).

As part of the movement toward sexual liberation that occurred in the 1960s, gay subcultures were able to flourish more openly in Europe and the United States. Members of these subcultures questioned existing definitions of masculinity and femininity and experimented with gender identities and lifestyles (Segal 1990:147, 146). By the mid-1970s, these subcultures were large enough to constitute markets for cultural products that formerly were stigmatized as effeminate. Using a technique that has been dubbed "gay window" advertising, advertisers targeted them using specific cues that are meaningful to gays but often unrecognized by straight men, in advertisements aimed at mainstream audiences (Clark 1993:188).[18] As sophisticated poachers, members of gay subcultures became tastemakers for the rest of the population, popularizing products (including perfume and jewelry for men), clothes, and haircuts (Segal 1990:155).

They were not necessarily effeminate or androgynous. In some gay subcultures, gay men attempted to look more masculine than straight men, affecting a look that included leather and denim, boots, short hair, and mustaches. At the same time, many heterosexual men were becoming more fashion conscious and more androgynous in their appearance (Segal 1990: 149). The gay minority, like the African-American minority, is an important source of stylistic innovation for appearances constructed to express leisure identities. Once they have been assimilated by the dominant culture, these items lose the specific connotations that they possessed for members of gay subcultures (Freitas, Kaiser, and Hammidi 1996:99).

A relatively late by-product of changes in men's attitudes and behavior toward sexuality, women, and their own bodies, French designer fashion for men emerged in the early 1980s (Chenoune 1993:302). It comments on changes that have taken place in men's perceptions of themselves and of their sexual roles and pushes for further change. Viewed with considerable distrust by most men (Piganeau 1994:33; Spencer 1992:45; Costil 1991; Pujol 1994), the designer fashion clientele is drawn primarily from sophisticated poachers. Many of the traditional items in the dandy's wardrobe appear in these collections: white suits, patterned or flowered vests, knickers and plus fours, lace collars and cuffs, embroidery, and feminine materials such as satin and silk (see fig. 49). While previously the dandy had worn white or black with discreet touches of bright color, avant-garde designers in the late 1980s and early 1990s began to show suits and jackets in bright colors formerly reserved for women: salmon, yellow, and turquoise. This was seen by fashion commentators as breaking one of the last boundaries separating male and female fashion (Menkes 1990). Colors other than black, dark gray, and dark blue had not been used in men's fashion (other than sportswear) since the middle of the nineteenth century.[19]

European luxury fashion design for men is in the vanguard of changes in the expression of men's sexual identity. For approximately the past one hundred years, the expression of sexuality in men's clothes has been largely taboo, while women's clothes throughout the period remained sexually expressive. In the 1970s, sportswear in the form of the blue jean provided a form of sexual expression for men. In the 1980s, a few designers attempted to deal with the theme of sexual expressiveness for men in other ways. Pants were skin tight and, in some cases, completely open on one side from ankle to thigh. This was another men's style that had been dormant since the early nineteenth century, when "inexpressibles" were very tight.[20] Shorts, Bermudas, and tight-fitting bicycle pants for city use were other examples of the ways in which men's bodies were being revealed. Miniskirts and minishorts were designed to reveal rather than conceal the genitals.[21] Long hair in the form of eighteenth-century powdered wigs completed the allusions to femininity. In the late 1980s, French designer Jean-Paul Gaultier revived the codpiece, sometimes with lace trim, revealed polka-dotted boxers (a staple of the gay subculture for half a century, according to Savage [1988:168–69]), bared models' torsos or partially hid them behind a "grille" of military braiding, and used tight-fitting T-shirts. The objective was to present the male as a sex object. These challenges to hegemonic masculinity continued in the 1990s, using materials and accessories identified with women, such as costume jewelry, satin ribbons, pink gingham checks, and pale blue nylon tops (Sabas 1999). According to one designer, "Whether clothes are for men or women is all in the head" (Menkes 1999).

While, in the past, men's fashion supported dominant cultural norms about the expression of male identity and sexuality, contemporary men's avant-garde fashion participates in a discourse that cross-cuts popular music and gay subcultures. This discourse is attempting to push men beyond androgyny, normalizing rather than marginalizing the dandy. In this sense, men's fashion design is identifying itself with the margins rather than the center of contemporary culture, particularly in the United States. In France, a small percentage of the population (perhaps 5–10 percent) use "cross wear," which involves the exchange of clothes between men and women (Piganeau 1999). Sixty-three percent of the French population have positive attitudes toward homosexuality, compared with 20 percent in a recent American study (Jaffré 1999; Wolfe 1998:46). The average American is less accepting of homosexuals than of any other minority group (Wolfe 1998). An advertising executive commented on men's luxury fashion advertisements: "They're trying to remold how people think about gender. . . . But you can't be successful at advertising by trying to re-create the human condition. You can't alter men's minds, particularly on subjects like sexuality. It'll never happen" (Gladwell 1997b:64).

CLOTHING BEHAVIOR, EXPENDITURES, AND WARDROBES IN THE LATE TWENTIETH CENTURY

In a postmodern society, in which men are concerned with redefining and renegotiating their images, as postmodernist theory suggests, clothing might be expected to constitute a more important expenditure than in an industrial society where a person's image was presumably more consistent, necessitating a lower level of expenditure for clothing. At first glance, this seems not to be the case. Since 1900, statistics indicate that the portion of personal expenditures spent on clothing in the United States has steadily declined, from 13.7 percent in 1900 to 6.4 percent in 1990 (Lebergott 1993:91). Most of this decline has occurred since 1950.

However, figures on declining personal expenditures allocated for clothing mask the increase in per-capita expenditure (measured in 1987 dollars) in the United States as consumption has increased and personal income has expanded. Per-capita expenditures on clothing have increased 4.5 times since 1900 (see table 6.1). The period when the largest increase in per-capita expenditures occurred was 1960–90 (1.5 times), while relatively little change occurred between 1930 and 1950. By comparison, expenditures on recreation, another means of expressing personal identity, have increased even more than expenditures for clothing (11.4 times since 1900 and 2.5 times since 1960). Per-capita expenditures on food have been relatively stable: they have increased only 70 percent since 1900 and 21 percent since 1960 (see table 6.1).

Changes in the types of clothing that were purchased are also indicative of the social and cultural changes that were occurring. Studies in France revealed changes in the styles of clothing worn by members of different social classes. Herpin and Verger (1988:52) identified two principal styles of clothing, classic and sport. The former included the business suit and its accessories; the latter included clothing for sports and other leisure activities. In the 1950s, men in all social classes in France selected clothing items defined as classic. In the 1980s, the middle class continued to purchase traditional,

TABLE 6.1

INCREASES IN PER-CAPITA EXPENDITURES IN THE UNITED STATES FOR CLOTHING, RECREATION, AND FOOD, 1900–1990 (in percentages)

		Clothing			
	Clothing	Men	Women	Recreation	Food
1900–20	54	—	—	120	−11
1930–50	5	7	2	32	26
1960–90	150	120	160	250	21
Totals, 1900–90	450	—	—	1,140	70

Note: Table is based on figures contained in Lebergott (1993:148–63).

classic styles of clothing, though in smaller amounts than before, and were also buying substantial quantities of sports clothes. However, the working class now opted almost exclusively for the latter despite reductions in the cost of men's suits and other items of classic apparel (Herpin 1986:72–73; Herpin and Verger 1988:51–52, 55). Since business suits are primarily worn in the workplace, these data are consistent with the thesis that occupational clothing is class coded, but leisure clothing is not.[22]

Similar changes took place in the United States. In 1950, middle-class men were buying suits somewhat more frequently than working-class men (one suit every two years as compared with one suit every three years). By 1988, middle-class men were buying suits and sport coats twice as often as working class men (Brown 1994:383). However, by 1973, working-class men were buying larger quantities of leisure clothes, such as jeans, sports shirts, and sports clothing, compared with middle-class men.[23] Assuming that sports clothes reflect a postmodernist sensibility more than business clothes, these findings suggest that the working class has increased its consumption of clothing with postmodernist connotations, while the middle class has retained its consumption of styles of clothing identified with industrial society.

In both countries, after 1960, women's per-capita expenditures for clothing increased substantially more than men's. In the United States, women's per-capita expenditures increased 1.6 times and men's 1.2 times (see table 6.1). In 1990, American women were spending almost twice as much on clothing as men (Lebergott 1993:162). In France, by 1984, women were spending 30 percent more than men (Herpin and Verger 1988:48). An explanation for these differences between men and women is suggested by recent psychological studies indicating that women are likely to be more adept than men at deciphering the increasingly diverse codes underlying fashion (Gladwell 1997b). These studies show that men prefer to process information selectively from, for example, advertising or personal encounters and are particularly likely to ignore nonverbal information. Unlike men, women attempt to synthesize a variety of clues embedded in both visual and verbal materials by integrating different types of information. Consequently, women are more likely to excel at the highly skilled decoding the postmodern fashion context requires. This in turn may be reflected in clothing behavior.

CONCLUSION

Since clothing choices are one of the ways in which people make sense of their personal lives, men's selections of clothing express their interpretations of their social positions. Men's clothing behavior is a barometer of social and cultural changes that indicate the emergence of a postindustrial society. Changes in men's clothing behavior in the postwar period reveal changes in the relationships between social classes and between age groups. Hierarchical relationships between social classes are reflected in clothing worn in the workplace, but, outside the workplace, leisure activities have become increasingly important and are characterized more by age-graded than by class-coded clothing. Clothes intended for younger age groups are becoming increasingly differentiated from those oriented toward middle-aged adults. In Europe, as well as the United States, age has become the most important factor in selling clothes (Guyot 1999). In contrast to the 1950s, industrial fashion today is oriented primarily toward the tastes of the young.

This type of age segmentation will continue in the future as the population ages. Instead of the upper class seeking to differentiate itself from other social classes, the young seek to differentiate themselves from the middle-aged and the elderly. As trends diffuse to older age groups, younger age groups adopt new styles. At the same time, each of the major consumer groups will continue to be divided into numerous lifestyles, which will vary in turn by region.

In this age-graded culture, the poor and the underprivileged, formerly perceived as passive recipients of the dominant culture, have under certain circumstances become fashion leaders. The postmodern construction of nonoccupational identities through clothing appears most strongly among the young and among racial and sexual minorities, whose members view themselves as marginal or exceptional in relation to the dominant culture. Designer fashion for men attempts to extend the boundaries of acceptable forms of sexual expression for men. The rest of the male population dresses conservatively in the workplace, although leisure clothing is gradually replacing traditional business clothing.

The nature of clothing itself has undergone important changes. In the nineteenth century, the hat expressed social status, actual or desired. In the twentieth century, clothes worn in the workplace express social status, while leisure clothes, particularly the T-shirt, express other attributes of the individual's identity. Jeans and T-shirts express disparate meanings, but a major item of men's clothing, the business suit, is "closed." Its range of meanings has steadily narrowed. At the same time, certain types of clothing that have acquired closed but strongly negative connotations, such as the black leather motorcycle jacket, have been used as symbolic challenges to the dominant culture.

42. *"Pauperist" style by Jean Colonna (1994). The construction of the jacket is deliberately imperfect. Courtesy of Marcio Madeira*

43. *Postmodernist reconstruction of fashion history, combining elements of a seventeenth-century musketeer's costume (jacket, boots, and hat) with a miniskirt and train (John Galliano, 1992). Courtesy of Marcio Madeira*

44. *Nudity in luxury fashion design (Martine Sitbon, 1992). Courtesy of Marcio Madeira*

45. *Androgynous costume incorporating ribbon tie and boater from the nineteenth-century "alternative" style (Yves Saint Laurent, 1996). Courtesy of Marcio Madeira*

46. *T-shirts expressing a variety of themes. (1) "Things to Do," an ironic comment on social and ecological activists. (LoF Inactive Wear.) (2) "Sisters for Life," used in a campaign to increase awareness of AIDS among black female adolescents in Boston, 1993. (3) "Bob Marley," for fans of the late reggae singer. Many T-shirts express themes related to popular music. (4) T-shirts showing surfers are very popular among practitioners of the sport on the West Coast of the United States. (Model: Eric Ruelas.) (5) "Be happy." (6) "Garlic Eater's Anonymous," a T-shirt for a very specific constituency. Courtesy of Still 'n Motion Picture Company, Phoenix, AZ (1, 3, 4, 5); Massachusetts Department of Public Health HIV/AIDS Education Bureau, Boston, and Colette Phillips Communications, Needham, MA (2); and Tilka Design, Minneapolis (6)*

47. *The zoot suit expressed African-American and Hispanic men's "pride, defiance, and yearnings" in the face of persecution and subordination (Chibnall 1985:61). This is a 1994 replica by Chris Sullivan of a 1943 zoot suit. Photo by Daniel McGrath. Courtesy of the Victoria and Albert Picture Library, London*

48. *"Psychobilly" subcultural style outfit incorporates references to several street-culture icons, such as the black leather jacket, T-shirt, ripped jeans, and Doc Martens' boots (UK), 1980. Photo by Daniel McGrath. Courtesy of the Victoria and Albert Picture Library, London*

49. *A contemporary French dandy, wearing costume jewelry and earrings, as visualized by Jean-Paul Gaultier (1996). Courtesy of Marcio Madeira*

50. Vogue *fashion editorial photograph (1947). The model is shown with the standard ac-cessories of the period: gloves, hat, purse, and umbrella. The importance of domestic pursuits is suggested by the knitting in her purse.*

Spring's attitude
for evening?
Seductive
nonchalance
in clothes cropped
or draped
to bare the body's
sexiest joint:
the shoulder.
Photographed
by Mario Testino.

51. Vogue *fashion editorial photograph: "Strap Happy" (1997). Photo by Mario Testino*

52. Vogue *clothing advertisement: Chanel (1997). Photo by Karl Lagerfeld*

53. Vogue *fashion editorial photograph: two women (1997). Photo by Steven Meisel*

54. Vogue *clothing advertisement: Donna Karan (1997).*

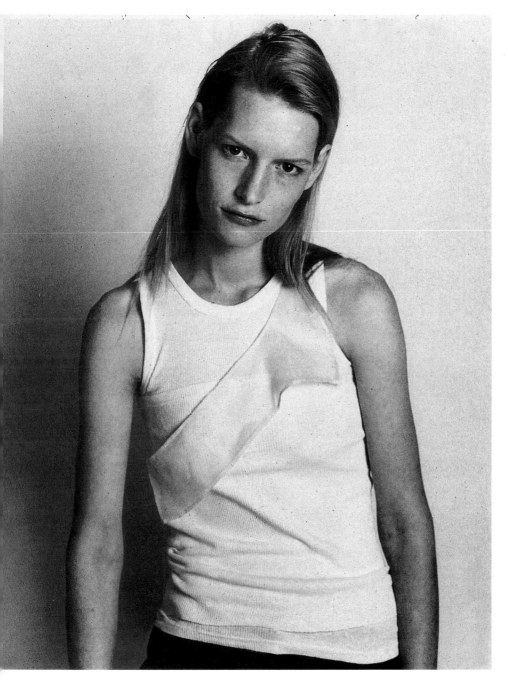

55. Vogue *clothing advertisement: Helmut Lang (1997). Model: Kirsten Owen; photo by Bruce Weber*

416

56. Vogue *fashion editorial photograph: woman lying down* (1997). *Photo by Steven Meisel*

57. Vogue *clothing advertisement: Carolina Herrera (1997).*

58. Vogue *fashion editorial photograph: black model* (1997). *Photo by Bruce Weber*

The increasingly intricate links between subcultural fashion and two major popular culture industries — music and clothing — take two forms. On the one hand, industrial popular culture (film, popular music) has endowed certain types of clothing with subversive meanings, which members of urban subcultures continue to use. On the other hand, new ideas generated by these subcultures are continually co-opted and recycled by various forms of media culture and the clothing industry, but the level of subcultural subversion is diminished. By contrast, in the past, because the ethnic subcultures in which the zoot suit, for example, flourished were more isolated from the dominant culture than today, the use of the zoot suit was restricted to members of those subcultures and was able to communicate a more powerful political message.

In comparison with the nineteenth century, late twentieth-century clothing codes are more complex. Nineteenth-century codes were primarily based on distinctions related to class and region. In cities, class codes were easy to recognize and interpret, although many people did not have the means to dress in the style of the middle class. Regional codes were irrelevant in cities, as were the codes governing the clothing of ethnic subgroups, whose members were generally immigrants and, consequently, marginal.

At the end of the twentieth century, clothes worn for different types of occupations are relatively easy to decipher. The basic distinction, as summarized by Spencer (1992:47), is between men "who wear suits to work and those who don't." However, the "street" is much more chaotic in its clothing codes than in the nineteenth century. Leisure clothes are more difficult than occupational clothes to read, because they are a vehicle for self-expression and a greater variety of codes is operating.[24]

The shift to a postindustrial social structure with a postmodern media culture has increased possibilities for self-expression and diminished traditional social and organizational constraints. In this new type of cultural terrain, cultural codes have proliferated, as groups seek to establish cultural niches in which their members can selectively assimilate cultural influences emanating from the media and from their immediate environments. The result is a complex, multicode culture of which leisure clothes are one example. Specific items are understood by those who use them but not necessarily by all those who merely encounter them. Nevertheless, the street is not postmodernist in Baudrillard's sense of the term; codes are not inherently ambiguous or meaningless, although many codes are opaque for most people.

NOTES

1. Comparable rules governing appropriate hemlines for women's clothes have disappeared.

2. According to experts, there is an appropriate size for each of these details—lapels: 3.5′; vents in jackets: 7′–9′ (depending upon a man's height); and size of trouser cuffs: 1.63′–1.75′ (Flusser 1989:32, 36, 51).

3. Leisure clothes for the upper class existed in the nineteenth and early twentieth centuries, but they were similar to the business suit in that their styles were dictated by precise rules.

4. Marx observed that leisure was more meaningful than work for members of the working class; this observation could be generalized to members of other classes today.

5. The photographic records of the Magnum photographers, a small organization of leading photographers from a number of countries, reveal the gradual shift in the nature of their attire at their annual meetings, from dark business suits in the 1930s through the 1950s to the adoption of leisure attire in the 1970s and 1980s (Manchester 1989).

6. The first short-sleeved T-shirts—white, crew-necked, and without lettering or designs—were marketed by Sears, Roebuck in 1938 (Giovannini 1984:14, 17). Green T-shirts without lettering were used by the American military during the Second World War; some soldiers added their own lettering. Long-sleeved cotton T-shirts were first manufactured in France at the beginning of the twentieth century and were used by the American military in the First World War.

7. Europeans consume fewer T-shirts than Americans. They buy an average of 1.5 T-shirts per person per year compared with 6.5 per person purchased annually by Americans (Germain 1997).

8. "Poaching" refers to the ways in which readers interpret material in texts to suit their own interests and needs (Jenkins 1992). It implies assimilating items without modifying them, as compared with "bricolage," which is more characteristic of subcultures that put existing items together in such a way that their original meanings are modified (Hebdige 1979).

9. The study was based on 2,800 interviews with men aged fifteen and over (Pujol 1992:39).

10. For a study of personal clothing that had special significance for women, see Kaiser, Freeman, and Chandler (1993).

11. These films include: *The Wild One* (with Marlon Brando), *Rebel without A Cause* (with James Dean), and *Jailhouse Rock* (with Elvis Presley).

12. In 1948, mainstream men's suit styles adopted a modified form of the zoot style (Chibnall 1985:61).

13. T-shirts and other types of clothes related to themes in the story lines of Hollywood "blockbuster" films in the 1980s and 1990s have sold very well, but these products have not produced a widespread transformation in popular styles.

14. Examples of this phenomenon include Michael Jackson and Prince, Bob Dylan and Jim Morrison (Jones 1987:99, 166).

15. Youth subcultures are generally defined as subgroups with identifiable social structures, distinctive sets of shared beliefs and values, and characteristic rituals and modes of symbolic expression.

16. The exhibition focused on specific outfits belonging to members of these sub-cultures, which were obtained through personal contacts and from specialty stores, sec-ondhand clothing stores, and designers serving these markets. The objective of the exhi-bition was to present a broad overview of subcultural clothing styles. For a discussion of recent trends in styles worn by youth cultures in France, see Mopin (1997).

17. Polhemus (1994) lists forty-five street styles, ten of them not included in De la Haye and Dingwell (1996). When asked with what style they identified, a national sample of French boys and men aged twelve to twenty-four named thirty-five labels, although many were mentioned by a tiny percentage (Piganeau 1988; see also Obalk, Soral, and Pasche 1984).

18. These ads often rely on sartorial signs that gays use to identify themselves to other gays in public places, such as bootlaces or a bandanna of a certain color or the way a particular type of garment may be buttoned or unbuttoned (Freitas, Kaiser, and Hammidi 1996:96).

19. Byrde (1979:72): "Colour and decoration, so noticeably absent from twentieth century men's suits, were usual until the middle of the nineteenth century. Both silks and cloth in bright colors were worn by men in the seventeenth and eighteenth centuries and although black or dark-coloured cloth became fashionable at the beginning of the nine-teenth century, shades of blue, green, red and white were still worn for evening wear for the first few decades."

20. D'Orsay, a French dandy in the early nineteenth century, is described by Laver (1968:55) as wearing "a sky-blue cravat, yards of gold chain, white French gloves, light drab greatcoat lined with velvet of the same colour, invisible inexpressibles (trousers), skin-coloured and fitting like a glove."

21. The market for experiments in the presentation of masculine gender identity is small, as suggested by sales of 3,000 men's skirts from Gaultier's collection in 1984 (Chen-oune 1993:302). Worn with boots and over trousers in New York City, skirts on men were said to attract little attention in the mid-1980s (New York Times 1985).

22. What is missing in Herpin's analysis is the role of uniforms in the wardrobes of employed working-class men and women.

23. See Brown (1984:287). Similar data for 1988 do not appear in Brown's book.

24. On the basis of a study of informants' interpretations of conventional and uncon-ventional outfits, McCracken (1988:64–67) argues that clothing codes are extremely lim-ited in what they can communicate. Alternatively, it can be argued that clothing codes are very diverse and that respondents' interpretations of specific combinations of clothing are inhibited by their inevitable lack of familiarity with codes used by social groups other than their own.

In postmodern culture, only a picture can testify that we exist, that we matter.
Tetzlaff (1993:262)

7 FASHION IMAGES AND THE STRUGGLE FOR WOMEN'S IDENTITY

At the end of the twentieth century, the goal of fashion is to project images that are intended to attribute meanings to items of clothing, as well as to propose changes in the cut, shape, or color of garments. Images created by fashion designers in their seasonal shows and in their stores coexist with images of clothing created by photographers for fashion magazines, advertisements, and catalogues of clothing manufacturers, and with images of women projected on television, in film, and in music videos. These image makers scavenge a wide range of sources, from the history of film, television, and the arts to street cultures, gay subcultures, and pornography (Kaplan 1987; Myers 1987).

In the nineteenth century, the primary focus of designers and purveyors of fashion was on the clothing itself rather than the use of clothing to evoke distinctive images. Fashionable clothes were displayed in highly stylized drawings in fashion magazines; photographs were not used until the end of the century (Breward 1994:88). Armed with considerable expertise in dressmaking, regardless of whether they made their own clothes, most women examined these fashion plates from the point of view of reproducing the clothes themselves or having them reproduced by others.

Not only are fashionable clothes themselves now less important than the images the clothes are intended to convey, but images of women projected by fashion designers and fashion magazines are very different from the innocuous images of women associated with fashion, even in the relatively recent past, as seen in Barthes's (1983) study of a French fashion magazine in the late 1960s. Today, fashion, as presented in fashion magazines, has several diverse and inconsistent social agendas. Fashion photographers have synchronized their themes and images with those that circulate in youth cultures and that are disseminated by the media, particularly of rock music. The content of popular music and its videos is heavily oriented toward subversion: drugs, crime, violence, sexual orientations that are not widely accepted, and negative attitudes toward women. Rape, abuse, and humiliation of women are staples of many music lyrics, particularly in rap. In music videos, women are frequently portrayed as sex objects, partially nude, and the object of overt sexual advances as well as the "male gaze" (Signorielli, McLeod, and Healy 1994).[1] As one feminist writer commented, "In virtually all rock videos, the female body is offered to the viewer purely as a spectacle, an object of sight, a visual commodity to be consumed" (Bordo 1993:312). In the 1990s, drug subcultures influenced fashion photographers, partly because of the photographs of Nan Goldin, resulting in shots of "concentration-camp-thin models with pasty complexions sporting blackened eyes, limp hair, and designer outfits" (Summer 1996:14; Brubach 1997; Spindler 1997).

The level of subversion in fashion imagery has also risen, as fashion designers and photographers have incorporated themes from S&M and pornography. This has resulted in trends for items such as underwear as outwear and body piercing, as well as fashion photographs and clothing advertisements that incorporate poses from pornographic publications (Steele 1996). These poses include sexual cues, such as closed eyes, open mouth, legs spread to reveal the genital area, and nudity or seminudity, particularly in the areas of the breasts and genitals (Myers 1987). A study of advertisements in fashion magazines covering a ten-year period, from 1985 to 1994, found a substantial increase in the extent to which parts of women's bodies were exposed and their bodies were shown in low-status, animal-like positions (Plous and Neptune 1997).

An alternative fashion agenda that appears in fashion magazines is to portray women as empowered and successful, capable of achieving goals and managing others (Davis 1992). Here women are likely to be presented wearing business suits and other costumes derived from masculine attire. Still another agenda is to present the assumed reader of the magazine as a postmodernist role player who "produces a self through a proliferation of theatrical roles created through a judicious use of costume and masquerade" (Rabine 1994:64). Here a woman is not conceptualized as a fixed identity but as a creator of "heterogeneous and contradictory" identities when experimenting with clothes and products, such as perfume, that project different images of herself (Partington 1996:215; Rabine 1994). From the perspective of postmodernist theories of gender, which view gender as constructed through playacting and performance (Butler 1990), female gender may be performed in different ways. This perspective implies an important role for fashion in providing the wherewithal for commenting upon, parodying, and destabilizing gender identities, without necessarily alleviating the social constraints imposed by gender .

Rabine (1994) argues that this concern with adopting and changing identities is also encouraged by other types of content that have appeared in the magazine since the early 1970s. The *Vogue* reader is exposed in the pages of the magazine to discussions and debates about social and political issues, both those affecting her directly, such as the Equal Rights Amendment and abortion rights, and those affecting her less directly. The magazine no longer attempts to preserve a protected, apolitical space for women in which they perform conventional roles. Instead it encourages women to adopt a "masculine subjectivity" regarding the social order and social problems involving women within that social order while at the same time showing them how to view and present their bodies according to masculine interpretations of female sexuality embodied in the dominant culture.

In this chapter, I will use women's responses in focus groups to representations of gender in fashion photographs and clothing advertisements to explore whether their perceptions of themselves correspond to the ways women are represented in these images. Do they see themselves as being able to project identities offered by the fashion press, or do they seek clothing that corresponds to their own conception of their identities? How do they interpret complex visual messages that represent a highly conflicted dominant culture in which female identity is subject to continual negotiation? In the past, fashion has been viewed as hegemonic by encouraging women to be dissatisfied with their appearance and to make regular changes in their clothing in order to conform to changing definitions of style. As fashion ceases to represent a social ideal and instead disseminates a variety of choices, some of them representing marginal lifestyles, can fashion still be said to be hegemonic?

IS CONTEMPORARY FASHION HEGEMONIC?

Fashion has generally been seen as exerting an obligation to conform that weighs heavily on the female population (Wolf 1991). Lakoff and Scherr (1984:114) claim that fashion photographs generate enormous dissatisfaction among women because they create unrealistic expectations that most women are unable to meet. However, recent changes in the nature of fashion, in the content of fashion magazines, and in the ways women perceive fashion and fashion magazines raise questions about the accuracy of this interpretation.

The nature and presumed effects of images of women in the media, particularly in advertising, have been the subject of numerous studies and intense debate for several decades (Plous and Neptune 1997). Feminists argue that media images of women are always directed at men. They view hegemonic femininity as incorporating masculine standards for female appearance that emphasize physical attributes and sexuality. Images that express hegemonic femininity present women in sexualized and demeaning poses (Davis 1997). Media images are constructed for the male spectator's gaze and embody his expectations of women and of male-female relationships (Mulvey 1975). Other observers argue that cultures from which contemporary fashion photography draws its inspiration define women as sexual objects and impose standards of bodily perfection that induce them to subject their bodies to cosmetic surgery and the risk of anorexia nervosa and bulimia (Stephens et al. 1994; Wolf 1991).

The classic analysis of codes that are used for female subjects is Goffman's (1979) study of "gender advertisements," in which he identified characteristic hegemonic poses in advertisements that show women as subordinate or inferior to men. According to Goffman, these poses are instantly understood by the public, because they represent in an exaggerated manner stereotypical images of women that correspond to the ways in which women's roles are understood in American culture. One set of codes, "ritualization of subordination," relies on positions that subtly demean the female subject, such as showing the subject lying on her side or her back, smiling in a ritualistically exaggerated manner, or assuming awkward stances with arms and legs thrust upward or to the side of the picture frame. Another stereotype is the female subject with a vacant gaze, seemingly directed at an unseen object outside the picture frame. Goffman interprets this gaze as "licensed withdrawal," implying that the subject is passive, alienated from, and not in control of the situation.

Recently, some authors have suggested that women in their teens and twenties view hegemonic femininity differently from the way middle-aged women and feminists interpret it (Winship 1985; Skeggs 1993). They suggest that the feminist critique of fashion is no longer relevant. Younger women are said to view images identified with hegemonic femininity not as signs of weakness and passivity but as indications of being "in control" of their sexuality. Madonna's attitude toward her sexuality exemplifies this point of view. According to Myers (1987), rather than indicating passivity and weakness, fashion images celebrate a kind of power to be obtained from physical beauty and sexuality. In an attempt to theorize this position, Skeggs (1993) argues that hegemonic femininity assumes women are all alike — passive recipients of the male gaze. She points to Madonna as a role model for women who challenge male definitions of female sexuality.

Still another version of hegemonic femininity can be found in traditional standards of feminine demeanor, according to which women are expected to be constrained and passive, but not sexually available. Henley (1977) shows that norms for nonverbal behavior are different for each gender. Women, as a consequence of their inferior status, are expected to occupy less space than men and to exert greater control over their bodies and facial expressions. This is seen in the expectation that clothing should be neat and well put together and limbs placed in disciplined postures. Women's legs are supposed to be closed rather than apart and arms close to the sides of the body. Nudity and displays of breasts and genital areas are also defined as inappropriate. Henley (1977:90) comments: "Girls' postural training . . . emphasizes propriety — keeping the legs properly closed when sitting, not leaning over so as to reveal breasts, keeping the skirt down to whatever is its current accepted leg coverage."

Norms about eye contact proscribe staring on the part of women, since staring is a gesture that indicates dominance. Women are expected to avert their eyes, particularly if the other person is male. They are expected to smile and to show pleasant emotions rather than indifference (Henley 1977:194). Since gender is the primary factor determining how people relate to one another in social interaction, Henley (93) argues that gender ambiguity is highly disturbing for many people. The norm is that gender identification should be unambiguous. If traditional standards of feminine demeanor are still accepted by women, they are likely to respond negatively to images that do not conform to these standards.

These contrasting views challenge the usual claim that there is a single hegemony in contemporary culture whose definitions of reality, norms, and standards appear "natural" rather than contestable. Instead, Kellner's (1990b) concept of conflicted hegemony in contemporary media and popular culture is more useful in understanding the impact of the fashion press. As we have seen, in the 1990s, there is no single fashion standard; the consumer chooses from different interpretations of fashion depending on her social affiliations and ethnic background. Thompson and Haytko (1997:17) describe fashion as a form of culture characterized by opposition between "two counter-vailing, historically established, cultural discourses," one of which romanticizes fashion while the other trivializes it, using a moralistic, inner-directed perspective.

It can also be argued that postmodernist elements in contemporary fashion contribute to a conflicted hegemony. Postmodernist fashion, as it is presented in fashion magazines and embodied in products, does not offer women a specific identity. Instead the heterogeneity of contemporary styles allows women to assume a variety of possibly contradictory identities (Rabine 1994:64; Partington 1996). The content of contemporary fashion magazines conveys contradictory rather than consistent messages to the reader. Some feminists have been disturbed by these developments in contemporary fashion on these grounds. Because postmodernist texts manipulate dominant and subversive cultural codes but rarely take a clear-cut oppositional stance, feminists have been skeptical of the implications of postmodernist culture for feminism and feminist politics as leading to an "endless dance of noncommitment" (Mandziuk 1993:182). By contrast, Butler (1990:146) suggests that the vacillation between gender categories that is characteristic of postmodernism may lead to the eventual disappearance of norms imposing compulsory heterosexuality.

To summarize, hegemony in the fashion press is a multidimensional phenomenon. It can be interpreted in a variety of ways, depending on the commitment of the commentator to traditional, feminist, or postfeminist views.

INTERPRETING FASHION PHOTOGRAPHS

Understanding how women "read" fashion photographs requires a theoretical interpretation of media content. The content of the media is subject to a variety of interpretations by the public (Hall 1980). Polysemy results from the fact that media content is multivocal, incorporating themes that are meaningful to a variety of publics. Studies of film, television dramas, and novels suggest that women's responses cannot be characterized entirely by either acceptance of hegemonic values or resistance (e.g., Press 1994). There is considerable variation, depending on the nature of the text and on the age, social class, and ethnicity of the viewer or reader. In general, older women are more critical of media representations than younger women, but women from different social classes or ethnic groups tend to respond positively or negatively to different aspects of the material according to its relevance and significance for their lives. Bobo (1988) suggests that responses to popular culture by African-American women are particularly complex, because of the difficulties experienced by black women in identifying with predominantly white images or with images of black women created by whites.

If, indeed, clothing expresses ambivalences surrounding social identities (Davis 1992:17–18), fashion photographs are likely to be subject to different interpretations, because they present diverse and crosscutting identities that reflect the complexities of defining identities in contemporary culture. Subtle meanings may be embedded in the way a model is posed or in the clothing itself. As an example of the former, the presence of two models rather than one in a photograph has been interpreted as implying a lesbian relationship between the two women (Lewis and Rolley 1996).

Some authors see postmodernism in fashion as liberating for women. Because a great variety of styles are fashionable at the same time, women are able to construct personal styles that are meaningful to them, using specific elements of fashionable styles rather than merely following a new and well-defined style (Kaiser, Nagasawa, and Hutton 1991). This suggests that women are likely to adopt certain aspects of fashionable styles they see in fashion magazines but that they will not necessarily see the style in its entirety as appropriate for themselves. A study of attitudes toward "least favorite" clothes suggests that people tend to reject certain types of clothing that are associated with specific statuses (e.g., age, race, sexual orientation) as a way of indicating their *lack* of connections with specific groups (Freitas et al. 1997). This may also occur when fashionable clothes and photographs of such clothes suggest ambiguous or unconventional interpretations of identities.

Thompson and Haytko (1997) found that college students whom they interviewed in depth used the conflicts and contradictions surrounding fashion to counteract the potentially hegemonic aspects of fashion consumption and to construct distinct and nonconformist styles, in contrast to being "passive trend-following consumers." Because women, more than men, are socialized to pay attention to appearance and fashion, they seem to have an emotional investment in looking attractive, but, at the same time, they, like men, tend to resist fashionable ideals. Thompson and Haytko (1997:30) found that women in their study "invoked a number of critical narratives that problematized these idealized representations, particularly those featured in fashion magazines and advertisements. . . . Their use of fashion discourse involves a continuous juxtaposition of divergent fashion discourses that are directed at resisting and contesting specific fashion meanings and images they deem as exerting a negative influence on their self-conceptions and those around them."

Thompson and Haytko concluded that while young consumers construct styles from a wide array of fashionable choices, they are not postmodernist role players in the sense of assuming a variety of contradictory identities, expressed through artificial, improbable, or inconsistent appearances. Instead, they concluded that their student consumers used fashion discourses to render fragmentary, disparate styles coherent and to construct meaningful self-identities using clothing. Through their commitment to the construction of coherent self-identities and their emphasis on the importance of their ties to social groups (Bellah et al. 1985), these young consumers were expressing values associated with modernism rather than postmodernism. Their interviewees stressed (1997:35) "the sanctity of individuality and self-directed reason, the individual as a locus of control. . . , a commitment to progressive improvement. . . , the belief in meritocracy and social mobility, and a generally optimistic outlook on the future."

As we have seen, other studies suggest that the types of consumers described by Kaiser, Nagasawa, and Hutton and Thompson and Haytko constitute a minority of the population. Using a sample of over 6,000 women, one study found that only one-third were interested in fashionable clothes (Gutman and Mills 1982). Even within the fashion-oriented group, women had very different attitudes toward fashion. Almost one-half of this subgroup considered themselves fashion "leaders" because they liked to identify and try new fashion trends but were primarily interested in mainstream fashion. Another 25 percent identified themselves as fashion "followers," who adopted new styles only when they were widely accepted. They were also interested in mainstream fashion. Only 32 percent of this subgroup were "fashion independents," who were interested in fashion but disliked mainstream fashion and therefore seemed likely to engage in either modern or postmodern appearance management.[2]

These studies provide conflicting indications of how women might be expected to respond to fashion photographs and clothing advertisements that are likely to be postmodernist stylistically and conflicted in their interpretations of women's roles. The present state of theory in the field lacks consensus on whether women respond to fashion imagery as modernist or postmodernist consumers, and whether they challenge, negotiate, or ultimately accept what fashion magazines have to offer. Lutz and Collins (1993:187) argue that a magazine photograph is "a dynamic site at which many gazes or viewpoints intersect," allowing viewers to interpret the identities of subjects of photographs in different ways and to construct interpretations of the subject matter appropriate for their own identities.

GENDER IMAGERY IN *VOGUE*

The existence of diverse and contradictory social agendas in fashion magazines is consistent with both the interpretation of contemporary fashion as postmodernist and with the conception of media culture as expressing a conflicted hegemony. Fashion magazines must please both advertisers, who represent media culture, and consumers. The primary source of profit for these magazines is advertising, and therefore editorial content must supplement and reinforce advertising while attempting to maintain or increase readership (McCracken 1993).

As one of the leading fashion magazines throughout the twentieth century, *Vogue*, in its fashion photographs, exemplifies changes that have taken place in the representation of the fashionable woman and her clothing.[3] In 1947, the magazine's fashion photographs documented an upper-middle-class world with great precision. Fashion photographs were taken in identifiable settings, such as city streets or beaches. Unclothed legs, thighs, or breasts were rare. There were no close-ups. Models rarely assumed demeaning or childlike poses. The camera was generally placed at eye level. The models were young women but not adolescents, as is frequently the case today. This was a milieu viewed almost entirely from a feminine perspective. No men appeared in the fashion photographs. Women were almost invariably photographed singly.

The center of attention in most of these photographs was the clothing rather than the model. The presentation of clothing corresponded to a recent characterization of the work by a leading photographer of the period, Horst (Hochswender 1991): "Because of his lighting effects, it is possible to really see the cut of a long skirt, to appreciate the sweep of a curved hem; to read the pattern on the suit, the story in the seams." The character of these photographs is epitomized by a photograph of a woman reading a newspaper while leaning against a chair in a park (see fig. 50). The focus is on the clothing rather than on the personality of the model; her face is seen in profile. She is holding a simple and natural pose in an outdoor setting.

By 1957, changes in certain aspects of *Vogue*'s fashion photography were beginning to be noticeable. More models were photographed looking directly at the camera, an indication of inferior status. According to some analysts (e.g., Lutz and Collins 1993), a challenging or confrontational expression may be read as implying that the subject is in control of the situation, but a more docile, passive expression is often read as the subject's consent to be observed.[4] Few photographs were set in urban or suburban locations. Many more women assumed contorted or exaggerated positions, typical of Goffman's (1979) "ritualization of subordination." There were occasional close-ups. However, there was still virtually no nudity, and men almost never appeared. The major focus of the photographs remained the clothing. By 1967, the magazine was showing close-ups of models in bathing suits. There was increasing emphasis on youth, youth cultures, and popular music stars as trendsetters (Lakoff and Scherr 1984:96–97). The supermodel rather than the society woman was becoming the role model.

By 1977, the character of the magazine had changed radically from 1947. The proportion of advertising pages had doubled, and, as a result, the visual impression of the magazine was conveyed more by advertising than by editorial content. The magazine's circulation had more than doubled since 1967.[5] Both advertisements and editorial pages appeared to be oriented toward a male gaze (Rabine 1994:65; Mulvey 1975). Men were more likely to be included in the photographs, along with pairs or groups of women. Models generally looked directly at the camera and often assumed childlike or contorted positions. Most photographs were not contextualized. The vantage point of the camera was less likely to be at eye level and more likely to be looking down or looking up at its subject.

By 1987, the model's body was much more likely to be partially nude, either breasts or thighs, and more likely to be the focus of the photographs than the clothing. The camera's vantage point was frequently below its subjects, emphasizing legs and thighs. Models wearing bathing suits were photographed in close-ups, resembling pin-ups. In many photographs, models looked directly at the camera without smiling and frequently assumed the exaggerated poses that exemplify the ritualization of subordination. Models were expected "to look sexually provocative. . . . Modern beauty is deeply embedded in sexual politics — the woman acting out male fantasies, engaging in purposeful provocation" (Lakoff and Scherr 1984:106). Contextualization had virtually disappeared; most photographs were not located in any recognizable geographical space. These trends continued in the 1990s. In 1997, advertisements outnumbered editorial pages by more than three to one. Women in fashion layouts and clothing advertisements were frequently presented as sexually provocative, androgynous, or homoerotic.

Over time, the fashion photographs in the magazine appeared to have changed their function. Exhibiting the latest trends in appropriate clothing for women of means ceased to be the primary goal of the magazine; instead fashion photographs offered a kind of visual entertainment analogous to other forms of media culture, such as Hollywood films and music videos (for changes in *Vogue* covers during this period, see Lloyd 1986).

SELECTION OF PHOTOGRAPHS
AND QUESTIONS FOR RESEARCH

There has been little research how women interpret representations of gender in fashion photographs.[6] The goal of this study is to examine responses to representations of gender in fashion photographs and clothing advertisements among young and middle-aged women, representing diverse ethnicities and nationalities.[7] Eighteen photographs were selected from the February, March, and September 1997 issues of *Vogue*, of which a subset of six to nine photographs was shown to members of each focus group. The photographs were divided almost equally between fashion editorial photos and clothing advertisements. The clothing in these photographs had, in most cases, been produced by companies headed by leading American, French, and Italian designers. The photographs were selected to exemplify different aspects of hegemony as it has been conceptualized in fashion magazines: (1) hegemonic femininity: sexuality/pornography, (2) hegemonic poses as interpreted by Goffman: ritualization of subordination and licensed withdrawal, (3) violations of traditional norms of feminine demeanor (traditional hegemonic femininity): frontal gaze and eye contact, nudity, and androgyny and gender ambiguity, as well as subjects who conformed to these norms (e.g., exaggerated smiles). In addition to gender stereotypes, two of the photographs could be interpreted as representing racial stereotypes. At least one photograph appeared to represent empowerment and success. Several photographs could be categorized as postmodern on the basis of ambiguities and contradictions in their imagery or in the nature of the clothing they depicted.

Members of focus groups were asked several questions designed to elicit their perceptions of these photographs and the extent to which they were able to identify with the models in the photographs. Before the focus group began, they were asked to complete a short questionnaire that tapped their level of interest in fashion and their techniques for following fashion.

Participants' responses were analyzed according to the following questions: (1) Did these women accept the "authority" of fashion as exemplified by the fashion press? (2) How did they respond to the different social agendas that were represented in the photographs? (3) Did age, race, and ethnicity affect women's responses to the photographs? (4) Were participants able to detect the presence of gender and racial stereotypes? (5) As fashion ceases to represent a social ideal and instead disseminates a variety of choices, some of them representing marginal lifestyles, can fashion still be said to be hegemonic?

THE "AUTHORITY" OF FASHION

Has fashion retained the "authority" that it appears to have exerted in the past? On the questionnaire, almost all (84 percent) of these women responded positively to the question: "Do you attempt to keep up with current fashions?"[8] Asked what aspects of fashion they specifically followed, the majority checked "specific styles" (65 percent) and "accessories" (55 percent). About one-quarter (24 percent) checked "brand names" and 18 percent, "hemlines."

According to their responses to the questionnaires, these women relied on three different types of sources for information about fashion. The first was their social milieu, broadly defined. This category included "cool friends and relatives" (chosen by 53 percent) and "what people are wearing on the street" (chosen by 59 percent). Sixty-nine percent of the women relied on one or both of these sources. The second type of source was the media, including fashion magazines, television, and clothes worn by popular singers. Sixty-nine percent of the women relied on some form of media for information about fashion. The third type of source was also the most important: 76 percent relied on local stores for information about fashion.

Most of the women relied on more than one source for information about fashion (80 percent) and many relied on all three (43 percent). This suggests that the authority to transmit information about fashion today is widely diffused. Only 15 percent of the women relied on cool friends or the street and not the media, while only one person relied on the media but not social contacts. Eighty-one percent of the women read fashion magazines at least occasionally, but fashion magazines were a source of information for only 55 percent of the women. Magazines were apparently not considered sufficiently authoritative to be used as a woman's only source of information. Only 16 percent relied on fashion magazines without using other types of media, and only 4 percent relied only on fashion magazines (i.e., excluding all other sources of information). However, 10 percent relied only on stores for information. *Vogue* appeared to be the fashion magazine of preference, being read by 71 percent of the women, but 57 percent read about a dozen other fashion magazines. Only 10 percent read other fashion magazines but not *Vogue*.

These findings suggest a certain ambivalence about fashion magazines, which was also expressed during the focus groups. Very rarely in the focus-group discussions was there any suggestion that these women viewed fashion editors as authorities on fashion. Rather, some women questioned fashion editors' judgments. A black undergraduate said: "Like the image that they always set, that everyone is alike, which everyone is not."

Some of these women doubted the capacity of fashion editors to understand or express the perspective of women: "Even though the fashion editors in the magazines are usually women, I still think it's not really a woman's point of view. It's what a woman thinks a man wants to see or something like that" (white undergraduate). Some white undergraduates perceived fashion as something remote from their own experience: "These outfits remind me of the newer style that is coming out . . . 'bandish,' faddish type stuff that I don't see around me that often. It is kind of removed from me is what I am trying to say." Another young white woman asserted that the fashion standards set in these magazines were impossible for normal women to achieve: "Anything in these magazines, especially high fashion, W and *Vogue* to a certain extent, nobody who is normal can wear any of those clothes. You cannot look good in those clothes. You just can't" (white college student).

An older woman complained that fashion photographs were almost useless for figuring out what was really taking place in fashion, because they were often too dark and did not show details of how the clothes were constructed. Other women saw these images as unnatural: "I see the point of view of the fashion people . . . because it doesn't look natural . . ." (white undergraduate). Some women suggested that fashion photographs should be viewed as a form of art and fantasy rather than as representations of fashion: "It's just like a dream, because you know that 90 percent, probably 98 percent of the clothes, are unattainable."

However, one woman admitted that she was susceptible to trends: "I think if you're flipping through a magazine and you continually see the same type of outfit on different pages, you might, I might try to alter what I'm wearing. Because you see it's like a new trend" (white undergraduate). Another young woman expressed the idea that the pictures in fashion magazines might be capable of influencing her "unconsciously." She stated that she might be inclined to wear a particular combination of clothing, without remembering the source of the idea, because an advertisement in a fashion magazine showed it: "This is something that can be done; it's allowed to be done."

Other comments referred to a preference for assembling outfits by taking items from a variety of sources (see Kaiser, Nagasawa, and Hutton 1991): "I like looking like that, and I like feeling that way sometimes, but I wouldn't necessarily go to that extreme. . . . But I like that direction. You can take elements of that." "I sometimes imitate the style of models and musicians but with second-hand clothes." Some women said they liked to know what was in fashion without necessarily being "in fashion" themselves. Several college students echoed a comment on one of the questionnaires: "By 'keeping up with fashion,' I mean that I like to *know* what is popular but I don't always adjust my style." Others differed: "It really doesn't interest me—keeping in touch with the latest styles." "I wear what looks good on me, not what looks good on Cindy Crawford when she's on the runway." An older participant said: "I'm not really interested in fashion. I just want to look presentable."

Other women were able to distance themselves from these photographs because of personal constraints. A few mentioned financial limitations. Older women admitted that they were incapable of meeting the standards set by models in these photographs but attributed this failure to age differences rather than to personal failings. Almost half the middle-aged women said they did not attempt to follow fashion. One older woman said: "Anyone who's got any kind of flaws in her body doesn't stand a chance in that dress."

Several women criticized current conceptions of the fashionable body as depicted in the photographs. The simplicity of contemporary clothing styles has the effect of highlighting the body and its perfections and imperfections. The body confers a kind of social status, revealing who has the time, money, and inclination to work on their bodies and perfect them.

Almost half the African Americans also said they did not attempt to follow fashion. The comments of African-American women suggested that they perceived fashionable styles as being created for white women and particularly for white bodies rather than black: "This look is impossible for us to achieve. Genetically, that is not how we are mapped out, and so if we are in the right frame of mind within ourselves, we know that it is going to be unlikely that we could achieve it through working out and what have you."

Only very occasionally did younger white women admit to being critical of themselves for not being able to meet the standards of beauty and physical perfection set by these photographs. A comment such as the following from a white undergraduate was rare: "I know I'll never, never be able to look like her, and it really pisses me off." Some of these women may not have felt sufficiently comfortable in the social situation created in the focus groups to acknowledge their failure to meet these standards and to attribute this failure to their own inadequacies. Alternatively, some images in these photographs may have been too extreme to elicit identification on the part of the viewer.

THE FASHION MAGAZINE AND ITS SOCIAL AGENDAS: Images of Blatant and Marginal Sexuality

Some of the photographs presented women in highly sexualized poses, suggesting that a woman's role is that of sex object. Other photographs presented subjects whose sexuality was ambiguous — possibly lesbian or transvestite. To what extent did participants in the focus groups accept this agenda? If women subscribe to traditional norms of feminine demeanor (Henley 1977), one might expect them to reject images that depict overt sexuality, nudity, and sexual ambiguity.

One photograph showed a woman wearing a very short, sleeveless, flesh-colored dress and very high-heeled shoes, with her body bent forward, leaning her buttocks against a wall (see fig. 51). Many of these women, both young and middle-aged, did not identify with the level of sexuality expressed in the photograph, as suggested by the comments of two undergraduates.

Interviewer: What aspects of this photograph do you like?

Tracee (black college student): Quite honestly, nothing, nothing.

Nathalie (white college student): I would categorize it as an image of a slut or a prostitute or just not a good girl.

Tracee: It's trying to be very seductive, and I guess that's kind of what I associate with being a supermodel or just a model in general.

Nathalie: Like a negative sexy.

Another undergraduate, while stating that she did not like the photograph in general, expressed a somewhat more positive attitude toward the model: "She has a seductive feel. She gives off this aura. So like there are times when I'd want to feel like — going to a black-tie party you want to feel seductive or sexy, but, in my own way. Not like that."

A few younger white women associated the sexuality in this photograph with strength rather than weakness in a manner that was consistent with discussions of sexuality as an indication of power rather than passivity.

Sandy: There's something strong about her. I mean she doesn't look lost, you know. She's not the lost sex symbol. She's more like she wanted to be that way. It's not that she is the victim of something.

Helen: I think this photograph expresses a woman's point of view. She's ready to take on the world and she can "live-on-the-edge" kind of thing. Because it's sexy in a way that it's powerful — she's the one in control. It's not sexy like you know, she's lying on a bed half naked.

In a group of middle-aged women, participants objected to the emphasis on the body rather than the clothing in the photograph.

Christine: I don't like the way the model is posed. Because I think it's showing the body rather than the clothing. That's the first thing you see. The dress is barely there. Not that there's anything wrong, but it's the photograph itself that suggests that they're not showing the clothes; they're showing the woman's body. And without that, the clothing would be nothing.

Nina: She's selling herself. This woman's selling her body.

Dorothy: From a distance she could be naked. The dress almost blends into her body.

In keeping with norms of traditional feminine demeanor that sanction nudity, many of the women disliked nudity and transparent materials that revealed breasts and genital hair: "They're selling it to women. And we all have this body. We don't need to see her without a shirt on. Which I never understood. You know? That doesn't really excite me, being a girl, without her shirt on." Their objections to transparent materials were not so much on the basis of modesty or prudishness but because they could not visualize themselves wearing such revealing clothes.

Interviewer: Would you like to look like this woman?

Tracee: No. Like she's going out of her way to be sexy, and I tend to prefer things that are more [. . .] You weren't trying to be sexy. . . . Whereas this almost seems as though they had to really work to make her look sexy, and so there's just something very negative about that.

Joan: I wouldn't ever wear something that let boobs show, but I think for the image she's trying to convey, it's appropriate.

Another photograph showed an African-American model, entirely nude except for costume jewelry, sitting on the floor. African-American women disagreed in their evaluations of this photograph. Several of these participants did not like the fact that the model was nude. One women in this group said: "I think the person who created this must be a man, because he is just trying to expose her body, and I doubt a woman would ever do this." Another African-American woman had a different viewpoint: "It's redefining nudity. It is not done in poor taste. I think that she is proud of her body, and she is not afraid to — it is not really sexual — she is showing off the accessories."

A third photograph contained elements that could be interpreted as androgynous or homosexual. An advertisement for Chanel, it showed a woman wearing black jeans and an unbuttoned suit jacket over a very pale, bare, flat torso (see fig. 52). The face was heavily made up, particularly around the eyes, which were obscured by a shadow. The overall impression that participants received from this photograph was one of gender ambiguity. Most participants were puzzled by it, critical of it, and to some extent disturbed by it. The following comments by white undergraduates illustrate a desire to distance themselves from this image and particularly its connotations of marginality and gender ambiguity:

Lauren: Is it a man?

Rosanne: I think it's a man.

Lauren: A man?

Barbara: No, it's a woman.

Evelyn: No, it's definitely not a woman.

Lauren: Yes, it is.

Barbara: You don't see the crevices of her chest.

Rosanne: I think it looks like a man to me.

Evelyn: Look at the hands! It's a man's hands.

Barbara: It's a woman's hands.

Evelyn: It's a man's hands. It's a transvestite. I'm telling you it's a transvestite.

Interviewer: What aspects of the photo do you not like?

Lauren: That we can't figure out if it's a man or a woman.

Anne: That face really scares me.

Ruth: It looks very androgynous. She doesn't have a chest at all. Like you see a glimpse of something. It's all pale and wiped out. Like a ghost. And her face looks very like a guy dressed in drag.

Nathalie: I would say scary, unnatural, and witchlike. And neither masculine nor feminine, because this just seems so unnatural to me that it doesn't seem like it would appeal to any regular man or woman.

Tracee: I don't like the makeup. I don't like the heavy eyeliner, heavy mascara like black around the eye. The "I'm dying, I'm on drugs" look. And then they really do contrast that with like the kind of bloody red lipstick. And then she has very pale skin. So that whole combination, I just really don't like.

Older women also tended to attribute marginal connotations to the subject of this photograph. One woman commented on the model's expression, which connoted "licensed withdrawal," while another woman indicated she could not identify with her:

Dorothy: And that vacuous look she has — like she's almost dead. She looks like corpses I've seen.

Mary: I wouldn't want to look like her. There is something very harsh about her.

Another older woman was dismissive: "This isn't a serious fashion statement at all. They just want your attention."

A fourth photograph showed two women, wearing long, transparent outfits and standing close together, one behind the other (see fig. 53). The second woman's right hand was placed over the first woman's stomach. In keeping with Lewis and Rolley's (1996) attribution of lesbian connotations to photographs showing two female models in the same photograph, some participants did in fact detect overtones of lesbianism in the photograph: "They look easy, and maybe there is a hint of homosexuality. I just see where the hand is placed, and it doesn't look very friendly or sisterlike; it looks like they are girlfriends. It's a hard image, like a heavy metal type of look, and it is just something that I don't aspire to." A middle-aged viewer had a different impression: "There's this fake sort of lesbianism in there too, the way the person had those two women pose. And I always associate that with men."

Members of an African-American focus group did not respond to any homosexual overtones in this photograph but interpreted it as representing a culture very removed from their own.

Tamara: Drug-addict club models. I see them as being in a club.

Michelle: Rock star chicks.

Dina: I see these stereotypical, tall, skinny, anorexic-looking white females.

Discussions in the focus groups did not suggest that there were substantial differences between women in different generations in their conceptions of their gender identities. Younger participants were not more inclined than older women to accept as appropriate for themselves a wider range of sexual orientations. Most of these women tended to reject images that suggested bisexuality, lesbianism, and transvestitism. Displays of nudity were generally sanctioned as inappropriate for their own lives. In general, their reactions were explicable on the basis of traditional norms of feminine demeanor, as described by Henley (1977). However, they were ambivalent toward a photograph of a woman in a very seductive pose. Some younger women admired her appearance of being in control, an interpretation that was consistent with recent changes in the ways expressions of sexuality by women are understood. Others interpreted her pose as demeaning.

THE FASHION MAGAZINE AND ITS SOCIAL AGENDAS: Images of Empowerment

Members of several focus groups were shown a Donna Karan advertisement that consisted of a black and white photograph of a woman in a pants suit staring directly at the camera (see fig. 54). This woman's image could be interpreted as empowered, successful, and androgynous, another of the magazine's agendas. A male participant summed up what he viewed as the rationale underlying the way this model was being presented: "Look, she's made it. It's not about her sexuality. It's not about her breasts. She's a working woman. Her clothes are about working woman's clothing. If you're successful and you're smart, I've got clothes for you. You don't have to put on tons of makeup. It's like you're the boss, darn it, and you can do what you want."

Most participants responded to this photograph on the basis of the model's personality, although their assessments of her personality varied. Some groups were repelled and others were attracted by the image the model appeared to convey. The model's stare violated a norm of appropriate female expressive behavior (Henley 1977), and this appeared to be a major factor in their reactions to this image. The effect of the model's facial expression on a focus group composed of white undergraduates is shown in the following discussion:

Interviewer: Are there any aspects of the photograph you don't like?

Ruth: The expression on her face.

Judy: I think she looks kind of aggressive. It's kind of portraying the attitude that the clothes are like, well you know I'm an elitist, like you can't touch me. I still like the clothes but the attitude the model is portraying.

Another undergraduate stated a preference for the type of expression that women have traditionally been expected to show: "I like that she's powerful, but I don't like [. . .] She's not smiling. She's not happy." Asked whether on some occasions they might want to look like the model, younger women found it difficult to identify with the woman in the Karan ad, as indicated by the comments from two focus groups.

Interviewer: Would you like to look like this woman?

Judy: This facial expression? No way.

Tracee: For me it's just like the whole image. I don't think I could ever be like that. . . . And I don't want to be like her.

Nathalie: I don't like her attitude. I think it's something that I don't relate to. I don't see myself as having that type of attitude in general. Although I do agree that there might be times in certain situations, certain office situations, where I might feel that it might be to my advantage to look a little bit more like her, to be strong, and to seem to have a sense of identity like that and confidence in myself.

A young woman doubted that she could convey an attitude of empowerment successfully by wearing those clothes: "If I was wearing that, I wouldn't look like that. I'm not saying I wouldn't look good, but I wouldn't feel like, 'Listen to me. I am woman. Hear me roar. I'm the boss.'" In other words, adopting a type of clothing appropriate for the role would not necessarily allow her to perform the role convincingly. By contrast, a group of middle-aged women also interpreted the model's image as strong and confident but reacted more positively to it. One woman commented: "I wouldn't mind looking like that on a lot of occasions. Not just because she's beautiful but because of the message that she's giving: strong and don't contradict me."

THE FASHION MAGAZINE AND ITS SOCIAL AGENDAS: Postmodernist Role Playing

In contrast to the fashion magazine, which proposed a postmodernist conception of multiple identities, women in the focus groups appeared to have a distinctly modernist outlook toward their identities and, consequently, toward fashionable clothing. They perceived the selection of suitable clothing as an expression of stable identities and as a task for which they possessed the requisite skills. They evaluated fashionable clothing in terms of its usefulness for the types of occasions in which they participated but not in terms of adopting a series of distinctly different roles. In response to the woman in a business suit in the Donna Karan ad, one young woman did not see these clothes as new, but as appropriate in certain situations: "I think I am wearing that style already. I would wear this kind of suit in a business situation but not because I saw the advertisement." Another young woman, looking at a photograph of a model in a transparent dress, said: "These types of photos really bother me. I don't like them at all. I never met anyone that would actually wear them. It's like what would you wear that to?"

Off-beat clothes were assessed according to how they would look in a specific setting: "I wouldn't go outside dressed like that." "I don't think I would see anybody dressed like this except in New York." A major criterion these women expressed was that of comfort: "I think that generally women like to have the option of being able to wear clothing that is more comfortable and casual and not actually having to be so confined to clothing that is just about how your body is shaped." Some young women were very concerned about exposing their bodies: "I wouldn't wear something that would show so much of my body."

Consciously or unconsciously, these participants seemed to believe that clothes represent the self, which they perceived as consistent and unchanging. This attitude underlies the following comment by an African-American college student about an African-American model: "I like the fact that she looks a lot like me. . . . So the question is not if I want to look like her but the fact that she looks like me and that is what is appealing to me about her." It was also seen in a phrase that was used many times, referring to an outfit: "It's not *me*." "I just don't really like what she is wearing, the general style of it. . . .

I guess also it is the attitude, the stance she is taking *is not really me at all.*" Or, referring to a model: "I think it's *her.*"

One result of the variety of stylistic standards that postmodernist fashion proposes is that particular styles and costumes are likely to be difficult to interpret (Davis 1992; Kaiser, Nagasawa, and Hutton 1991). In some of the photographs, certain aspects of the model's clothing were considered puzzling or difficult to comprehend by members of the focus groups. For example, participants commented on ambiguous qualities in the clothes portrayed in a photograph of a rather feminine woman on a beach, such as the use of untied sneakers, combined with a very baggy man's suit, a necktie, and an untucked shirt.

> *Interviewer:* What aspects of this photograph do you not like?
>
> *Tracee:* The disorder, the shirt untucked. Kind of like, she was confused. What were they really trying to go for? Why is the shirt untucked? What's the point of the tie?"
>
> *Ruth:* When would you wear a suit with the shirt hanging out with sneakers?
>
> *Anne:* I think the whole outfit is out of place. Like the shoes with the suit and the entire thing on the beach."
>
> *Interviewer:* What meanings do you think the clothing in the photograph conveys?
>
> *Elena:* Androgyny and professionalism, because she's in a suit.
>
> *Joan:* But she's in sneakers.

When the level of ambiguity in a model's appearance was very high, participants tended to reject it vehemently. One photograph showed a model with a highly toned, muscular body and very dark eyeshadow, wearing a very sheer, transparent dress of indeterminate color. The dress had connotations of fairytales and fantasy for participants that seemed incongruous with the model's almost masculine body. Two older participants commented:

> *Catherine:* The dress is soft and gauzy but she looks very hard. . . . It's kind of an aggressive pose and there's that little wispy dress on her.
>
> *Elizabeth:* She looks a little grotesque.

Younger participants were particularly negative toward this photo:

> *Beth:* She doesn't even look human.
>
> *Barbara:* I wouldn't stay on that page for more than a second.
>
> *Evelyn:* Her body's sick. Like she's so toned that it's disgusting.
>
> *Rosanne:* It looks like she got slimed
>
> *Lauren:* Distasteful.
>
> *Rosanne:* Prehistoric.
>
> *Evelyn:* Out of touch.

Participants' conceptions of their own appearance appeared to be shaped by practical considerations and by conformity to traditional norms of feminine personal demeanor. These women were seeking comfortable, useful clothing and rejecting elements of ambiguity and subversion. They were not postmodernist role players, manipulating visual codes to simulate different identities.

THE MODEL AS ROLE MODEL

Rather than the clothes or fashion itself, the focus of attention in these photographs for most of the women was the model. Many of the women, particularly younger women, recognized well-known models and identified them by name. Almost invariably, the models elicited strong reactions on the part of these women, sometimes positive, often negative. The model as a physical presence and as a personality served both as the channel for the transmission of fashion ideals, along with whatever hegemony that might have entailed, and as the justification for rejecting these ideals on the grounds that the model projected a negative and undesirable image. Younger participants in the focus groups seemed to find it quite natural to make comparisons between themselves and the models in the photographs. They were inclined to identify with the models and seemed disappointed when they were unable to identify with them.

Participants discussed at length the models' physical attributes, their facial expressions, and their gender identifications. The models' bodies were analyzed in terms of body frame, height, weight, and skin. Body parts, such as feet, legs, arms, hands, waistlines, and bustlines, were examined, along with facial characteristics such as eyes, eyebrows, and expressions. Haircuts, makeup, and nail polish were also subjected to scrutiny. On the basis of physical characteristics and facial expressions, members of the focus groups almost invariably drew inferences about the models' personalities (e.g., strong, aggressive, confident, aloof, carefree, fun loving). These women responded to the models as individuals, as people with distinct identities apart from the clothing they were wearing.

Facial expressions were a major factor that determined how participants reacted to the models and whether they appeared to identify with them. Only one woman (a white college student) said that for her the models' facial expressions were not important, because "I know they're not real." Most women responded positively to one of the few models who was smiling and who appeared to be enjoying herself. A college student said:

> *Evelyn:* She looks natural.
>
> *Interviewer:* Why does she look natural to you?
>
> *Evelyn:* She's smiling.

In keeping with norms about women's demeanor, the absence of positive facial expressions was perceived as disturbing. An older viewer complained that two models in a photograph looked unhappy.

> *Interviewer:* Do you think the fact that they look unhappy influences the way you respond to the photograph?
>
> *Louise:* Yes, I do. It looks unnatural. The one on the left looks miserable.

Another older viewer observed: "Her face is very cold. . . . That's why I don't like this photo. It's because of her face, not because of her clothes." An African-American student said: "She is sort of dehumanized by not showing any emotions."

Some focus groups were shown an advertisement for Helmut Lang which was in black and white, depicting a very young model, head canted, shoulders slouched, wearing a sleeveless T-shirt (see fig. 55). The young woman was not wearing any makeup. The presence of small wrinkles around the mouth indicated that the photograph had not been airbrushed. Her shoulder-length blond hair was not parted and appeared to be uncombed. Although she was looking toward the camera, there were elements of "licensed withdrawal" in her serious, self-absorbed, alienated expression. Members of a group of white undergraduates close to the model's age described her as "mean," "upset," "unhappy," and "asexual." A middle-aged viewer thought the model's body suggested drug addiction. A college student said: "I think she just looks like a heroin addict."

The model's personality, as suggested by her facial expression, her personal demeanor, as indicated by her stance, or the extent to which her image expressed sexuality or other aspects of gender often had more impact on these participants than her clothes. Their vocabulary for discussing clothing was limited. Among the characteristics of clothing as defined by experts — fabric, texture, color, pattern, volume, silhouette, and occasion (Kaiser, Nagasawa, and Hutton 1991 : 171) — they were mainly concerned with color and occasion, and secondarily with fabric and pattern. Clothes were described in very general terms as: comfortable, nice, attractive, pretty, sexy, modern, trendy, funky, cutting edge, classy, elegant, and sophisticated. Negative adjectives included: chintzy, cheesy, tacky, and ugly.

Contrary to what is generally believed to be the effect of fashion images on women, these women were not intimidated by them. Models were not necessarily perceived as beautiful or as being exemplars of physical perfection. Their bodies were often criticized as being too thin, too muscular, or otherwise unappealing. Their clothes, hair, and makeup were frequently described as bizarre, inappropriate, or unattractive. Even though participants were as interested in the models as in their clothing and attempted to attribute distinct personalities and identities to the models on the basis of their physical appearance, these women did not often wish to emulate their appearance. When asked whether they would like to look like the models in these photographs on certain occasions, participants generally replied negatively. The images projected by these photographs were not ones that these women wished to project themselves. These images were often incompatible with their attitudes or preferences. The image younger participants accepted most readily was that of the woman in a transparent dress leaning provocatively against a wall even though many of them made critical remarks about the level of sexuality in her appearance. By contrast, the disheveled woman in a man's suit with sneakers was almost unanimously rejected.

These issues were particularly pertinent for African-American women, as suggested by these comments from an African-American group:

Interviewer: Does this photograph represent your point of view at all?

All: No.

Interviewer: Why not?

Tamara: She is blond-haired.

Kyla: I can't relate to her.

Interviewer: Why not?

Kyla: She is just different from me.

Tamara: She is six foot, very thin, pale [. . .]

By contrast, these women interpreted a photograph of a black African model as representing "the black woman's point of view." One of these women said: "I like her figure. It's an obvious African figure, the hips, butt, her arms. . . . She's an African woman. She's an elegant African woman."

THE VISIBILITY/INVISIBILITY OF THE POSE

Strongly implicated in the ways the models were perceived by participants were the kinds of poses in which they were placed and, in general, the various techniques underlying the social construction of the photographs. To what extent were these poses and techniques visible or invisible to these participants? These photographs, like many others in the issues of *Vogue* from which they were taken, relied on a small number of stereotypical poses that have been interpreted by social scientists as demeaning to women.

Members of the focus groups indicated their awareness of the social construction of these photographs through comments such as the following: "You can tell there's obviously a fan or wind machine blowing the hair." "I'm sure that they took a hundred pictures to get that and still her smile's not perfect. But like they tried hard to make it look natural." "It's intended to make you wonder if it's a man or a woman. It's meant to grab our attention. That's how they're going to get you into their ad."

Participants were clearly sensitive to the fact that these photographs were designed to sell clothing or at least the image of the designer or brand-name. At the same time, they expected these photographs to meet certain standards of realism, to match their conceptions of how young women actually behaved. The following comments are an example of this attitude: "It looks like a fashion photograph, whereas the other two photographs we just saw could be real." "She looks like a mannequin. She doesn't really look real."

Members of the focus groups sometimes interpreted the "evidence" in these photographs in different ways. They varied in their sensitivity to the meanings of the stereotypical poses that appeared in certain photographs. Some photographs illustrated an aspect of what Goffman called the ritualization of subordination, the use of childlike, passive, awkward, or ridiculous body positions. In response to a photograph showing a model barefoot in midair, with her arms outspread, one woman found the pose amusing: "I think the photograph is nice. . . . It's kind of arresting—how they have her jumping. It looks kind of fun." Other participants who appeared to have a sense of the underlying connotations in the photograph said: "She looks like a marionette." "She looks like Peter Pan because she's jumping."

One photograph included a man in a position characteristic of the ritualization of subordination: in midair with arms outstretched. Possibly because it is very unusual to see a man rather than a woman presented in this manner, viewers were unanimously critical. Significantly, they were critical of him as an individual rather than of the pose per se: "That kid. That guy in the picture is annoying." "Yeah, he looks like he's going horseback riding but he kind of missed the horse or something."

If the stereotypical pose appeared to have sexual connotations or violated norms about bodily exposure, these participants were more likely to be critical of it. One of the photographs projected contradictory images. It showed a woman wearing a short black dress, lying supine on a chair (see fig. 56). The upper part of the woman's body, her hair and her face were neat, sleek, and well-groomed. The lower part of the photograph showed her legs slightly open, revealing the inside of her right thigh, violating the norm against exposing this part of a woman's body (Henley 1977). Participants responded differently, depending upon which part of the picture seemed most important to them:

Mark: She's pretty. Her face is the focal point.

Robin: You can totally see her crotch.

Laurie: You see her entire right thigh.

The following exchange of comments is generally favorable but reveals a slight ambivalence toward the pose.

Beth: She looks very pulled together and relaxed. She's obviously reclining but I like it. . . .

Interviewer: Whose point of view does this photograph express?

Robin: I'd say a man's. . . . I don't know. I see her lying there.

Beth: Submissive.

Interviewer: Does this photograph express your point of view?

All: No.

Other participants were more critical of this pose:

Nathalie: It seems like she's giving herself away or something.

Tracee: I don't like the pose. . . . I just don't like the whole laid back look and it's almost as though her legs are gaped open, and that's what really kind of offends me.

Still another group interpreted the pose favorably, because they perceived the woman as being in control of the situation, consistent with "revised" interpretations of hegemonic femininity.

Interviewer: So does this represent the way a man sees a woman or the way a woman sees a woman?

Helen: I think women want to be like this. . . . She's a strong woman. It's not the traditional kind of weak woman idea. She's a strong woman there.

Another photo that illustrated Goffman's category of the ritualization of subordination and that also had subtle sexual connotations showed the back of a young woman who was bent forward with her buttocks in the foreground of the picture. She was wearing a long dress in a colorful fabric (see fig. 57). Again reactions to this photograph were mixed.

Interviewer: What adjectives would you use to describe the image of the woman?

Elena: I think she's sexual, but it's not a very slutty sexual. . . . I think it's nice and I think it's feminine.

Another white participant was more critical of this pose:

Courtney: I don't like the pose. It's a sexualized pose.

Interviewer: Would you like to look like this woman on certain occasions?

Courtney: No. I don't care to be in that position.

African-American students were also critical of the pose in this photograph:

> *Lisa:* I don't like what she is doing. Why does her butt have to be in our faces?

> *Toyah:* It's like she's an animal. She looks like a lizard.

An African-American participant pointed to the racist aspects of a photograph that showed a black African model in a pose that also fit Goffman's category of the ritualization of subordination—seated on the floor, wearing a long, elegant dress, smiling broadly, and holding a musical instrument (see fig. 58):

> I really like the dress, and I think she is definitely very attractive. I guess mostly I have more negative feelings. I really don't like how she is sitting in this picture. It just looks really unnatural. . . . It just seems that there is a definite attempt to portray her as some kind of oddity. . . . I really don't like the expression on her face and I don't like the instrument in her hand because it brings up like a negative stereotype of a samba image, where they have the little pickaninny with a musical instrument or just with watermelon, and it is to kind of make you think of that image. . . . If you were in a dress like this, you wouldn't be sitting on the floor in this kind of pose. You would be standing, you wouldn't actually be in that position. . . . It just seems so forced. It just seems like there could be a better picture to take of her, and there is a definite attempt to make sure she looks kind of like this strange oddity of a person so that you can keep thinking she is different, she is not like the other models that you are going to see in a spread, or whatever.

This comment was unusual, because the speaker was able to imagine other poses that would have been preferable to the stereotypical pose.

Another African-American participant was critical of the racist implications in a photograph of an entirely nude African American model: "I don't really like the fact that she is naked. I think being naked in a photograph, that is not the problem, but usually when they have a black woman in a photograph and she is naked, she looks like a complete sex object, and it is just like in an animalistic way. . . . I see it as connecting with really negative stereotypes of kind of like this sexual animal thing. . . . To me it just doesn't really say anything good."

In general, participants appeared to be more sensitive to the sexual or racist connotations of stereotypical poses than to connotations of childishness or passivity. Demeaning poses with sexual connotations were rejected unless the sexual aspects of the photograph were offset by elements in the photograph that had more positive implications for the participants.

CONCLUSION

The findings from this study raise questions about the extent to which fashion photographs constitute a form of hegemonic femininity that is accepted as natural and uncontestable by readers. As exemplified by *Vogue*, the fashion magazine presents a wider range of social identities and "agendas" than was the case several decades ago. The overall effect is closer to conflicted hegemony than hegemonic femininity and probably facilitates the expression of negative attitudes toward these images. Judging from the responses of a racially and ethnically varied group of women of different ages, the authority of fashion magazines as arbiters of fashion is no greater than that of the television screen, the street, and local stores. Fashion editors were viewed as one source of information about fashion but not as being particularly authoritative.

The responses of most of the participants in the focus groups to images representing hegemonic femininity and feminine empowerment suggested that they had internalized traditional norms of feminine demeanor and perceived these photographs as violating these norms. These taboos about appropriate gender behavior for women led many of them to reject exaggerated expressions of sexuality, both heterosexual and androgynous, and images that implied gender ambiguity. A few women interpreted overt sexuality as an indication of strength rather than passivity. Images that conveyed feminine empowerment and dominance evoked ambivalent responses. On the one hand, they admired women who appeared to be strong, but expressions of strength that deviated from norms of feminine personal demeanor evoked negative responses. Participants varied in their sensitivity to demeaning hegemonic poses that carried connotations of childishness and sexual availability. African Americans were adept at decoding racial stereotypes and expressed explicitly their perception that these styles were not intended for women of color. Participants' attitudes toward the models were curiously ambivalent: they appeared to want to identify with them, but they were not intimidated by their beauty, the perfection of their bodies, or their clothing.

Criticism of the images in these photographs came not just from women who, on the basis of age or ethnicity, might have perceived themselves as being outside the youthful audience for whom the clothing in the photographs was presumably intended but also from young, white college women. The often-strident tone of their critiques may have resulted from an underlying emotional involvement in fashionable images and in the culturally prescribed requirement to look feminine and attractive (Thompson and Haytko 1997:30). However, a group consisting of younger and less educated women might have responded differently to these photographs.[9]

This study suggests that women respond critically to the fashion press in part because these magazines are expressing the tensions and contradictions of a conflicted hegemony and in part because traditional values and perceptions of personal demeanor (another form of hegemony) and modernist conceptions of social identity continue to shape women's perceptions of postmodern culture. These women did not appear likely to engage in postmodernist role playing; they evaluated fashionable clothing with a strong sense of stable personal identities. Instead of reveling in postmodernist ambiguity, they disliked outfits that appeared to be conveying conflicting messages. They examined clothes for their relevance to their personal lives and rejected postmodernist confusion of styles and genders.

It is difficult to generalize these findings to women's clothing behavior in other contexts, such as shopping, where they are exposed directly to the clothing. Fashion photographs incorporate clothes into a complex gestalt of imagery that often overshadows the clothes themselves, so that participants respond as much to the setting in which the clothes are placed as to the clothes themselves. Seeing clothes in these unfamiliar contexts, they may be more likely to reject the identities that are being associated with them than they would in a shopping mall. In other words, they may be responding to the ambiguities in the identities projected by these photographs by emphasizing their lack of connection with them (Freitas et al. 1997). Participants in the focus groups were sensitive to the ways in which their reactions to these photographs were affected by seeing them outside the covers of the magazine. Several participants commented that their responses would have been different if they had seen the photographs while flipping through the pages of the magazine, because they claimed they would have looked less carefully at certain photographs under those circumstances. Such comments raise important issues about hegemony and resistance. To what extent do images and texts in the media affect audiences if they are barely attentive? Under what circumstances does media content penetrate a person's consciousness? Are messages superficially scanned because they appear to be familiar and therefore do not need to be processed or because they appear to be threatening to a person's mental set and are consequently rejected in order to avoid the necessity of reassessing basic assumptions?

NOTES

1. One of the most thorough analyses of the sexual content of music videos on MTV is found in the video *Dreamworlds*, directed and produced by Sut Jhally. For his account of what he was trying to accomplish in making the video, see Jhally (1994).

2. A similar study, of over 2,000 women, in 1991 found five consumer segments in a sample of women between eighteen and fifty-five: "fashion enthusiasts" and "style seekers," who represented 20 percent of the population but 58 percent of all clothing expenditures; "classics," who represented 20 percent of the population and 20 percent of all clothing expenditures; and the "timid" and the "uninvolved," who represented 59 percent of the population but only 25 percent of clothing expenditures (Krafft 1991:11; see also Gadel 1985). In France a study of women aged fifteen to fifty-five found that 65 percent had not followed fashion in the year of the study (Valmont 1993). Thirty-four percent of the women were critical of fashion and opposed to it; 21 percent considered that fashion was acceptable for other women but unwearable for themselves; and 10 percent declared fashion to be sad, uncreative, and difficult to wear but attempted to be aware of current styles. Another French study, conducted for a company which publishes fashion magazines, found that 18.9 percent of the female population were very interested in fashion, 49.1 percent were somewhat interested, and 32 percent were not interested (Pujol 1992).

3. *Vogue* was founded in 1893. For a brief history of *Vogue*, see Lakoff and Scherr (1984:chap. 4). This discussion is based on an analysis of the first three issues of the following years: 1947, 1957, 1967, 1977, 1987, and 1997.

4. In their analyses of photographs in *National Geographic* magazine, Lutz and Collins (1993:199) found that "those who are culturally defined as weak—women, children, people of color, the poor, the tribal rather than modern, those without technology—are more likely to face the camera, the more powerful to be represented looking elsewhere."

5. *Vogue's* circulation was 449,722 in 1968; 970,084 in 1978; and 1,126,193 in 1997 (the last date for which such figures are available) (*World Almanac and Book of Facts* 1969, 1980, and 1999).

6. A different type of research on women's perceptions of advertisements in fashion magazines has attempted to ascertain the effects of ads showing images of highly attractive models on college women's perceived levels of satisfaction with their appearance (Richins 1991). McCracken (1988) showed college students fashion ads and asked them to try to explain how they interpreted them.

7. Focus groups rather than interviews were used as a means of obtaining responses to fashion photographs, because the task of commenting on photographs was unfamiliar to respondents. In developing their opinions, members of the groups were stimulated by the comments of other respondents in the focus-group setting. They were not obligated to participate to meet the requirements of a course. They varied in age, racial background,

and nationality: 83 percent were college age (the rest were middle-aged); 33 percent were African American, African, East and West Indian, Eurasian, and Asian American (the remainder were Caucasian); and 13 percent were not American (they were from Ghana, Indonesia, Iran, Lebanon, and Panama). Three of the respondents were male. Undergraduates were students in classes in sociology and communication. A total of forty-five people participated. The fifteen focus groups varied in size from two to four and were conducted in college classrooms or in private homes. Each session typically lasted from half an hour to an hour. As far as possible, each focus group was homogenous in age and racial background. Focus-group leaders for the college students were graduate students in most cases. An African-American graduate student led the focus groups of African Americans. The other groups were led by the author. All focus groups were recorded and transcribed. All names used in the text are fictitious.

8. This figure is substantially higher than comparable figures obtained in American surveys (one-third and one-fifth) (Gutman and Mills 1982; Krafft 1991) and is probably because the majority of the women who participated in the study were under twenty-five. It is also likely that most women who agreed to participate in the study had some interest in fashion.

9. Although the numbers were small, it appeared that race was a more important influence than nationality on participants' responses to these images.

8 FASHION AND CLOTHING CHOICES IN TWO CENTURIES

Social scientists have not reached a consensus about the character of contemporary Western societies. A number of recent labels circulate, such as "postindustrial," "postmodern," and "fragmented," to be contrasted with older labels, such as "industrial," "modern," and "class," which have not been discarded. The nature of the "new" society is in part a result of economic changes that have altered the definition of work and the relationship between work and leisure, changes that correspond to the definition of postindustrial society. The character of contemporary society is also the result of postmodern electronic media, which have changed the relationship between public and private space and redefined the way we view images from the past and the present. The complexity of the new society arises from the fact that various segments of the population have been affected in different ways by recent social, economic, and cultural changes, leading to new and more complex forms of social fragmentation. An additional level of complexity has been added to contemporary society by its increasing susceptibility to external economic and social trends and to "global" cultural influences, both of which have increased the level of competition for survival among national economic and cultural organizations, as well as the variety and level of dissonance among cultural texts and nonverbal codes.

Tracing changes in the nature of fashion and in the criteria for clothing choices is one way of understanding the differences between the type of society that has been gradually disappearing and the one that is slowly emerging. On the one hand, fashionable clothes embody the hegemonic ideals and values of a particular period. On the other hand, clothing choices objectify the ways in which members of social groups and groupings at different social levels perceive themselves in relation to the dominant values.

Analyzing how changes in fashion and clothing choices are related to other aspects of social and cultural change requires a combination of theoretical approaches, since these cultural phenomena can be viewed from different perspectives. In this book, I have examined clothing as a type of consumption; clothing as a form of nonverbal culture; the use of clothes in public locations for the presentation of self, specifically the effects of urban, organizational, and electronic spaces; and the impact of various ways in which the production of fashion is organized upon the meanings of clothing and the diffusion of fashionable styles. Within each of these perspectives, different theoretical approaches have been invoked.

Under the influence of Simmel's paradigmatic essay, the consumption of fashion has usually been viewed as a diffusion process, one that is constantly being renewed. Diffusion models have focused on the social characteristics of adopters defined in terms of social class and social status in a specific group, age, or gender. Arguing that the extent of the diffusion of fashion tends to be overestimated, I have shown that in nineteenth-century class societies the diffusion of fashion tended to be aided or prevented by a person's identification with her own or with another social class or social group. Relationships between social classes have been interpreted using theories of symbolic boundaries and class reproduction, which attempt to explain the nature of class cultures and their relationships to one another. I have also argued that relationships between social class strata cannot be conceptualized as a linear progression from high to low status. Relationships between social strata change over time in ways that disrupt perceptions of relative status and affect the adoption of fashionable clothing.

Because of the enormous complexity of diffusion processes on a societal level in the late twentieth century, attention has shifted away from the process of diffusion itself to an analysis of the responses to clothing by consumers and to the role of clothes in the construction of personal identity. The concept of "reception" endows the consumer with a greater level of agency than was the case in the older diffusion models, the consumer now actively making selections rather than passively responding to what is available.

For women, clothes were in the nineteenth century, and are still, powerful expressions of gender hegemonies. One way to understand the hegemonic effects of clothing is by examining discourses surrounding clothing, specifically the controversies and conflicts over the expression of gender in clothing that change from one period to another. Here I have examined how gender hegemonies were actually experienced and in what ways they were resisted. Clothing has performed important roles in maintaining the visibility of alternative discourses about gender roles.

Explaining the construction of identity and resistance to hegemony through clothing requires an interpretation of how clothes express meaning. Clothing as a form of nonverbal, visual communication is a powerful means of making subversive social statements, because these statements are not necessarily constructed or received on a conscious or rational level. Changes in the significance of certain types of clothing and in the ways clothes communicate meanings are indications of major alterations in how social groups and groupings perceive their relationships to one another. As a result of the almost symbiotic connections between fashion industries and media industries, fashion producers draw on and contribute to the multiplicity of visual codes that circulate in the electronic spaces of contemporary societies.

Clothes are intended to be worn in public space; we dress for others not for ourselves. Therefore, the nature of public space influences the ways in which people use fashionable and nonfashionable clothes to express their identities and to make subversive statements. Changes in the characteristics of urban spaces and in the availability of "alternative" public spaces affect people's perceptions of how it is necessary to present themselves in public. Such changes often have the effect of increasing or decreasing opportunities to use clothing as a means of subverting the dominant culture. In contemporary society, the electronic media increasingly monopolize public space to an extent that was not possible for nonelectronic media and influence the ways in which we use other types of spaces.

Finally, changes in the production of fashionable styles are indicative of changes in the relationships among contemporary societies. Fashion was one of the earliest forms of global culture but in a type of global economy that differed from the present one. In the late nineteenth century, global culture spread from center to periphery: styles in men's clothes from London and in women's clothes from Paris were followed in other European countries and in America. In the past, the production of fashion was an activity of social communities or "fashion worlds" of culture creators who attempted to establish themselves as "quasi-artists." In the late twentieth century, global culture is multicentered: styles flow from centers to peripheries and vice versa. Today, the production of fashion takes place in sets of organizations in different countries that operate on a global scale and that are subject to the competitive pressures of the global marketplace.

Too often in studies of various forms of culture, consumption, meaning, space, and production are considered separately. As a result, our understanding of how cultural forms influence and are influenced by their social contexts is greatly reduced. Although I will organize the following section by paired terms that summarize specific types of changes, it is important to remember that social change is actually cumulative rather than discontinuous. Older forms and patterns seldom entirely disappear as newer ones emerge. In the following section, I will recapitulate the major findings from the previous chapters and, in the final section, speculate about their significance.

FASHION AND CLOTHING CHOICES IN TWO TYPES OF SOCIETIES: A Recapitulation

From Class Cultures to Segmented Cultures.   The classical diffusion model of fashion proposes that styles were adopted by elites and gradually disseminated to subordinate classes. This theory implies that clothing was a crucial element in status striving, the attempt to claim a higher social status than might otherwise have been attributed to a person as a way of indicating improvements in his or her situation. In fact, symbolic boundaries were difficult to transgress in the nineteenth century because of the relative lack of social contacts between social classes, the scarcity of disposable income, and unfamiliarity with certain forms of etiquette used in other class cultures. Instead, clothing was an important means of "claiming" social status, for indicating one's actual social position in societies where small gradations in social status were taken seriously. This suggests that identification with a social class was a major aspect of one's sense of self.

The use of hats by different strata in the French working class in the nineteenth century was one indication of the importance of status striving as compared with status maintenance. French working-class men were more likely to own hats identified with the working class than with the upper or middle class. Wearing hats identified with the upper or middle class appeared to be a means of signifying improvements in social position, but most men preferred working-class hats.

Variations in clothing choices in nineteenth-century France and the United States were the result of differences in the nature of and interrelationships between class cultures. In France, before 1875, some working-class strata were cut off from the national culture by regional dialects and illiteracy, accentuating the differences in clothing behavior between Paris and the provinces. After 1875, changes in outlook that reshaped the existing cultures of working-class strata led to new types of clothing behavior. The cultures of working-class strata in the provinces changed in response to increases in the standard of living, higher levels of literacy, and access to new sources of information.

In the United States, high rates of geographical mobility from East to West and of immigration from other countries heightened the salience of clothing, which was reflected in expenditures for clothing that were higher than in Europe. The level of concern with clothing appeared anomalous in a society that was considered more democratic and less stratified than European societies. Political democratization might have led to democratization of clothing, but, instead, there were pronounced differences by region. American farmers in the Middle West, even in remote areas, attempted to emulate the lifestyle and clothing of the middle class on the East Coast. On the East Coast, there were different class strata within the working class whose members had different levels of opportunity to emulate the middle class.

Although differences in types of clothing worn in different social classes in the nineteenth century decreased in both the United States and France, the adoption or nonadoption of certain types of accessories remained an indication of social class affiliation. Silk ties, watches, and watch chains were more readily adopted by the working class than canes, gloves, and top hats.

Technological changes in the production of clothing beginning in the middle of the century led to the simplification of clothing styles, which eventually contributed to a gradual democratization of clothing. However, these changes were offset by the increasing use of uniforms in the workplace and for domestic workers in the home. Ironically, uniforms reinforced social class differences at a time when changes in other types of clothing were beginning to diminish them.

Clothing appears to have mattered in nineteenth-century class societies in ways it has gradually lost in the twentieth. As the first widely available consumer good, it was coveted both as a marker of achieved status and as a means of indicating a person's identity within a social stratum. As regional and ethnic costumes disappeared, clothing also contributed to the development of a sense of identity based on nationwide cultures, as did public education and the media.

In highly fragmented societies in the late twentieth century, clothing behavior indicates a major disjunction between work and leisure. These institutional spheres constitute different social and sartorial worlds. The values expressed by clothing worn in the economic sector in the late twentieth century are not very different from those expressed by clothing in the economic sector in the late nineteenth century. Regulated by dress codes, clothing behavior in the workplace expresses the hierarchical style of organization, compatible with clear divisions between social classes. This type of clothing indicates an individual's position in an organizational hierarchy. The meanings of clothing worn in the workplace are relatively fixed: well-defined rules specify how clothing items, such as men's suits, women's suits, and uniforms for specific occupations, are to be worn.

Leisure activities transmit values that are usually very different from the values of the workplace and the traditional work ethic. Leisure cultures are diverse and fragmented into social segments based on age, race, ethnicity, gender, and sexual orientation that are reflected in clothing behavior. Social class identity is less salient, because, at the same economic level in social classes, differences in attitudes and tastes that result from other aspects of social identity are likely to be as great as differences between social classes. Consumption cannot be interpreted entirely in terms of a particular category. Instead, these different types of classifications overlap, contributing to the complexity of meanings expressed by clothing. Some people identify with particular social groups; others engage in "identity work," choosing or creating ways to express their changing understandings of themselves. For many adolescents and young adults, clothing is a means of expressing identity rather than social class status and, to some extent, a means of locating identity, of making sense of their personal lives. The latter occurs through appropriation of items of clothing that film and popular music personalities have endowed with symbolic significance and through various activities, such as *bricolage*, fantasy, and aesthetic expression, that redefine the meanings of clothing. Older, affluent dandies use highly coded avant-garde and postmodernist clothing for similar purposes.

Democratization of clothing has led to diversity, not standardization. Consequently, trajectories representing the diffusion of specific styles are shorter and more erratic. Age is more salient than class. As fashionable clothing, designed for the young and often based on styles they have developed themselves, diffuse to older groups, the young move on to newer styles, as did the upper class in the nineteenth century. Clothing behavior suggests the intricacies of relationships between social groups within and between social classes and dispels the illusion of social integration fostered by media culture.

From Hegemonic Gender Ideals to Conflicted Gender Hegemonies.   Industrial societies were characterized by distinct gender cultures. Fashion represented upper-class conceptions of how women and men should look and behave. Depending on their social class or stratum within a social class, women had different degrees of access to fashionable clothing and used it in different ways.

Upper- and middle-class wives, who represented their families at numerous social functions, attempted to dress fashionably and frequently spent substantially more of the family income for this purpose than did their husbands. Working-class wives, when not employed outside the home, tended to have more limited resources for clothing than other members of their families, an indication of their relative exclusion from the public sphere and of their positions in the family and the community. They were less likely than their husbands or their daughters to own items of middle-class dress, because both husbands and daughters were more likely to participate in social life outside the home.

By contrast, unmarried, employed working-class women in cities often spent their disposable income on extravagant and flamboyant clothing, presumably designed to attract attention to themselves. Their efforts to dress fashionably were frequently disparaged at the time but appear to have been forerunners of a type of late twentieth-century consumption as a means of expressing personal identity.

In the late nineteenth century, fashionable clothing embodied gender ideals that no longer corresponded to the realities of women's lives, as women became better educated, entered the workplace in greater numbers, and participated in political activities. Fashionable styles were created in Paris for upper-class women and courtesans, whose attitudes and behavior conformed to hegemonic gender ideals that were being challenged in other countries. The emancipation of women progressed more rapidly in the United States and England, where women adopted items of clothing that did not originate in France and that were more appropriate for their new lifestyles. At the beginning of the twentieth century, French styles became somewhat less elaborate and physically constraining, but a new gender ideal that combined elements of both the dominant and alternative nineteenth-century styles did not appear in fashionable clothing until after the First World War.

While fashion is still viewed as a form of hegemonic oppression for women, it no longer expresses the gender ideals of the entire culture, as is indicated by the fact that the majority of women are not interested in fashion. The fashion press projects an image of fashion as a kind of entertainment similar to other types of media entertainment directed at young consumers. Stereotypical gender images in photographs provide dissonant commentaries on feminist agendas expressed in articles. The ideal feminine body is

Caucasian; photographs make subtle distinctions between bodies identified with different races.

In keeping with the conflicted nature of hegemony in fragmented societies, in which pluralistic elites disagree among themselves, luxury fashion design deliberately invokes a variety of social agendas, ranging from those that empower women to those that appear to disempower them. These agendas include the female executive, the woman as object of the male gaze, and the postmodernist role player, continually constructing new identities in response to new consumer products. The fashion industry and the fashion press construct their goals as proposing rather than dictating appearances while at the same time implying that the consumer will want to be whatever she can manage to appear to be. Customers, as described by luxury fashion designers, appeared to have a strong sense of their personal identities and how they wished to express themselves through their clothes.

Women who discussed fashion photographs in focus groups did not seem to have a postmodern outlook in the sense of deriving their identities from the consumption of clothing and other goods. The standards frequently invoked by the majority of these women, both young and middle-aged, were based on traditional hegemonic norms about feminine demeanor which define as deviant appearances that are sexually ambiguous, displays of nudity, and provocative sexuality. In evaluating clothing in the photographs, these women sought to express their identities and to remain faithful to their conceptions of their identities. They found postmodernist ambiguity unsettling, because they were committed to a sense of self that they attempted to enhance rather than conceal. They did not perceive their identities as fluid, but at the same time the construction of a gender image that fit their conceptions of their identities was a way of expressing agency.

Fashion in the nineteenth century expressed male hegemonic values. In the late twentieth century, men's gender hegemony is revised, satirized, and subverted by clothing choices of men belonging to youth subcultures and to racial and sexual minorities. French luxury fashion, in particular, highlights the clothing choices of the traditional dandy, emphasizing aspects of male identity that are unacceptable to conventional male hegemonic values. Here fashion expresses its subversive tendencies, pushing toward a redefinition of masculinity.

Clothes as "Texts": From Closed to Open. Analysis of clothing behavior reveals the importance of conceptualizing the cultures of contemporary societies as complex aggregations of codes, sets of clothing items to which social groups have attributed interrelated meanings. Since the same items of clothing may be used in different ways with different meanings in different social groups, contemporary fragmented societies are difficult to read; individuals successfully read the groups to which they belong but are often unaware of codes used by other groups.

"Closed" texts, garments with fixed meanings, were typical of class societies. "Open" texts, garments that continually acquire new meanings, are more likely to appear in fragmented societies, because different social groups wish to express different meanings using the same type of garment. Jeans have continually acquired new meanings during the twentieth century as they have been appropriated by different social groups and worn in different social contexts. However, closed texts have not disappeared. For example, jeans signal both conformity and opposition in comparison with garments such as the black leather jacket. The latter projected only one meaning, resistance to the dominant culture, until recently, when its widespread adoption at all social class levels diluted its countercultural implications.

How changes in social structures have affected the presentation of social identity is seen in the shift from the hat, a closed text, as an obligatory item of male attire to the widespread use of the T-shirt, an open text. Until the 1960s, a man's hat, as the most immediately visible part of his costume, was a major signal of social identity and social class. Specific styles of hats were associated with different class strata. In the late twentieth century, men's hats have become a relic of a class society based on face-to-face relationships in public spaces that has largely disappeared.

In contemporary societies, the sartorial equivalent of the hat is the T-shirt, which expresses social identity in many different ways, ranging from identity politics to lifestyle. Unlike hats, whose meanings were universally understood, T-shirts speak to like-minded people; a particular T-shirt may not be meaningful to those with different views and affiliations. This reflects the fragmentation of leisure cultures into lifestyles and subcultures and other groupings whose members respond to the enormous cultural complexity of their surroundings by orienting themselves toward those who are like rather than those who are unlike themselves.

Subcultures and marginal groups manipulate clothing texts to express their attitudes toward themselves and society. In both the nineteenth and twentieth centuries, the expression of nonverbal symbols through clothing was a means of challenging a repressive gender ideology. Unmarried, employed middle-class "surplus" women in the nineteenth century relied on a form of symbolic inversion. Items of masculine clothing, incorporated into feminine styles, acquired new meanings, signifying feminine independence. The result was a nonverbal commentary on the ideal gender role for women that could be read in different ways: ignored, assimilated unconsciously, or understood. In the late twentieth century, the clothing choices of gay subcultures have offered an analogous commentary on heterosexual gender roles, which has influenced the clothing of heterosexual men.

Members of youth subcultures use a relatively small number of "iconic" garments that enable them to make sense of their experiences, drawing on decades of previous experiments with subcultural clothing styles. The media, in the form of film and popular music, perform important roles in creating the meanings of garments and of combinations of garments. Electronic culture worlds provide networks that relay meanings created in street cultures to larger publics via popular music. Youth subcultures produce music and street styles that are in turn popularized by the media and marketed by clothing industries.

Both luxury fashion and industrial fashion are closely linked to media culture, incorporating its icons, motifs, and themes. Media culture (film, television, and popular music) and the clothing industry, both on the luxury and industrial levels, are engaged in similar activities — creating new meanings by appropriating and recycling meanings from other sectors of culture, past and present. Some fashionable styles are highly subversive; others are intended to represent specific lifestyles that are related in varying degrees to the way people actually live.

The media and fashion in the aggregate fit definitions of the postmodern as a result of the enormous variety and incongruity of styles and codes, but these codes are not inherently meaningless or ambiguous, as some postmodernists have suggested. Instead, some clothing codes are understood primarily by those who share the same identities and are opaque to outsiders. Women and minorities appear to be more skillful "decoders" than white men.

From Urban to Electronic Space.   Clothing in class societies was more salient than it is in contemporary postclass societies, in part because of the significance of urban space. Status striving and status maintenance were facilitated by the nature of social relationships in public places. The street was an important element of social life: when people walked in the streets, they felt themselves to be on display. Clothes were of central importance in the presentation of self in these public spaces. Social elites promenaded frequently on certain streets and in parks. According to a French costume historian (Delbourg-Delphis 1981:76): "It was necessary to visit regularly certain places in order to be seen. . . . Social life was a perpetual stage." French designers hired women, wearing their newest styles, to walk in areas frequented by elites. Some working-class people refrained from engaging in

Sunday promenades, when it was customary to wear one's most elegant clothing, because they could not meet minimal standards of appearance. Immigrants in the United States advised relatives who were coming over to discard
their traditional costumes as soon as they disembarked so they wouldn't be
seen wearing inappropriate clothing. Deviations from clothing norms, particularly by women, were strongly sanctioned by crowds in the streets.

The visibility of certain categories of working-class people in urban public spaces influenced the ways in which the working class as a whole was
perceived by other social classes. The relative visibility of men belonging to
the more affluent strata of the working class and of young, employed, unmarried working-class women led middle-class observers to assume that their
styles of clothing were typical of the working class.

Secluded, marginal, and liminal spaces offered opportunities for women
to experiment with otherwise unacceptable clothing, such as trousered bathing suits and gym suits. Employed working-class women who worked in "secluded" spaces, outside urban public space, sometimes adopted men's clothing, including trousers, the item that was most taboo for women in the
nineteenth century. The popularity of the bicycle at the end of the century
led women to begin wearing types of clothes in urban public spaces that had
formerly been worn only in marginal spaces, leading to considerable resistance on the part of the public, but eventual acceptance of clothing that
implied a different conception of women's behavior.

As cities have increased in size, the environments they provide have become more impersonal. The nature of urban space has changed, rendering
clothes less salient as an indication of social status or social identity. The
majority of transactions in public places occur between strangers. Presentation of social status through clothing is less important than other types of
identification, such as credit cards, automobile licenses, social security numbers, passports, identity cards, and e-mail addresses. Faceless identities are
preserved and transmitted in electronic space. Consequently, we are less
likely to perceive our clothes as being subject to the critical gaze of others on
the street. One result has been the widespread adoption of the practice of
"dressing down," wearing informal, casual clothes, generally associated with
leisure rather than work, in settings where formerly a person would have felt
constrained to claim social status through more formal dress. Exceptions to this
trend are marginal and liminal spaces in urban settings that are "colonized" by
specific groups, often racial and sexual minorities, where the presentation of
self through dress becomes a major preoccupation. For example, clubs and
bars in certain neighborhoods develop dress codes that challenge the expression of sexuality and sexual orientation in dress. By contrast, television and the

internet create new versions of public space, ones which represent the public selectively.

From Urban Fashion Worlds to Global Production Systems.   The creation and production of fashionable clothing has shifted from a system that was highly centralized to one which is more decentralized and pluralistic. The existence of well-defined styles of fashionable clothing in the nineteenth and early twentieth centuries required a highly centralized and visible system of fashion creation and diffusion. Nineteenth-century fashion originated in major cities, among which Paris dominated. With its long history of leadership in the decorative arts, France was uniquely placed to play this role. Fashionable clothes expressed the outlook and gender ideals of elites and were designed for the social activities in which they participated. Continually circulating, parading, and socializing in particular types of urban spaces, these elites expected clothing to meet high standards of creativity and craftsmanship. French fashion was created in an urban culture in which designers knew their clients and understood the social milieus in which they moved. These styles were disseminated to other countries through personal contacts and by fashion magazines. French designers continued to set fashion in other countries in the twentieth century despite the development of ready-to-wear clothing and the increasing standardization of clothing that entailed. As styles became less complicated, it became easier to market variations of these styles to different social strata. Consensus about fashionable styles was possible because class-based ideals of behavior and appearance were widely accepted in Western industrial countries.

"Consumer" fashion, which replaced "class" fashion, is much more amorphous and unpredictable than class fashion. Luxury fashion emerges from fashion worlds in several countries and generally expresses the outlook of particular subcultures in the middle and upper classes, while industrial fashion targets distinct age groups, lifestyles, and ethnic cultures. Styles and fads originate in different class strata, but their trajectories vary, depending in part on the ways they are presented in the media and in part on their being interpreted in many different ways by members of different social groups.

Luxury fashion designers present themselves as daring and creative artists, but their activities are embedded in organizations that require high levels of investment to penetrate global markets and that use fashionable clothing styles to confer images on other products. Designers whose activities are "subsidized" by successful lines of luxury products are free to engage in innovative but often erratic experiments with avant-garde and postmodern themes.

Those who are attempting to enter highly competitive markets sometimes engage in similar types of innovation, as a market strategy, but face high risk.

In the past, fashion as a form of global culture radiated from a center to peripheries, which were located largely, although not entirely, in Western industrial countries. Today, as in many other forms of global culture, fashion is dominated by, but has no clear center in, Western culture while at the same time it continually absorbs influences from non-Western cultures.

CONCLUSION

Fashion's social agendas always speak to and for certain social groups and exclude others. In the nineteenth century, the bases for exclusion were inferior social class status and lack of conformity to a specific gender ideal. In the late twentieth century, exclusion is more likely to be based on age and sometimes race. More subtle forms of exclusion are expressed in the selection and definition of target customers for sophisticated or esoteric clothing. Alternative clothing codes and discourses emerge to provide a means of speaking about ourselves in ways that fashion neglects. Women in the nineteenth century and minorities in the late twentieth century developed their own styles of communication through clothing. Eventually, these alternative agendas are likely to be assimilated by fashion, if only as stereotypes or caricatures. Social identities and the material cultures associated with them are constantly being redefined.

Material cultures such as clothing provide clues for "grounding" notions of postindustrial society and postmodernist culture. Like postindustrial societies, industrial societies were poorly integrated, but the lack of social integration was different. Class cultures were less segmented; urban spaces were more representative. In class societies, the meanings of most items of clothing were readily understood in different social classes. In fragmented societies, clothes worn in workplaces are intended to convey messages that are inconsistent and even incongruous with those conveyed by clothes in leisure spaces. Postmodern leisure cultures are chaotic aggregations of codes that are not universally understood. Clothing worn by a specific social group or segment is likely to be interpreted in different ways within and outside such groups, raising the question of how well different groups are able to understand one another. Clothing as a form of communication has become a set of dialects rather than a universal language. Urban public spaces formerly provided sites for visual representations of groups that competed for control of the public sphere but have been displaced by electronic media. Such media represent social groups and segments selectively and create new types of spaces in which local spaces are less meaningful.

The studies in this book suggest that in order to understand contemporary societies, we need to pay more attention to how meanings for cultural goods are produced, by whom, and in what contexts; to how widely specific sets of meanings embodied in particular types of cultural goods circulate; and to the nature of the public spaces in which they diffuse. We need to know more about how consumers of culture interpret ambiguous codes and how they choose to identify with certain cultural goods rather than others. Are fragmented societies frustrating because people are continually exposed to codes they do not understand and from which they feel excluded? Or, alternatively, are these societies liberating because people are able to find or create codes that express their identities? Are conflicted hegemonies less oppressive than traditional hegemonies because pressures to conform in one's choices of cultural goods are generally weaker?

We also need to ask how creators of culture are able to maneuver among the intricate networks of social affiliations in fragmented societies. It is likely to be increasingly difficult for them to discern emerging worldviews that crosscut different social segments. A few creators have organizational power bases that permit them to expose their interpretations of the worldviews of their social groups or segments to large publics. The activities of most creators are limited to tiny "niches" carved from their own experiences and backgrounds.

Fashion and clothing, like litmus paper, offer clues to discerning links between social structure and culture and to tracing the itineraries of material cultures in fragmented societies. In the increasingly multicultural societies of the twenty-first century, clothing codes will continue to proliferate as a means of expressing relationships within and between social groups and segments and of indicating responses to even more conflicted hegemonies.

APPENDIX 1: List of Monographs of Nineteenth-Century French Working-Class Families Published by Frédéric Le Play and His Associates

The analysis of clothing owned by French working-class families in chapters 2 and 3 is based on eighty-one monographs on French families, forty-two completed between 1850 and 1874 and thirty-nine between 1875 and 1910. They were published in a series of volumes entitled *Ouvriers Européens* (Le Play 1877–79) and *Ouvriers des Deux Mondes* (La Société Internationale des Etudes Pratiques d'Economie Sociale 1857–1928).

Each case was coded as a set of variables designed for the analysis of clothing behavior and in terms of social and economic variables. Applying techniques of empirical analysis to these data permits me to draw conclusions about the frequency of different types of clothing choices and about the factors associated with different types of clothing behavior. Clothing behavior, analyzed in its social and economic context, emerges as a significant and meaningful facet of nineteenth-century social life, in other words, as an expression of the social situation of the family, as well as the goals and desires of its individual members.

A complete list of Le Play monographs used in the study (in the text, monographs are identified by number and year)[1] is presented below, followed by two tables that present information about levels of income and wealth (table A1.1) and expenditures for and value of clothing owned by families in the various working-class strata (table A1.2).

Ouvriers Européens, vol. 3[2]
   I (1851): Cutler (London)
   II (1851): Cutler (Sheffield)
   III (1842–51): Carpenter (Sheffield)
   IV (1850): Smelter (Derbyshire)

Ouvriers Européens, vol. 4
   V (1851): Farm laborer (Brittany)
   VI (1851): Farm laborer (Armagnac)

1. Missing numbers represent cases that were inappropriate for this study (i.e., the families were not located in France, England, or the United States).
2. The numbers used in this section were assigned to the cases in these volumes.

Ouvriers Européens, vol. 5
  VII (1850): Miner (Auvergne)
  VIII (1856): Farmer (Basque)
  IX (1855): Unskilled laborer (Nivernais)
  X (1855): Wood smelter (Nivernais)
  XI (1852): Laundryman (Clichy)
  XII (1852): Marshal (Maine)

Ouvriers Européens, vol. 6
  XIII (1850): Farm laborer (Laonnais)
  XIV (1848–50): Unskilled laborer (Maine)
  XV (1850): Weaver (Maine)
  XVI (1854): Ragpicker (Paris)

Ouvriers des Deux Mondes
  First series, vol. 1:
    1 (1856): Carpenter (Paris)
    2 (1856): Unskilled farm laborer (Champagne)
    3 (1856): Community of farmers (Hautes Pyrénées)
    4 (1856): Farmer (Basses Pyrénées)
    6 (1857): Dairyman (Surrey)
    7 (1857): Weaver (shawls) (Paris)
    8 (1856): Tenant farmer (Nottingham)
  First series, vol. 2:
    10 (1857): Tin worker (Aix-les-Bains)
    11 (1856): Quarryman (suburbs of Paris)
    13 (1856): Tailor (Paris)
    15 (1858): Unskilled steelworker (Doubs)
    16 (1858): Skilled steelworker (Doubs)
    17 (1858): Water carrier (Paris)
    19 (1858): Chalk loader (suburbs of Paris)
  First series, vol. 3:
    20 (1859): Embroiderer (Vosges)
    21 (1859): Farmer and soap boiler (Provence)
    22 (1859): Miner (California)
    23 (1858–60): Unskilled laborer/winegrower (Charente)
    24 (1858): Seamstress (Lille)
    26 (1860): Country teacher (Eure)
    27 (1860): Unskilled laborer (Paris)
  First series, vol. 4:
    29 (1861): Farmer (Laonnais)
    32 (1860): Unskilled laborer/winegrower (Burgundy)
    33 (1861): Typesetter (Paris)

34 (1861): Junk-shop owner (Paris)

36 (1862): Weaver (Vosges)

First series, vol. 5:

38 (1860): Extended family of farmers (Nivernais)

40 (1863): Fan maker (Oise)

41 (1878): Shoemaker (Seine)

41A (1878): Ragpicker (Paris)

42 (1878): Locksmith/blacksmith (Paris)

42A (1878): Unskilled bronze worker (Paris)

43 (1881): Corporal in the Republican Guard (Paris)

44 (1881): Farmer/resin tapper (Landes)

Second series, vol. 1:

47 (1883): Salt maker (Loire)

49 (1884): Wheelwright/factory worker (Oise)

50 (1864): Crockery maker (Nièvre)

51 (1885): Market gardener (Seine-et-Oise)

52 (1879): Fisherman (Bouches-du-Rhône)

53 (1879): Small farmer (Gascogne)

55 (1865): Glove maker (Grenoble)

Second series, vol. 2:

58 (1861): Fisherman (Seine)

59 (1862): Small farmer (Provence)

59 *bis* (1885): Farmer and bricklayer (Creuse)

62 (1887): Flint maker (Loir-et-Cher)

65 (1888): Extended family of small farmers (Charente)

Second series, vol. 3:

66 (1888): Winegrowers (Alsace)

69 (1888): Tanner (England)

70 (1889–90): Carpenter (Paris)

Second series, vol. 4:

73 (1884–90): Factory supervisor (Aisne)

74 (1891): Luxury cabinetmaker (Paris)

75 (1891): Small farmer (Texas)

76 (1892): Skilled toymaker (Paris)

78 (1890): Workman, paper factory (Angoulême)

80 (1892–93): Mountain farmers (Loire)

81 (1893): Lamplighter (Nancy)

Second series, vol. 5:

83 (1894): Spinner (Marne)

86 (1893): Miner (Pas-de-Calais)

87 (1893): Farmer (Pas-de-Calais)

88 (1895): Locksmith/blacksmith (Paris)

88 *bis* (1897): Installer of Venetian shutters (Paris)

89 (1895): Overseer/miner (Loire)

91 (1863–64): Small farmer (Bas-Limousin)

Third series, vol. 1:

93 (1899): Piano tuner (Paris)

94 (1897–99): Brandy distiller (Charente)

98 (1901): Porcelain decorator (Limoges)

99 (1901–2): Railway roadman (Paris)

Third series, vol. 2:

104 (1904–5): Dyer, glove factory (Haute-Vienne)

105 (1902–3): Gardener (Tarn-et-Garonne)

106 (1904–5): Corset maker (Paris suburbs)

107 (1889–1905): Tinner (Allier)

Third series, vol. 3:

109 (1908): Weaver (Aisne)

110 (1909): Brush maker (Cher)

Bailhache, *La Science Sociale* (May 1905): 3–84.[3]

115 (1896–97): Factory worker (Paris)

3. This case study was used because it was conducted according to the techniques developed by Le Play, although it does not appear in the volumes published by Le Play or by La Société Internationale des Etudes Pratiques d'Economie Sociale.

APPENDIX TABLE 1.1
INCOME AND WEALTH BY WORKING-CLASS STRATA, 1850–74 AND 1875–1909
(in francs)

		Median Income	Range	Median Wealth	Range
1850–1874					
Prov. farmers	(8)	3,464	1,656–10,199	19,162	5,451–37,584
Paris skilled	(6)	2,777	1,751–10,765	5,834	748–85,405
Paris unskilled	(5)	1,962	970– 2,469	1,557	432– 6,268
Prov. skilled	(14)	1,596	544– 2,985	3,139	447–12,481
Prov. unskilled	(8)	837	460– 2,356	1,578	328– 5,678
All strata	(41)	1,842	460–10,765	3,688	447–85,405
1875–1909					
Prov. farm owners	(6)	7,165	3,382–13,624	48,081	13,773–141,299
Prov. farm tenants	(5)	4,402	1,700– 6,996	17,743	2,442– 28,446
Paris unskilled	(6)	3,854	2,669– 4,645	2,832	84– 22,157
Paris skilled	(6)	3,342	2,132– 4,144	4,160	1,612– 6,346
Prov. unskilled	(7)	2,782	1,904– 5,619	1,384	900– 18,866
Prov. skilled	(6)	2,299	1,074– 8,417	6,678	901– 20,316
All strata	(36)	3,604	1,074–13,624	5,446	900–141,299

Notes: Table is based on case studies collected by Le Play and his associates. Medians rather than means were used because the ranges were very large. Median wealth includes property, buildings, equipment, furniture, utensils, and clothes. Ns are in parentheses, and total excludes one female head of household in the first period and three in the second period.

APPENDIX TABLE 1.2

EXPENDITURES AND VALUES OF CLOTHING BY WORKING-CLASS STRATA, 1850–1874 AND 1875–1909

		Median Percentage of Income Spent on Clothing	Median Value of Clothing as Percentage of Wealth
1850–74			
Prov. farmers	(8)	9.0	9.0
Paris skilled	(6)	7.5	16.5
Paris unskilled	(5)	7.0	43.0
Prov. skilled	(14)	9.5	13.0
Prov. unskilled	(8)	10.5	13.5
All strata	(41)	8.0	13.0
1875–1909			
Prov. farm owners	(6)	7.5	5.5
Prov. farm tenants	(5)	6.5	14.5
Paris skilled	(6)	11.5	26.5
Paris unskilled	(6)	7.0	27.0
Prov. skilled	(6)	7.5	10.0
Prov. unskilled	(7)	8.0	27.0
All strata	(36)	8.0	16.5

Notes: Table is based on case studies collected by Le Play and his associates. Wealth includes property, buildings, equipment, furniture, utensils, and clothes. Ns are in parentheses, and total excludes one female head of household in the first period and three in the second period.

APPENDIX 2: Interview Schedules; Questionnaire for Focus Groups

INTERVIEW SCHEDULE

Note: Participants in the focus groups were shown a series of six to nine photographs. They were asked to respond to the following series of questions for each photograph.

1. What aspects of this photograph do you like?
2. What aspects of this photograph do you not like?
3. What adjectives would you use to describe the image of the woman (women) in this photograph?
4. a. Whose point of view is this photograph intended to represent?
      A man's point of view?
      A woman's point of view?
   b. Does it represent your point of view?
   c. Whose point of view does this photograph actually represent?
      The fashion editor's point of view?
      The fashion designer's point of view?
      The advertising account executive's point of view?
      The photographer's point of view?
5. Would you like to look like this woman (women) on certain occasions?
      Why? or why not?
6. What meanings does the clothing in the photograph convey?
      Masculinity
      Femininity
      Androgyny
      Sexuality
      Professionalism
      Other?
7. Would the clothes in this photograph influence in some way how you dress?
      If yes: How? If no: Why not?

QUESTIONNAIRE

Before we show the photographs, we would like you to respond to a few questions about your interests and background. All answers will be kept entirely **confidential.** If you need more space, please write on back of page.

255

1. How frequently do you read *Vogue?*
    _____ every month
    _____ several issues a year
    _____ occasionally
    _____ never

2. Do you read any other fashion magazines regularly (at least several issues a year)?   _____ Yes   _____ No
    If Yes: Which ones? _____
    _____

3. Do you attempt to keep up with current fashions?
    _____ Yes   _____ No
    If yes: In what sense? (Please check as many as apply)
    _____ specific styles of the season
    _____ specific accessories (shoes, bags, belts)
    _____ clothing items displaying brand names
    _____ adjusting hemlines
    _____ other; please explain: _____
    _____
    _____

    If no: Why not? _____
    _____
    _____

4. How do you find out about fashion? (Please check as many as apply)
    _____ "cool" friends, relatives
    _____ television
    _____ fashion magazines
    _____ what pop singers are wearing
    _____ what people are wearing on the street
    _____ what's in my favorite store
        please give name _____
    _____ catalogues: which ones? _____
        other: please explain _____
    _____

5. What are you wearing right now?

    _____
    _____

6. What is your favorite outfit at the moment?

_____

_____

7. What color clothing do you usually wear? _____

8. What is your major? _____

9. What year are you in? _____

10. What career do you hope to pursue after college?

_____

11. What is your father's occupation? _____

12. What is your mother's occupation? _____

13. Where are you from? _____   _____
                              (city)   (state)

14. Where did you grow up? _____   _____
                                   (city)   (state)

15. What is your race? _____

FOCUS-GROUP INTERVIEW:

During the focus-group interview, you will be asked to respond to clothing advertisements and editorial photos taken from recent issues of *Vogue* magazine. All comments will be kept entirely **confidential**. No one will be identified by name in any publications based on this research.

INTERVIEW SCHEDULE (for Luxury Fashion Designers)

I am conducting a study of fashion designers, especially focusing on influences on their work and the conditions under which they work. You will not be identified by name in publications based on this research without your permission.

1. How did you get started as a fashion designer?
2. Did you go to design school?
3. How do you go about creating a new model?

4. When you are creating new models, where do your ideas come from?
   a. Are you influenced by any of the following?
      The visual arts?
      The work of other designers? Who?
      Your customers?
      People you see on the streets?
      Other?
5. Do you look at books or magazines showing fashion plates from the past?
6. What are your goals for your clothes?
   a. Can they be described in terms of any of the following?
      Constant change from year to year?
      Long-lasting, classic, timeless clothes?
      Provide an "image" that will appeal to the customer?
      Provide clothes that will fit into a certain lifestyle?
7. How much do the clothes change from season to season?
   a. In what ways do they change? Examples?
8. Are the clothes designed for a particular group of women?
   a. How would you describe these women?
9. Do you have any ways of being in touch with your customers in order to find out how they are responding to the clothes?
10. What are the prices of your clothes?
11. What country has the most influence on women's styles today?
12. In your opinion, who are the most important designers in the world today?
    a. Why are they so important?
13. What do you think of the work of Japanese designers such as Rei Kawakubo and Yoji Yamamoto?
14. Do you know designers working in other companies in the city or in other parts of the country?
    a. Do you discuss fashion with them from time to time?
15. Do you have any friends who are working in the arts?
    a. If so, which arts?
    b. Are you influenced at all by their work?
16. Do you ever do clothes for films, theater, or pop music stars?
17. How many collections do you do per year?
    a. What is the timing of those collections?
18. How elaborate are your fashion shows?
    a. Do you have specially composed music? Special lighting effects?
    b. How much do you spend on shows?
19. Are there any fashion writers who consistently do stories about your collections? Who?
20. Do you advertise? Where?
21. How many employees does your firm have?
    a. How many of those participate in the design process?

22. Do you have a financial backer?
23. Do you have any licenses? How many?
24. In which countries are your clothes sold?
25. In how many stores in this country are your clothes sold?
26. In your opinion, what is the future of fashion?
    a. What sorts of clothes will we be wearing in the twenty-first century?
27. Could you suggest other people I might talk to about the fashion business, either designers or people connected with the fashion business?

REFERENCES

Adburgham, Alison. 1987. *Shops and Shopping, 1800–1914.* London: Barrie and Jenkins.

Adler, Laure. 1979. *Les Premières Journalistes, 1830–1850.* Paris: Payot.

Akom, Antwi. 1997. "Life in a Segregated High School: Exploring Social and Cultural Capital at Eastern High School." Unpublished master's paper, Department of Sociology, University of Pennsylvania.

Albrecht, Juliana, Jane Farrell-Beck, and Geitel Winakor. 1988. "Function, Fashion, and Convention in American Women's Riding Costume, 1880–1930." *Dress* 14:56–67.

American Demographics. 1993. "Hot Clothes." *American Demographics Desk Reference*, series no. 5, 15 (July): 10–11.

Arbus, Doon, and Marvin Israel, eds. 1984. *Diane Arbus: Magazine Work.* Millerton, NY: Aperture.

Archer, M., and Judith Blau. 1993. "Class Formation in Nineteenth-Century America: The Case of the Middle Class." *Annual Review of Sociology* 19:17–41.

Ash, Juliet. 1992. "Philosophy of the Catwalk: The Making and Wearing of Vivienne Westwood's Clothes." Pp. 169–85 in *Chic Thrills: A Fashion Reader*, ed. Juliet Ash and Elizabeth Wilson. Berkeley: University of California Press.

Bagdikian, Ben H. 1997. *The Media Monopoly.* Boston: Beacon Press.

Bailhache, J. 1905. "Un Type d'ouvrier anarchiste: Monographie d'une famille d'ouvriers parisiens." *La Science Sociale*, série 3, deuxième période, 14e fascicule.

Ballaster, Ros, Margaret Beetham, Elizabeth Frager, and Sandra Hebron. 1991. *Women's World: Ideology, Femininity and the Women's Magazine.* London: Macmillan.

Banner, Lois W. 1984. *American Beauty.* Chicago: University of Chicago Press.

Barber, Bernard, and L. S. Lobel. 1952. "'Fashion' in Women's Clothes and the American Social System." *Social Forces* 31:124–31.

Barbera, Annie. 1990. "Des journeaux et des modes." Pp. 103–18 in *Femmes Fin de Siècle, 1885–1895*, Paris: Musée de la Mode et du Costume, Palais Galliera.

Barmé, Geremie. 1993. "Culture at Large: Consuming T-Shirts in Beijing." *China Information* 8 (nos.1/2): 1–44.

Baron, Ava, and Susan E. Klepp. 1984. "'If I Didn't Have My Sewing Machine . . .': Women and Sewing Machine Technology." Pp. 20–59 in *A Needle, a Bobbin, a Strike: Women Needleworkers in America*, ed. Joan M. Jensen and Sue Davidson. Philadelphia: Temple University Press.

Barringer, Felicity. 1990. "Pinstripes of the Power Elite." *International Herald Tribune*, Jan. 12.

Barthes, Roland. 1977. *Image, Music, Text.* New York: Hill and Wang.

———. 1983 [1967]. *The Fashion System.* Trans. Matthew Ward and Richard Howard. New York: Hill and Wang.

Bassett, Caroline. 1997. "Virtually Gendered: Life in an On-line World." Pp. 537–550 in *The Subcultures Reader,* ed. Ken Gelder and Sarah Thornton. New York: Routledge.

Baudrillard, Jean. 1988. *Selected Writings.* Ed. Mark Poster. Stanford, CA: Stanford University Press.

Becker, Howard. 1982. *Art Worlds.* Berkeley: University of California Press.

Bédarida, François. 1967. "Londres au milieu du XIXe siècle." *Diogène,* no. 60:268–95.

Behling, Dorothy U., and Lois E. Dickey. 1980. "Haute Couture: A 25-year Perspective of Fashion Influences, 1900–1925." *Home Economics Research Journal* 8:28–36.

Bell, Daniel. 1976. *The Cultural Contradictions of Capitalism.* New York: Basic Books.

Bellah, Robert N., Richard Madsen, William M. Sullivan, Ann Swidler, and Steven M. Tipton. 1985. *Habits of the Heart: Individualism and Commitment in American Life.* New York: Harper and Row.

Benaïm, Laurence. 1988. *L'Année de la Mode, '87–'88.* Paris: La Manufacture.

———. 1994. "Forêt de songes." *Le Monde,* July 23, p. 13.

———. 1995. "La mode d'hiver a defilé dans une ambience de fin de siècle." *Le Monde,* July 16–17, p. 16.

———. 1997. "Paris règne sur la mode sans gouverner." *Le Monde,* Mar. 17, p. 21.

Berendt, John. 1988. "The Straw Boater." *Esquire* 110 (Aug.): 24.

Bertin, Célia. 1956. *Haute couture: Terre inconnu.* Paris: Hachette.

Bischoff, J.-L. 1989. "La Planète jeune est sous influence musicale." *Journal du Textile,* no. 1169 (Aug. 24): 95–96.

Blum, André, and Charles Chassé. 1931. *Histoire du costume: Les modes au XIXe siècle.* Paris: Librairie Hachette.

Blumer, Herbert. 1969. "Fashion: From Class Differentiation to Collective Selection." *Sociological Quarterly* 10:275–91.

Bobo, Jacqueline. 1988. "The Color Purple: Black Women as Cultural Readers." Pp. 93–109 in *Female Spectators,* ed. D. Pribram. London: Verso.

Bocock, Robert. 1993. *Consumption.* New York: Routledge.

Bondi, Nicole. 1995. "Going Casual." *Automotive News,* Sept. 4, p. 3.

Booth, Charles. 1903. *Life and Labor of the People in London.* London: Macmillan.

Bordo, Susan. 1993. "'Material Girl': The Effacements of Postmodern Culture." Pp. 265–90 in *The Madonna Connection: Representational Politics, Subcultural Identities, and Cultural Theory,* ed. Cathy Schwichtenberg. Boulder, CO: Westview Press.

Borgé, Jacques, and Nicolas Viasnoff. 1993. *Archives de Paris.* Paris: Editions Michèle Trinckvel.

Bourdieu, Pierre. 1984. *Distinction: A Social Critique of the Judgement of Taste.* Trans. Richard Nice. Cambridge, MA: Harvard University Press.

———. 1993. *The Field of Cultural Production.* Ed. Randal Johnson. New York: Columbia University Press.

Bourdieu, Pierre, and Yvette Delsaut. 1975. "Le Couturier et sa griffe: Contribution à une théorie de la magie." *Actes de la Recherche en Sciences Sociales* 1:7–36.

Bradfield, Nancy. 1981. *Costume in Detail: Women's Dress, 1730–1930.* London: Harrap.

Branch, Shelly. 1993. "How Hip-Hop Fashion Won over Mainstream America." *Black Enterprise* 23 (June): 110–20.

Brew, Margaret L. 1945. "American Clothing Consumption, 1879–1909." Ph.D. diss., Department of Home Economics, University of Chicago.

Breward, Christopher. 1994. "Femininity and Consumption: The Problem of the Late Nineteenth-Century Fashion Journal." *Journal of Design History* 7:71–89.

Brittain, J. W., and John H. Freeman. 1980. "Organizational Proliferation and Density Dependent Selection." Pp. 291–338 in *The Organizational Life Cycle: Issues in the Creation, Transformation, and Decline of Organizations,* ed. John R. Kimberly, R. H. Miles, et al. San Francisco: Jossey-Bass.

Brown, Clare. 1994. *American Standards of Living, 1918–1988.* Oxford: Blackwell.

Brown, Jane D., Carol Reese Dykers, Jeanne Rogge Steele, and Ann Barton White. 1994. "Teenage Room Culture: Where Media and Identities Intersect." *Communication Research* 21:813–27.

Brubach, Holly. 1987. "Ralph Lauren's Achievement." *New Yorker* 63 (April): 70–73.

———. 1993. "Mail-Order America." *New York Times Magazine,* Nov. 21, pp. 54–61, 68–70.

———. 1997. "Beyond Shocking." *New York Times Magazine,* May 18, pp. 24, 26, 28.

Buchmann, Marlis. 1989. *The Script of Life in Modern Society.* Chicago: University of Chicago Press.

Buckley, Richard. 1997. "Tracking Hip: Blink and It's Gone." *International Herald Tribune,* Oct. 16, pp. 17, 19.

Bulger, Margery A. 1982. "American Sportswomen in the 19th Century." *Journal of Popular Culture* 16:1–16.

Burnett, John, ed. 1974. *Annals of Labour: Autobiographies of British Working-Class People, 1820–1920.* Bloomington: Indiana University Press.

Burnett, Robert. 1992. "Concentration and Diversity in the International Phonogram Industry." *Communication Research* 19:749–69.

Butler, Judith. 1990. *Gender Trouble: Feminism and the Subversion of Identity.* New York: Routledge.

Byrde, Penelope. 1979. *The Male Image: Men's Fashion in Britain, 1300–1970.* London: B. T. Batsford.

———. 1992. *Nineteenth Century Fashion.* London: B.T. Batsford.

Cabasset, Patrick 1989. "Paris sert de rampe de lancement." *Journal du Textile,* no. 1178 (Nov. 6): 26–27.

———. 1990. "La Violence urbaine ne se laisse pas oublier." *Journal du Textile,* no. 1211 (Aug. 22): 226.

Caldwell, John C. 1995. *Televisuality: Style, Crisis and Authority in American Television.* New Brunswick, NJ: Rutgers University Press.

Calhoun, Craig. 1994. "Introduction: Habermas and the Public Sphere." Pp. 1–48 in *Habermas and the Public Sphere*, ed. Craig Calhoun. Cambridge, MA: MIT Press.

Casey, Allie. 1997. "Why Men Find 'Casual Fridays' Suitable." [Letter]. *New York Times*, April 13, p. 14.

Cassell, Joan. 1974. "Externalities of Change: Deference and Demeanor in Contemporary Feminism." *Human Organization* 33:85–94.

Charles-Roux, Edmonde. 1975. *Chanel: Her Life, Her World, and the Woman behind the Legend She Herself Created*. Trans. Nancy Amphoux. New York: Knopf.

Chaumette, Xavier. 1995. *Le Costume Tailleur: La culture vestimentaire en France aux XIXème Siècle*. Paris: Esmod Edition.

Chenoune, Farid. 1993. *A History of Men's Fashion*. Trans. Deke Dusinberre. Paris: Flammarion.

Chibnell, Steve. 1985. "Whistle and Zoot: The Changing Meaning of a Suit of Clothes." *History Workshop*, no. 20:56–81.

Clark, Danae. 1993. "Commodity Lesbianism." Pp. 186–201 in *The Lesbian and Gay Studies Reader*, ed. Henry Abelove, Michèle Aina Barale, and David M. Halperin. New York: Routledge.

Clark, Terry N., and Seymour M. Lipset. 1991. "Are Social Classes Dying?" *International Sociology* 6:397–410.

Clarke, John. 1976. "Style." Pp. 175–91 in *Resistance through Rituals*, ed. Stuart Hall and Tony Jefferson. London: Hutchinson.

Clark-Lewis, Elizabeth. 1994. *Living In, Living Out: African American Domestics in Washington, D.C., 1910–1940*. Washington, DC: Smithsonian Institution Press.

Coffin, Judith G. 1994. "Credit, Consumption, and Images of Women's Desires: Selling the Sewing Machine in Late Nineteenth-Century France." *French Historical Studies* 18:749–83.

———. 1996a. "Consumption, Production, and Gender: The Sewing Machine in Nineteenth-Century France." Pp. 111–41 in *Gender and Class in Modern Europe*, ed. Sonya O. Rose. Ithaca, NY: Cornell University Press.

———. 1996b. *The Politics of Women's Work: The Paris Garment Trades, 1750–1915*. Princeton, NJ: Princeton University Press.

Coleman, Elisabeth Ann. 1990. "Pourvu que vos robes vous aillent: Quand les Américaines s'habillaient à Paris." Pp. 133–44 in *Femmes Fin de Siècle, 1885–1895*. Paris: Musée de la Mode et du Costume, Palais Galliera.

Condé, Françoise. 1992. "Les Femmes photographes en France, 1839–1914." Master's thesis, Université Jussieu-Paris VII-UFR d'Histoire.

Connor, Steven. 1989. *Postmodernist Culture: An Introduction to Theories of the Contemporary*. Oxford: Basil Blackwell.

Cookingham, Mary. 1984. "Bluestockings, Spinsters, and Pedagogues: Women College Graduates, 1965–1910." *Population Studies* 38:349–64.

Cose, Ellis. 1993. "Brutality as a Teen Fashion Statement." *Newsweek* 122 (Aug. 23): 61.

Cosgrove, Stuart. 1988. "The Zoot Suit and Style Warfare." Pp. 3–22 in *Zoot Suits and Second-Hand Dresses*, ed. Angela McRobbie. Boston: Unwin and Hyman.

Costil, Olivier. 1991. "Vendre des griffes masculines est un métier à hauts risques." *Journal du Textile*, no. 1252 (July 1): 23.

Crane, Diana. 1987. *The Transformation of the Avant-Garde: The New York Art World, 1940–1985*. Chicago: University of Chicago Press.

———. 1992. *The Production of Culture: Media and the Urban Arts*. Newbury Park, CA: Sage.

———. 1993. "Fashion Design as an Occupation: A Cross-National Approach." *Current Research on Occupations and Professions* 8: 55–73.

———. 1997a. "Postmodernism and the Avant-Garde: Stylistic Change in Fashion Design." *Modernism/Modernity* 4, no. 3: 123–40.

———. 1997b. "Globalization, Organizational Size, and Innovation in the French Luxury Fashion Industry: Production of Culture Theory Revisited." *Poetics* 24: 393–414.

Crispell, Diane. 1992. "Diversity . . . and How to Manage It." *American Demographics* 14 [online] (May): C01(1).

Cross, Gary, and Peter R. Shergold. 1986. "The Family Economy and the Market: Wages and Residence of Pennsylvania Women in the 1890s." *Journal of Family History* 11: 245–65.

Crowe, Duncan. 1971. *The Victorian Woman*. London: George Allen and Unwin.

———. 1978. *The Edwardian Woman*. London: George Allen and Unwin.

Cunnington, C. Willett, and Phillis Cunnington. 1959. *Handbook of English Costume in the Nineteenth Century*. London: Faber and Faber.

Cunnington, Phillis. 1974. *Costume of Household Servants from the Middle Ages to 1900*. New York: Harper and Row.

Cunnington, Phillis, and Catherine Lucas. 1967. *Occupational Costume in England from the Eleventh Century to 1914*. London: Adam and Charles Black.

Davis, Fred. 1992. *Fashion, Culture, and Identity*. Chicago: University of Chicago Press.

Davis, Laurel R. 1997. *The Swimsuit Issue and Sport: Hegemonic Masculinity in "Sports Illustrated."* Albany: State University of New York Press.

Davray-Piekolek, Renée. 1990. "Les Modes triomphantes, 1885–1895." Pp. 29–64 in *Femmes Fin de Siècle, 1885–1895*. Paris: Musée de la Mode et du Costume, Palais Galliera.

Debrosse, Juliette. 1994. "La Mode populaire citadine à travers les catalogues et les prospectus des magasins et bazars (1880–1914)." Master's thesis, Paris IV Sorbonne et Institut Catholique de Paris.

de la Haye, Amy. 1994. *Chanel: The Couturière at Work*. Woodstock, NY: Overlook Press.

———. 1997. *The Cutting Edge: 50 Years of British Fashion, 1947–1997*. Woodstock, NY: Overlook Press.

de la Haye, Amy, and Cathie Dingwall. 1996. *Surfers, Soulies, Skinheads & Skaters: Subcultural Style from the Forties to the Nineties*. Woodstock, NY: Overlook Press.

Delbourg-Delphis, Marylène. 1981. *Le Chic et le look: Histoire de la mode feminine et des moeurs de 1850 à nos jours*. Paris: Hachette.

———. 1983. *La Mode pour la vie*. Paris: Editions Autrement.

——. 1984. "Trombinoscope." Humeur de Mode. Special Issue of *Autrement*, no. 62 (Sept.): 165–80.

——. 1985. "Radioscope de la coupe Balenciaga." Pp.21–24 in *Hommage à Balenciaga*. [Exhibition, Musée Historique des Tissus de Lyon, Sept. 28, 1985–Jan. 6, 1986]. Paris: Editions Herscher.

Delpierre, Madeleine. 1990. *Le Costume: De la Restauration à la Belle Epoque*. Paris: Flammarion.

——. 1991. *Le Costume: La haute couture de 1940 à nos jours*. Paris: Flammarion.

de Marly, Diana. 1980. *The History of Haute Couture, 1850–1950*. New York: Holmes and Meier.

——. 1985. *Fashion for Men: An Illustrated History*. New York: Holmes and Meier.

——. 1986. *Working Dress: A History of Occupational Clothing*. New York: Holmes and Meier.

——. 1990a. *Christian Dior*. London: B. T. Batsford.

——. 1990b. *Worth: Father of Haute Couture*. New York: Holmes and Meier.

Derko, Scott. 1994. *The Value of a Dollar, 1860–1989*. Detroit: Gale.

Déslandres, Yvonne, and Florence Müller. 1986. *Histoire de la mode au XXe siècle*. Paris: Editions Somogy.

Diamonstein, Barbara. 1985. *Fashion: The Inside Story*. New York: Rizzoli.

Dike, Catherine, and Guy Bezzaz. 1988. *La Canne Objet d'art*. Paris: Editions de l'Amateur.

DiMaggio, Paul. 1987. "Classification in Art." *American Sociological Review* 52:440–55.

Dowd, Maureen. 1997. "Dressing for Contempt." *New York Times*, Sept. 17, p. A31.

Dudden, Faye E. 1983. *Serving Women: Household Service in Nineteenth Century America*. Middletown, CT: Wesleyan University Press.

Dumazedier, Joffre. 1989. "France: Leisure Sociology in the 1980s." Pp. 143–61 in *Leisure and Life-Style: A Comparative Analysis of Free Time*, ed. Anna Olszewska and K. Roberts. Sage Studies in International Sociology 38. London: Sage.

Duroselle, J.-B. 1972. *La France et les Français, 1900–1914*. Paris: Editions Richelieu.

Duveau, G. 1946. *La Vie ouvrière en France sous le Second Empire*. Paris: Gallimard.

Editions de la Réunion des Musées nationaux. *Costume, Coutume*. 1987. [Galéries nationales du Grand Palais, March 16–June 15]. Paris: Editions de la Réunion des Musées nationaux.

Ehrenreich, Barbara. 1989. *Fear of Falling: The Inner Life of the Middle Class*. New York: Harper.

Erickson, Bonnie H. 1996. "Culture, Class, and Connections." *American Journal of Sociology* 102:217–51.

Evans, Caroline, and Minna Thornton. 1989. *Women and Fashion: A New Look*. London: Quarter Books.

Ewen, Elizabeth. 1985. *Immigrant Women in the Land of Dollars: Life and Culture on the Lower East Side, 1890–1925*. New York: Monthly Review Press.

Ewing, Elizabeth. 1975. *Women in Uniform through the Centuries*. Totowa, NJ: Rowman and Littlefield.

——. 1984. *Everyday Dress, 1650–1900*. London: B. T. Batsford.

Falluel, Fabienne. 1990. "Les Grands Magasins et la confection féminine." Pp. 75–117 in *Femmes Fin de Siècle, 1885–1895*. Paris: Musée de la Mode et du Costume, Palais Galliera.

Farren, Mick. 1985. *The Black Leather Jacket*. New York: Abbeville Press.

Fatout, Paul. 1952. "Amelia Bloomer and Bloomerism." *New York Historical Society Quarterly* 36:361–73.

Featherstone, Mike. 1991. *Consumer Culture and Postmodernism*. Newbury Park, CA: Sage.

Field, George A. 1970. "The Status Float Phenomenon: The Upward Diffusion of Innovation." *Business Horizons* 13 (Aug.): 45–52.

Firat, A. Fuat. 1995. "Consumer Culture or Culture Consumed?" Pp. 105–25 in *Marketing in a Multicultural World*, ed. Janeen Arnold Costa and Gary J. Bamossy. Thousand Oaks, CA: Sage.

Fisher, Andrea. 1987. *Let Us Now Praise Famous Women*. London: Pandora.

Fishlow, Albert. 1973. "Comparative Consumption Patterns, the Extent of the Market, and Alternative Development Strategies." Pp. 41–80 in *Micro Aspects of Development*, ed. E. B. Ayal. New York: Praeger.

Fiske, John. 1984. "Popularity and Ideology: A Structuralist Reading of *Dr. Who.*" Pp. 165–98 in *Interpreting Television: Current Research Perspectives*, ed. Willard. D. Rowland Jr. and Bruce Watkins. Beverly Hills, CA: Sage.

——. 1989. *Understanding Popular Culture*. Boston: Unwin Hyman.

——. 1997. "Global, National, Local? Some Problems of Culture in a Postmodern World." *Velvet Light Trap*, no. 40: 56–66.

Fitoussi, M. 1991. "Giorgio Armani lance le pret-à-porter sur mesure." *Elle*, no. 2393 (Nov. 18): 39–40, 42, 44–45.

Flamant-Paparatti, Danièlle. 1984. *Bien-pensantes, cocodettes et bas-bleus: La femme bourgeoise à travers la presse féminine et familiale (1873–1887)*. Paris: Denoël.

Flusser, Alan. 1989. *Clothes and the Man: The Principles of Fine Men's Dress*. New York: Villard Books.

Foote, Shelly. 1980. "Bloomers." *Dress* 5:1–12.

Foote, Shelly, and Claudia B. Kidwell. 1994. "Du travail au loisir, le denim, et l'evolution de l'Amérique." Pp. 69–78 in *Histoires du jeans de 1750 à 1994*. Paris: Editions des musées de la ville de Paris.

Foucault, Michel. 1978. *The History of Sexuality*. Trans. Robert Hurley. New York: Pantheon.

Foucher, Nicole. 1994. "Le Jeans au cinéma." Pp. 95–103 in *Histoires du jeans de 1750 à 1994*. Paris: Editions des musées de la ville de Paris.

Fox, Kathryn J. 1987. "Real Punks and Pretenders: The Social Organization of a Counterculture." *Journal of Contemporary Ethnography* 16:344–70.

Freitas, Anthony, Susan Kaiser, and Tania Hammidi. 1996. "Communities, Commodities, Cultural Space, and Style." *Journal of Homosexuality* 31:83–107.

Freitas, Anthony, Susan Kaiser, Joan Chandler, Carol Hall, Jung-Won Kim, and Tania Hammidi. 1997. "Appearance Management as Border Construction: Least Favorite Clothing, Group Distancing, and Identity . . . Not!" *Sociological Inquiry* 67 : 323–35.

Freeman, John. 1990. "Ecological Analysis of Semiconductor Firm Mortality." Pp. 53–78 in *Organizational Evolution: New Directions*, ed. Jitendra V. Singh. Newbury Park, CA: Sage.

Freeman, Ruth, and Patricia Klaus. 1984. "Blessed or Not? The New Spinster in England and the United States in the Late Nineteenth and Early Twentieth Centuries." *Journal of Family History* 9 : 394–414.

Friedmann, Daniel. 1987. *Une histoire du blue-jean.* Paris: Editions Ramsay.

Frith, Simon. 1987. *Art into Pop.* London: Methuen.

Fuchs, Rachel G. 1995. "France in a Comparative Perspective." Pp. 157–87 in *Gender and the Politics of Social Reform in France, 1870–1914*, ed. Elinor A. Accampo. Baltimore: Johns Hopkins University Press.

Gadel, Marguerite S. 1985. "Commentary: Style-oriented Apparel Customers." Pp. 155–57 in *The Psychology of Fashion*, ed. Michael R. Solomon. Lexington, MA: Lexington Books.

Garnier, Guillaume. 1987. *Paris-Couture-Années Trente.* Paris: Edition Paris-Musées et Societé de l'Histoire du Costume.

Gaskell, Elizabeth. 1994 [1853]. *Cranford.* London: Penguin Books.

Germain, Isabelle. 1997. "Les Tee-shirts Hanes passent à la TV." *Journal du Textile*, no. 1482 (Jan. 20): 153.

Gernsheim, Alison. 1963. *Fashion and Reality, 1840–1914.* London: Faber and Faber.

Gibbings, Sarah. 1990. *The Tie: Trends and Traditions.* Hauppauge, NY: Barron's Educational Series.

Giddens, Anthony. 1991. *Modernity and Self-Identity.* Cambridge: Polity Press.

Giles, Judy. 1995. *Women, Identity, and Private Life in Britain, 1900–50.* New York: St. Martin's Press.

Ginsburg, Madeleine. 1988. *Victorian Dress in Photographs.* London: B. T. Batsford.

———. 1990. *The Hat: Trends and Traditions.* London: Studio Editions.

Giovannini, Marco. 1984. "Is the T-shirt Already a Legend?" Pp. 13–24 in *T-shirt t-Show*, ed. Omar Calabrese. [Exhibition, Studio Marconi Gallery, Milan, April 1984]. Milan: Electa Editrice.

Gladwell, Malcolm. 1997a. "Annals of Style: The Coolhunt." *New Yorker* 73 (Mar. 17): 78–88.

———. 1997b. "Listening to Khakis." *New Yorker* 73 (July 28): 54–65.

Godard, Colette. 1993. "La Mode en état de crise." *Le Monde*, Mar. 11, p. 30.

Goffman, Erving. 1966. *Behavior in Public Places: Notes on the Social Organization of Gatherings.* New York: Free Press.

———. 1979. *Gender Advertisements.* Cambridge, MA: Harvard University Press.

Goldin, Claudia. 1980. "The Work and Wages of Single Women, 1870 to 1920." *Journal of Economic History* 40 : 81–88.

Goldman, Robert. 1992. *Reading Ads Socially.* New York: Routledge.

Goldman, Robert, Deborah Heath, and Sharon L. Smith. 1991. "Commodity Feminism." *Critical Studies in Mass Communication* 8:71–89.

Goldthorpe, John H. 1987. *Social Mobility and Class Structure in Modern Britain.* New York: Oxford University Press.

Gordon, Beverly. 1991. "American Denim: Blue Jeans and Their Multiple Layers of Meaning." Pp. 31–45 in *Dress and Popular Culture*, ed. Patricia A. Cunningham and Susan Voso Lab. Bowling Green, OH: Bowling Green State University Popular Press.

Gordon, Maryellen. 1998. "It's Fitted Skaters vs. Baggy Ravers." *New York Times*, Jan. 18, sect. 9, p. 2.

Gorguet-Ballesteros, Pascale, and Sophie Rosset. 1994. "Album d'images." Pp. 53–68 in *Histoires du jeans de 1750 à 1994.* Paris: Editions des musées de la ville de Paris.

Gorsline, Douglas. 1952. *What People Wore: A Visual History of Dress from Ancient Times to Twentieth Century America.* New York: Bonanza Books.

Goulène, Pierre. 1974. *Evolution des pouvoirs d'achat en France, 1830–1972.* Paris: Bordas.

Green, Nancy L. 1997. *Ready-to-Wear and Ready-to-Work: A Century of Industry and Immigrants in Paris and New York.* Durham, NC: Duke University Press.

Grumbach, Didier. 1993. *Histoires de la mode.* Paris: Seuil.

Guiral, Pierre. 1976. *La Vie quotidienne en France à l'âge d'or du capitalisme, 1852–1879.* Paris: Hachette.

Guiral, Pierre, and Guy Thuillier. 1978. *La Vie quotidienne des domestiques en France au XIXe siècle.* Paris: Hachette.

Gutman, Jonathan, and Michael K. Mills. 1982. "Fashion Life Style, Self-Concept, Shopping Orientation, and Store Patronage: An Integrative Analysis." *Journal of Retailing* 58 (Summer): 64–86.

Guyot, Catherine. 1993. "Des Liens commencent à se nouer entre industriels et jeunes créateurs." *Journal du Textile*, no. 1335 (June 21): 34.

———. 1999. "Le Jean n'est plus un vêtement-culte et il lui faut lutter pour trouver une nouvelle identité." *Journal du Textile*, no. 1576 (April 12): 31.

Hall, John R. 1992. "The Capital(s) of Cultures: A Nonholistic Approach to Status Situations, Class, Gender, and Ethnicity." Pp. 257–285 in *Cultivating Differences: Symbolic Boundaries and the Making of Inequality*, ed. Michèle Lamont and Marcel Fournier. Chicago: University of Chicago Press.

Hall, Lee. 1992. *Common Threads: A Parade of American Clothing.* Boston: Little, Brown.

Hall, Stuart. 1980. "Encoding/Decoding." Pp. 128–138 in *Culture, Media, Language: Working Papers in Cultural Studies, 1972–79*, ed. Stuart Hall et al. London: Hutchison.

Halle, David. 1984. *America's Working Man.* Chicago: University of Chicago Press.

Hause, Steven C., and Anne R. Kenney. 1981. "The Limits of Suffragist Behavior: Legalism and Militancy in France, 1876–1922." *American Historical Review* 86:781–866.

Hebdige, Dick. 1979. *Subculture: The Meaning of Style.* London: Methuen.

Heinze, Andrew R. 1990. *Adapting to Abundance.* New York: Columbia University Press.

Helvenston, Sally. 1980. "Popular Advice for Well-Dressed Women in the Nineteenth Century." *Dress* 5:31–47.

Hénin, Janine. 1990. *Paris Haute Couture.* Paris: Editions Philippe Olivier.

Henley, Nancy M. 1977. *Body Politics: Power, Sex and Nonverbal Communication.* Englewood Cliffs, NJ: Prentice-Hall.

Herpin, Nicolas. 1986. "L'Habillement: Une dépense sur le declin." *Economie et Statistique,* no. 192 (Oct.): 65–74.

Herpin, Nicolas, and Daniel Verger. 1988. *La Consommation des Français.* Paris: Editions La Découverte.

Herreros, Fernando M. 1985. "Balenciaga le maître." Pp. 41–42 in *Hommage à Balenciaga.* [Exhibition, Musée Historique des Tissus de Lyon, Sept. 28, 1985–Jan. 6, 1986]. Paris: Editions Herscher.

Hetzel, Patrick. 1995. "Le Rôle de la mode et du dessin dans la société de consommation postmoderne: Quels enjeux pour les entreprises." *Revue Française du Marketing,* no. 151: 19–33.

Hiley, Michael. 1979. *Victorian Working Women: Portraits from Life.* London: G. Fraser.

Hine, Lewis W. 1977 [1932]. *Men at Work: Photographic Studies of Modern Men and Machines.* New York: Dover.

Hirschberg, Lynn. 1997. "The Little Rubber Dress, among Others." *New York Times Magazine,* Feb. 2, pp. 26–29.

Hochschild, Arlie R. 1983. *The Managed Heart: Commercialization of Human Feeling.* Berkeley: University of California Press.

———. 1997. *The Time Bind: When Work Becomes Home and Home Becomes Work.* New York: Henry Holt.

Hochswender, Woody. 1988. "American Accents." *New York Times Magazine,* "Men's Fashions of the Times," Sept. 18, pp. 72–75, 101–2.

———. 1989. "Trade Stocks or Bonds but Beware of Trading Your Suit for a Blazer." *New York Times,* Feb. 26, p. 54.

———. 1991. "Horst's Vision: Glamour Defined." *International Herald Tribune,* Sept. 10.

———. 1993. *Men in Style: The Golden Age of Fashion from "Esquire."* New York: Rizzoli.

Holcombe, Lee. 1973. *Victorian Ladies at Work: Middle-Class Working Women in England and Wales, 1850–1914.* Hamden, CT: Archon Books.

Hollander, Anne. 1994. *Sex and Suits.* New York: Alfred A. Knopf.

Holloman, Lillian O., Velma LaPoint, Sylvan I. Alleyne, Ruth J. Palmer, and Kathy Sanders-Phillips. 1996. "Dress-related Behavioral Problems and Violence in the Public School Setting: Prevention, Intervention, and Policy: A Holistic Approach." *Journal of Negro Education* 65:267–81.

Holt, Douglas B. 1997a. "Poststructuralist Lifestyle Analysis: Conceptualizing the Social Patterning of Consumption in Postmodernity." *Journal of Consumer Research* 23: 326–350.

———. 1997b. "Distinction in America? Recovering Bourdieu's Theory of Tastes from Its Critics." *Poetics* 25:93–121.

Horyn, Cathy. 1992. "Summer Shapes Up: The Baggier the Better." *International Herald Tribune*, Aug. 11, p. 7.

———. 1996. "Gender Flap." *Vogue* 186 (May): 114–15.

Hurlock, E. B. 1965. "Sumptuary Law." Pp. 295–301 in *Dress, Adornment and the Social Order*, ed. M. E. Roach and J. Eicher. New York: Wiley.

Jaffré, Jérôme. 1999. "La Gauche accepte le marché; la droite admet la différence." *Le Monde*, Aug. 15–16, p. 5.

Janus, Teresa, Susan B. Kaiser, and Gordon Gray. 1999. "Negotiations @ Work: The Casual Businesswear Trend." In *The Meanings of Dress*, ed. Mary Lynn Damhorst, Kimberly Miller, and Susan Michelman. New York: Fairchild.

Jenkins, Henry. 1992. *Textual Poachers: Television Fans and Participatory Culture*. New York: Routledge.

Jensen, Joan M. 1984. "Needlework as Art, Craft, and Livelihood before 1900." Pp. 3–19 in *A Needle, A Bobbin, A Strike: Women Needleworkers in America*, ed. Joan M. Jensen and Sue Davidson. Philadelphia: Temple University Press.

Jerde, J. 1980. "Mary Molloy: St. Paul's Extraordinary Dressmaker." *Minnesota History* (Fall): 82–89.

Jhally, Sut. 1994. "Intersections of Discourse: MTV, Sexual Politics, and *Dreamworlds*." Pp. 151–68 in *Viewing, Reading, Listening: Audiences and Cultural Reception*, ed. Jon Cruz and Justin Lewis. Boulder, CO: Westview Press.

John, Angela V. 1980. *By the Sweat of Their Brow: Women Workers at Victorian Coal Mines*. London: Croom Helm.

Jones, Mablen. 1987. *Getting It On: The Clothing of Rock 'n' Roll*. New York: Abbeville Press.

Joseph, Nathan. 1986. *Uniforms and Nonuniforms: Communication through Clothing*. Westport, CT: Greenwood Press.

Journal du Textile. 1991. "Autopsie des 20 collections leaders." *Journal du Textile*, no. 1265 (Nov. 11): 80–95.

Juin, Hubert. 1994. *Le Livre de Paris 1900*. Paris: Editions Michèle Trinckvel.

Kaelble, H. 1986. *Social Mobility in the 19th and 20th Centuries*. New York: St. Martin's Press.

Kaiser, Susan B. 1990. *The Social Psychology of Clothes: Symbolic Appearances in Context*. 2d ed. New York: Macmillan.

Kaiser, Susan B., Richard H. Nagasawa, and Sandra S. Hutton. 1991. "Fashion, Postmodernity and Personal Appearance: A Symbolic Interactionist Formulation." *Symbolic Interaction* 14: 165–85.

Kaiser, Susan B., Carla M. Freeman, and Joan L. Chandler. 1993. "Favorite Clothes and Gendered Subjectivities: Multiple Readings." *Symbolic Interaction* 15: 27–50.

Kalaora, Bernard, and Antoine Savoye. 1989. *Les Inventeurs oubliés: Le Play et ses continuateurs aux origines des sciences sociales*. Seyssel: Editions Champ Vallon.

Kaplan, E. Ann. 1987. *Rocking round the Clock: Music Television, Postmodernism, and Consumer Culture*. New York: Methuen.

Katzman, David M. 1978. *Seven Days a Week: Women and Domestic Service in Industrializing America.* New York: Oxford University Press.

Kelley, Robin D. G. 1992. "The Riddle of the Zoot: Malcolm Little and Black Cultural Politics during World War II." Pp. 155–82 in *Malcolm X: In Our Own Image*, ed. Joe Wood. New York: St. Martin's Press.

Kellner, Douglas. 1989. *Jean Baudrillard: From Marxism to Postmodernism and Beyond.* Cambridge: Polity Press.

———. 1990a. "The Postmodern Turn: Positions, Problems, and Prospects." Pp. 255–86 in *Frontiers of Social Theory*, ed. George Ritzer. New York: Columbia University Press.

———. 1990b. *Television and the Crisis of Democracy.* Boulder, CO: Westview Press.

Kemeny, Lydia. 1984. "St. Martin's School of Art." Pp. 91–98 in *The Fashion Year*, vol. 2, ed. Emily White. London: Zomba Books.

Kent, Susan Kingsley. 1988. "The Politics of Sexual Difference: World War I and the Demise of British Feminism." *Journal of British Studies* 27:232–53.

Kidwell, Claudia, and Margaret Christman. 1974. *Suiting Everyone: The Democratization of Clothing in America.* Washington, DC: Smithsonian Institution Press.

Kidwell, Claudia, and Valerie Steele. 1989. *Men and Women: Dressing the Part.* Washington, DC: Smithsonian Institution Press.

Kiechel, Walter, III. 1983. "The Management Dress Code." *Fortune*, April 14, pp. 193–94, 196.

Kimle, Patricia A., and Mary Lynn Damhorst. 1997. "A Grounded Theory Model of the Ideal Business Image for Women." *Symbolic Interaction* 20:45–68.

King, Sharon R. 1998. "Designers Stumble on the Catwalk: Small Fashion Houses Fall Victim to Tough Economic Conditions." *International Herald Tribune*, Nov. 5, pp. 15, 19.

Kingston, Paul W. 1994. "Are There Classes in the United States?" *Research in Social Stratification and Mobility* 13:3–41.

Klüver, Billy, and Julie Martin. 1989. *Kiki's Paris: Artists and Lovers, 1900–1930.* New York: Harry N. Abrams.

Kotarba, Joseph A. 1994. "The Postmodernization of Rock and Roll Music: The Case of Metallica." Pp. 141–64 in *Adolescents and Their Music: If It's Too Loud, You're Too Old*, ed. Jonathon S. Epstein. New York: Garland.

Krafft, Susan. 1991. "Discounts Drive Clothes." *American Demographics* 13 (July): 11.

LaBalme, Corinne. 1984. "The Other Collections." *Paris Passion* (Nov.): 48.

Labovitch, Carey, and Simon Tesler. 1984. "*Blitz* Magazine: Style as an End in Itself." Pp. 107–14 in *The Fashion Year*, vol. 2, ed. Emily White. London: Zomba Books.

Lacroix, Christian. 1998. Interview. *Mode in France.* TF1 [French television], July 24.

Lakoff, Robin T., and Raquel L. Scherr. 1984. *Face Value: The Politics of Beauty.* Boston: Routledge.

Lambert, Miles. 1991. *Fashion in Photographs 1860–1880.* London: B. T. Batsford.

Lamont, Michèle, John Schmalzbauer, Maureen Waller, and Daniel Weber. 1996. "Cultural and Moral Boundaries in the United States: Structural Position, Geographic Location, and Lifestyle Explanations." *Poetics* 24:31–56.

Latour, Bruno. 1988. "Mixing Humans and Nonhumans Together: The Sociology of a Door-Closer." *Social Problems* 35:298–310.

Lauer, Jeanette C., and Robert H. Lauer. 1981. *Fashion Power: The Meaning of Fashion in American Society*. Englewood Cliffs, NJ: Prentice-Hall.

Laver, James. 1968. *Dandies*. London: Weidenfeld and Nicolson.

Lebergott, Stanley. 1993. *Pursuing Happiness: American Consumers in the Twentieth Century*. Princeton, NJ: Princeton University Press.

Lecompte-Boinet, Guillaume. 1991. "La Difficile Union des rêveurs et des comptables." *Journal du Textile*, no. 1261 (Oct. 14): 74.

Lencek, Lena, and Gideon Bosker. 1989. *Making Waves: Swimsuits and the Undressing of America*. San Francisco: Chronicle Books.

Le Play, Frédéric. 1862. "Instruction sur la méthode d'observation." In *Les Ouvriers des deux mondes*, vol. 4, 1st series. Paris: Au Secretariat de la Société d'Economie Sociale.

———. 1877–79. *Les Ouvriers Européens*. 6 vols. 2d ed. Tours: Alfred Mame et fils.

Leroy, Jean-Paul. 1994. "Les Jeanneries disent adieu aux années 50." *Journal du Textile*, no. 1368 (April 11): 33–34.

Levitt, Sarah. 1986. *Victorians Unbuttoned: Registered Designs for Clothing, Their Makers and Wearers, 1839–1900*. London: George Allen and Unwin.

———. 1991. *Fashion in Photographs, 1880–1900*. London: B. T. Batsford.

Lewis, Reina, and Katrina Rolley. 1996. "Ad(dressing) the Dyke: Lesbian Looks and Lesbian Looking." Pp. 178–89 in *Outlooks: Lesbian and Gay Sexualities and Visual Cultures*, ed. Peter Horne and Reina Lewis. London: Routledge.

Lister, Margot. 1972. *Costumes of Everyday Life: An Illustrated History of Working Clothes*. London: Barrie and Jenkins.

Lloyd, Valerie. 1986. *The Art of Vogue Photography Covers: Fifty Years of Fashion and Design*. New York: Harmony Books.

Lopes, Paul D. 1992. "Innovation and Diversity in the Popular Music Industry." *American Sociological Review* 57:561–71.

Lutz, Catherine A., and Jane L. Collins. 1993. *Reading National Geographic*. Chicago: University of Chicago Press.

McBride, Theresa. 1976. *The Domestic Revolution: The Modernisation of Household Service in England and France, 1820–1920*. London: Croom Helm.

———. 1978. "A Woman's World: Department Stores and the Evolution of Women's Employment, 1870–1920." *French Historical Studies* 10:664–83.

———. 1986. "Servants and Domestic Laborers: Status and Conditions of, 1879–1970." Pp. 929–30 in *Historical Dictionary of the Third French Republic*. Westport, CT: Greenwood Press.

McCannell, Dean. 1973. "A Note on Hat Tipping." *Semiotica* 7:300–312.

McCracken, Ellen. 1993. *Decoding Women's Magazines: From "Mademoiselle" to "Ms."* New York: St. Martin's Press.

McCracken, Grant D. 1985. "The Trickle-Down Theory Rehabilitated." Pp. 39–54 in

The Psychology of Fashion, ed. Michael R. Solomon. Lexington, MA: Lexington Books.

———. 1988. *Culture and Consumption*. Bloomington: Indiana University Press.

McCrone, Kathleen E. 1987. "Play Up! Play Up! And Play the Game! Sport at the Late Victorian Girls' Public Schools." Pp. 97–129 in *From Fair Sex to Feminism: Sport and the Socialization of Women in the Industrial and Post-Industrial Eras*, ed. J. A. Mangan and Roberta J. Park. London: Frank Cass.

———. 1988. *Sport and the Physical Emancipation of English Women, 1870–1914*. London: Routledge.

McDowell, Colin. 1987. *McDowell's Directory of Twentieth Century Fashion*. London: Frederick Müller.

———. 1997. *The Man of Fashion: Peacock Males and Perfect Gentlemen*. London: Thames and Hudson.

McDowell, Linda. 1997. *Capital Culture: Gender at Work in the City*. Oxford: Blackwell.

MacFarquhar, Neil. 1996. "Backlash of Intolerance Stirring Fear in Iran." *New York Times*, Sept. 20, pp. A1, A6.

McGraw, Dan. 1996. "Dressing down for Dollars: The Booming $10 Billion T-Shirt Industry Is Now a Big-time Business." *U.S. News and World Report* 120 (May 13): 64.

McKinley, James C., Jr. 1996. "Where Castoff Clothes Turn into Cash." *New York Times*, Mar. 15, pp. 1, 10.

Mackrell, Alice. 1992. *Coco Chanel*. London: B. T. Batsford.

McMillan, James F. 1980. *Housewife or Harlot: The Place of Women in French Society, 1870–1940*. New York: St. Martin's Press.

McRobbie, Angela. 1988. "Second-Hand Dresses and the Role of the Ragmarket." Pp. 23–49 in *Zoot Suits and Second-Hand Dresses*, ed. Angela McRobbie. Boston: Unwin and Hyman.

———. 1998. *British Fashion Design: Rag Trade or Image Industry?* London: Routledge.

Maisel, S. 1991. "Le Consommateur masculin s'est émancipé." *Journal du Textile*, no. 1230 (Jan. 21): 76, 78.

Manchester, William. 1989. *In Our Time: The World as Seen by Magnum Photographers*. New York: American Federation of Arts/W. W. Norton.

Mandziuk, Roseann. 1993. "Feminist Politics and Postmodern Seductions: Madonna and the Struggle for Political Articulation." Pp. 167–87 in *The Madonna Connection: Representational Politics, Subcultural Identities and Cultural Theory*, ed. Cathy Schwichtenberg. Boulder, CO: Westview Press.

Martin, Richard. 1987a. "Aesthetic Dress: The Art of Rei Kawakubo." *Arts* 61 (Mar.): 64–65.

———. 1987b. *Fashion and Surrealism*. New York: Rizzoli.

———. 1998. *American Ingenuity: Sportswear, 1930s–1970s*. New York: Metropolitan Museum of Art.

Martin, Richard, and Harold Koda. 1989. *Jocks and Nerds: Men's Style in the Twentieth Century*. New York: Rizzoli.

Martin-Fugier, Anne. 1979. *La Place des bonnes: La domesticité féminine à Paris en 1900.* Paris: Grasset.

Massachusetts Bureau of Labor Statistics [Carroll D. Wright, chief]. 1875. *Sixth Annual Report of the Bureau of Labor Statistics.* Massachusetts Public Document no. 31. Boston: Wright and Potter.

Massey, Mary Elizabeth. 1994. *Women in the Civil War.* Lincoln: University of Nebraska Press.

Mathews, J. 1993. "Fashion Note: Dressing Down for Work." *International Herald Tribune*, Dec. 30, pp. 1, 6.

Melinkoff, Ellen. 1984. *What We Wore: An Offbeat Social History of Women's Clothing, 1950–1980.* New York: William Morrow.

La Mémoire de Paris, 1919–1939. 1993. Paris: La Mairie de Paris.

Menkes, Suzy. 1989. "Creating Another New Look for Dior." *International Herald Tribune*, Jan. 17, p. 7.

———. 1990. "30 Years of Men's Fashion: A Tribute." *International Herald Tribune*, Sept. 4, p. 6.

———. 1992. "As Couture Shows Open, Some Battles Rage On." *International Herald Tribune*, July 25–26, p. 7.

———. 1995. "Why Not Couture by Women?" *New York Times*, Feb. 5, "Styles," pp. 49, 51.

———. 1996. "Galliano's Theatrics at Givenchy." *International Herald Tribune*, Jan. 22, pp. 1, 8.

———. 1999a. "Luxurious Gowns for the Ultimate Party." *International Herald Tribune*, July 20, p. 10.

———. 1999b. "What Is Man? Eclecticism and Whimsy Flourish in Paris." *International Herald Tribune*, July 6, p. 10.

Meyrowitz, Joshua. 1985. *No Sense of Place: The Impact of Electronic Media on Social Behavior.* New York: Oxford University Press.

Middleton, William. 1999. "A Peaceful Revolution for the French Male." *International Herald Tribune*, "Men's Fashion: A Special Report," Jan. 13, p. 4.

Milbank, Caroline. 1985. *Couture: The Great Designers.* New York: Stewart, Tabori, and Chang.

Mitchell, B. R. 1981. *European Historical Statistics, 1750–1975.* London: Macmillan.

Modell, John. 1978. "Patterns of Consumption, Acculturation, and Family Income Strategies in Late Nineteenth Century America." Pp. 206–40 in *Family and Population in Nineteenth Century America*, ed. Tamara K. Hareven and Maris A. Vinovskis. Princeton, NJ: Princeton University Press.

Monier, Véronique. 1990. "Balbec, essai sur l'apparition d'une mode sportive en littérature." Pp. 119–32 in *Femmes Fin de Siècle, 1885–1895.* Paris: Musée de la Mode et du Costume, Palais Galliera.

Montagné-Villette, Solange. 1990. *Le Sentier: Un Espace ambigü.* Paris: Masson.

Mopin, Odile. 1997. "Les Modes jeunes jaillissent en tous sens." *Journal du Textile*, no. 1481 (Jan. 13): 89–90.

More, Louise B. 1907. *Wage-Earners' Budgets: A Study of Standards and Cost of Living in New York City*. New York: Holt.

Morokvasic, Mirjana, Roger Waldinger, and Annie Phizacklea. 1990. "Business on the Ragged Edge: Immigrant and Minority Business in the Garment Industries of Paris, London, and New York." Pp. 157–76 in *Ethnic Entrepreneurs: Immigrant Business in Industrial Societies*, ed. Roger Waldinger et al. Newbury Park, CA: Sage.

Moses, Claire Goldberg. 1984. *French Feminism in the Nineteenth Century*. Albany: State University of New York Press.

Mrozek, Donald J. 1987. "The 'Amazon' and the American 'Lady': Sexual Fears of Women as Athletes." Pp. 282–98 in *From Fair Sex to Feminism: Sport and the Socialization of Women in the Industrial and Post-Industrial Eras*, ed. J. A. Mangan and Roberta J. Park. London: Frank Cass.

Mulvey, Laura. 1975–76. "Visual Pleasure and Narrative Cinema." *Screen* 16:6–18.

Musée de la Mode et du Costume. 1983. *Uniformes civiles Français: Ceremoniales et circonstances, 1750–1980*. [Exhibition, Dec. 16, 1982–April 17, 1983, Paris]. Paris: Musée de la Mode et du Costume.

Myers, Kathy. 1987. "Fashion 'n' Passion." Pp. 58–65 in *Looking On: Images of Femininity in the Visual Arts and Media*, ed. Rosemary Betterton. London: Pandora.

Nabers, William. 1995. "The New Corporate Uniform." *Fortune*, Nov. 13, pp. 132–37.

Nelton, Sharon. 1991. "The Man Who Transformed T-Shirts from Underwear into Fashion." *Nation's Business* 79 (Jan.): 14.

New York Times. 1985. "About Town: Skirts for Men." *New York Times*, Feb. 19, p. C24.

———. 1995. "On the Street: Highly Evolved." *New York Times*, April 23, "Styles," p. 52.

Newton, Stella M. 1974. *Health, Art and Reason: Dress Reformers of the 19th Century*. London: John Murray.

Nordquist, Barbara K. 1991. "Punks." Pp. 74–84 in *Dress and Popular Culture*, ed. Patricia A. Cunningham and Susan Voso Lab. Bowling Green, OH: Bowling Green State University Popular Press.

Normand, Jean-Michel. 1999a. "Le Jean prend un coup de vieux." *Le Monde*, Feb. 12, p. 25.

———. 1999b. "Du 'look cow-boy' au 'look chantier.'" *Le Monde*, Feb. 12, p. 25.

Nye, Robert A. 1993. *Masculinity and Male Codes of Honor in Modern France*. New York: Oxford University Press.

Obalk, Hector, Alain Soral, and Alexandre Pasche. 1984. *Les Mouvements de mode expliquées aux parents*. Paris: Robert Lafont.

Oberschall, Anthony, ed. 1972. *The Establishment of Empirical Sociology*. New York: Harper and Row.

O'Donnol, Shirley M. 1982. *American Costume, 1915–1970*. Bloomington: Indiana University Press.

Offen, Karen M. 1984. "Depopulation, Nationalism, and Feminism in Fin-de-siècle France." *American Historical Review* 89:648–76.

Olian, JoAnne. 1992. *Everyday Fashions of the Forties as Pictured in Sears Catalogs*. New York: Dover.

Ostrowski, Constance J. 1996. "The Clothesline Project: Women's Stories of Gender-related Violence." *Women and Language* 19:37–41.

Papayanis, Nicholas. 1993. *The Coachmen of Nineteenth Century Paris: Service Workers and Class Consciousness*. Baton Rouge: Louisiana State University Press.

Pareles, Jon. 1993. "'90s Rock: A Mess, but Not Bad." *International Herald Tribune*, Jan. 6, p. 8.

Parisi, Peter. 1993. "'Black Bart' Simpson: Appropriation and Revitalization in Commodity Culture." *Journal of Popular Culture* 27 (Summer): 125–42.

Partington, Angela. 1996. "Perfume: Pleasure, Packaging and Postmodernity." Pp. 204–18 in *The Gendered Object*, ed. Pat Kirkham. Manchester: Manchester University Press.

Pasquet, P. 1990. "Le Parcours des jeunes créateurs reste semé d'embûches." *Journal du Textile*, no. 1188 (Jan. 29): 80, 82, 91.

Pellegrin, Nicole. 1989. *Les Vêtements de la liberté*. Paris: Alinea.

Perrot, Marguerite. 1982. *Le Mode de vie des familles bourgeoises, 1873–1953*. Paris: Presses de la Fondation Nationale des Sciences Politiques.

Perrot, Philippe. 1981. *Les Dessus et les dessous de la bourgeoisie: Une Histoire du vêtement aux XIXe siècle*. Paris: Fayard.

Peterson, Richard. 1994. "Culture Studies through the Production Perspective: Progress and Prospects." Pp.163–90 in *The Sociology of Culture: Emerging Theoretical Perspectives*, ed. Diana Crane. Cambridge, MA: Blackwell.

Phizacklea, Annie. 1990. *Unpacking the Fashion Industry: Gender, Racism and Class in Production*. London: Routledge.

Piganeau, Joëlle. 1988. "Les Garçons jugent la mode." *Journal du Textile*, no. 1099 (Jan. 18): 24.

———. 1989. "Le Créateur des collections Benetton s'explique." *Journal du Textile*, no. 1146 (Feb. 13): 30.

———. 1991. "Le Nom est plus vendeur que la mode." *Journal du Textile*, no. 1255 (Aug. 26): 72–73.

———. 1994. "Qu'y a-t-il dans les placards des hommes en devenir?" *Journal du Textile*, no. 1378 (June 27): 28.

———. 1996. "Les Modes junior ont leur porte-parole." *Journal du Textile*, no. 1464 (Aug. 30): 126–28.

———. 1998. "La Période est difficile pour les jeunes créateurs." *Journal du Textile*, no. 1528 (Feb. 13): 12.

———. 1999. "Les Professionnels de la mode vont devoir se servir de nouvelles clés." *Journal du Textile*, no. 1586 (June 28): 2–3.

Piirto, Rebecca. 1990. "Why They Buy Clothes with Attitude." *American Demographics* 12 (Oct.): 10, 52, 54.

Plous, S., and Dominique Neptune. 1997. "Racial and Gender Biases in Magazine Advertising." *Psychology of Women Quarterly* 21:627–44.

Polhemus, Ted. 1994. *Street Style: From Sidewalk to Catwalk*. London: Thames and Hudson.

Press, Andrea. 1994. "The Sociology of Cultural Reception: Notes toward an Emerging Paradigm." Pp. 221–45 in *The Sociology of Culture: Emerging Theoretical Perspectives*, ed. Diana Crane. Cambridge, MA: Blackwell.

Pujol, Pascale. 1989. "Pour créer il faut d'abord capter." *Journal du Textile*, no. 1170 (Aug. 28): 98, 100–101.

———. 1992a. "Le Cca voit les hommes de plus en plus conservateurs." *Journal du Textile*, no. 1275 (Jan. 10): 39.

———. 1992b. "L'univers des femmes est formé de cinq groupes." *Journal du Textile*, no. 1301 (Sept. 28): 47.

———. 1994. "L'Introuvable Marché des créateurs masculins." *Journal du Textile*, no. 1378 (June 27): 34–35.

———. 1995. "L'Avenir des jeunes griffes reste incertain." *Journal du Textile*, no. 1404 (Feb. 27): 46, 51.

Quant, Mary. 1965. *Quant by Quant*. New York: G. P. Putnam's.

Quilleriet, Anne-Laure. 1999. "Le 'Off' en hausse." *Le Monde*, July 24, p. 22.

Rabine, Leslie. 1994. "A Woman's Two Bodies: Fashion Magazines, Consumerism, and Feminism." Pp. 59–75 in *On Fashion*, ed. Shari Benstock and Suzanne Ferris. New Brunswick, NJ: Rutgers University Press.

Reberioux, Madeleine. 1980. "L'Ouvrière." Pp. 59–78 in *Misérable et glorieuse: La Femme de XIXe siècle*, ed. Jean-Paul Aron. Paris: Fayard.

Rendall, Jane. 1985. *The Origins of Modern Feminism: Women in Britain, France, and the United States, 1780–1860*. London: Macmillan.

Ribeiro, Aileen. 1988. *Fashion in the French Revolution*. New York: Holmes and Meier.

Richardson, Joanna. 1967. *The Courtesans: The Demi-Monde in Nineteenth Century France*. Cleveland: World Publishing.

Richins, Marsha L. 1991. "Social Comparison and the Idealized Images of Advertising." *Journal of Consumer Research* 18 : 71–83.

Riegel, Robert E. 1963. "Women's Clothes and Women's Rights." *American Quarterly* 15 : 390–401.

Riot-Sarcey, Michèle, and Marie-Hélène Zylberberg-Hocquard. 1987. *L'Autre Travail: Travaux de femmes au XIXe siècle*. Paris: CRDP, Musée d'Orsay.

Robb, Graham. 1994. *Balzac: A Life*. New York: W. W. Norton.

Robert, Jean-Louis. 1988. "Women and Work in France during the First World War." Pp. 251–66 in *The Upheaval of War: Family, Work, and Welfare in Europe, 1914–1918*, ed. Richard Wall and Jay Winter. New York: Cambridge University Press.

Roberts, Mary Louise. 1994. *Civilization without Sexes: Reconstructing Gender in Postwar France, 1917–1927*. Chicago: University of Chicago Press.

Robinson, Fred Miller. 1993. *The Man in the Bowler Hat: Its History and Iconography*. Chapel Hill: University of North Carolina Press.

Roche, Daniel. 1994. *The Culture of Clothing: Dress and Fashion in the Ancien Regime*. Cambridge: Cambridge University Press.

Rolley, Katrina. 1990a. "Fashion, Femininity and the Fight for the Vote." *Art History* 13 : 47–71.

———. 1990b. "Cutting a Dash: The Dress of Radclyffe Hall and Una Troubridge." *Feminist Review*, no. 35 (Summer): 54–66.

Rubinstein, David. 1977. "Cycling in the 1890s." *Victorian Studies* 21:47–71.

Runciman, W. G. 1990. "How Many Classes Are There in Contemporary British Society?" *Sociology* 24:377–96.

Russell, Frances E. 1892. "A Brief Survey of the American Dress Reform Movements of the Past, with Views of Representative Women." *Arena* 7:325–39.

Russett, Cynthia E. 1989. *Sexual Science: The Victorian Construction of Womanhood.* Cambridge, MA: Harvard University Press.

Ryan, Mary P. 1994. "Gender and Public Access: Women's Politics in Nineteenth-Century America." Pp. 259–88 in *Habermas and the Public Sphere*, ed. Craig Calhoun. Cambridge: MIT Press.

Sabas, Carole. 1999. "La Mode masculine intègre sans états d'âme le Répertoire des Valeurs féminines." *Journal du Textile*, no. 1586 (June 28): 48, 50.

Samet, Jamie. 1989. "Les Mystères dévoilés des 6,000 robes les plus chéres du monde." *Le Figaro*, Jan. 19, p. 33.

Sandler, Irving. 1976. *The Triumph of American Painting: A History of Abstract Expressionism.* New York: Harper and Row.

Saporito, Bill. 1993. "Unsuit Yourself: Management Goes Informal." *Fortune* 128 (Sept. 20): 118–19.

Savage, J. 1988. "Sex, Rock and Identity." Pp. 131–72 in *Facing the Music*, ed. Simon Frith. New York: Pantheon.

Schreier, Barbara. A. 1989. "Sporting Wear." Pp. 92–123 in *Men and Women: Dressing the Part*, ed. Claudia Brush Kidwell and Valerie Steele. Washington, DC: Smithsonian Institution Press.

———. 1994. *Becoming American Women: Clothing and the Jewish Immigrant Experience.* Chicago: Chicago Historical Society.

Schudson, Michael. 1994. "Culture and the Integration of National Societies." Pp. 21–44 in *The Sociology of Culture: Emerging Theoretical Perspectives*, ed. Diana Crane. Oxford: Blackwell.

Schwartzman, A. 1993. "Arnold Glimcher and His Art World All-Stars: Carrying Salesmanship to the Level of Art." *New York Times Magazine*, Oct. 3, sect. 6, p. 22.

Scott, Joan W., and Louise A. Tilly. 1975. "Women's Work and the Family in Nineteenth-Century Europe." *Comparative Studies in Society and History* 17:36–64.

Segal, Lynne. 1990. *Slow Motion: Changing Masculinities, Changing Men.* New Brunswick, NJ: Rutgers University Press.

Senes, Alexandra. 1997. "New York: Haute pression à Manhattan." *Le Monde*, Oct. 16, "Styles," p. 6.

Sepulchre, Cécile.1992. "Le Filon vert pourrait deboucher sur une Impasse." *Journal du Textile*, no. 1298 (Sept. 1): 60–64.

———. 1994a. "Martin Margiela invente une nouvelle forme de présentation." *Journal du Textile*, no. 1372 (May 9–16): 84–85.

———. 1994b. "Les Tee-shirts prennent la parole." *Journal du Textile*, no. 1395 (Dec. 5): 27.

———. 1997. "La Temple de la haute couture s'ouvre aux créateurs." *Journal du Textile* no. 1481 (Jan. 13): 3–4.

Service Nationale de la Statistique. 1906. *Résultats statistiques du recensement général de la population, effectué le 24 mars, 1901*, vol. 4. Paris: Imprimerie Nationale.

Severa, Joan L. 1995. *Dressed for the Photographer: Ordinary Americans and Fashion.* Kent, OH: Kent State University Press.

Shaffer, John W. 1978. "Family, Class, and Young Women: Occupational Expectations in Nineteenth-Century Paris." *Journal of Family History* 3:62–77.

Shergold, Peter R. 1982. *Working-Class Life: The "American Standard" in Comparative Perspective.* Pittsburgh: University of Pittsburgh Press.

Sichel, Marion. 1978. *Costume Reference, Vol. 8: 1918 to 1939.* London: B. T. Batsford.

——— 1979. *Costume Reference, Vol. 10: 1950 to the Present Day.* London: B. T. Batsford.

Signorielli, Nancy, Douglas McLeod, and Elaine Healy. 1994. "Gender Stereotypes in MTV Commercials: The Beat Goes On." *Journal of Broadcasting and Electronic Media* 38:91–101.

Silver, Catherine B. 1982. *Frédéric Le Play: On Family, Work and Social Change.* Chicago: University of Chicago Press.

Silverman, Debora. 1991. "The 'New Woman,' Feminism, and the Decorative Arts in Fin-de-siècle France." Pp. 144–63 in *Eroticism and the Body Politic*, ed. Lynn Hunt. Baltimore: Johns Hopkins University Press.

Simmel, Georg. 1957 [1904]. "Fashion." *American Journal of Sociology* 62 (May): 541–58.

Sims, Sally. 1991. "The Bicycle, the Bloomer, and Dress Reform in the 1890s." Pp. 125–45 in *Dress and Popular Culture*, ed. Patricia A. Cunningham and Susan Voso Lab. Bowling Green, OH: Bowling Green State University Popular Press.

Siroto, Janet. 1993. "Punk Rocks Again." *Vogue* 183 (Sept.): 248, 258.

Skeggs, Beverly. 1993. "A Good Time for Women Only." Pp. 61–73 in *Deconstructing Madonna*, ed. Fran Lloyd. London: B. T. Batsford.

Smith, Bonnie G. 1981. *Ladies of the Leisure Class: The Bourgeoises of Northern France in the Nineteenth Century.* Princeton, NJ: Princeton University Press.

Smith, Dorothy E. 1988. "Femininity as Discourse." Pp. 37–59 in *Becoming Feminine: The Politics of Popular Culture*, ed. Leslie G. Roman et al. London: Falmer Press.

Smith, D. S. 1994. "A Higher Quality of Life for Whom? Mouths to Feed and Clothes to Wear in the Families of Late Nineteenth-Century American Workers." *Journal of Family History* 19:1–33.

Smith, J. Walker, and Ann Clurman. 1997. *Rocking the Ages: The Yankelovich Report on Generational Marketing.* New York: Harper Business.

La Société Internationale des Etudes Pratiques d'Economie Sociale. 1857–1928. *Les Ouvriers des Deux Mondes.* Paris: Secretariat de la Société d'Economie Sociale.

Sonenscher, Michael. 1987. *The Hatters of Eighteenth-Century France.* Berkeley: University of California Press.

Spencer, Neil. 1992. "Menswear in the 1980s: Revolt into Conformity." Pp. 40–48 in *Chic Thrills: A Fashion Reader*, ed. Juliet Ash and Elizabeth Wilson. Berkeley: University of California Press.

Spindler, Amy. 1995. "Four Who Have No Use for Trends." *New York Times*, Mar. 20, p. B10.

———. 1996a. "The Look: Tough, Maybe Tattered." *New York Times*, Oct. 11, p. B8.

———. 1996b. "Sensuality, Not Practicality." *New York Times*, Oct. 22, p. B8.

———. 1997. "A Death Tarnishes Fashion's 'Heroin Look.'" *New York Times*, May 20, pp. A1, B7.

Stallybrass, Peter. 1993. "Worn Worlds: Clothes, Mourning and the Life of Things." *Yale Review* 81 : 35–50.

Stansell, Christine. 1987. *City of Women: Sex and Class in New York, 1789–1860*. Urbana: University of Illinois Press.

Statistical Office of the European Communities. 1993. *Eurostat-CD 1993: Electronic Statistical Yearbook of the European Communities*. 2d ed. Luxembourg: Amt flr Amtliche Vervffertlichungen des Europaoschen Gemeinschaften.

Stearns, Peter N. 1972. "Working-Class Women in Britain, 1890–1914." Pp. 100–20 in *Suffer and Be Still: Women in the Victorian Age*, ed. Martha Vicinus. Bloomington: Indiana University Press.

Steele, Valerie. 1985. *Fashion and Eroticism*. New York: Oxford University Press.

———. 1989a. "Dressing for Work." Pp. 69–91 in *Men and Women: Dressing the Part*, ed. Claudia B. Kidwell and Valerie Steele. Washington, DC: Smithsonian Institution Press.

———. 1989b. *Paris Fashion*. New York: Oxford University Press.

———. 1991. *Women of Fashion: Twentieth-Century Designers*. New York: Rizzoli.

———. 1996. *Fetish: Fashion, Sex and Power*. New York: Oxford University Press.

Stegemeyer, Anne. 1988. *Who's Who in Fashion*. 2d ed. New York: Fairchild Publications.

Steinhauer, Jennifer, and Constance C. R. White. 1996. "Women's New Relationship with Fashion." *New York Times*, Aug. 5, sect. A, p. 1.

Stephens, Debra Lynn, et al. 1994. "The Beauty Myth and Female Consumers: The Controversial Role of Advertising." *Journal of Consumer Affairs* 28 : 137–53.

Sudjic, Deyan. 1990. *Rei Kawakubo and Comme des Garçons*. New York: Rizzoli.

Summer, Christine C. 1996. "Tracking the Junkie Chic Look." *Psychology Today* (Sept. / Oct.): 14.

Sutherland, Daniel E. 1981. *Americans and Their Servants: Domestic Service in the United States from 1800 to 1920*. Baton Rouge: Louisiana State University Press.

Swartz, Mimi 1998. "Victoria's Secret." *New Yorker* 74 (Mar. 30): 94–98, 100–101.

Tarrant, N. 1994. *The Development of Costume*. London: Routledge / National Museums of Scotland, Edinburgh.

Tetzlaff, David. 1993. "Metatextual Girl: ⇒ Patriarchy ⇒ Postmodernism ⇒ Power ⇒ Money ⇒ Madonna." Pp. 239–64 in *The Madonna Connection: Representational Politics, Subcultural Identities, and Cultural Theory*, ed. Cathy Schwichtenberg. Boulder, CO: Westview Press.

Thébaud, Françoise. 1986. *La Femme au temps de la guerre de 14*. Paris: Stock/Laurence Pernoud.

Thim, Dennis. 1987. "Magic Christian." W [Women's Wear Daily], Dec. 10, p. 65.

Thompson, Craig J., and Diana L. Haytko. 1997. "Speaking of Fashion: Consumers' Uses of Fashion Discourses and the Appropriation of Countervailing Cultural Meanings." *Journal of Consumer Research* 24 (June): 15–42.

Tickner, Lisa. 1988. *The Spectacle of Women: Imagery of the Suffrage Campaign, 1907–14*. Chicago: University of Chicago Press.

Time. 1992. "Gun Shirts Are Out." *Time* 140 (Oct. 19): 24.

Toner, Robin. 1994. "Fond Memory: The Family Doctor Is Rarely In." *New York Times*, Feb. 6, sect. 4, p. 1.

Toussaint-Samat, Maguelonne. 1990. *Histoire technique et morale du vêtement*. Paris: Bordas.

Trautman, Julianne, and Marilyn DeLong. 1997. "Design and Fashion Theory in the Work of Madame Boyd, Dressmaker, 1887–1917." Paper presented at the meeting of the International Textile and Apparel Association, Université de la Mode, Lyon, France, July 11.

Trautman, Pat. 1979. "Personal Clothiers: A Demographic Study of Dressmakers, Seamstresses and Tailors, 1880–1920." *Dress* 4:74–95.

Tredre, Roger. 1999. "Jeans Makers Get the Blues as Sales Sag." *International Herald Tribune*, Jan. 13, "Men's Fashion: A Special Report," p. I.

Trujillo, Nick. 1991. "Hegemonic Masculinity on the Mound: Media Representations of Nolan Ryan and American Sports Culture." *Critical Studies in Mass Communication* 8:290–308.

Turim, Maureen. 1985. "Gentlemen Consume Blondes." Pp. 369–78 in *Movies and Methods: An Anthology*, Vol. 2, ed. Bill Nichols. Berkeley: University of California Press.

Turow, Joseph. 1997. *Breaking Up America: Advertisers and the New Media World*. Chicago: University of Chicago Press.

U.S. Bureau of the Census. 1975. *Historical Statistics of the United States: Colonial Times to 1970*. Washington, DC: Government Printing Office.

U.S. Commissioner of Labor. 1891. *Sixth Annual Report: 1890*. Washington, DC: Government Printing Office.

U.S. Department of Labor, Bureau of Labor Statistics. 1990. "Detailed Occupation by Race, Hispanic Origin, and Sex: 1990 Census of Population and Housing." Equal Employment Opportunity File/U.S. Bureau of the Census. [Accessed via CenStats: An Electronic Subscription Service, Sept. 28, 1999.] Washington, DC: Government Printing Office. (URL: http://tier2.census.gov/eeo.htm)

Valette-Florence, Pierre. 1994. *Les Styles de vie Bilan critique et perspectives: Du mythe à la réalité*. Paris: Nathan.

Valmont, Martine. 1993. "La Consommatrice est mise sous surveillance." *Journal du Textile*, no. 1349 (Nov. 8): 94.

———. 1994. "La Vague du streetwear est prête à déferler." *Journal du Textile*, no. 1368 (April 11): 21–22, 25.

Vanneman, Reeve, and Lynn Weber Cannon. 1987. *The American Perception of Class.* Philadelphia: Temple University Press.

Veblen, Thorstein. 1899. *The Theory of the Leisure Class.* New York: Macmillan.

Vettraino-Soulard, Marie-Claude. 1998. "L'internationalisation de la mode." *Communication et langages*, no. 118: 70–84.

Vicinus, Martha. 1985. *Independent Women: Work and Community for Single Women, 1850–1920.* Chicago: University of Chicago Press.

Vidich, Arthur J. 1995. "Class and Politics in an Epoch of Declining Abundance." Pp. 364–86 in *The New Middle Classes: Life-Styles, Status Claims and Political Orientations*, ed. Arthur J. Vidich. New York: Macmillan.

Villacampa, E. 1989. "Les Hommes: Sont-ils plus receptifs à la Mode?" *Journal du Textile*, no. 1169 (Aug. 24): 98, 100.

Waldrop, Judith. 1994. "Markets with Attitude." *American Demographics* 16 (July): 22–32.

Walsh, Margaret. 1979. "The Democratization of Fashion: The Emergence of the Women's Dress Pattern Industry." *Journal of American History* 66 (Sept.): 299–313.

Walz, Barbara, and Bernadine Morris. 1978. *The Fashion Makers.* New York: Random House.

Warner, Patricia Campbell. 1993. "The Gym Suit: Freedom at Last." Pp. 140–179 in *Dress in American Culture*, ed. Patricia A. Cunningham and Susan Voso Lab. Bowling Green, OH: Bowling Green State University Popular Press.

Weiss, Andrea. 1995. *Paris Was a Woman: Portraits from the Left Bank.* San Francisco: Harper.

Weiss, Michael J. 1989. *The Clustering of America.* New York: Harper and Row.

White, Constance R. 1997. "If It Sings, Wear It." *New York Times*, Oct. 26, sect. 9, pp. 1, 4.

———. 1998. "Isaac Mizrahi to Close His Doors." *International Herald Tribune*, Oct. 3/4.

White, Palmer. 1986. *Elsa Schiaparelli: Empress of Paris Fashion.* New York: Rizzoli.

White, Shane, and Graham White. 1998. *Stylin': African American Expressive Culture from Its Beginnings to the Zoot Suit.* Ithaca: Cornell University Press.

Wilcox, R. Turner. 1945. *The Mode in Hats and Headdress.* New York: Charles Scribner's.

Williamson, Jeffrey G. 1967. "Consumer Behavior in the Nineteenth Century: Carroll D. Wright's Massachusetts Workers in 1875." *Explorations in Entrepreneurial History*, 2d series, 4:98–135.

Wilson, Brian, and Robert Sparks. 1996. "'It's Gotta Be the Shoes': Youth, Race, and Sneaker Commercials." *Sociology of Sport Journal* 13:398–427.

Wilson, Elizabeth. 1987. *Adorned in Dreams: Fashion and Modernity.* Berkeley: University of California Press.

———. 1990. "These New Components of the Spectacle: Fashion and Postmodernism." Pp. 209–37 in *Postmodernism and Society*, ed. Roy Boyne and Ali Rattansi. London: Macmillan.

Winship, Janice. 1985. "'A Girl Needs to Get Street-Wise': Magazines for the 1980's." *Feminist Review*, no. 21: 25–46.

Wolf, Naomi. 1991. *The Beauty Myth: How Images of Beauty Are Used Against Women.* New York: Anchor Books.

Wolfe, Alan. 1998. "The Homosexual Exception." *New York Times Magazine*, Feb. 8, pp. 46–47.

Wood, George. 1903. "Appendix A: The Course of Women's Wages during the Nineteenth Century." Pp. 257–308 in B. L. Hutchins and A. Harrison, *A History of Factory Legislation.* P. S. King and Son.

Worcester, Wood F., and Daisy W. Worcester. 1911. *Report on Conditions of Woman and Child Wage-Earners in the United States.* Vol. 16: *Family Budgets of Typical Cotton-Mill Workers.* Washington, DC: Government Printing Office.

World Almanac and Book of Facts. 1969, 1980. New York: Newspaper Enterprise Association, Inc.

———. 1999. Mahwah, NJ: World Almanac Books.

Worth, Jean-Philippe. 1928. *A Century of Fashion.* Boston: Little, Brown.

Wright, Carroll D. 1969 [1889]. *The Working Girls of Boston.* New York: Arno/New York Times.

Yardley, Jonathan. 1996. "Hot Color for Men: Gray Pinstripe." *International Herald Tribune*, May 28, p. 10.

York, Peter. 1983. *Style Wars.* London: Sidgewick and Jackson.

Young, Agnes B. 1937. *Recurring Cycles of Fashion, 1760–1937.* New York: Harper.

Young, Malcolm. 1992. "Dress and Modes of Address: Structural Forms for Policewomen." Pp. 266–85 in *Dress and Gender: Making and Meaning in Cultural Contexts,* ed. Ruth Barnes and Joanne B. Eicher. New York: Berg.

Ziegert, Beate. 1991. "American Clothing: Identity in Mass Culture, 1840–1990." *Human Ecology Forum* 19 (Spring): 5–9, 31–32.

INDEX

Designers, when discussed as individuals, are listed by surname; their companies are listed by brand name, which generally means by given name.